Family in America

Family in America

Advisory Editors: David J. Rothman

Professor of History,
Columbia University

Sheila M. Rothman

THE
COMPANIONATE
MARRIAGE

By
JUDGE BEN B. LINDSEY
& WAINWRIGHT EVANS

Introduction by
Charles Larsen

ARNO PRESS & THE NEW YORK TIMES

New York 1972

INTRODUCTION

When Boni and Liveright published *The Companionate Marriage* in 1927, Judge Ben Lindsey (1869-1943) needed no introduction to the American public. For almost two decades he had been the best-known juvenile court judge in the country and the leading spokesman of the burgeoning juvenile court movement. His activities were never confined to his adopted city of Denver. From the beginning of his judicial career in 1901, he was involved in national causes such as woman suffrage, prison reform, abolition of capital punishment, and the evolving Progressive movement. In 1909, with the help of a professional writer for *Everybody's Magazine,* he prepared a series of articles on political corruption in Colorado which was subsequently published in book form as *The Beast* (1910). Lindsey had now added the dimension of muckraker to his national reputation as reformer and juvenile court judge.

By the middle 1920s, Lindsey was well on his way to playing a new role as the outstanding American spokesman for the "sexual revolution" that was being heralded in a growing number of novels, motion pictures, and popular magazines. Lindsey's identification with "the revolution in manners and morals," as social historian Frederick Lewis Allen labeled it, began in late 1925 when Boni and Liveright published *The Revolt of Modern Youth.* The book had its origins in a series of magazine articles prepared by the judge and his literary collaborator, Wainwright Evans. Since Evans did all the actual writing of both *The Revolt of Modern Youth* and *The Companionate Marriage,* the Lindsey-Evans collaboration deserves a brief description.

It began in January 1924, when Lindsey visited New York City on a lecture tour. He consulted some old friends about the possibility of writing a series of articles on his courtroom experiences, with particular emphasis on the sexual problems and attitudes of the younger generation. His two closest friends in New York were George Creel, an old ally in Denver reform movements who had later become chief propagandist for the American government during World War I, and Harvey O'Higgins, who had collaborated with the judge in writing *The Beast*. Both men agreed that the best outlet for the articles Lindsey had in mind would be the publishing firm of Bernarr Macfadden. Lindsey recognized that he would again need a literary collaborator. A self-made man with a very modest formal education, he did not feel capable of writing a book by himself, but he was aware that his national reputation would be an asset in selling anything that carried his name. He had no difficulty in persuading Macfadden, who was known chiefly for the sensationalism of his publications, that he was being presented with a golden opportunity. A meeting was arranged between Lindsey and Wainwright Evans, a writer for Macfadden Publications, and the two men "got each other" immediately, as Evans later described their working relationship.

The writing procedure for the Lindsey-Evans collaboration was essentially the same for both *The Revolt of Modern Youth* and *The Companionate Marriage*. The judge, either by correspondence or in conversations in Denver and New York, supplied Evans with a seemingly inexhaustible fund of anecdotes from his encounters with young people—and sometimes with adults —and Evans put the material in acceptable form. Evans was listed as junior author of both books, but the first person singular was always used since the stories were Lindsey's. The publishing history of the two books was also similar. *The Revolt of Modern Youth* was first serialized in Macfadden's *Physical Culture Magazine*. *The Companionate Marriage* first appeared in *The Red Book Magazine*. Both books were published by Boni and Liveright.

The Companionate Marriage was, in a sense, a sequel to the earlier book. In *The Revolt of Modern Youth,* Lindsey had described some of the cruelties and injustices that grew out of existing laws and practices regarding divorce, alimony, and birth control. Another recurrent theme was the difficulty faced by young people who were ready and eager to begin the sexual side of life but not prepared from either a financial or psychological standpoint for conventional marriage. Lindsey sympathetically described a few instances where young couples had formed "trial marriages" without benefit of clergy. Lindsey defended such unions as being more virtuous than some legal marriages that were held together only by economic considerations. He did not, however, unreservedly endorse such arrangements, nor did he take a final position on the institution of marriage itself. In *The Companionate Marriage,* he attempted to answer the questions left unresolved in *The Revolt of Modern Youth.*

On one level, *The Companionate Marriage* was a fairly conservative book. The basic proposal Lindsey advocated was described as "legal marriage with legalized birth control, and with the right to divorce by mutual consent for childless couples, usually without payment of alimony." As Lindsey pointed out, much of his "program" was already followed by educated Americans who practiced birth control and got divorces when they wanted them. In a decade when the institution of marriage was under attack by radical thinkers, Lindsey was merely proposing to extend its benefits to the young and underprivileged, who often found it most difficult to obtain reliable information about birth control. Bertrand Russell typified the more avant-garde reaction when he wrote to Lindsey that companionate marriage was better than the status quo but that it did not go far enough.

Why, then, was *The Companionate Marriage* denounced from so many pulpits as a book that was corrupting the youth of the land? Why did various chapters of the Daughters of the American Revolution attempt to have it suppressed? Why did a congressman introduce a bill to make it a crime "to practice companionate marriage" in Washington, D.C.? The answer lies not so much in Lindsey's proposals but in his vigorous defense of moral relativism in regard to sexual conduct and in the belligerent nature of his attack on defenders of the status quo (in politics as well as sexual morality), whom he generally portrayed as reactionary dullards or self-serving hypocrites. When, for good measure, the judge added that some of them could improve their mental health by having some of the experiences that the "flaming youth" of the era were enjoying, he added fuel to the flames. While Lindsey was careful to avoid giving overt approval to the numerous acts of premarital and extramarital sexual relations described in *The Companionate Marriage,* those who engaged in them were usually the strongest and most attractive characters in the book. Viewed in this light, it is not surprising that *The Companionate Marriage* was so widely regarded as a handbook and guide to "the revolution in manners and morals" that was being enthusiastically reported in the popular media.

The Companionate Marriage had a considerable vogue for about three years following its publication in 1927. Movie magazines and Sunday supplements used prurient synonyms such as "jazz marriage," "pal marriage," and "trial marriage" interchangeably with companionate marriage to describe almost any kind of illicit sexual relationship. The fame of the book spread abroad as it was translated into half a dozen European languages as well as Japanese. The judge, who had considerable ability and experience as a public lecturer, spoke or debated on the subject in many parts of the country. Sometimes the debates were held on a college campus, and when a vote was taken afterward, the judge was usually declared the winner. Undoubtedly, the most dramatic confrontation involving the book occurred after a sermon in the Cathedral of St. John the Divine in New York City on December 8, 1930. On that day, Episcopal bishop William T. Manning denounced the book as "one of the most filthy, insidious, and cleverly written pieces of propaganda ever published in behalf of lewdness, promiscuity, and unrestrained sexual gratification." The sermon occurred as an aftermath of a controversy between the bishop and a group of liberal Episcopal clergymen who had invited Lindsey to speak to them about marriage and divorce. Warned in advance of Manning's intention to discuss the matter publicly at a Sunday service, Lindsey unobtrusively entered the cathedral and startled the congregation by standing up and demanding a right to reply to the bishop's attack. Before the judge could finish more than two sentences, he was forcibly ejected from the church. A year later, Lindsey described the episode in his autobiography, *The Dangerous Life,* written in collaboration with a Los Angeles journalist, Reuben Borough. By 1931, however, the attention span of the public, weakened in part by the deepening economic depression, was diverted from the "sexual revolution" of the 1920s, and the sales of Lindsey's new book were disappointingly low.

From the perspective of the 1970s, *The Companionate Marriage,* in spite of the sensationalism of its style and format, will appear even more conservative than it did to Bertrand Russell. Young People who wish to live together without a formal commitment to a permanent relationship will have no need of an institution called companionate marriage. Ironically, the improvement of birth control techniques and a wider knowledge of their use, which Lindsey so strongly endorsed in the book, make the need for companionate marriage less urgent that it was in the 1920s, when birth control clinics were still occasionally raided by the police. Nevertheless, the book retains its interest as a significant item of Americana. Also, by its emphasis on the need for greater candor in discussing sexual matters and by its pervasive hostility toward the use of the sanctions of criminal law in treating the private conduct of consenting adults, *The Companionate Marriage* was prophetic of prevailing sentiment among psychologists and the legal profession today.

Charles E. Larsen
Mills College
Oakland, California
1971

THE COMPANIONATE MARRIAGE

THE
COMPANIONATE
MARRIAGE

By

JUDGE BEN B. LINDSEY
& WAINWRIGHT EVANS

BONI & LIVERIGHT : NEW YORK

1927

Printed in the United States of America

PREFACE

Companionate Marriage is legal marriage, with legalized Birth Control, and with the right to divorce by mutual consent for childless couples, usually without payment of alimony.

Companionate Marriage is already an established social fact in this country. It is conventionally respectable. Sophisticated people are, without incurring social reproach, everywhere practicing Birth Control and are also obtaining collusive divorce, outside the law, whenever they want it. They will continue the practice, and no amount of prohibitive legislation can stop them.

My thought is that we should put an end to this hypocritical pretense, under which we profess one thing and do another; that the Companionate Marriage, now largely monopolized by educated people who understand scientific contraception, and who can employ skilled lawyers in the obtaining of collusive divorces, ought to be made legally and openly available to all people—particularly to the poor and the socially unfit, who need it most.

Scientific contraception promises what may develop into the most revolutionary change in human affairs that history has ever recorded. It would be difficult to overstate the economic, the eugenic, the broad social significance, of a discovery which is even to-day changing marriage in some of its most fundamental aspects. Birth control has brought the Companionate into existence. It has made possible between men and women a relationship which has never before, in the history of the world, been practicable for multitudes of people.

To protest against this colossal phenomenon is like trying to stop the tide by scolding it. I suggest that if we rationalize this new thing, and use it intelligently, we may be able to derive from it a degree of social and spiritual power capable of creating for our descendants a better world than we have been able to fashion for our own use and happiness.

v

I am putting this explanation into a preface because I want, so far as possible, to forestall misunderstanding and prejudice on the part of readers who have been told by ill-informed critics of my views that I advocate men and women living together in free love unions, without marriage, and that they should remain in that unmarried status till the birth of d child.

Another version is that I advocate "Trial Marriage." What these critics mean by "Trial Marriage," apparently, is a technically legal marriage which is entered with the intention that it shall be, not an enduring union, but merely a temporary sex episode, similar in spirit to what we commonly call the "unmarried union." The parties to a "Trial Marriage" would be marrying, that is to say, strictly on a basis which would emphasize the "trial" element in the union, and create in it a psychology of impermanence. The very name "Trial Marriage" indicates this; and it suggests to those who believe that marriage should be as permanent as possible, the thought that persons so doubtful as that of their ability to remain married, had better not marry in the first place. An unmarried union would suit the needs of such couples better than any sort of legal union, one would think. The fact is that the distinction between "Trial Marriage" and Free Love is nominal. A Trial Marriage is really a Free Love union which avails itself of a legal form. I am not here concerned to criticize it. I merely insist on this identity between Free Love and Trial Marriage; and I further insist that Free Love and Trial Marriage are by no means to be confused with Companionate Marriage.

Technically *the Companionate and Trial Marriage have certain features in common but* one *is not the* other. *Both would normally avail themselves of Birth Control and divorce by mutual consent. Both would place a minimum of obstruction in the way of childless couples wishing a divorce. And both recognize the fact that when men and women marry they can never be perfectly certain that their marriage will turn out to be a permanent success. But there the similarity ends.*

For the emphasis—*the psychological emphasis—is altogether different. All men and women who are sensible and honest know when they marry that there is at least a possibility of failure ahead. But*

*they assume that the chance is remote. They have confidence in
their ability to weather all storms and make port. It is their intention to do that, and to make such adjustments as may be necessary to that end. That is* marriage. *That is the spirit of marriage.
It involves the same recognition of risk that goes into trial marriage,
but it stoutly proposes to overcome and nullify that risk. It emphatically does not propose to seek divorce the moment the flame
of romantic passion begins to cool.*

*Now the trouble with this attitude in ordinary marriage is that
not enough account is taken of the risk. If the Trial Marriage
psychology puts too much emphasis on the risk, the psychology
of traditional marriage bull-headedly ignores it altogether. The
result is that couples who make a mistake in their choice of each
other find that in getting into marriage they have walked into a trap.*

*There is room for sane compromise between these two extremes.
Men and women who enter marriage should be encouraged to do it
under conditions that would best insure the success and permanence
of the marriage, but which would also afford a line of retreat in case
the marriage failed. They should not have children, for instance,
till they have been married long enough to be reasonably sure of
their ability to carry on together; and they should not have them
till they can afford them. This is common sense. It is not Free
Love or Trial Marriage at all. It may, as I have indicated, have
a technical similarity to Trial Marriage, but legal technicalities
are not what make a marriage. What makes a marriage is the spirit
and intent of it. And the Companionate as described in this book
is genuinely, if not technically, a different thing from Trial Marriage.*

*I do not deny that it would be possible for people to enter the
Companionate with a Trial Marriage psychology. But so is it possible for them to enter traditional marriage with a Trial Marriage
psychology. Some do it; but they are not many. For such persons
the unmarried union, achieved secretly, is easier, and involves less
responsibility before society. The Companionate would not invite
many such persons. Nor, since it would offer small hope of alimony,
would it attract ladies of the "gold-digger" type. It would give
Marriage a chance to breathe and live; it would give it room in*

*which to grow; it would give it soil in which to put forth roots;
and it would establish it on a better basis than it has yet known.*

This book, like The Revolt of Modern Youth, *has been written
in collaboration with Wainwright Evans. Mr. Evans has contributed
to this book more than his skill as a writer. He has brought to the
work a mind which is strongly in agreement with my views. His
whole-hearted sympathy with what I am trying to do has given him
a penetrating—almost an instinctive—insight into the deeper implications and meanings of the principles on which I have done
my work in Denver; and he has thus made articulate much which
might otherwise have gone unsaid. In short, Mr. Evans has put a
creative effort into this book which, along with the effort of my
own mind, and my own unique fund of experience, has made the
whole thing possible. It is a true collaboration. I am grateful for
that; and it is a matter of concern to me that the reader should be
mindful of it as he reads these pages, and grateful for it too.*

BEN B. LINDSEY.

The Juvenile and Family Court of Denver.
    May 30, 1927.

CONTENTS

CHAPTER X.   THE SPIRIT OF MONOGAMY . . .

CHAPTER XI.   CHASTITY: WHAT IT IS NOT . .

THE COMPANIONATE MARRIAGE

THE COMPANIONATE
MARRIAGE

CHAPTER I

THE REVOLT OF MIDDLE AGE

1.

DURING a recent trip to New York I went to a notorious play which the "play jury" a few weeks later threatened to discipline.

It was crude melodrama. It was composed of a raw title, raw sex situations, and mediocre acting. It served no valid artistic end; it was there to make money by going as far in the way of bad taste passing for "truth" as the police would permit and the public tolerate.

The truth was that the play was a cheap imitation, by incompetent persons, of certain other excellent plays which dealt with a similar theme gracefully and with good taste, and which had thus met with legitimate success, because they were enlightening, and because they gave people who saw them a better insight into themselves and into other persons.

This play stood at the absolute zero of vapidity. Professing to reveal and illuminate the human heart, it sold a gold brick to people so badly educated in the values of life that they couldn't spot the fake. It had no genuine heights and depths to justify it.

Nevertheless the play packed a great thrill for the audience. This was particularly true in the second act, when there came a scene in which it really looked as if the palpitating man and woman behind the footlights would forget that the footlights were lighted and the shades not drawn. But fortunately there was a room in the rear of the stage. You could see, through the open door of it, that it contained a bed.

3

"I think," said the lady, "that we would be more comfortable in there."—Whereupon the two retreated before the smirking face of *almost* outraged Virtue, and shut the door.

None of this particularly interested me—it was flat, stale, and unprofitable as compared with scores of the real life situations I encounter daily in the Juvenile and Family Court of Denver.

What did interest me beyond words was the audience. I had come there to watch that audience; and what I observed at first hand richly repaid the price I had had to put up for my ticket.

The people around me were of various ages. The Thirties and Forties—particularly the Forties—predominated. Sometimes they edged into the Fifties. Collectively they represented what I here call Middle Age: Forty, more or less. It seemed symbolic that even the theater where the play was shown was situated in "The Roaring Forties."

They were obviously conventional folk: middle class for the most part—prosperous, moral, correct. A large number of them were doubtless married, and had adolescent sons and daughters—members of the well-known Younger Generation, concerning whose morals and immorals they were probably greatly worried. Some of these youngsters were present, without their parents.

In short, it was outwardly a typical, respectable, and conventional audience, the older part of it reared in the Eighties and the Nineties, and still suffering from the hang-over without quite knowing what to do about it.

Now note what happened. The play, dramatically untrue and spurious as it was, had in it just enough truth to hit them with a kick like a battering ram.

This was not so evident in the case of the men. After the manner of men, they sat silent and absorbed. It was the women who gave visible and audible expression to what they felt, in the most astounding exhibition of sex emotion that I have ever witnessed in a public gathering.

2.

The atmosphere was electric—more like the air of an old fashioned religious revival meeting than anything I can think of. Women sitting so near that I could have reached out and touched them nearly had hysterics. Choking sounds came from them which might have been sobs or nervous laughter. Others seemed to be in a kind of ecstasy, as if, in the person of the woman on the stage—"sisters under their skins"—they were going through a vicarious thrill such as few of them had ever known in their own ill-educated, ill-regulated, unintelligent love-lives. Some of them broke suddenly into shrieks of laughter or lapsed into absorbed, fast-breathing silence.

It was a curious and intriguing thing to watch. But it doubled the interest for me when I suddenly realized that the phenomenon I was observing was confined to the decorous Older Generation. There they sat, clad modestly in the long bombazine Mantle of the Golden Nineties, and found that the blending of this play with the ancient taboos of their own youth involved consequences of a bio-chemical-psychological sort, which for any one wrapped in that chaste and protecting mantle, were very warm indeed.

Among those present, as I have already indicated, were engaging members of the Younger Generation, wearing no Mantle—spiffy, un-chaperoned little Flappers with their "boy-friends," some of them candidly "necking," others behaving for the time being, at least, with perfect propriety, and none of them manifesting any interest in the play other than the interest which people usually do manifest in any play. They were quite calm, entirely relaxed, and evidently free from whatever internal turmoil had rendered some of their elders almost beside themselves.

The contrast was startling. Where, I asked myself, were the riotous and hectic passions of Youth? Where that heat within the blood for which solicitous censors would provide an Ice Pack? Where the devastating Flame that would send these youngsters out through the doors of this theater burning with unwonted desire?

The answer was that in these youngsters I saw no evidence of anything of the sort; but that in the oldsters I saw plenty. So far as Youth was concerned I saw what I constantly encounter in my court in dealing with youngsters: a cool, sophisticated, impersonal appraisal of the passing show, as if to say, "Don't worry about us, Old Dears; we can take it or let it alone. But watch *your* step, Old Dears!"

My mind went back to a Motion Picture Conference I had recently attended in Chicago. I had there come into rather violent collision with some excellent people who wailed a doleful ditty, the burden of which was: "Our boys and girls are being corrupted by the motion pictures and the stage; they are in peril of hell-fire. We, who are old and steady and wise in all these matters, must come to the rescue and save these ignorant, guileless and unsophisticated boys and girls!"

Boys and girls! Can you beat that? Why not themselves! Here at this play was evidence that if censorship measures were necessary it was up to the Younger Generation to come to the rescue and save its sinning and wayward elders from their own riotous passions. I laughed aloud as I thought of it; and I could imagine some Flapper sitting behind me observing to her boy-friend, "Look at that middle-aged guy two seats ahead. What a kick he's getting out of that bedroom stuff! And just lamp those crazy dames on our left! Oh—hum—it makes me wish I were old! We haven't reached it yet, Freddie. We're too young!"

Such sex spectacles, when concretely presented on the stage, are supposed to shatter the poise and self-control of Youth, and to leave the tepid blood of Age, or Middle Age, still tepid. Yet here, before my eyes, was the exhibit of Middle Age shaken like a reed in the wind, by that which left Youth *blasé* and tranquil.

3.

Now, of course, I realize that this is too unqualified a picture to be wholly true. For the sake of speed and emphasis I have painted in the high-lights without qualification, trusting to the reader's common sense to do the qualifying. But substantially I have stated the situation as it really was, to wit, an almost complete reversal of what, off-hand, one would expect to see happening to a theater audience looking at a raw play.

It was Youth exhibiting something of the sophistication, poise, maturity, and restraint which are supposed to go with years; and it was Middle Age exhibiting the classic symptoms of Adolescence. It was Middle Age more adolescent than Adolescence itself; Middle Age in pin-feathers, capering there, callow and ungraceful; an exhibit of adult infantilism, of deferred maturity, that was surely a sight for men and angels to take a lesson from.

And oh, the pity of it! What a blend of tragedy and comedy for the pen of a Rabelais! What a theme of laughter salted with tears! What an indictment of that dead and gone social period which Mrs. Wharton has felicitously called "The Age of Innocence," and whose walking ghost still haunts us here even amid the clangs and alarums of Science.

How grotesque, how fraught with pathos and bathos—and yet how fraught with hope! For even Middle Age is growing up. The fact that it nearly threw a fit before my eyes I consider symptomatic. It is leaving its adult infantilism behind, and these were growing pains.

In the meantime, while it grows, behold it, a Gargantua the like of which was never seen before, a gigantic infant that plays with steam and electricity, that flies the air, that swims the seas, that girdles the world with wonders, and yet sees in the Girdle of Aphrodite only a wicked bauble whose dangerous magic it understands not at all.

There are thus two major dramas going forward in American life to-day. Concerning one of them, I have, with my collaborator, Wainwright Evans, already written a book, "The Revolt of Modern Youth." Concerning the other, I propose to say something here. It is the more dramatic of the two, and yet few persons clearly realize that it is going on.

It all happens like a play beside a play or within it. On the open stage we have the drama of Youth in Revolt, popping with spurts of red fire behind the footlights, where everybody can see it. But behind the scenes, enacted furtively, in a half light, behold another drama among the stage hands, old wheel horses whose acting days are popularly supposed to be over. This is the drama of Adult restiveness, of the Adult struggle with inclinations, with forbidden choices, with tabooed ideas, and with lifetime habits of thought and action—some of them stupid and some not so stupid—that were bred in their bones as children.

4.

The way of that drama is secret; and it is the more dramatic for that reason. The actors in it keep sedulously out of your range of vision; but you can find them, if you have insight and sympathy, and an inquiring mind, in every nook and cranny of American life. The confidences imparted in the Domestic Relations Department of my court bring many of them to view; and for the hundreds of cases I review there, I know there are thousands that neither I nor anybody else, save those immediately concerned, ever hear of.

But what makes all this dramatic is not its secrecy. What makes it dramatic is that it is a travail; that its fruits, regardless of whether they be good or bad, are brought forth in pain, and with wrenchings of the spirit.

In this respect it is very different from what is most characteristic in the revolt of Youth. Youth is pliant. It was born to the new order, the Twentieth Century order of things, in the first place; and such adaptations as it has had to make in order to live simul- taneously with the new order and the old, it has made easily, as easily and inevitably as it has learned to dance the Charleston, which Middle Age finds difficult.

Moreover, Youth has support in its innovations. It has formed a world of its own, a segmented, cohesive thing which speaks its own peculiar tongue, has its own well-recognized customs and moral sanctions—and even, if you will, its emerging culture. Some of that culture is destined, in my judgment, to be permanent; and part of it will serve as a stepping stone to changes in social custom that promise to be radical beyond anything even the most wild-eyed prophets among us dare try to specify.

Children, as they grow up, step into this new order of things naturally. They learn its language as they learn their native tongue, without cramming a grammar and a dictionary into their heads, as one ordinarily does when one learns a language in later life.

The process for Youth, therefore, involves little or no subjective violence. There is little or no wrenching, warping, or displacement of the delicate internal machinery of the personal life. That is why, with a minimum of damage to itself, Youth has been able, not merely to talk about Freedom but to take it, in defiance of customs and traditions which it regards as irrational, unsuitable, and wanting in genuine authority. Thus Youth, at small cost, has Freedom in large measure; for it is true in proverb and in fact, that possession is nine points of law.

Not so with Middle Age. From the beginning Adults are under a kind of psychic coercion that reaches out for them like a long arm of the Past. It is the most powerful coercion known; it has an all but hypnotic power; it is based on *suggestions* received, believed, and habitually obeyed—as of divine origin—from childhood on.

It is the coercion of life habits, life fears, life customs and unquestioning beliefs. It springs from the Folkways, and, regardless of whether it be rational or irrational, its grip is one of iron. And that grip holds the ordinary individual fast, however much he may objectively dissent and avow that his rational beliefs and personal philosophy are different. He may call them superstitions, but something within, something subjective which he is quite likely to call his conscience, tends automatically to *obey*—with a hypnotized and uncritical obedience.

5.

This grip of the Past is broken, in most cases, only at the cost of subjective anxieties and fears which may manifest themselves physically as well as mentally—*fears which, if they prove too strong and persistent, may wreck the health and happiness of the person who has miscalculated their strength and his own weakness.* Later I shall tell of some instances in which I have known this to happen.

To call this phenomenon an uneasy *"conscience"* is to misuse and sentimentalize a noble word. The whole thing is too often irrational, unintelligent, to be other than genuinely sinful to the last degree.

To call such a thing "conscience" is a kind of blasphemy. This thing is gross. It lacks intelligence, discipline, courage, and other elements that compose a valid culture in the lives of individuals. It must be reckoned with, and, in the end, *usually obeyed.* For most persons, particularly for most adult persons, the cost of disobedience is too great to make it advisable even when the individual may rationally be convinced that such disobedience would be right and conformity wrong.

6.

We ought always to be conscious that mere subjective habit is not genuinely ethical; that it travels in a rut of tradition; that *conduct determined by it is not thought-out conduct*. What it prescribes may, or may not, be wise and expedient; but whichever it is, it involves no moral decision or rational choice.

Very little of our social conduct is determined by rational choice, as we quickly find if we attempt to mix brains with conduct. Such attempts not only involve head-on collision with the social order, but they involve, as I have said, collisions within, collisions with one's own Fears and ingrained Habits. And such internal conflicts often do more harm to the individual than does the state of smothered rebellion in which he essays obedience to that which does him spiritual violence and outrages at once his desires, his rational beliefs, and his sense of right and wrong.

In our present state of social evolution Intelligence and Courage remain at a heavy discount. Obviously they are difficult and genuine virtues. On the other hand, instinctive or *uncritical* obedience to racial and social suggestions, regardless of their demonstrable and proven worth, is a very easy "virtue" and is not genuine at all. It produces temporary comfort, like any other opiate, and many of the miseries of life spring from it.

The terrible power of the subjective mind is well known in this day when psycho-analysis is a household word. Everybody knows, in a general way, the broad fact that when the average mature person, grown to conform to a given social mold, attempts revolt, his whole subjective background constitutes a massive obstacle, capable of resisting new convictions and beliefs, however clear cut these may be. This is true even among persons of very high culture and independence, whose minds are well disciplined; and it is doubly true among those who lack these difficult qualities.

7.

I remember a case that illustrates not only how powerful is the grip of custom on the subjective mind, but also how irrational, unintelligent, and *unethical* it often is.

A fine looking, blonde, blue-eyed Scandinavian girl called at the court one day and asked to see me. Suppose I call her Helga, because that wasn't her name. Helga was "in trouble." At first she accused a young fellow who worked in a garage, and who was married and had two young children, with a third on the way. She wanted him to put up $500 to pay for her confinement, and then she wanted me to have the baby adopted into a good home. But young men who work in garages and are married are not likely to have that much money in their jeans; and I was therefore anxious to fix things, if possible, so that there would be a minimum of inconvenience for all concerned.

I had the young man up to see me. He admitted his relations with the girl and was nearly frantic for fear his wife would learn about it—the reason for this being that he was in love with his wife.

"That damn' girl," he wailed, while tears brimmed out his eyes; "I went to a show with her. No harm in that. And she just naturally got me. I'd give a million dollars if I'd never seen her. But I'll do all I can to square it, Judge—only I don't know where the money's coming from, with my wife's confinement approaching. Judge," he added, leaning forward, "I think she's been having relations with the chap that employs her; and I'll bet he's just as likely to be the father of that kid as I am. And he's rich. Let him put up the coin."

"Who is he?" I asked.

"James Burton," he answered—the real name he gave me being that of a leading business man, who belonged to most of the important organizations and clubs in town, and was, besides, extremely active in church work, and had an important lay position in a large Denver church.

"Leave that to me," I said.

I immediately sent for Helga. She owned up about the other man. Her object in not mentioning him before was that she liked

him, and was afraid of getting him and his social position into trouble.
It was with the young garage worker that she had last been before
she discovered her pregnancy, and so she had attributed it to him,
though it was evident that it might have been either of the two men.

8.

Her relations with Burton were in consequence of the fact that she
was a maid in his household. His wife, some months before, had
gone on a trip, and had taken with her the other of their two maids,
leaving Helga in charge, and, of course, unchaperoned. And Burton
was tempted by her beauty and fell.

I knew him well, and considered him a very fine fellow; and I
thought it likely that he would do the generous thing if approached
generously. I therefore instructed Helga to go to him, confess to him
her affair with the young garage man, admit that either of them might
be responsible for her pregnancy, and ask him to do the sporting thing
and pay the freight, since the other man was poor. I told her to
make it clear to him that she had no intention of betraying him
whether he would put up the money or not, and not even to let him
know that I knew of it. I explained what blackmail was, and warned
her that she must avoid anything that even savored of it.

The girl followed my instructions to a dot, and the man responded
as I was sure he would. Helga had her baby under arrangements
I made in her behalf at the home of her married sister, whom I had
once helped through a sex scrape—though Helga knew nothing of
that. It was a fine boy, who was later adopted by a man who is
an intimate friend and neighbor of James Burton. The two men
belong to the same club and the same church and the same business organizations. The day may come when the boy, growing
up, will enter the Sunday School class in which his father takes
such an interest. But none of the parties concerned know where
the boy came from.

So much for Helga. Now for the psychology of the tale, which
is my justification for telling it. Helga told me that she was not
the only lady who had had attentions from Mr. Burton. She had
accidentally discovered that he had had an intrigue during another

absence of his wife from home, with a woman who was the wife of a friend of his.

Helga had discussed the matter with him, and was surprised and amused to find that he was conscience-stricken about the whole affair. He told her he felt like a dog.

"I said to him," she told me, and I shall try to quote her as exactly as my memory permits, "that I couldn't see why he was so stirred up over his affair with this other woman and didn't seem to worry at all about *me*. He told me that it was because she was married and I wasn't, and her husband was a friend of his to boot. He said his conscience hurt him something fierce. All on account of that woman—see, Judge, not a thought about me, and I'd been a good girl till then! And that married woman knew just what she was doing and how to take care of herself and everything. I can't make it out, Judge. It looked like he thought he was headed for hell or something on account of that married woman—but not on account of me."

I explained to her as best I could that his distress was due to his consciousness of having violated his code—*not* his code about women, but his code about friendship. "How did you feel, Helga," I asked, "about having such relations with the husband of the woman who employed you? I notice you speak of her very affectionately, and that you have been most anxious that she should not hear of this for fear it would hurt her happiness. Don't you feel any similar qualms?"

She shook her head and showed her white teeth in a smile. "No, Judge, I don't. I think it's foolishness. He sure loves her. Seems like he cares all the more for her. He only *likes* me. I'm satisfied and he's satisfied. So what about it?"

"But what of the wife of the garage man?"

"I don't even know her," she replied. "But I know he's awfully fond of her and he talks about her all the time. Pooh," she finished. "Mr. Burton was foolish. I guess it's just because he's a church member."

9.

I can see her yet, leaving my office with a step as light as air—

no fears, no conviction of sin, no tweakings of conscience, none of the stresses and struggles that had apparently gone so hard with my friend Burton.

This seems to me admirably to illustrate the point, the very vital and fundamental point, I have been trying to make—that Middle Age not only finds it hard to break with custom, but that it finds it hard to be rational or discriminating as to different customs. Burton distinguished sharply between this affair with Helga and his affair with his friend's wife simply because custom distinguishes between them, and not through any genuine moral discrimination on his own part. As a matter of fact it was socially far more reprehensible for him to seduce that girl left alone with him in his own home, than it was to have an affair with an already married woman who presumably knew what she was about. But in the one case he had no misgivings, and in the other less reprehensible one he felt like a dog.

Whatever else can be said of all this, it seems to me that the ability to think clearly in matters of conduct was no part of Mr. Burton's education. He wasn't thinking of the women involved, *but of a man whose property he conceived he had stolen.*

It must not be fogotten that our strict guardianship of the chastity of women, together with the relatively slight value which we attach to chastity in men, is based on the notion that women are property and that men are not, and that men want to be sure that their children, being also property, are theirs by blood, and of their own begetting. This has nothing to do with rational ethics. It is simply custom that has come down to us from sources so remote that we can't trace its beginnings. James Burton's misgivings had nothing to do with chastity; they concerned what he had been taught was thievery—theft from another man.

Am I wrong in saying that our dependence on this background of received tradition, and on these irrational compulsions of the subjective mind, is one of the worst forms of immorality that we practice? Am I wrong in insisting that there is hope in the fact that Youth is discarding all that for some degree of conscious rationalism, and that there is further hope in the signs that Middle Age now feels the same impulse first thoroughly to examine "goodness" of every sort to see if it really be goodness? But of course that is adventure, and it is fraught with peril. And I have no wish to minimize that peril. Social innovation may easily lead to social ruin for individuals who undertake it and who don't watch their step. It is certainly not a thing which I would recommend indiscriminately.

The truth is that some persons have a gift for social innovation and that some lack it. Some are impervious to the shafts of criticism and genuinely thrive on opposition; others—most of us, in fact—weaken and collapse under social reprimand. This is especially true in Middle Age. Fear holds most of us in line—till the line itself moves, and we can go safely forward with the mass.

But, of course, that is a slow business. It was of small profit to the unhappy married woman in the Golden Nineties that if she waited till 1927 or thereabouts she could divorce her husband because she loved another man and then marry the other man without her neighbors regarding her as little better than a harlot. Indeed, the mere fact of divorce, even on grounds of infidelity, was sufficient to give a woman a shady reputation in those days. In the Golden Nineties the woman who wanted a divorce, for whatever cause, made the break with custom at terrific personal cost, or she submitted and hoped for better luck for her grandchildren.

10.

I know a very respectable, very aristocratic, very firm-minded maiden lady of about fifty who lives in an Eastern university town, where her blue-blooded ancestors have always lived. About the year 1900—she was young and pretty then—she decided that skirts were too long for comfortable walking; and she shortened her petticoats to a point well in excess of the prevailing mode. She told me about it years later—how she dared the disrespectful stares of loungers before the village stores and on the campus, and how she set her square little jaw and stuck to her convictions till they got used to her and her peculiarities, and till fashion caught up with her. But the ordeal upset her health—trivial as the matter was. Nervousness, indisposition, and other disorders of unquestionably psychic origin beset her while the struggle with custom and the idiocies of society lasted.

Our apparently free and independent Younger Generation are no more free from this coercion of custom than their elders. It is merely that they have a different set of customs. Youth defies the shibboleths of its elders, but it has shibboleths of its own which are as tyrannous as anything it has escaped from. Most young people wear the same clothes, they do the same things in the same way, and are so lacking in individual initiative and originality in their relations to each other that I count it one of the clearest evidences of the painful crudity and want of culture which are an outstanding characteristic of their present stage of development. I believe, however, that this is a phase which will pass. Just now they have to hang together, knowing that if they don't they will, as Franklin put it, hang separately.

Generally speaking I am not afraid of Revolt. I believe in that sort of thing on general principles, as against conformity. I think it gets somewhere, even at the cost of occasional disaster to individuals; and I think conformity, except when it is well and rationally grounded, tends to get nowhere. We must have conformity, of course. It has a conserving function—as the word "Conservative" indicates. It is quite as necessary as Revolt. The one is inconceivable without the other. But just now we are suffering from an overdose of it. Conformity has been a national vice with us—again the Vice of Virtue—and I think our lack of moral backbone when the restraints of law and custom are removed demonstrates how too much law and supervision has weakened our ability as individuals to travel on our own power.

Excesses of all sorts are usually a rebound from an excess of forced conformity. The only sort of conformity that does not work this mischief is the willing, voluntary, chosen conformity which is grounded in culture and springs from it. That is the only kind of conformity for which we should have any use in America; but it is, I sometimes think, the kind for which we have the least use.

This is natural, for to have free conformity to any sort of culture you must first catch your Culture, and that is difficult. It is much easier to send a lobby down to Washington and legislate a fake culture, like Censorship, or an Obscenity Law, into fake existence. By the same token it is easier to have anti-divorce laws or legislation for the restriction of divorce, than it is to produce a social order and a system of education—a culture, in short—wherein real marriage would be natural, easy, and possible; and one way to make it so would be to make divorce also natural, easy, and possible whenever divorce was indicated and desired. Rather than take this chance with human beings, and rather than register our faith in the dignity of human nature to that extent, we prefer our present system of fake marriage, based *wholly* on Bell, Book, Candle, and the Law.

II.

It is easier to force married persons to go on living together when they don't love each other than it is to weld love and marriage into an identical thing, two sides of a shield that would be capable of really protecting the "Home" that we talk so much about and do so much to destroy by our barbarous stupidities and our ignoble fears of overthrowing "custom."

We want marriage and no divorce; we want to eat our cake and have it too. We prate of Freedom and we take it on ourselves to forbid the free play of human relationships. We are drunken with the irrational and dangerous sentimentalities which cluster like slimy barnacles about our conception of Love. We base ninety-eight per cent of our social customs, particularly the important ones, on folkways which we should by this time be capable of rationalizing and adapting without recklessly destroying them. The folkways are good servants but cruel masters.

The reason I like the signs of restiveness on the part of Middle Age is that Middle Age shows a glimmering realization of these facts; a slow waking up to the notion that after all the control and intelligent direction of custom is a function of the living, and that it does not lie with the ancestral ghosts.

Youth has already been on the warpath for some little time. If now there shall come an awakening of Middle Age, it will bring into the field a mightier army than the forces of Youth, and the change will then have in it the seeds of permanence. For this would impart to Youth, not only fresh courage, but also a philosophical conception of the significance and fruitfulness of its present course, so that it might avoid the trap of conformity when it, itself, reaches Middle Age.

At present the opposition Youth meets from the Older Generation constitutes a malign suggestion that what Youth is doing is wholly futile and wrong. This suggestion, however little Youth may now seem to heed it, tends to sprout and grow subjectively. And later, as present day Youth edges into Middle Age, these old notions, long suppressed, may spring up like toadstools. There is danger that Youth will thus succumb to a spell of malignant virtue, and in an access of fear, teach it to a generation yet to be born. That has been the way of it from time immemorial. It is thus that independent and hopeful Youth, instead of growing into Middle Age, degenerates into Muddle Age. It is my hope and belief, however, that the Youth of this generation will resist this subjective influence of the more irrational of our folkways better than any preceding generation has ever done. I think the findings of science may put enough starch into the racial backbone for that.

12.

In the meantime the issue, so far as Middle Age is concerned, is acute. It involves a readjustment, a bending of stiffened mental fibers, difficult in the last degree. Thousands of adults to-day, many of whom I come into direct personal contact with in the Domestic Relations Department of my court, are struggling to rationalize their attitude toward traditions whose hold upon them is independent of reason and intelligent conviction. This is true of their daily conduct and it is true of their religious life. The part of the struggle which concerns religion versus theology is being fought out under the banners of Modernism and Fundamentalism. But it is the vast, silent change in men's private thoughts about these matters that counts the most. No age has ever been so strongly interested in religion as this age, and no age has ever been less satisfied with theology as a substitute for religion.

But the difficulty becomes more and more acute when one gets into the field of personal conduct. Used as I am to this sort of thing, I never cease to be startled at the evidence, forever pouring in, that the number of adults who are consciously chafing against the old notions and consciously resenting them, is enormous. If it keeps on the number of innovators may become so large that what they do will be the "custom" and therefore "right"; and concealment will be at an end.

It is my purpose here to speculate somewhat upon that change and to shed what light I can upon it from my extended experience in dealing with the Older Generation in the domestic relations part of my work.

The Revolt of Youth and the Revolt of Middle Age have one capital, central, and important biological fact in common: both are very largely based on the fact that modern society, on the surface at least, is governed by a body of sex convention which, however well or ill it may have worked in bygone ages, was never designed to cope with the social problems of this age.

It is amazing how Sex bobs up even in those court cases which on the surface apparently have nothing whatever to do with Sex. That Sex and the Need for Money are the two great main causes which bring individuals into collision with society and the laws of society is a truism which I need not stop to develop here. The two things usually go hand in hand, but in that class of cases which have chiefly to do with people in their social and personal human relationships with other men and women, Sex is usually the mainspring of whatever is dramatic in it.

I want to make this clear because I have already had much to say about Sex in "The Revolt of Modern Youth," and I shall have more to say about it here; and I don't want the reader to misconstrue this emphasis on an unconventional topic or to interpret it as a personal obsession on my part. The thing is there; and if I am to discuss the domestic relations of people with any degree of honesty and candor, I can't avoid Sex.

Sex is, moreover, a thing that badly needs to be talked about; and though I want to offend the reader's sensibilities as little as possible, I propose to talk plainly.

13.

What I may call the Revolt of Middle Age presents itself to me chiefly in concrete pictures, actual incidents, from which I draw certain conclusions, and upon which I am compelled to speculate. These incidents have certain characteristics now that they did not have years ago. The attitude of the persons involved is different from what it used to be in other, similar circumstances. And that change of attitude, in my judgment, indicates a change in the spirit of the times, an astonishing revolution in our way of thought— even the way of thought of the man on the street, who, though he does not consciously rationalize or philosophize, does unconsciously mirror the common drift of human behavior. He has caught it by a kind of contagion, God knows where, and thus he contributes his bit toward that shift in the mores, the customs, which is now so overwhelmingly upon us.

I should say that of all the remarkable things that are happening to-day in American society the change that has come about in the popular attitude toward adultery is the most striking, and in some respects the most perilous.

Only they don't call it "adultery" any more. They don't even call it "infidelity" or "unfaithfulness" or "philandering," or any of the other more or less opprobrious names by which this human, ancient and modern failing has always been known.

The thing seems to have taken a new turn. It used to be that I seldom or never came across a married couple who, in theory, did not both take it for granted that absolute "faithfulness" in marriage was a *sine qua non,* that the thing was not debatable, and that who-ever departed from that rule sinned against society and against the other party to the marriage contract. This stood, regardless of the amount of illicit sex experience the man or the woman or both might have had before their marriage. After marriage they, in theory, quit all outside relations. If they violated the rule and failed to play the game according to the agreement, they would admit with-out qualification that the thing was wrong and sinful, and would excuse themselves as best they could for having done what they admitted was unjustifiable. They didn't debate that it might be otherwise. Well, they debate it now. They do more than commit adultery; they defend it and seek to justify it. They assert that they see no reason why it should not be compatible with marriage, and even why it should not considerably improve marriage.

I have heard such assertions from men who would not dare say such a thing to their wives, and from wives who would not dare breathe it to their husbands. And I even know a few married couples who agree in this view, and who conduct their marriage on that basis. They insist that they are in love with each other, and that they don't love anybody else, but that they both like variety, and that they see no harm in what they call "intimate friendships."

Usually, however, it is either the man or the woman that feels this way, and not both together. And, of course, it more often happens in the case of the men. Most women have such a horror of unchastity, and of the traditionally *smirching* effects of sex relations that are not sanctioned by society, that they less often permit such desires, if they have them, to rise into the field of consciousness. And even if that happens, they are still a long way from acting on the thought.

But the couples who mutually agree that adultery is all right are a strange and interesting phenomenon in American life to-day. And what I have so far observed leads me to believe that such agreements are far more common than even students of these matters have any idea of. There is no means of telling to what extent the thing is happening, of course, because such agreements, when they exist, are sedulously secret. In many cases I have no doubt there is no candid agreement, but simply a tacit ignoring of the facts. In other cases, where the couple no longer care for each other, there may be some such agreement, with no further sex relations in their own marriage. But when couples that love each other enter on such an apparently anomalous course, that is surely indicative that something extraordinary is happening to one of the most firmly established of our customs.

14.

One of the most remarkable and clear-cut cases of this sort that has ever come to my attention through the statements of the parties themselves was that of a couple whom I will call Mr. and Mrs. Frederick Blank. They have wealth, education, and enough leisure to think about things, and, if you will, get into mischief. Their social position is first rate. They don't run with a fast set; they go to social functions only occasionally; and they apparently stick pretty closely to their home.

Mrs. Blank is a very attractive woman, and men are attentive wherever she appears. She divorced her first husband on grounds of incompatibility. Apparently there is no prospect that she will ever separate from her second husband for a similar cause—for most 'persons, I think, would consider them compatible to a fault.

She had called to see me about a young girl in whom she was interested. The child had gotten into "trouble," and she proposed to pay whatever expenses were involved in connection with the confinement. We discussed the question of having the baby adopted out. From that the talk turned back to the girl herself, and from the girl to the general problem involved in her conduct.

Presently Mrs. Blank began to tell me some things about herself. Her husband, she said, had recently had an affair with a girl—not this girl; and she on her part had been through similar experiences, after her present marriage, with men she liked.

"Does your husband know it?" I asked.

"Of course," she said placidly. "We agree on these things. We love each other, but we enjoy these outside experiences; so why not take them? I think we care more for each other on account of them."

It isn't often that I get paralysis of the tongue, but I got it then. I simply sat and looked at her. I had suspected this kind of thing was going on, but here was the evidence. Here was a new one. Sex scrapes were old stuff; collusion for the obtaining of a divorce was as old as divorce laws; statutory rape was an item of my daily routine; and unbelievable coincidences in human lives were the kind of thing I expected as a matter of course. But here was collusion in adultery on the part of people who were as far from gross vulgarity as any you would be likely to find in a day's run.

Perceiving my astonishment Mrs. Blank smiled.

"This is a new one on me," I said at last. "I have suspected it might be going on. I have known of such cases where neither party admitted it to the other. I have known cases where they admitted it because they had ceased to care for each other. I have known women who tolerated unfaithfulness on the part of their husbands;

and a few husbands who tolerated it on the part of their wives. But this—in a marriage you say is a love-match—" I could proceed no farther.

"Oh, Judge," she exclaimed. "What's the harm—aside from the fact that we have always been told that it was wrong? If he has an affair with a girl he takes a fancy to, it really means nothing more to him or to me than if he took her to dinner or the ....eater. It is all casual and harmless unless one *thinks* harm into it. Society says there is harm in it, and that it strikes at the roots of the Home. But as a matter of simple, biological fact does it do any harm whatever in our particular case; and as a matter of sociological fact, does it strike at the roots of our Home? I maintain that it makes us both happier, and that our Home is a lot better off than the virtuous homes where husbands and wives chafe and fret in bondage. We are free, and our married life is ideal,—in spite of the whole world saying, 'It can't be done!'

"This thing," she went on, "is what thinking makes it—not what society's thinking makes it, but what his thinking makes it, and the girl's thinking, and my thinking, and the thinking of the men who win my friendship to that ultimate degree. And if the thing is what *thinking* makes it rather than what *custom* makes it, then custom has no authority in this matter unless we are obligated to agree with custom and obey it. I deny that it has any such authority. We propose to disagree with custom in our thoughts as much as we see fit, and in our acts up to any point where we don't infringe on other people's rights."

"But that's just the point, isn't it?" I suggested. "Other people's rights—and society's rights."

"We have not violated any such rights," she answered. "What we have done is our own business and that of the friends with whom we have shared our intimacies. It concerns nobody else."—Then she added with a laugh, "The minister of my church will stand up and tell you that such and such an Old Testament worthy had concubines and several wives; and if you ask him he'll tell you further that this was perfectly moral *then*—right in the sight of God, but one of the seven deadly sins *now*. To which I answer: Even the customs of God seem to change. Why not those of men?—Custom is always pronouncing something right in one age or country, and wrong in another. What is pure in one region is impure in another. Which is which? And when even the Bible changes face on the matter, who is to decide? The individual, of course. That's the way I look at it, Judge. I think there is no such intrinsic thing as Purity and Impurity. They are abstractions; and they have been one and the same thing repeatedly in human history."

"I should like to know," I said, "how you came around to this way of thinking. You were strictly brought up. I take it that you did not break away from all that early training without a struggle and some misery. How did it come about?"

"I found out that he was having an intrigue with a girl," she answered. "He looked it. He went around like a whipped dog, and he would never look me in the eye. When I accused him he went white, and tried to deny it; but I told him what I knew, and then, when there was no way out, he owned up.

"I went cold all over, so furiously angry that I could only look at him in a way to freeze him. Then, without a word I went to my room, packed my trunk, and telephoned for a taxi. He, in the meantime, was sitting in the library with his head in his hands. Not a word did he say. As we saw it then, indeed, there was nothing he could say.

"At last, just as I was ready to go, I went to him. 'I am going over to my mother's,' I told him. 'I'll engage a lawyer and sue for divorce. Of course you won't object to that. It needn't be on any unpleasant ground. We'll call it incompatibility.'

"I'll never forget how he looked at me. Something within me began to melt. 'I have no right to object,' he said. 'And I haven't any right to go on loving you; but I do—both.'

"Then what did you do it for?" I demanded furiously to hide what was happening inside of me. "You *couldn't* if you loved me, only me."

"Well, I did," he said sullenly. "That's the truth, and you can take or leave it. I never loved that girl. I liked being with her— but that had nothing to do with *you*—nothing at all."

"Well, Judge, I sat down in a chair to think. And, besides, if he loved me—why, that was what I wanted, you see. And a woman likes to be told she is loved.

"So we began to reason together. I found he could talk all right as soon as he found I was ready to listen. It was an agonizing business, but the upshot, after many hours, during which the taxi called and was dismissed, was that I agreed to condone what he had done. Only he was never to do it again—never—never.

"That quarrel lasted us for six months. Outwardly everything was calm, but the air in our house was tense. I wondered what Frederick was thinking about; but if I asked him,—well, of course, you can't find out that way.

" 'Frederick,' I said to him one day, 'you're under a strain. There's something on your mind. I think I can guess it. Have you been out with any one?'

"He jumped up furiously. 'I told you I was through,' he snarled, 'and I'm keeping my word. So forget it.'

" 'Are you keeping it in your thoughts?' I asked. And then, without giving him a chance to answer, I added, 'I've been thinking things over, Frederick. This present arrangement won't do. Telling people they mustn't do things makes them want to do them. I've made that mistake with you. Suppose we arrange it this way—that I'm to give you full liberty—and that you are to give me the same.'

"Judge, I wish you could have seen his face. It was a study. The utter conflict of emotions! On the one hand a yearning for the freedom he craved for himself; and on the other the old notion about female chastity—the double standard. He *owned* me; for *me* to go adventuring was quite different. I'd be polluted and unclean."

" 'I don't want it,' he said shortly. 'I wish you'd drop it and forget it.'

" 'Oh,' I said. 'You don't want it. Are you sure? Or is it that you want it for yourself but not for me—exactly like a man!' And I felt myself going into a rage.

" 'Well,' he asked, 'would you like me to say that I'd be willing to share you with some one else? You know you wouldn't! You'd feel insulted.'

"With that I realized that that was just the way I would have felt. I didn't know whether to laugh or cry, I was so mixed up.

" 'Wouldn't you?' he reiterated.

" 'Yes,' I owned, 'I would. But that's one way of looking at it, and an irrational way at that. We can't go on the way we have been; and I'm not going to let you get away with any double standard. We couldn't live together on that basis either. If you want to drop your masculine notions about purity and property and meet me on the level, we'll try out the thing *you* started.'

"He looked at me just the way you looked at me, Judge, a few minutes ago—dumbfounded. 'But—but—' he said naïvely, 'I didn't know—*that you wanted other men.*' "

"I laughed.

" 'Oh, you needn't!' he growled. 'I know it was a damn' fool thing to say. Only—you never gave any sign of it, somehow. I didn't mean that *I* was so all important.'

"At that I relented. 'You *are* all important,' I said. 'But hereafter, if I feel in an experimental frame of mind I'll do as I choose, and you are at liberty to do the same. You want it, and I think I may want it. Let's not be hypocrites, and let's not take offense at facts. And there won't be any concealments, you understand. This is your prescription, and we'll separately give it a fair trial. If it doesn't work, we'll drop it. But you'll never be satisfied till you try it; and as for me, well, you've made me curious—and so you've got yourself to thank.'

"So, Judge, that's the way it came about. Nobody could be more surprised than I am at the outcome. After the first shock was over the tension in our home disappeared. We had no reservations. We were able to speak our minds on all this. Little mishaps ceased to irritate us. Everything was different. We felt like free souls in voluntary service to each other.—As for these outside affairs, there have not been many.

"The world would say we are wrong. It would call *me* unclean, and my husband merely unconventional. It would receive him socially and make me an outcast for the very same conduct. And yet it has not affected me any differently from what it has him—though we have a social superstition which says it has.

"But why should I pay any attention to that? I know this thing has not affected me or made me any different from what I was. I know the way I think and feel. Why should I let the outside world tell me that I'm different when I know at first hand that I am not?"

She paused a moment, a curious agitation visible on her face.

"Still," I said, "you find the suggestion hard to resist, don't you,— a life-long subjective habit that is hard to ignore or put by?"

She nodded. "That's true, Judge. You've put your finger on the weak spot in my armor. I have to fight it down, and keep on fighting. I think the thing that enables me to sit tight is that my husband understands and believes as I do. We support each other. And it isn't as hard to fight as it was. The old habit of thought has gradually broken down. It is only at times that it returns to disturb me.—On the whole, I think I can say that this departure from convention works with *us*. I think if more people would break with tradition, and in the direction of their own secret convictions, which they don't dare breathe to anybody, marriage would be happier and divorces rare."

"So you recommend adultery as a cure for divorce," I observed. "Very interesting. You know, of course, that in some states adultery is the one ground on which divorce is allowed; so that when two persons want a divorce they have to fake an adultery if they can't produce evidence of a real one. Every one guesses that they are committing perjury, which is a penitentiary offense, but nobody seems to have the heart to do anything about it.

"Now, Mrs. Blank, I am not going to preach. I appreciate your having told me these facts. Facts are what I am looking for. I know that, being satisfied of the rightness of your own conduct, you are not asking me to pass judgment on it or to offer you gratuitous advice.

"It is my custom in matters of this kind to view every human situation much as a physician views a case, with as much impersonal tolerance as I can muster. If I should attempt to counsel you, I could not, as a Judge, commend you in a course which runs so flatly counter to a basic custom in our civilization. I am sure, that whatever you may feel about the rightness of what you are doing, you will agree with me that so violent a tampering with an established social custom, and with one's own habits of thought and feeling, is dangerous in a high degree—dangerous to the happiness of those who attempt it, and possibly dangerous to the stability of society."

"It all depends on whether one knows how to handle dynamite," she answered. "Some persons should not touch it. What makes our course safe is that we understand each other, and that we don't impose our opinions, and, if you like, our bad example, on the outside world. We are very careful not to get found out. I don't mean that in any cynical spirit, but I mean it."

"Perhaps," I ventured, "you will permit me to say that your story sounds more like promiscuity than what you call many marriages."

She flushed. "I'm not afraid of the word," she said with spirit. "That's all it is—a word. If you mean by promiscuity that I am to be had for the asking, you are mistaken. But I know you don't think that. I know you understand the thought in my mind better than that. These are genuine attachments, deep friendships, intimate companionships. The sex part is an incident, and a rather rare one so far as I am concerned. I am very particular, though I may not sound like it. I suppose most persons would not believe me when I say that sex, as such, plays a very minor rôle in these affairs, and often no rôle at all. But that is because most persons are so repressed that they can't think of intimate friendship between a man and a woman in anything but the sex sense. I was that way. But I've genuinely gotten beyond it, simply by letting go.

"What I mean is that I do what I want to do, and that I find it increasingly easy to do it without my fears and my old habits of thought tearing me to pieces inside. Save for the restraints contingent on other people's rights, there isn't a repression in my body. I think that is the way one should be in order to be healthy and happy. One must not disregard the rights of other persons, and one must be obedient always to one's own genuine instinct for what is seemly and in good taste. I honestly don't think my husband and I have violated either of these fundamentals of conduct; and I don't see how any one, thinking the thing through without bias, could say we had."

"Is it a line of conduct that you would prescribe for society in general?" I asked.

"Certainly I would—if society could think it through the way we do," she replied.

"Still," I persisted, "you would admit that what you are doing would be impracticable and dangerous for most persons, wouldn't you?"

"Yes," she acknowledged. "It is largely a question of expediency. My husband and I form, if you like, an ideal case; we are a miniature social laboratory into which I have permitted you to look. All the needful conditions happen to be present. We have money, and leisure, and sufficient culture, and we are of a speculative turn of mind.

"If my husband fancies what to him and to me seems an innocent and natural intimacy with some other woman, from whose companionship he can derive joy and inspiration, he is able to pay for his fancy, and he robs me of no material support. If we were poor that would not be true.

"I too have money and leisure—time to get into mischief, I suppose you would call it. I have servants. If we had children—we are thinking of it—I could employ expert nurses to attend to the nursery routine.

"You see our situation is parallel, in a sense, with the conditions travelers report in some paradises of the South Seas, where everybody has enough to eat, and where economics do not interfere with people when they want to gratify their normal impulses. Ethics have nothing to do with our sex taboos, but economics have a lot to do with them. I suppose that can't be altogether avoided; but the interference goes to unreasonable extremes. The taboos are without restraint, rime, or reason."

"In short," I suggested, "you are rich enough to afford the simple life. You agree, then, that all this is out of reach of persons who are either poor or only moderately well-to-do?"

"Not out of reach," she said, "but more difficult. I know women who can't afford servants, and who have to make a little money go a long way. But they can entertain guests as gracefully as I can with all my money. Why?—Simply because they make brains, skill, and culture serve in place of money. I think such persons could also introduce brains, skill, and culture into their domestic and sex lives in just that manner, and that they would get away with it. The trouble is that they have never seen fit to bend their energies in that direction. They don't know they can. They accept things as they find them, and they think what they call 'infidelity' is undebatable. I hope my candor does not offend you."

"On the contrary," I said, "I wish more people would speak their minds. If one thinks a thing one should be able honestly to say it.

"I confess that your case is in a way unique in my experience. I know married persons who secretly think much as you do, but who never admit it to each other. It is particularly extraordinary that a husband should be willing to grant his wife the sort of liberty he feels is permissible for himself. I congratulate you and your husband on having at least gotten onto the same level, regardless of whether it is high or low.

"I have also known many women," I continued, "who were ready to condone the outside affairs of their husbands under certain conditions. I know one who is violently jealous if her husband pays attention to any other woman. But consider her reason: 'What right,' she said to me, 'has he to be spending money on other women when I have to make over my last year's hats, and skimp and save in every way I can. If we had money, perhaps I'd feel differently. But this isn't fair.'

"Now I suppose, Mrs. Blank, that if you were making over your last year's hats, you would take some such view, wouldn't you?"

"Perhaps," she admitted. "If there were no way to get more money."

"I know another woman," I continued, "who knows that her husband has outside affairs; but she is not disturbed by them. 'So long as Sam provides adequately for me and the children,' she said to me, 'I shall not interfere.'

" 'Do you feel that he loves you?' I asked her.

" 'Oh, certainly,' she said. 'He's as good as gold to all of us.'

" 'And you would not feel justified in doing as he does?' I asked.

" 'Sam would never see that,' she said with a shrug. 'With a woman, it's different, somehow.'

"But, as a matter of fact, though she never admitted it to me,

I am satisfied that that woman was secretly doing what she allowed her husband to do openly. They just couldn't face such a thing together, though they could manage it separately and did."

Mrs. Blank laughed, a trifle bitterly I thought. "Oh, Judge, lies are such terrible things. Why can't we all speak the truth? Tell *me* the truth, Judge. What do you think of me?"

"I think you're rich but honest," I said. "You would like to have me tell you that I think you are doing right. In like manner most conventional persons would reproach me bitterly for not telling you that you are an impure woman and a highly immoral person. But I could not do the work I am engaged in if I permitted my mind to form fixed judgments on human behavior. You must excuse me therefore from taking sides. It is part of my job not to take sides. I simply note the facts; and I find them interesting because they are among the indications that some sort of a social change is on the way.

"That there are people in the world with your convictions seems to me significant and not necessarily alarming. There are some persons who regard as alarming every aberration of social conduct with which they don't happen to agree; but I am not of their number. I am greatly obliged to you for the truth. I hope you will keep me informed of future developments in your way of life if there are any."

I have not talked with Mrs. Blank since that interview; but so far as I know she and her husband continue with apparent success in their individualistic scheme of living.

CHAPTER II

OLD DOGS AND NEW TRICKS

I.

To the possibly shocked and angry reader I can only say the same thing that I said to Mrs. Blank. I do not extract the truth from people by passing gratuitous judgments on their conduct. Mrs. Blank talked to me freely because she felt sure that I would not promptly begin to belabor her with the club of convention. I wish that in putting down my talk with her in these pages I could do it with the assurance that all who read the account would likewise hold judgment in suspension, and be content to regard such departures simply as things that are happening, and which no amount of mere denunciation can prevent from happening.

Mrs. Blank's story constitutes a part of the social data which I think I should lay before the readers of this book; but if I am to present such material I must necessarily assume from the start that my readers prefer to be treated as adults rather than as children. This is clinical material, and it must be treated as such, without sentimentality, either in the direction of assent or dissent. I trust I make this clear.

The facts I have so far set down, together with other facts which I have not set down as yet, make it evident that marriage is changing. That there has come about a loosening and an alteration of the marriage bond all are agreed, particularly those of the clergy who are so alarmed about it.

Generally speaking, I think—as I shall try to show in this book— that a reasonable amount of such loosening, particularly in the direction of legalized birth control and divorce by mutual consent for childless couples, might well make the bonds of marriage tighter, and reduce the number of divorces. A reasonable freedom for the individual in thought, conduct, and daily life is the only bondage that can really bind. I think we are very far indeed from having that kind of freedom—and that the story of Mr. and Mrs. Blank is one instance of a violent reaction away from marriage as society and the church insist on having it. What makes the conduct of Mr. and Mrs. Blank startling is that its apparent violence and recklessness has about it a kind of rationality, a daring reasonableness, which makes it doubly effective and, perhaps, doubly perilous in a world where the vast majority of persons don't seem to use any rationality at all.

2.

Personally, I am satisfied that society should leave to the individuals who compose it a very large liberty to do the shocking thing, the socially revolutionary thing, if that thing seems right and expedient to them, and if it does not patently infringe on the social rights of others—particularly children.

I readily grant that Mr. and Mrs. Blank are engaged in an exceedingly dangerous experiment. But let us consider the reasons why it is dangerous, who is endangered by it.

In the first place, since Mr. and Mrs. Blank are childless, and since their mode of life remains their own private business, the effects of their experiment may be considered to be individual rather than social. I know some persons would argue that their "example" and influence is a sinister thing, and that it extends at least to the persons they know intimately, and perhaps beyond.

This view seems to me considerably more dangerous, socially, than the possible bad example of Mr. and Mrs. Blank. It starts with the assumption that Mr. and Mrs. Blank are doing a thing which is necessarily pernicious; which is the very point at issue. On that theory no innovator would ever be justified. It is much better, I think, to assume that if the theory of marital conduct held by Mr. and Mrs. Blank is false or impracticable, it will fall of its own weight, and contains the seeds of its own destruction. And if their perilous *example* threatens to lead others into peril and possible disaster, that happens to be one of the conditions attached to every sort of progress. Nobody suggests that we put a stop to aviation because the path to discovery in this field is marked with the gravestones of those who took their chance with the Unknown.

3.

Social experimentation by those who care to risk it seems to me quite as well justified as experimentation in other dangerous fields. Society ought to sanction it and tolerate it and even encourage it.

Incredible as it may seem, there are still people who look upon experimentation in the scientific fields as immoral and displeasing to God. Their theory is that what God has not "revealed" we are not intended to inquire into. And even among persons who are heartily in favor of scientific inquiry into most things, there are many who shrink with superstitious terror from investigations in the psychic realm. That's where *they* draw the line. Others object to experimentation in psychology. The whole business is "dangerous," say they. Granted! But what of it? If we have not the courage to live dangerously, no amount of safety can make up to us for that spiritual lack.

I hold, therefore, that if Mr. and Mrs. Blank choose to risk their happiness and their health and well being in putting to the test certain traditions from which few of us are able to break away without disaster, they may be quite as justified in their search for the real truth as any one else who dares exploration in the fields less ringed about with taboos. In short, I think that the intolerance which society would show toward Mr. and Mrs. Blank if it knew their names hasn't a shred of justification, and that, like all intolerance, it is based on Fear. Society is afraid Mr. and Mrs. Blank might turn out to be right in their theory; and it isn't willing to take that chance. Society has always crucified its truth-seekers because it fears them. It rightly regards adjustment to new facts as a great inconvenience.

4.

This brings me to the second reason why Mr. and Mrs. Blank ran a grave risk in embarking on their unconventional adventure, a risk which must be pointed out to any who might contemplate following their course. What this second reason is I have already indicated in my statement that adult persons who attempt to break away from those subjective habits of mind which function independently of the reason, and which are so deep within us that they are difficult to touch or alter by any intellectual process, *do it at their peril.* I don't say it can't be done. Some persons do it and get away with it. But often the results of such a break with ingrained tradition are profoundly disturbing and often demoralizing. The nervous tensions that result from a sudden plunge into conduct at variance with beliefs held unquestioningly since childhood are often so terrific that they upset the physical and mental health of the experimenter.

That is why most of us find it necessary to merge ourselves into new customs gradually if at all. Young people find it easy to take on the new quickly; adults draw back from it. Middle-aged women to-day have come gradually to short skirts and bobbed hair, which our flappers were able to adopt, without much emotional strain, almost overnight. In like manner the younger generation is able, without psychic strain, to adopt new sex conventions and standards which are often devastating in their effect on adults who attempt to adopt them suddenly, as many do.

It is of grave importance that adults should understand this fact. It is this that introduces the greatest element of peril into the effort which so many of the older generation are making to adapt themselves to the new order. It does not necessarily prove that the effort at change is morally wrong, but simply that it may be inexpedient and ill-advised.

This peril reaches even into the ranks of the younger generation. Many of our youth, brought up in conventional homes, find crumbling within them ideals that are, so to speak, an organic part of them. That those ideals may be false and divorced from reality has nothing to do with the fact that they are *there,* and that they have to be reckoned with, regardless of whether the intellect of the individual pronounces them false or not.

I think this violation of inner, subjective habit has had much to do with the epidemic of youthful suicide in this country. Something within has crumbled; the process of change, speeded up by new conditions in our civilization, has been too quick and violent; the plant dies in the transplanting. The shock of transplantation is great, even for a plant; try transplanting a full-grown tree if you want a problem in horticulture. First you dig down and cut the roots on one side of the tree, and leave it thus for many months, till it puts forth a mass of new, short rootlets on that side. Then you cut the roots on the other side, and wait again. And when the tree has thus put forth a ball of such fine roots, you prune it severely, and you dig it up and move it. If you do this skillfully, the tree will live. But it is hard to do. It is much easier to set out a *young* tree where you want it, and be content with the thought that it will give shade to those who will follow you.

5.

By the same token, those who attempt sudden spiritual transplantations in their own lives need to know what they are about. For some can achieve it and some cannot. Each must judge the thing he finds within him, and take his own risk.

For instance, I know of a certain woman who learned that her husband desired an outside affair. She made up her mind to follow her convictions, and to put jealousy out of her life. She therefore told her husband that it would be all right with her; and she even went so far as to bring the other woman into her home, sincerely telling her husband, the other woman, and *herself* that it was perfectly all right. Intellectually and rationally she was convinced that it was, and that she could overcome the thing within her, the irrational thing within her, that rebelled. Outwardly she did overcome it; outwardly everything was all right. But a few days later she was found lying unconscious in the driveway in front of their garage, *with her head in the rut worn by her husband's car*.

What had happened was that her subconscious mind had taken control, intellect or no intellect; that she had gone into a kind of a trance, and had laid herself down in that position as a symbol of the degradation and humiliation to which, according to her ingrained habits of thought and feeling, she had been subjected.

Within her was something stronger than her mind. It wasn't rational; it had nothing to do with what her mind assured her was the *reality* of the situation; it was simply a fixed subjective habit which refused to yield to her judgment. Subjected to gradual education over a long period of time, it might have yielded. I know many persons who by slow degrees have swung around to views and to conduct which they would once have found impossible. But this woman found it impossible to do, in this case, what she sincerely believed to be right.

I know a woman who was once a notorious courtesan. She is a very extraordinary person, and she has written a book which is a classic in the annals of the under-world. She abandoned her ancient profession, married a man who knew all about her past, and "settled down." The man who married her had it all thought out. He loved her, he respected her, and his judgment told him there was no reason why her misguided and unfortunate past should be an impediment to their marriage. He was fully convinced of this. They lived together in complete concord; and the only evidence that part of him continued to turn from her, with a sense of repulsion which his intellectual convictions could not change, was the fact that when away from the house he was constantly telephoning to see where his wife was, *and that he could never eat any food that was warmed over.*

The subjective mind again, with its fixed, traditional habits! His intellect had repudiated such traditions; it rejected the old notions which ascribe inferiority to every woman who has been in the arms of a man or men to whom she is unmarried; but his subjective consciousness had been taught the old standards from childhood, and there they were. And they expressed themselves in symbolism since his objective mind had denied them direct expression. It wasn't rational. It had nothing to do with what his intellect conceived to be the reality of the matter. But there it was. A younger man, brought up in a different tradition, might not have reacted that way. I have known many young men who have married girls whom they know to have had many sex intimacies with other men, and who find no subjective impediment in the fact. They have grown up in a different tradition, that is all—fundamentally, a much sounder tradition, in my opinion.

6.

All this works out rather curiously in some cases of mutually condoned infidelity. The husband who condones the infidelity of his wife often becomes ill; the wife who condones similar unconventional conduct on the part of her husband often becomes ill. But a husband can be unfaithful, either with or without his wife's knowledge, with no apparent ill effects on him, and she can do likewise with no ill effects on her. Where the infidelity is mutually condoned, both may become ill, he because of what his subjective mind by habit regards as *her* dereliction, and she because of *his* dereliction.

One explanation advanced by psycho-analysts is this: A boy grows up, through his early childhood, with the Mother Image predominant in his mind. He expects fidelity and constancy from his mother because he always gets it, and because that is the tradition he is taught as early as he can learn anything. He expects constancy and fidelity from her, but he does not yield those qualities to her. Children are notoriously that way in their relations with their parents.

Similarly, a girl grows up with the Father Image predominant in her life. She expects constancy and fidelity from her father, but she does not yield those qualities to him. At least she does not regard them as obligatory.

When the boy grows up, he tends to choose a girl who conforms, more or less, to the ideal expressed by his Mother Image; and he transfers to her the same kind of regard that he has for his mother. There is more to his regard than that, of course, but that is an essential element in it. In like manner, the girl marries a man who conforms, usually, to the Father Image, and she confers on him the kind of regard she has for her father.

Hence it comes about the boy expects constancy and fidelity from the Mother Image in his wife, but does not subjectively yield those qualities; and the girl expects constancy and fidelity from the Father Image in her husband, but does not subjectively yield those qualities. Thus either may be unfaithful to a mate without necessarily experiencing any very profound or injurious violation of subjective habit; *but neither can encounter or condone unfaithfulness in a mate without such violation, and without danger of ill results from it.*

In consequence there are many couples who both of them philander successfully so long as they keep the fact secret from each other, *or studiously ignore it;* whereas, if they attempt to face the facts candidly, they become ill.

Some of them seem to feel the danger of this instinctively. I have had many a woman say to me, "If George goes with other women, I don't want to interfere; I simply want him to keep it to himself and not let me know it. I am afraid it would make me ill."

7.

A young woman recently related to me that she was married to a young man she had met in college. They had lived together for some time before marriage, largely because of her insistence that she did not want to marry. Finally she changed her mind. They had three children. The first few years of the married life they found ideal. But at last the husband became surly, and finally brutal. He developed a sadistic streak, and would beat her and then shower her with caresses. Naturally she refused to put up with that, and the strain between them became steadily worse.

At last he was attracted by another woman, and promptly informed his wife of this fact. She told him by all means to live with the other woman if he chose; and she persuaded herself that this was the wise and right course for her to take under the circumstances. As it turned out, he soon tired of the other woman, and came back to his wife; and then their difficulties began afresh. It was in connection with those difficulties that she sought consultation with me.

The interesting thing in her story was this: Her husband had come back to her, and she still loved him, and always had. *But, every time she saw the other woman she (the wife) would vomit, and become violently ill.* She had nothing against the other woman so far as she knew. The thing simply happened, independently of her wish or conscious volition.

"I wouldn't have cared about the other woman if I hadn't known," she said. "But looking at the thing in the light of day was too much for me. My husband wanted me to go out with other men. I think he thought that would ease his conscience—if we were both doing it."

In this particular case, with the man as inclined to violence and cruelty as this man was, there is little doubt that if his wife had taken him at his word he would probably have killed her in a fit of rage; and that if he hadn't done that he would have divorced her at the first opportunity.

I have seen many instances of such resentment on the part of persons who have told their mates to take any outside liberty they might desire. They *think* they mean it; and with their minds they do. But they can't overcome the habit within them.

In the case of couples where one or both partners condone outside affairs, everything may be all right on the surface; but often an internal tension develops such that the slightest irritating cause will lead to a break, and to divorce. And of course, in extremely neurotic cases, violence and even murder may follow.

When I say that illness often results from the effort of husband and wife to condone infidelity in each other, I don't mean "mere nervousness." The nervous tension in these cases may be so terrific as to produce glandular imbalance and profound disturbances of physiological function that can result in almost anything. Among the diseases that often result are asthma, tuberculosis, acute digestive disorders, defects of eyesight, and a long list of other troubles. Consider, for example, the remoter consequences that might come from such digestive disturbances. It is well known that some digestive disorders readily lead to duodenal ulcer, and that duodenal ulcer in turn frequently ends in cancer. Thus the chain of cause and effect may be a long and tragic one. Physical health is intimately linked up with mental health; and violations of custom, however rational they may seem, *can* ruin health, shorten life, and destroy happiness.

8.

Of course, it does not follow that this is the outcome for *everybody*. It is merely a possibility that every rebel against the existing order has to reckon with. The outcome varies with the individual. Particularly does it vary according to ideas that people have grown up with. There are persons who *little by little* have completely broken with traditions from which they dissent. There are others who never can accomplish it where the emotional life is deeply and intimately involved.

I want to make it clear that this enforced obedience to subjective habit has nothing to do with what the *reason* pronounces right or wrong. These rooted habits may be, and often are, irrational. That is to say, they are not *thought out*. That makes no difference. They are there; they often function independent of the sanctions of reason; and every man has to reckon with the individual problem they happen to present in his case. I can't make this warning too emphatic. It should be taken into account in connection with everything I have to say in these pages about the changes coming about in our sex code; particularly those changes which are coming about in the views and conduct of an increasingly large number of individuals in the older generation.

In general, I think it is unquestionably a fact that any sudden break on the part of an individual with his own deeply rooted subjective habits involves stress and strain which, if too severe, may injure health and work demoralization in the innovator.

The average person lacks the physical and nervous stability, and the reserves of nervous energy necessary to the withstanding of such a drain upon his strength. Consequently most adult persons find it necessary and expedient, regardless of their thought-out convictions, to submit to their ingrained habits, which are the habits of society, and to change only as fast as society itself changes.

On the other hand there are some who are so constituted that they are capable of innovation. Their number is increasing, if my personal observations of men and women mean anything; and as they increase they form circles among themselves and lend each other mutual support, aid, and comfort.

These innovators, I maintain, are valuable to society. They are violently denounced by "moral" people, but they are valuable just the same. They may blunder, but they do break trail.

Among them I should number such persons as Mr. and Mrs. Blank, regardless of whether or not Mr. and Mrs. Blank's theories are right or wrong.

CHAPTER III

MARRIAGE AND MORALS

1.

I STOPPED not long ago at a hotel in an important midwestern city where another Denver man, whom I will call Ewing, since that was not his name, was also staying. I knew him well; and rather early in the morning I dropped in at his room.

For a time we chatted of this and that. Presently I went to the window to take in the fine view that it commanded.

Near that window was a dresser; and on the dresser was the usual early-morning litter: a collar, a comb, a razor, and other items that would normally be there—together with others that would normally be quite somewhere else than on the dresser of a man a thousand miles from wife and home. Several hairpins, for instance, of the sort used for controlling bobbed hair; and a long-toothed comb in which a few golden strands were visible, shining like gold threads there in the morning sun.

I looked away as quickly as I could, but our eyes met, and he grinned sheepishly.

"I own up, Judge," he said. "I know you won't peach—or preach."

"You can be at ease on that score, Ewing," I said. "But what's the trouble? I would have said that among all the married couples I know you and your wife would be about the last to have such a thing happen as this. I have always thought of your marriage as showing that marriage isn't, after all, a failure, other evidence to the contrary notwithstanding. And here you pull this on me!"

My eyes turned again to the dresser. I was further from it now, but even at that distance one could see that gleam of hair, like

43

spun gold. His eyes followed mine, and for a moment we looked in thoughtful silence.

"You see—it's beautiful," he said at last, defensively.

"A blind man could see that," said I. "But what I'd like to know is how long it will take, at this rate, before you and your wife and two fine children (who have equities in the integrity of their home) appear in my court with business to transact."

"We'd be there right away if my wife ever found this out," he admitted. Then he added with a groan, "Oh, Lord, what a mess! I love and worship her; but would she believe it if she knew about this? Never!"

"There is a line in the Marriage Service of the Church of England," I observed, "that has been partly expurgated from the Marriage Service of the Book of Common Prayer in this country. In substance, if my memory serves me, it runs, 'with this Ring I thee wed, with my body I thee worship, and with all my worldly goods I thee endow.' A fine, specific use of language, don't you think?—I once heard a high-bred American woman say of it that she thought it indecent; but if marriage is to mean that, then we ought to be specific about it in our own minds, should we not; and if it is to mean something different, to correspond to the changes in this different age, then we ought to be specific about that also."

"True enough," he said gloomily. "But it's darned hard to switch from one angle to the other. It's been a wrench for me; and it would be impossible for my wife. And yet I think I'm right. I do worship her—with all of me. But in love you deal with infinity. I rob her of nothing when I go with this girl. And as for all my worldly goods, why, she has everything in the way of material comfort and provision that money can buy; and I have not violated the spirit of the agreement there, unless the dog-in-the-manger philosophy enters in. Of course I have violated the letter of the agreement. I admit that. But the letter killeth, while the spirit giveth life. I repeat, I rob her of nothing."

"Do you love the girl?"

"I love my wife," he answered. "As for the girl, why that depends on what you call love. I like her; and if she had more mental capacity I might come nearer to loving her. But even then she would not usurp the place held by my wife because one reacts toward individuals individually and uniquely. There is no duplicating in one woman the love one feels toward another woman. That is why this talk about exclusiveness in love seems to me a lie, a jealous lie.

"No, I don't love this girl in any deep or vital sense. We could part to-morrow and never see each other again, and we would feel no more regret than one feels ordinarily when separated from persons one is fond of. I simply like her. I have an affection for her. I enjoy her company. She attracts me. I enjoy taking her out to dinner and to see a show. That's innocent enough, isn't it? Well, I have enjoyed being completely *en rapport* with her, and for the same reason. The dinner and the show by themselves were not complete, and this other made it all complete and lovely.

"For the life of me I can't find any *rational* reason against it. We gave each other pleasure. We took what heaven gave, and we found it good; but society would step in and defile this beautiful thing by calling it unclean. . . . Damn it, Judge, I won't stand for it!

"She and I have enriched each other's lives. I am more of a man than I was and she is more of a woman than she was, because of it. People enrich each other by knowing each other, don't they? When you really know people, you know their mannerisms, their gestures, their way of thought, their emotional responses, the color of their hair, the lights in their eyes. One knows these things emotionally, and by experiencing them. But they can't be experienced completely without sex. They can't be grasped merely by the mind. And if society requires of such understandings between men and women that they must stop short of physical sex expression, then that nips in the bud what, in many instances, should be permitted to grow. No exchange short of the complete exchange, no merely mental exchange, can suffice."

"If your wife heard you," I remarked, "she would say that such remarks, if they applied to her, would be the philosophy of the ideal husband."

"They would apply to her if she'd let them," he said, beginning to pace the room furiously. "But she'd say, 'I want *all* of you, physically and spiritually; and if there is more of you left over after I am completely sufficed, then I want that, too. No other woman must have it. I have enough; but if I can't use the surplus, no one else shall.' "

"She would deny the existence of the surplus," I said. "She would say that you were dissipating your energies, and that it is the essence of love that it is exclusive."

"Quantitative thinking," he retorted; "as if one measured love in a bushel. Erotic avarice!—I've done no wrong, I tell you. I have a right to think for myself, and I'm going to do it. I guess I know what goes on inside of me."

"You are a rare one if you do," I observed. "Does all this upset you inside—pull you to pieces, so to speak? I ask because I have a belief that your subjective mind plays hob with you when you violate the habits and fears it was bred to."

He laughed. "Does it! Why, at first it made a wreck of me. I was nervous as a cat and I felt like a criminal. It was as if I had committed murder or burgled a house. But I'm getting over that; and I'd be over it completely if my wife knew—and approved what I'm doing.—Gee, if I could only tell her!"

"I take no sides in these matters," I said. "And my questions are less intended to express disapproval than they are to draw you out. I'd be interested to know how this situation came about."

He lit a cigarette and sat down. "It will be a relief to open up. Here's the way I see it—honestly, Judge. Margaret and I had reached a humdrum condition of life. Sex was humdrum. I didn't realize this, but she did; and she resented it, as a woman will, because she interpreted it to mean that I didn't care for her as I once did. She didn't realize that it was merely human; and that daily habit may deaden sensibility. Or, if she did realize it she resented it, and felt that where she was concerned such a thing should not happen.

"She figured that the glow of our courting days had passed; and that we had settled down to an arrangement from which all romance and beauty had fled. And she said so; and of course that created the very lack of romance and beauty of which she complained. My vehement denials did no good. She didn't believe me.

"The net result was a strained atmosphere in our home, with periodic outbreaks of exasperation from her, which storm I weathered as best I could.

"You can't force love, you know, and you can't force the active manifestations of sex. The more pressure she applied the deader I went inside. Fear, anxiety, the sense of strain, and the consciousness that I was in a false position, all conspired to inhibit me.— She, being, as you know, an exceptionally intelligent person, realized all this with her mind; but that didn't serve to control the instinctive something within her that impelled her to sting like a gadfly when her resentment came to the surface.

"Then, of course, she began, without meaning to, to look for causes of offense. It was a defensive measure, I suppose, as it tended to justify her in her own eyes. And when one looks for causes of offense in this life, one finds plenty. Little faults in me that had formerly had her indulgence became enormously significant. Mostly they were fresh evidence that I had ceased to love her as a normal woman wants to be loved, wanted, and courted.

"I could see how she felt, but the element of compulsion which she had introduced into the situation without meaning to, had put me under an evil spell.

"We had violent quarrels, during which she would nearly drive me to frenzy, nagging and prodding me with her tongue. And then, under that abnormal tension, the quarrel would dissolve in tears, and for a time after that we would seem to understand each other and would be happy in each other again.

"I have come to the conclusion, Judge, that when a woman lashes out at a man with her tongue the way she did at me, she is obeying a very profound biological impulse—and a very effective one; for those hours of misery did seem to have the effect of bringing us together. The trouble was it didn't last. Usually within a week we'd have it all to do over again.

"At last she began to wonder if there wasn't some other woman in my life, who was taking from her the love I would otherwise have given her. I don't know how long she had been wondering about this, but now she openly speculated about it.

"I want particularly to call your attention to the fact that up to that time there was no other woman, and that I had never contemplated such a thing,—save perhaps as every married man is at times tempted by women he meets casually and fancies he might like to know them better—thoughts he is careful to hide from his wife. At least I hid them from mine. She wouldn't understand it in a million years."

He paused in bitter silence.

"Don't be an ass, Ewing," I said. "You ought to know better than to underestimate her intelligence like that. That's a much bigger insult to her than any *liaison* could be. The trouble is you've never had the nerve to tell her the truth. It's a pity she can't hear this conversation. In fact, it's a pity a lot of wives can't overhear it. They might learn something.—Take your nerve in hand and tell her the truth. She's a wonderful woman; she has a fine mind and a big heart. She'd get it!"

He raised his hands despairingly. "Sure she's wonderful. Mentally she's a whizz. Sometimes she makes me feel like ten cents in comparison. But damn it, Judge, she's a *woman!* Moreover, her whole background and training have blinded her to just this kind of thing, though they have opened her eyes to a lot of other things. What goes on inside of me is simply outside of her ken. I'm sure of it. If she could read my mind she'd be shocked beyond anything she could put in words.—And besides, this is a one-sided business. I'd have to do all the confessing. *She* hasn't got anything to confess. Hell's bells! Why, she's like Cæsar's wife; she's a sort of an unapproachable Diana. She's as chaste as Lucrece. And if I owned up, she'd be judge and jury in one. How can I possibly meet a prospect like that?"

"Perhaps she isn't so oppressively good as you think," I said. "At least let's hope not. I'll wager she's human, and you ought to know it for sure. Anyhow, go ahead with your story."

He resumed, "She put the idea of other women into my head. She suggested it by her accusations, and I suddenly found myself getting a kick out of it. I think a lot of women do this, and virtually drive their husbands to it."

"And some husbands?" I queried. "Do they drive their wives to it?"

"I suppose so. But I never thought of such a thing in connection with her. I've never seen the least evidence that other men attract her. I have no doubt, however, I could put the idea into her head all right by saying to her things such as she has said to me. It might teach her a lesson.

"At any rate, the notion grew in my mind. I had an instinctive feeling that it might be the way out. So I took up with this girl— a nice little girl, Judge. She used to work in my office.—And here, far from home, we can be together without anxiety or fear.

"Now, Judge, I come to the heart of the matter. You can believe it or not; but a very curious thing happened when I made that break.—It was, of course, a fresh and unusual experience; and one grows by fresh and unusual experiences. They renew one's ability to find interesting meanings in life.

"This experience, after the first shock of fear and doubt, and what I may call remorse, was over, seemed to rehabilitate me. It stirred me up inside. Above all it took sex out of the routine and humdrum it had fallen into and gave it back the meaning and the compelling charm it had for me formerly. In fact it gave my love-life such a fillip that it transformed things at home. It all carried over into my relations with my wife; as if I had come back to her with the honeymoon point of view of which time and habit had robbed me.

"My wife is now happy. She has remarked repeatedly on the change in me. Naturally I have ventured no explanations. I am rather surprised that she hasn't asked more questions. But she is apparently perfectly happy, and she seems to have gotten over the notion that I have transferred my affections from her to some one else. If she has any secret theory about it I imagine it is to the effect that I may have had another woman on the string, but that I have now abandoned my wild ways, have dropped the other woman or women, and have come back to her. Which is exactly opposite to the facts.—Think of the irony of it, Judge! What would she say if she knew to what she owes her present happiness?"

"And so you are satisfied?"

"Satisfied! I should say not. Look at the fix I'm in. Here

I've got to lie and go on lying for the rest of my life. I have to make a business of concealment; and in our most intimate moments I have this secret to hide, when it would be perfect if I could tell her. Even at that she is likely some time to stumble on the truth. And then her humiliation, and her hurt pride, and her feeling that she was not able to hold me—not attractive enough to compete with other women and with Youth—all that— Can't you imagine what would happen? Why, she'd diagnose me and herself and the situation dead wrong.

"So fear dogs my steps. The satisfaction and benefit I might derive from this *liaison,* though it is not destroyed, is nevertheless reduced from what it might be. The whole-souled and carefree pleasure I ought to feel has to be restrained and watchful. I carry a sort of weight in my heart. I can't reason this away. Subjective habit, as you say! As far back as I can remember I have been taught that what I am now doing is wrong, a heinous sin. I don't believe that; and yet I am haunted by a feeling of internal anxiety from which I think nothing could wholly relieve me except my wife's understanding and approval.—And I know that is a large order to place with any human, flesh and blood woman educated to the traditional code of society in these matters.—What do you think of it?"

"I can't say that I see anything unusual in your case," I answered, "unless it's your desire to confide in your wife. As for the subjective conflict within you, I have seen many instances of that.

"Of course this talk about a man being able to love two women at the same time is old stuff. They all say that. Many men say it can be done, and most women say it can't. Perhaps it is a matter of individual temperament."

"I didn't say I loved two women at once," he retorted. "I think you are trying to draw me out. I don't love this girl in any deep sense of the word. I like her. She's a pleasant companion; she's pretty as a picture, and desirable as a gift from heaven. It is pleasant and lovely to be with her. Why demand that our play together take on the seriousness and weight of a lifetime passion? We neither of us want that.—So, what's the harm, Judge?"

"Is she of age?" I asked.

He laughed. "She is. You have no call to show your judicial teeth.—Besides this is a private and personal matter, as I see it, between her and me. It concerns nobody else, neither our neighbors nor the law."

"I interfere in people's lives as little as I can," I replied. "And you need fear nothing of the sort from me. As to having it out with your wife, of course you know her better than I do; and I don't presume to advise you on that point. In general, however, I think truth is a fine thing if you can get people to understand it. Most of us, unfortunately, regard facts as very offensive things. You'll have to use your own judgment. But—don't underestimate your wife's intelligence and good sense. If you do underestimate it, that may account for part of the trouble you have had. Try telling her."

"And if she forbids this affair to go on?"

"Be a sport," I said. "Take a chance on her. Maybe you and she can build a practicable scheme of living out of the wreck. Now *that* would be interesting, wouldn't it?"

But he shook his head. "A foolish risk," he said. "The situation is too one-sided. I've done all the sinning. Still, almost thou persuadest me—almost!"

2.

Though the conversation ended there, the incident did not. Months later I chanced to meet Mrs. Ewing. Her hair was black, not golden; but it had a fine sheen of health and beauty. She had keen brown eyes, a fine forehead, a firm, sweet mouth, and a width of jaw that indicated vitality and energy.

Mrs. Ewing is a graduate of a world-known women's college in the East. Among the many splendid women I have met she stands out as possessing what I consider a distinguished intellect. I shall long remember my talk with her as one of the most remarkable experiences I have ever had among the many that have come my way. I have had conversations with distinguished men, many of them leaders in the thought of this nation; and some of these have expressed with skill and with fine logic ideas which I have found stimulating and suggestive. But what I am about to recount came from a quiet, high-bred Denver woman. I shall set it down as faithfully as my memory of the occasion will permit.

Let me explain in this connection that the conversations I recount in this book are necessarily reduced to their significant essentials. It would be impossible, in a reasonable space, to recount the details of talks which in their accomplishment often occupied hours of time and repeated interviews. Digging the truth out of people is sometimes a slow business; and I want the reader to understand that these stories as I tell them usually develop far more swiftly in these pages than did the actual events on which they are based. Such foreshortening of the picture is proper and necessary, but I want the reader to understand it.

The talk between Mrs. Ewing and myself turned at first on some phases of my work in which she was interested; and it drifted toward the subject of marriage, as I meet with it in my domestic relations work. I let it drift because I was curious to find out, if I could, what would be this woman's response if her husband should take his courage in his hands and tell her the truth, as I am satisfied all husbands and all wives should do if they are both of them intelligent enough to line up facts, and evaluate them. Not all persons are so qualified, but it seemed to me that the Ewings were. People who are sufficiently intelligent to understand the truth are entitled to know it. But the truth may wreck others who lack the intelligence to cope with it.

I cited to Mrs. Ewing a typical case of marital infidelity, sufficiently like that of her own husband to serve as a test of her way of thought in such matters.

She heard me through in silence. "Should he tell her?" I concluded. "Suppose you were the woman! Would you get his point of view?"

"If I were the woman," she said slowly, "I think I would understand, and that I might put up with the situation though I would not like it."

"But would that be understanding?" I asked. "Wouldn't such a grudging concession merely be a source of fresh trouble? Could he be happy in his *liaison*? Wouldn't he have to drop it; and wouldn't the second state be worse than the first?"

She shook her head. "I see that. But it's a lot to ask; a lot to expect."

"Might such a woman not feel," I continued, "that her husband's faith in her understanding and sympathy was rather a compliment, and pretty conclusive evidence that he valued his relations with her so highly that he was willing to take tremendous chances with them in order to have them on a sound basis of mutual understanding?"

"The question rather strikes home," she said. "You see, Judge—" She paused, faltered, and then went on, "I—I have reason to think that Henry is indulging in just such an affair as you have described. He doesn't dream I suspect it. Perhaps on the whole it is better that he doesn't tell me. I might not be able to weather it. That is why I have not been able to bring myself to investigating and finding out. I lack the courage, I guess."

"Still," I suggested, "you would feel that the truth, if he produced it, would be in a sense a tribute to you. You'd respect him if he told it."

She nodded. "I think I am hoping, in the back of my mind, that he will. In the meantime, I only suspect this affair; and I am not letting it come between us. We have been quite happy lately."

"Why do you suspect it?"

She shrugged. "Intuition, I guess. Little indications. And— well, he seems to care more for me, for one thing."

I held my breath, afraid even to look up for fear my face might betray me. Manifestly one never can tell about a woman.

"It sometimes makes me feel," she went on, "that if he knew that I knew about it, and that if I could convince myself and him that I grudged him and the possible other woman no pleasure they might take in each other, then he would love me beyond measure, he would care for me beyond anything he could express— far more than he could care for any other woman no matter how intimate a friendship he might have with her.

"Do you see what I mean, Judge? Does it sound shocking? I fear I put it clumsily, for I'm groping in the dark; and I don't know quite what I mean myself. All I know is that I have these ideas at times, and that I'm torn by this conflict between my reason and my emotions, the emotions natural to any woman when some other woman intrudes.

"I think what I mean is this: that love is never delivered on demand; and that the true way to get it is to claim nothing and demand nothing, and simply to welcome it as a gift, arbitrarily bestowed by the giver. After all, Sex as Sex is a more or less meaningless and worthless thing. What gives it meaning and emotional value is the love back of it—and Love is by no means synonymous with Sex, though we often use the word as if it were.— And so I think sometimes that if I could make him love me first of all, not as a woman but as a human being, because he found me truly sweet and lovable, then his desire for me would follow; and if his desire were conceived in that fashion, it would be a truly wonderful, constant, and permanent thing, would it not?—And of course it works both ways. I naturally love him primarily for what he is as a person; and my desire for him—as a man—must spring from that, and be conditioned by that, if it is to be real and spiritually fruitful.

"One thing that has made me think this might be so is that even the release I suspect him of having taken for himself seems to have made him care more for me. I think he feels that I no longer restrict him and deprive him of something his nature may crave—not just Sex, you know, but human intimacies. Things are better between us now than they have been in years. Sometimes he is just one great big desire for me, like the eager boy he was when I married him. And I can't tell you how I love to have him so. If this can happen as a result of his summarily and secretly *taking* his freedom, how much greater would be the result if he had not had to *take* it. Suppose we *both gave*, without stint!

"I have heard you say, Judge, that marriage should ideally mean the union of one man and one woman. Is that your conception of marriage?"

"Emphatically," I said.

She nodded. "I think that is right. That is the way marriage should be. But it begins to come to me, Judge, that Henry and I have not been attaining a genuinely monogamic marriage by the ways we were taught, the ways of enforced and jealous exclusiveness. I begin to think that these outsiders who may enter into his life, or who might, I suppose, enter into mine, don't necessarily enter into our marriage, or become a factor within it, or in any way disrupt it or share it with us, or otherwise come between us. Love remains in that sense truly exclusive—a thing which we two possess between us—a unique communion in which no third person could share. I begin to think that the only way outsiders could rob us of this would be for one or both of us to forbid them to come in. If one does that, they may break in, like thieves, and rob us of each other.

"I don't know whether there is any soundness in these notions; but they may interest you because they are what I am thinking about—and I know you are tolerant toward people and their thoughts."

"I'm tolerant toward them so long as they try to think," said I. "And I try even to be tolerant toward those who don't."

"I am at least trying," she smiled. "But though it all sounds very plausible and convincing, Judge, theories and feelings are two different things. I *theorize* bravely, but I don't know how far I dare trust myself in *doing*. It is what one *does* that counts—not how one speculates and philosophizes. But the doing is dangerous. I feel as if I were on the edge of a precipice with my eyes blindfolded."

"You won't get very far with all this, Mrs. Ewing," I answered, "so long as you and your husband conceal your thoughts from each other. He probably wishes he might talk honestly with you, just as you would like to talk honestly with him—if you could get over your fear of each other, and particularly if he could get rid of his fear of you. Men commonly believe that women can't possibly get the masculine point of view in these matters. But I think that is nonsense. You have just demonstrated it.

"Let me make one suggestion. Some time draw your husband into a general conversation about these matters, and express some of the views you have been putting to me. Do it in a wholly impersonal fashion."

"Can a woman talk impersonally?" she asked.

"Certainly, if they see the desirability of it," I replied. "The trouble is that they generally don't.—Let me make another suggestion: Between intelligent persons who owe each other the truth and are capable of making facts definitive, concealment is the worst form of infidelity I know of; and both you and your husband seem to have been guilty of that. Society puts no stigma on such infidelity, but it is none the less deadly It shuns the truth because it distrusts it, and thinks it may be a lie. This attitude is due to fear; and fear is death. Remember, too, that since jealousy is fear, jealousy, too, is death. Now, one other thing. Would *you* have anything to confide in *him?*"

She laughed. "I see the point, Judge. I almost wish I had. It would put us on a level. I suppose it wouldn't do for me to fabricate a sin. It's the solemn truth that I was once—well, tempted. I felt the impulse. I don't think Henry could imagine me being even that wicked. That's one trouble. A woman should never allow herself to seem *too* dependable in such matters. Certainties are so uninteresting."

"I think," I replied, "that both of you may be rather missing the point. Let's get this clear. Does this philosophy of yours mean that you would discard or discount monogamy?"

"I don't think it does," she answered, "though perhaps it sounds so."

"Some might interpret it that way," I commented.

"Please understand me," she said. "I haven't thought it through. I'm floundering about in an effort to be honest. If I run into an occasional logical *impasse* I can't help it. I refuse to give up monogamy, Judge. That's what I've been trying to say all along. Oh, what *do* I mean?" She finished with a despairing little laugh.

"Well," I said, "let's see first what can be said for monogamy. For my part, I think monogamy is the ideal for people to work toward in marriage. They should achieve monogamy, both physically and spiritually, if possible. I think that in a marriage which represents the *real* union of a man and woman they find each other so evidently preferable to anybody else, both physically and spiritually, that they feel no inclination for sex experiences outside their own marriage. They uniquely fill each other's lives. They are connoisseurs in love; they are so particular that nothing short of the authentic best, created by themselves to suit their own need and their own taste, can satisfy them. And such an authentic best, of course, is not often built out of casual contacts; it isn't the growth of an hour or of a whim. It usually comes to perfection slowly, like a tree. A lot of people discover for themselves the inferiority of substitutes for this slow-grown thing, and they quit their foolishness after a very little experimenting. I have known many such. They seem to want to experiment largely because they have been told they mustn't. They think they feel a need, a 'repression,' but that feeling is mostly an illusion."

"I agree—absolutely," she exclaimed.

"I'm glad you see it," I continued. "But if that is your ideal, why do you compromise with it? Why not live up to it? Personally, I have found it very satisfactory in my own marriage."

"Yes," she retorted, "but that is because you and your wife wish it so, and not because society wishes it on you.—That's what I want. But my idea is that such an end can't be achieved by coercion, by prohibitions, by society saying, 'you shall,' or by wives and husbands saying to each other, 'you shall not.' The first thing to be had is freedom of choice. Everything valuable in human conduct has to flow from that. Am I right?—If Henry and I achieve the kind of monogamy you speak of, it must be a genuine achievement; and it must come into being because we genuinely want it and not merely because society says we must have it whether we want it or not.

"People who hold themselves to a technical monogamy when their heart and soul don't prompt them to it are not finding monogamy. Their hearts are not in it, whatever may be said of their bodies. They fool themselves. They shut their eyes to the facts, because society tells them it would be sinful candidly to admit the truth. Thus they achieve a fake. That's the way with thousands of marriages to-day. I simply won't have it that way. I don't like paste jewelry or other imitations of precious things. Monogamy is precious, and in its most perfect form it is rare. It isn't to be had for the asking. It is a product of culture and of educated preference. It must be *made*. It is, therefore, difficult; but I think most persons could achieve genuinely monogamous marriages—spiritually monogamous marriages—if society would give them a chance.

"I want such a marriage in my own life, and I refuse to be fully content with less. I think it can be attained by freedom of choice, and the freedom, if necessary, to make mistakes—yes, even polygamous mistakes. I'd rather arrive at a monogamous marriage with my husband by that road than not arrive at all. Besides, I don't think either of us would run to the making of mistakes if we were free to make them. Freedom is the best preventive for that sort of thing."

"Of course you realize that given that sort of freedom, a lot of people would run amuck," I observed.

"It would have to come gradually," she answered. "In the meantime why not reckon with people and their tastes and capacities as they are? I dote on Brahms and Beethoven; but I don't expect everybody else to conform to my musical standards. And so I say, why ram monogamy down the throats of people who either want it in some modified form, or who just naturally object to being made to do things, or who don't want it at all? Their tastes may not be highly cultured tastes, but they have a right to them. Also, they may not have married just the right person, and so circumstances may prevent them from achieving a truly monogamous marriage. If so, why deny them the right to better their condition if they can, so long as they don't violate other people's rights? It's all terribly complex, Judge—but freedom—surely that is simple."

"Your idea, then," I said, "is that if the bars could be let down, everybody would stop jumping fences and would stay in the pasture. Is that it?"

"They would find the right pasture, and then they would stay put," she answered. "They would stay because they liked the pasture. Why not?"

"I think," I answered, "that a long talk between you and your husband might serve a useful, and possibly a monogamic purpose. I prescribe it. It might keep both of you in the pasture—because you like it, as you suggest. I shall be interested to observe the outcome."

"Thank you, Judge," she smiled. "And if we are not down here before long, you may infer that it is all right."

Some months have passed; I have not seen them yet.

3.

In this incident, as well as in the story of Mr. and Mrs. Blank, which I told awhile back, there is food for thought. I am constantly in contact with indications which reveal a tendency on the part of conservative and conventional persons to experiment with sex traditions which they sincerely feel are in need of revision.

Many would say that there is nothing new about that. But I hold there is. Adultery is ancient, of course; but this tendency to debate what has hitherto been undebatable is new. The tradition which forbids it is no longer being taken at its face value.

This is a fact; and as such it must be faced. I strongly disagree with those who hold that it must be faced in a hostile spirit, or with an attitude of unqualified condemnation. If the old traditions are right, let them prove it by fighting their battle in the open, with fair field and no favor. I have been bitterly condemned for discussing such matters, and for stating such facts, on the ground that no good purpose is served by such discussion, and that it will simply encourage many persons to follow the example of the people I tell of.

That is simply a begging of the question. It assumes that the old order is unqualifiedly right, and that these efforts at change are wholly wrong. I don't agree. I think that point needs investigation of a very unprejudiced sort, and discussion very much in the open. I do not pretend to say whether these new developments are right or wrong—though I recognize that many of them are dangerous. I do feel very sure, however, that the old order has in it plenty of room for improvement, and that by the efforts and— if you will—the mistakes, of such innovators as these, we may arrive finally at a sane readjustment of our sex code.

What that readjustment will be, I don't know; it may, and probably will, turn out to be vastly different from the experiments of the Blanks and Ewings; but I don't see how we are to get it if there are no innovators to blunder and make mistakes while the rest of us play safe, and denounce and persecute. Progress has always been attained that way.

That is why I value the strivings and the discontent that lead many such persons as these to break more or less with accepted codes. To say, as many do, that these people are merely actuated by "lust" and by their "animal natures" betrays a lack of understanding of the meaning and the values of Sex which is characteristic of persons who hate the discomfort of thinking. It is a very complicated matter; and it can't be disposed of in any such offhand manner.

The lives of thousands of well-intentioned, decent, well-balanced people are in a state of turmoil and tragic unhappiness because they are at odds with the existing sex code. To put this down to "original sin" is theological nonsense. What it means is that there is something wrong with the code; and that only by experimentation and discussion can we discover what it is. This is one of the most important problems before society; and yet there are tremendous, organized forces in this country bent on suppressing all honest and frank discussion of it.

The reason for this book is this: if some persons have the courage to try to think out their own private conduct for themselves and run the risk of the social swats which our semi-barbarous civilization visits on such independence, then it is up to somebody to tell about it and discuss it with an open mind, and, if necessary, take the swats that may be expected to result from that. I may add here and now that I am getting them. They descend in the form of denunciatory letters, most of which refer largely to the Bible by Chapter and Verse; denunciations from certain types of ministers who shy at a fact as a bird does the net of the fowler; denunciations from editors, some of whom tell me privately that privately they are for me, but don't dare say so;—denunciations, in short.

4.

In the meantime, I find that I do not lack for distinguished company. The change now upon us is finding expression, not merely in the conduct and talk of obscure persons who are amateurs and novices in the field of Ethics, but also in the writings of persons whose opinions are of the highest import. Bertrand Russell, for example, is one of the finest scientific and philosophic minds in England. One might disagree with his opinions, but nobody of any discrimination could treat them lightly. I quote from his recent book "Education and the Good Life":

"One other thing in teaching (children) about sex-love. Jealousy must not be regarded as a justifiable insistence upon right, but as a misfortune to the one who feels it and a wrong toward its object. Where possessive elements intrude upon love, it loses its vivifying power and eats up personality; where they are absent, it fulfills personality and brings a greater intensity of life. In former days, parents ruined their relations with their children by preaching love as a duty; husbands and wives still too often ruin their relations to each other by the same mistake. Love cannot be a duty, because it is not subject to the will. It is a gift from heaven, the best that heaven has to bestow. Those who shut it up in a cage destroy the beauty and joy which it can only display while it is free and spontaneous. Here, again, fear is the enemy. He who fears to lose that which makes the happiness of his life has already lost it. In this, as in other things, fearlessness is the essence of wisdom.

"For this reason, in teaching my own children, I shall try to prevent them from learning a moral code which I regard as harmful. Some people who themselves hold liberal views are willing that their children shall first acquire conventional morals, and become emancipated later, if at all. I cannot agree to this, because I hold that the traditional code not only forbids what is innocent, but also commands what is harmful. Those who have been taught conventionally will almost inevitably believe themselves justified in indulging jealousy when occasion arises; moreover they will probably be obsessed by sex either positively or negatively. I shall not teach that faithfulness to our partner through life is in any way desirable, or that a permanent marriage should be regarded as excluding temporary episodes. So long as jealousy is regarded as virtuous, such episodes cause grave friction; but they do not do so where a less restrictive morality is accepted on both sides. Relations involving children should be permanent if possible, but should not necessarily on that account be exclusive. Where there is mutual freedom and no pecuniary motive, love is good; where these conditions fail, it may often be bad. It is because they fail so frequently in the conventional marriage that a morality which is positive rather than restrictive, based upon hope rather than fear, is compelled, if it is logical, to disagree with the received code in matters of sex. And there can be no excuse for allowing our children to be taught a morality which we ourselves believe to be pernicious."

Among persons who have thought out their judgments less clearly than does Mr. Russell in the pregnant passage I have just quoted, the working of the social change to which he gives such clean-cut expression is a curious thing to watch. Thousands who feel the pull of the new conditions and influences lack the courage to say what they think. In fact, they deny that any such change is possible or desirable, and they enroll under the banners of conservatism with an *éclat* that deceives the very elect.

5.

I know, for example, a physician in Denver who is outwardly one of the pillars of the old order. Women's clubs swear by him; social workers buzz around him; dowagers, alarmed about the Younger Generation, look upon him as a steadfast and a shining light that reveals always which is the path of virtue; he is a king pin in one of the most important churches in Denver; and if any one wants to put over radical ideas sufficiently cloaked in the mantle of respectability to win conservative support, they turn to the eminent Dr. Archibald Fellowes for support—knowing that what he supports will be regarded as somehow safe and conservative by those who would sell their souls to the devil before they would abandon safety and conservatism.

If Dr. Archibald Fellowes were asked which passage in the above quotation from Bertrand Russell he most disapproved of, he would probably point to the part that reads, "I shall not teach that faithfulness to our partner through life is *in any way* desirable, or that permanent marriage is to be regarded as excluding temporary episodes. So long as jealousy is regarded as virtuous, such episodes cause grave friction; but they do not do so where a less restrictive morality is accepted on both sides."

And he would point to other passages which he would pronounce almost equally offensive, and equally evidential that the Home is in grave peril. He would add that unless something is done about it, society is going to the bow-wows.

I recall that once when a certain other Denver physician was prosecuted and convicted on the charge of having performed abortions, Dr. Archibald Fellowes was a leader among the physicians of Denver in encouraging the prosecution that finally resulted in the man's conviction.

A few months after this abortionist was safely behind the bars, where he could no longer be a social menace, Dr. Archibald Fellowes personally performed an abortion on a young married woman whom he himself had made pregnant. He performed the operation in a very respectable Denver hospital, and he gave out to those who knew about it that the girl had been consorting with her divorced husband, and had become pregnant that way.

He continued till recently his intimacy with this girl, whom I know very well, and who confided in me.

He has a wife and a family of four very fine children. His home is a happy one, so far as I know.

His intimacy with the girl of whom I have been telling arose as the result of her going to him for treatment. He cured her and then made love to her. He thereby violated, not merely the social code, but the ethical code of his own profession, of which he is a leading light. *And* by loudly demanding vigorous prosecution, he helped send another man to prison for doing unintelligently and clumsily what he himself thinks nothing of doing intelligently, and skillfully.

As a matter of fact, the real reason the abortionist was convicted by the jury was not that he had broken the law by committing an abortion, but that he had recklessly performed the operation on a woman so far advanced in pregnancy that she died—as a result of what he did. "We just figured," said one of the jurors afterward, "that if he was such a reckless damn' fool as that we'd better send him up."

Personally I am strongly against abortion except when, for certain clear reasons, connected usually with health, it is unmistakably indicated. In the meantime the reader will not fail to note two things— first, that the jury was very little concerned with punishing abortion, and sentenced the doctor for his recklessness and want of skill in practicing it; second, that Dr. Archibald Fellowes himself is apparently as little opposed to abortion as he is to other breaks with our established ways of thought and conduct.—Thirteen men, one of them a reputable doctor, you see, secretly *at odds with a code to which they still give outward assent.*

I know a doctor who performs in Denver an average of an abortion a day, mostly on married women; and I haven't a doubt that at an extremely conservative estimate, there are a thousand abortions a year performed in Denver.

For the benefit of those readers who demand why the doctors who perform these operations are not prosecuted, let me say that it is practically impossible to get women to testify in such prosecutions, and that district attorneys give it up as a bad job—except when the operation results, or threatens to result, fatally.

Now in setting down such facts as these I do it without the slightest animus toward Dr. Archibald Fellowes. Indeed, I regard him as an asset to the community; for he is an extremely competent physician. I have told about him because his case is typical. He is like thousands and thousands and thousands of others, in that his inner life, be it right or wrong, is different from his outer life. This fact he conceals. He has to. If he didn't he would lose caste. So he keeps up the sham. He secretly lives the thing he outwardly denies.

He accepts and practices, in private, the views which he would pillory a man like Bertrand Russell for boldly expressing in public. In his secret conduct and in his secret convictions, he conforms, for instance, to what Mr. Russell suggests as feasible and possibly desirable in permanent marriage. *In practice* he regards faithfulness to one's partner in life as in no way desirable, and he thinks permanent marriage should not be regarded as excluding temporary episodes. It is true that he apparently rejects Mr. Russell's suggestion that such episodes should be based on an honest mutual understanding between husbands and wives, and that a less restrictive morality be accepted *on both sides*. But possibly that is not because he dissents from this view, but rather because he fears the consequences of trying to convert his wife. Like my friend Ewing, he would doubtless convert her if he could—unless, as is quite likely, he is one of those males who hold to the double standard.

6.

The point I want to make is this—that people are *doing* these things; and that what they are *doing* constitutes the reality of this matter—not what they *profess* in order that they may avoid social destruction. If this reasoning is correct, then I believe I have enough evidence to justify the conclusion, not that this change in our sex morals is going to take place at some time in the future, but that it has already largely taken place, and is developing and crystallizing into a tacitly recognized and increasingly tolerated code. It is not that such practices are new or have never been known before, but that they have support from such a large segment of society.

We *have* this thing among us *now*. It can't be stopped. And to me it seems evident that the only course open to persons who are capable of rational thought is to accept the change, help guide it wisely, and transform it into a social asset as quickly as possible. In my judgment it is capable of becoming a social asset, and it is capable of bringing joy rather than destruction into human life.

Even the most casual survey of social history, and of the growth and development of folkways into moral customs, demonstrates conclusively, not only that such changes can't be stopped, but that they usually meet some established social need, and are therefore beneficent. They are not to be feared but to be welcomed.

I don't see how any one with the least capacity for honest thinking can ignore the fact that it is custom that makes this or that line of conduct "right," in the eyes of society, regardless of whether it is truly ethical or not. We have many customs which are "moral" but which are also unethical. To show how irrational the whole business is: within the last ten years we have had changes in women's dress, for instance, that were unthinkably "wrong" formerly. Only "lewd" women wore clothes then which are accepted now as a matter of course by the most conservative and conventional persons.

7.

Fifteen or twenty years ago no decent woman could appear in a one-piece bathing suit. The police would have arrested her if she had done so. I remember how in those days a well-known actress appeared in a play, during one episode of which she was supposed to wear a bathing suit—a heavily skirted and properly elongated bathing suit, on the stage. Dramatic critics mentioned it. Great excitement along the Great White Way. New York, that now yawns at the nude beauties in the revues, was interested. Would she dare do it? After a generous lot of publicity out of what her press agent had skillfully conveyed to the newspapers, the lady got around the difficulty by wearing a bath robe, through the folds of which the bathing suit occasionally and coyly showed that it was there. None of us thought we were prurient fools, but that is the only word, I think, that can describe such a state of the public mind.

To-day a one-piece bathing suit could be used in any play on any stage in New York if the drama called for it, and it wouldn't bring a comment from anybody except hopeless cases that belong in asylums, or in psychiatric clinics. Young girls, clad in one-piece bathing suits, now swarm our beaches, glowing with health, brown from the sun, lovely in their unhampered grace, chaste in the unashamed and unafraid uses of their fine, strong bodies. Nor do they bring umbrellas for fear it will rain on their bathing suits. Rather they swim and dive in a way that should bring clean delight to the heart and mind of any healthy-minded person. But who started it all—and in the teeth of what protests from the virtuous prudes who follow suit, now that some one else has had the nerve to make it easy and safe?

It was flappers who made these innovations in dress. Historians of the future will make due record of this fact, and will trace many a vital social change back to it: The derided flapper has turned out to be a major determining factor in the changes I am discussing in this book.

Who can forget the roar of disapproval the virtuous raised when the flappers raised their skirts even above the ankle line? How the morals of the innovators were called into question; and how, as we got used to it, we gradually discovered that we had been uttering unclean nonsense, and that this change in women's clothing was sane, reasonable, and clearly in the interest both of health and morals!

Clothes, when used for concealment, are one of the most fruitful sources of the sex obsessions that possess us. For my part I wish the day might come when we might strip every stitch from our bodies anywhere at any time without shame. If it were customary to expose the human body to public view, some of us would take better care of it, who need to, and would be less like what Carlyle called forked radishes.

Women and men bathe together naked in Japan. It is "right" there because it is the custom. In this country some people are said to do it at wild parties. Thus, what is clean and lovely in Japan we transform into obscenity perpetrated in silver pigsties.

It is interesting to note in this connection that thousands of ministers all over this country are beginning to defend the flapper and her innovations from the pulpit. I continually see in the newspapers accounts of sermons in which the Rev. Mr. So and So has pronounced the Younger Generation on the right track. There is hope for the Church in that attitude of mind; and it is growing. What I am wondering is how long it will take the clergy to support other changes which they as fiercely denounce to-day as they once did those now "moral" modes of dress.

The clergy have a great opportunity here, if they could only see it; and if they would take a chance on getting fired by their outraged congregations, whose leading members practice what they won't allow any one to preach.

8.

Thus the changes still go on, both in dress and in conduct; and still we have people who learn no lesson from the past, who absorb no wisdom from history, and who kick consistently and steadily and *stupidly* at every latest phase of change, while they *accept* those phases which they have gotten used to.

What applies so clearly in women's dress applies just as clearly in our sex code. That code is changing. In a few years the people who are holding up their hands in speechless horror at the "demoralization" which they see around them, will accept certain results of that "demoralization" as a matter of course; and in the same breath they will turn the guns of their wrath on some other change which is recent and therefore "wrong."

The facts which I am constantly observing lead me to believe that the day is not far off when these calamity howlers will find themselves acquiescing in a revolutionary conception of what marriage is and of what it is for. They will acquiesce in it because it will be "custom" and therefore "right"; and they won't have the least notion of the slow stages by which they got there after "immoral" people had done the dangerous work and made a broad highway for their tender feet and their flabby moral sinews. They don't know anything about covered wagons. They ride in automobiles and ballasted Pullmans.

In that perhaps not very distant day, I think it quite possible that society at large will accept Mr. Russell's drastic statement, which seems so significant of the present social drift.

9.

At the same time, there will come other changes. The conservatives of that day will accept the Companionate Marriage as a solution for men and women who want to live together without raising families; since legalized birth control and divorce by mutual consent for childless people will by then be the accepted thing.

They may even accept the notion that people should be taught "the facts of life"; and that since Love is what makes the world go 'round, it might be well to turn its enormous energy to some rational use, and that people should therefore be taught love as an art—not sex love merely, but Love. For Mrs. Ewing spoke truly when she suggested that sex love is a worthless thing unless Love be the source of it; and that men and women must love each other as personalities first,. and as men and women second, if sex is to retain permanent interest and freshness in their lives.

Since Love is an art, sex love is likewise an art. All persons, particularly young persons, should know this, and they should be taught in houses of human welfare, the biological and psychological essentials on which the activities of sex are based. To some the suggestion that sex love is an art and should be taught as such, will seem shocking. But the evidence that passes before me daily of the bungling and terrible stupidity and ignorance of men and women in their physical and spiritual relationships with each other is a far more shocking thing even than would be the old-fashioned pagan Temple of Venus in every town in place of the present Ford sedan. I sometimes feel that ninety per cent of the mountainous misery in the world is due to our lack of education in these matters.

The ancients were not so wholly lacking in common sense about some things as are we, with our Puritan civilization, and the tangle of pseudo-Christian theology which we are pleased to call religion. The ancients—some of them, at least—perfectly understood the importance of giving some practical, direct, and unashamed attention to making effective, rather than abortive, the fact of Sex.

They solved it in their own fashion, a fashion which seems repugnant to us. Where we regard virginity in a bride as a pearl of great price, for instance, some of the ancients bluntly pronounced it a perilous thing. They had conventions, in fact, which forbade it in a bride.

We have quite different and far more "virtuous" notions; hence the problem of sex ignorance is always with us. Some day we shall solve it, in our own fashion—a different fashion from that of the ancients, doubtless. And at present it is impossible to forecast what that solution will be. All that is certain is that some scientific and rational solution is needed.

CHAPTER IV

THE GREEN EYES OF MARRIAGE

1.

The papers were full, only the other day, of the story of a wealthy man who shot his wife and then himself. The pistol lay on the floor between the two bodies. At first it was uncertain which had fired the gun, and what was the cause of the quarrel. Later they found in the dead man's pocketbook the torn fragments of a letter written to his wife—a love letter from another man.

To ask whether this husband would have killed his wife and himself if custom had not taught him the savage lesson that such was the traditional and proper course for any real man to follow in such circumstances is to answer it. Men and women have been *taught* that line of conduct from childhood, precisely as a high class Japanese is taught from childhood that under certain conditions of conventional disgrace the only thing an honorable man can do is commit hara-kiri. He must not shoot himself nor take poison nor resort to drowning, mind you. The convention calls, not merely for suicide, but for suicide in a ritual manner, prescribed and painful. He must rip open his abdomen with a knife,—hardly a quick or an easy death.

We think such conduct senseless and irrational. When an American general loses a battle, for instance, our customs require nothing of the sort from him. We would consider it utterly preposterous. The conventional hara-kiri we think unworthy of intelligent human beings; and so it is, as judged by every reasonable standard of conduct that we in the western world know anything about. And yet we prescribe, and have prescribed in the past, other conventional courses which are equally unreasonable and irrational and unworthy of intelligent human beings. We grow up taking these

70

for granted as the proper thing to do if one has the nerve to do it.

For instance, men used to stand up at a set distance apart and try to kill each other with sword or pistol if one had called the other a liar or a coward or had flung his glove in the other's face, or done some other thing which was supposed to snuff out the other man's "honor" as a puff of wind extinguishes a candle flame. Obviously the flame had to be relighted—by a magic ritual; and the magic ritual was to fight a duel. A human life was thought to be a fit price for extinguishing or even causing to flicker the sacred flame of romantic "honor." It didn't matter how evilly a man might live. He was "honorable" till he refused to fight some one who said he wasn't. In the event of such refusal he was a "coward."

Well—we don't duel any more—not in America at least. We would call a killing in a duel murder, and would treat it as such. We no longer have any romantic illusions about what dueling *is*.

On the other hand, we still cling to the prompt and romantic use of a gun when "infidelity" shows its head in marriage. This hideous thing *still* remains among our sanctioned practices. It is, of course, contrary to our statute laws, but what are statute laws when they run counter to custom? It is founded in part on romantic love, and in part on the rooted notion, still extant, that women are property, and that marriage, on either side, confers the ownership of one's mate.

Here is a tradition of whose "respectability" there can be no possible question; and yet it has no possible value this side of Hell. It does not make men brave or women good. It merely makes beasts of us whenever we acknowledge that it has authority over us. For such sanctions as this are *War;* and War on any scale whatever, public or private, is an evil, degrading, and needless thing.

2.

The fact is that our marriage conventions, as they work out in the "unwritten law," *glorify jealousy and make a fetish of it.* I believe that jealousy, taking the form of a claim to the exclusive ownership and possession of a mate, is the cause of most divorce litigation whenever such litigation is based on a failure in the sex life of the parties involved. I am sure, too, that it is, directly or indirectly, the cause of ninety per cent of the unhappiness in married life.

Jealousy is simply another way of demanding one's place in the sun—or under the domestic spotlight—a place in the center of the stage, as an exclusive object of consideration and attention. It is an impossible claim, when made by one human being on another, and human relationships are unworkable in its presence.

At the very heart of this "Christian," but often very un-Christ-like, civilization of ours, we place this ugly thing, this mother of lies and abominations, on a throne beside the domestic hearth, and in so doing we exalt selfishness, exclusiveness, fear, suspicion, and raw egotism in the home to the position of cardinal domestic virtues.

Jesus said that he who makes himself least becomes thereby the greatest; that he who takes the lowliest seat is called higher; that the meek inherit the earth; and that those who stand and serve become the lords of life. Life is builded on such spiritual paradoxes as these.

But how can these paradoxical values of the spirit find their place in a marriage code which so often derives its authority and its compulsive control over human beings, not from the free will and mutual consent of the persons involved, but from jealousy?

Let me define here what I mean by this word. Jealousy must not be confused with the perfectly natural desire to keep and hold an important, and possibly a first, place in the heart of a person whom one loves. It consists rather in a willingness and a determination to hold such a place regardless of that free and spontaneous mutuality so necessary to love. It is a wish and a determination to possess another. Unlike love, jealousy does not give *first* place to the happiness of its object. It gives first place rather to the desire and self-interest of the person who feels it. Its object, often cleverly disguised, is personal advantage. Jealousy is concerned with one's own happiness. Love is concerned with the happiness of the loved one.

Jealousy has nothing to do with love though it masquerades as love. Animals often show it. It is common and instinctive even in very young children. Mothers often show it when their sons marry. The fact that it is biological does not justify it, for love is also biological, and it is the higher law, since it makes for greater intensity of life. Jealousy belongs to Nature "red of tooth and claw." In a thing so complicated as human life, jealousy is a triple-distilled spiritual poison; and where sex relations are concerned it ruthlessly murders every other spiritual quality that can make marriage either practicable or desirable.

I do not discount the fact that when two persons love each other unequally, so that the one pines for what the other cannot give, the situation is unfortunate and often tragic. But if love cannot be forced, that, surely, is no excuse for trying to force it. Such a course may be instinctive, but it is also irrational and wrong. We shall do well to face life as it is. I admit that it is not as we would like to have it.

3.

When the word "jealousy" is used with respect to husbands and wives, it is usually taken to mean an unfounded and therefore mean and ignoble suspicion. Othello is a classic example of jealousy in marriage in that sense. But had Desdemona been in fact "unfaithful," then we would not call Othello's emotional response "jealousy," unless within some carefully restricted meaning of the word. Rather we would think of it as the legitimate rage, the righteous wrath of a wronged man, whose wife had played him false, and whose friend had stolen from him a woman who was his particular and exclusive property—he being also hers, though less so.

Under the stress of such righteous wrath, he might, with that sanction of custom called "the unwritten law," properly kill her, kill her paramour, and then—if intended for High Tragedy—kill himself.

The customs now in force in our so-called civilization pronounce all this *morally impeccable.* If you don't believe me, try to assemble a jury that will pronounce guilty of murder the man or woman who slays in such a fit of *traditional, customary, socially sanctioned, homicidal rage.* I don't say that such a jury could not be found;

but it would be difficult; and a few decades ago it would have been all but impossible. The custom is changing—though slowly; and this change is extremely significant. I note that a jury in New York state has recently found guilty of murder a man who pleaded the "unwritten law."

Generally speaking, however, the fact stands that it would be hard to find a juryman, trying such a case, who would not feel that the person who did not experience such homicidal rage under such conditions was falling far short of his or her duty, and was either a coward or a cold-blooded fish.

And yet this attitude of mind is irrational and savage to the last degree. It assumes as a fact what is happily becoming less and less and less a fact, that one person can own and possess another person—as if anybody, under any conceivable human relationship, could have equities of so preposterous a nature. Such equities are fictitious, and the custom that has sanctioned them for ages has no genuine authority. That is why men and women in this age are beginning to snap their fingers at it.

4.

Phyllis, age twenty-two, married Bert, who is three years older than she. The marriage took place three years ago. Phyllis had already come to me with her troubles; and she came to me immediately with this. She was sorry she had married him. She told me with tears that she did it on impulse. "I felt I ought not to," she said, "and I called you by telephone for an engagement to ask you what you thought. But you were out of town, and—and—here I am. Can't you annul the marriage, Judge?"

"How can I, Phyllis?" I said. "You are over twenty-one. If you were less than that I could probably free you. As it is, you will have to submit to the cumbersome divorce machinery by which the state makes it as impossible as it can for adults to get a divorce."

Then she told her story: She had, as I knew, for a matter of two years had an affair with a man of forty whom I will call Bell. Mr. Bell had wealth, social position, and education; and he was very different from the callow youths of her own age with whom she was used to associating. He was attracted to her by her beauty and her

very real refinement. But he was married, and there could,· therefore, be nothing in such an affair for Phyllis but disappointment.
He wanted to divorce his wife and marry Phyllis; but as this would
mean his ruin as a professional man, in Denver, he did not dare take
such a step!—At the same time Phyllis's intimacy with him spoiled
her for the crude love-making she encountered elsewhere.

In the meantime Phyllis ran around a good deal with young
people of her own age. Among them was Bert, a young traveling
man. Bert made violent love to her; she yielded; and whenever he
was in town, about once in three weeks, their relations were of the
most intimate sort. And under this arrangement they were both
very happy. They had no quarrels, they parted reluctantly, and
Bert returned again to her happily after his trips as a hardware
salesman.

While they were apart neither tried to dictate to the other. Bert
of course knew that she went out with their "set." He also knew
of her already established affair with Bell, and that she confined
herself to that. He knew also that other young men took her to
dances and dinners. These things he took quite as a matter of
course, and with no manifestations of jealousy whatever. She on her
part never thought of restricting him in his association with other girls.

So far as their life together was concerned, marriage could apparently make no difference in it. Had they been married, their routine
would have been practically the same, since neither wanted children.
Marriage, however, would make the difference that they could live
together openly, and that the tie would be recognized and permanent.
Bert kept urging marriage, and she finally consented against her
better judgment.

And now note what Phyllis said to me: "Before I married him,
Judge, Bert was perfectly sweet and dear. I really loved him and he
loved me, and we were ever so happy when we were together. But
now we're miserable. He wants me to travel around with him
because he's afraid I'll go out with other men. I went out last
night to dinner with two girls and two men and another fellow.
There was nothing wrong with it. They were our old set. But
Bert would be furious if he knew it. He says he'll kill me and

himself if he ever finds that I have been unfaithful to him or that I have anything more to do with Mr. Bell. He never used to say such things; but now he watches me all the time, and he doesn't want me to go anywhere with anybody while he is away, or to have any pleasure. He'd like to lock me in a room when he starts on his trips and keep me there till he gets back. And he insists that I must give up my job and travel around with him. And I don't want to do that. Why should I, any more than before we were married? He can have me just as much now as he did then. Why were we happy then and unhappy now?"

"Do you feel the same about Bert and other women?" I asked.

"Of course. Why, I'd just die if I knew of his having anything to do with any other girl. I never felt that way till we got married.— And now I'm so afraid about Mr. Bell. Why, if I should so much as look that way, I don't know but what Bert would go and shoot him.—And, Judge, one reason why it might be better for me to travel with Bert is that Mr. Bell is sure to call me up as soon as he gets back from this trip he is on—to New York. And if he does— well, I'm afraid I can't resist him. He'll want me. I know he will, and I think as much of him as I ever did. He's different from all the others. Oh, if I could have married him! And, oh, if I hadn't married Bert! I'm so wretched. And now if I stay, and Mr. Bell comes back, and Bert ever finds out—he'll shoot, I know he will.— If only he'd let me step out."

"And what about you?" I demanded. "Would you let him step out?"

"I should say not!" she exclaimed. "If he stepped out I'd just about die. I'd go mad with jealousy. I know it's unreasonable, but I can't help it."

"You helped it before you married him, but you can't help it now. Is that it?"

"Yes."

"And now you two young fools are engaged in watching each other, and preventing each other from doing what you each want to do yourself. Now, Phyllis, listen to me. It goes without saying that you must keep away from Bell. When you married Bert you knew he would insist on that; and unless you had an understanding with him to the contrary your marriage constituted a clear-cut agreement to quit Bell.

"But Bert's insistence that you must not run around with your friends in his absence is all wrong. If he will have it that way he'll drive you to things you would never have thought of. Your marriage must not start on such a basis. If it does, you'll be on the rocks in no time. You and Bert must face this issue and be reasonable in your demands on each other.

"Since you both equally demand faithfulness of each other you must both be prepared to deliver in that respect right up to the hilt. Your jealousy of Bert in regard to other women, coupled as it is with your speculations about going back to Bell, is a preposterous thing. If you two can't be good sports and observe the elements of fair play and decency and honesty in dealing with each other, there is no destination for you short of the divorce court.

"I don't attempt to tell you what you can and cannot do. What arrangement you and Bert make between you in this matter is your own affair. But you must arrive at an understanding of one sort or another, and then abide by it. It must be voluntary on the part of both of you, and you must carry it out to the letter, not because somebody else says so but because you want to. If you and Bert don't care enough for each other to be square with each other, then the sooner you quit and go your ways, with divorce or without it, the better for both of you. I would think your present selfish behavior toward each other, each of you trying to take all and give nothing, was little short of caddish if I didn't realize how bewildered you are by the situation, and by your own defective training and education in these difficult matters. The fact is that you are both the victims of the traditions you were brought up in. It's a subjective habit. You'd better be careful how you try to break with it. In the meantime, I am sure that when you realize that all you and Bert need do is play fair, you will be far on the road to being happy together. Bring him up here and let's have a talk."

5.

Later I talked with Bert. I found him a nice enough boy turned into a jealous young pup by the notion that having married a girl he must begin exerting the traditional authority of a husband.   He had the support of our conventions in this, and it had never remotely occurred to him that he might be wrong, or that he could possibly take any other attitude.   He accepted it unquestioningly.   Phyllis, of course, had equal backing in her jealousy from a tradition only a little different from that which actuated Bert.

The situation amounted simply to this: Formerly these two had been happy because the conventions in which they live and move and have their being permitted them to be *free*.   This didn't mean that either of them felt free to indulge in sex orgies, but simply that whatever restraints they chose to place on their conduct were of their own making, and in accord, more or less, with their own sense of what was fitting and proper.   They may have made mistakes in deciding what was fitting and proper, but they at least made their own decisions, and their conduct flowed genuinely from that.   Under this system of deciding their own conduct and making their own moral decisions, they got along, on the whole, pretty well.   Moreover, they were fairly responsible in all that they did.   They were willingly subject at all times to the feeling *that among the things they must not do were things which evidently worked injury to other persons*.   In matters where they thought no injury to others was involved, they generally did as they chose, and even violated the sex conventions without feeling that it did harm either to themselves or any one else.   Such was their view as it worked out in practice. I don't mean that they consciously analyzed it as I have done, but that they acted on it, and that it worked reasonably well for them, without ruin or disaster or unhappiness.—Very good.   Such was the situation while they were unmarried.

With marriage this situation completely reversed itself.   They became immediately unhappy.   They immediately began forbidding each other to do things which formerly they had done as a matter of course, and in which they had never thought of restraining each other.

The convention of marriage, which they accepted at its face value as a thing to be acted on without question or debate, stepped in and created between these two an attitude of mind which proved destructive to their happiness. They didn't need such an attitude of mind; they had gotten along without it hitherto. But now they were both saddled with it. And it transformed what they had thought was good into something whose fruits were unmistakably evil.

On the one hand, the "unwritten law" laid certain obligations on Bert. As a self-respecting male, it had now become his duty to defend his home and his honor and his marriage bed; and if anybody slipped past his guard, then he must shoot things up. He didn't question this. Few men do.

Phyllis, on the other hand, was under a similar set of traditional obligations, somewhat modified. She had been taught, and had always taken for granted, that other women would rob her of Bert if he should pay too much attention to them. Bert had only so much love to give, and what he gave to any one else necessarily meant deprivation for her.

That there was something self-contradictory in this view of the matter she might have suspected from her own earnest affirmation to me that her liking for Bell did not make her think any the less of Bert. She really believed this; but she couldn't see how such a thing might logically work both ways. She was more than willing to continue with Bell, but she was crazy jealous at the thought of Bert taking a similar liberty with some other woman. Bert was her husband, and she owned him and wanted exclusive possession, even while she resented his wanting exclusive possession of her. She would watch; and if Bert formed any outside attachments, she proposed to raise hell. Those were her words to me.

6.

So here they were, each longing, like an imprisoned bird, for something they had both given up. They wanted the old freedom, the old sense of personal independence which had formerly been as the breath of life to them. They wanted it for themselves though they would not grant it to each other. Something had stepped in and said, "No more of that. You own each other now; and all these things you have liked and enjoyed, you must henceforth *forbid to each other* regardless of whether you mutually, and of your own will, renounce them in your hearts or not."

I submit that the reaction against a thing like that is inevitable, natural, and to be expected. It is utterly impossible to impose such restraints on people *from without* and not thereby create the internal feeling that the restraints are not reasonable. Resentment and rebellion are immediately in evidence, and these form a direct incitement to unconventional behavior.

Before marriage the personal life of these two was ruled, as I have said, by promptings and restraints that came from within and were voluntary. It was not perfect, but it was genuinely authoritative so far as it went. After marriage Bert substituted his commands for Phyllis's internal system of self-control, and she imposed hers on him in the same manner. Thus an invalid and ineffective kind of restraint replaced what had, in its way, been an effective and genuine personal code,—a code which was effective and genuine simply because it was created by Phyllis and Bert within their own hearts for their own personal use.

I am not saying it was an adequate code, or that it might not have been much improved. *I merely say that they obeyed it because they had made it. There is no other way in which human conduct can have any ethical quality whatever.* That any code, be it a marriage code or what you please, should thrust out of people's lives a thing which, though imperfect, is genuine, and substitute what is not genuine at all, is an outrage so unspeakable that I can find no words in which to denounce it adequately.

If it were not for this damnable interference by society in the private lives of Phyllis and Bert, they could have lived together in marriage just as happily as they did before marriage. In fact they would have been much happier in marriage than out of it, and their marriage would then have justified itself by giving them a fuller union in each other than before. Furthermore, they would both have been much more likely to forego outside sex relations and to lose all desire for them. As it was, the tight rein they kept on each other was a constant reminder of things forbidden, and it aroused the very desires it was intended to quench.

If these two could have persuaded themselves to forget that they were married; if they could have wiped it out of their minds by tearing up their marriage certificate, and if they could then *mentally* have gone back to the old free relationship, and picked up the threads of the old free intimacy, and resumed their respect for each other's personalities and each other's rights, they could have made a successful marriage of what was otherwise doomed to failure.

As it is, they have now struggled along bravely for three years. I have done what I can to set them right, but some persons can't think past a convention. Unconventional before marriage, because unconventionality was the convention of their social set, they are furtively unconventional now because furtive unconventionality is also the convention of their set. They must not be honest. Goodness, no! How shocking! That would not be conventional! Instead they must watch each other, and forestall each other, while they each play the game of slipping by with something.—And they do it. Phyllis went back to Bell, and Bert secretly indulges in his own affairs on the side; and so the tension grows. Each furiously suspects the other, and neither is willing fearlessly to accord to the other the liberty which was once as the breath of life in the nostrils of them both.

7.

I feel confident that if they had the courage and good sense to turn each other loose, so to speak, regardless of temporary consequences or of the first excessive rebound after so much restraint, they would presently find each other, no matter how many persons had apparently come between them. I think they would find their married intimacy, their mutual sympathy, and their bond of interest in each other so infinitely superior to any substitute they could find in outside relationships that they would cease their outside affairs from sheer indifference and *ennui*. The interest they now take in philandering would transfer itself to their marriage; and the boredom they now feel toward their marriage would transfer itself to their philandering, where it belongs.

But at present they are very far from this consummation. Their condition is quite otherwise. And Marriage, *as we have it and as we conceive it,* has done this thing to two persons whose minds have not been keen enough to penetrate the fact that society has not really married them at all, and that it has palmed off a fake on them.

They wanted bread, and they have been given a stone. Society is doing this thing to thousands whose minds seem to be no keener. There are yet others, however, who are beginning to see that a cast iron morality cannot take the place of genuine ethics; and some of these are repudiating the fraud and are experimenting with honesty and common sense in its place. This does not mean that they are discarding marriage. We shall never discard marriage. But they are beginning to insist that the thing be real.

Please understand me. I am speaking of *honesty* and *common sense*. I am not suggesting, directly or indirectly, that honesty and common sense point the way to philandering in marriage. Nor do I say they might not do so. I merely suggest that honesty and common sense are requisite no matter what they lead to, and that they must be accepted unconditionally as a basis for effective marriage. They may turn the world upside down for all I know; but I still maintain that honesty and common sense have a first claim on human loyalty.

I suggest further that the proper view for society to take of this matter is to recognize that some persons have an inclination toward varied sex experiences, and that some haven't; and that it is no function of society to discriminate against those who have such inclinations provided they duly respect and consider the genuine rights of other people. Within that limit, their conduct is as much a personal matter, to be personally determined, as the choice of one's politics and religion. An honest personal code which duly considers the rights of other people, and which submits voluntarily to whatever internal restraints are necessary for the observance of such rights, constitutes a very large order, believe me. Such a code is about as far removed from irresponsible license as could well be imagined. Its tendency would be to impose on the individual stricter and more genuine restraints than anything dreamed of in our conventions.

Let me now offset the story of Phyllis and Bert with the story of Phyllis's best friend, Esther, and of Esther's divorced husband, Archie, and her second husband, Bob.

8.

Esther, Archie, and Bob are intimate friends of Phyllis and Bert. The five of them run together inseparably. And the difference in their fundamental point of view is all the more remarkable on that account.

Esther married Archie at about the same time that her friend Phyllis married Bert. Archie, whom I have known for years, is a very fine boy, steady, hardworking, effective in all he does, well balanced, and gifted with a kindliness of nature which is a part of his stable and dependable make-up. In him Esther had picked a winner.

Esther knew this. She valued his fine qualities. She had chosen him in preference to Bob, who had also wanted to marry her. But after she tied up with Archie she began to repent. She realized that Archie was the finer of the two boys, and that he was in every way more worthy of her love than was Bob; but, as she told me later, there seemed to be a fundamental incompatibility which left her ill at ease when she was with him. They had different natures and a different point of view. They talked a different language. It was not that they quarreled, but rather that they had little in common. With Bob, on the other hand, she was always at her ease and perfectly happy. He never treated her as well as Archie did; he lacked Archie's fineness and chivalry, his considerateness and his innate courtesy. He treated her in the offhand fashion women usually detest. He neglected her when he felt like it. And yet she fell in love with Bob.

Archie presently took note of the fact that she was very largely in Bob's company. She went to shows with Bob. They found this and that excuse to be together. Bob was often at the house.

At last Archie said to her, "Esther, do you think you'd be happier with Bob than with me?"

She admitted that she would.

"All right," said Archie, "get a divorce from me and marry him. In the meantime, do as you please."

In due time she brought suit for divorce. They got by without the collusion being detected, and without otherwise betraying the fact that they were in cahoots. At last the interlocutory decree was granted. The final decree was to follow six months later—another senseless obstacle.

In the meantime, Esther and Bob had been living together secretly, though with Archie's knowledge; and when the final decree was granted, Esther was already pregnant by Bob. I married them a few months later.

Shortly before the birth of this baby, Archie gave a dinner party to his divorced wife Esther, now very obviously on the verge of motherhood. He invited Esther, Bob, Phyllis, and Bert. It was a thoroughly amicable occasion.

9.

A woman to whom I told these two contrasting stories about these five persons said, "You imply in this last story that because Archie left his wife free to follow her inclination and finally marry another man everybody was happy. I admit that his conduct seems to have made possible the avoidance of a lot of trouble. But what I want to know is, where does Archie get off? Archie had rights. Of course, if he didn't care about Esther, and was willing to let her go, that's another thing. But assume that he really loved her, and then found that she cared for another man. It seems to me that there are limits to what human nature can reasonably be expected to put up with. And I can't see that such an outcome provides Archie with the happiness he has a right to—assuming of course that he loved his wife and wanted to keep her. It looks to me as if in such a situation he had a right to be jealous, and put up a fight and assert his intention to fight off any man who might try to deprive him of the woman he loved."

I have no doubt that this same view of the matter will occur to many of my readers. I answer it this way: If he loved her, and wanted to keep her, the losing of her was a regrettable tragedy in his life. Such tragedies happen. We can't any of us help it. And in marriage, no matter how hard people try to pick the right mate, some of them make mistakes. Esther thought she loved Archie, because, recognizing his superior qualities, she thought she ought to love him, in preference to Bob. She made an honest mistake.

In this situation Archie had a perfect right, if he loved her, to want to keep her and to be first in her life. That goes without saying. But that desire is not jealousy. The point I make is that he was free from *jealousy*, and that he put her happiness before his own wishes.

A jealous husband would have tried to hold her because such a course fell within his conventional and legal rights. Archie had a sweetness of nature that made the course he took easier for him than it would be for some.—Besides, it is quite possible that when he found Esther didn't care for him, his own feelings toward her underwent a change. But whether they did or did not, it in no way alters the significance of what he did. *He accorded to another human being the freedom of action we should all be prepared to accord to other human beings, so long as such freedom does not infringe on other people's rights.* And you will note that in this case he did not feel that she was violating his right of ownership, as most men would have done.

If there had been children, the rights of those children would have been involved; and in that event the case would have had a different aspect. Esther's freedom would have been limited by the *right* of a child to both its parents. Quite another thing, you see—a real right instead of a fictitious one. In that case I don't know how they would have worked it out. Probably Archie and Esther would have continued their home with Bob entering in as a Tertium Quid. I know such a case in Denver right now—a wealthy couple. Only yesterday I saw them on the street. The husband was walking on ahead with a lovely four-year-old child tripping along beside him, her hand in his. The wife followed. She was accompanied by Tertium Quid.—I am not commending the arrangement. I merely say that the thing happens, and that these people seem to find it satisfactory. Before they arrived at the present understanding they were both miserable, as I happen to know.

Some persons would consider such a solution impossible and repugnant. But some persons don't. We differ in these matters, apparently, as we differ in politics and religion. I really don't see why Denver society should interfere with these people, or judge them, or ostracize them. But it would do just that—if it knew what I know. And among the people who would do the ostracizing would be many who also would be ostracized for this reason or that if *they* got found out, by people who, in their turn, would be ostracized if—etc. What a Merry-Go-Round!

In the long run the value of this or that kind of human behavior has to be determined by the test of human happiness. The stand society takes against such irregular domestic relations as I have been describing is based on the belief that that kind of thing if generally practiced would disrupt society. Some think God prohibits it, and that He does it for just that reason.

But society has not yet gotten to the point where it can see that anger, hatred, malice, jealousy, and the like are far more destructive to human happiness than any amount of sex irregularity.

I don't say the old view is all wrong. I merely say that it needs some sort of revision, and that it can make no just claim to being exempt from such revision. Present results do not support such a claim. And until such a revision shall have been worked out, I think it behooves us all to be tolerant of those who are finding their way out as best they can. Perhaps they are contributing to the revision. I think it would be preposterous to say that their conduct is wholly anti-social or wholly without value. Such persons are at least *doing* something. Perhaps they think there is something to the saying that heaven helps those who help themselves.

But to come back to this phenomenon that my friend Ewing called erotic avarice: I know a man named Harris. He is separated from his wife. She said to me once, "Mr. Harris can go his own way; and he can have affairs with as many women as he likes, so long as he continues to provide me and the children with that $200 a month he has agreed to."

Such is her view. Now note his view. Some time after the separation Harris found his wife sitting on another man's lap. Unmindful of his own affairs with other women, he flew into a terrific rage. His wife was his property. He neither used it nor cherished it himself, but he was quite clear that nobody else must touch it. He, being a man, might have outside affairs, and it would make no difference.

But for a woman to behave so—that was different. Enter the twin bugaboos, Purity and Impurity.

A woman recently separated from her husband said to an officer of my court, "I am glad to be separated from my husband at last. I don't love him. In fact, I hate, detest, and abominate him. But if he wants a divorce I shall refuse to let him have it. I won't have him marrying any other woman. He shan't have that satisfaction, ever, if I can prevent it."

10.

Mrs. Lindsey and I were once dining with a delightful French family. It consisted of a mother, her daughter, her son, and the son's wife, a bride. The son was well up in the twenties, and his bride was somewhat younger. They all spoke very good English, which they courteously used as their exclusive medium of conversation because Mrs. Lindsey and I do not speak French. With us was an English friend who knew these people very well, and who is familiar with French customs.

In the course of the evening this interesting family branched off, still speaking English, into conversation among themselves concerning a private matter. And we could hardly believe our ears when this respectable French dowager, a woman of first-rate social position, suddenly began vigorously reproaching her son for neglecting "Annette."

"Annette," murmured our English friend, grinning discreetly, "is this chap's mistress."

If the reader will try to imagine some stately matron in middle life, a leader in the social affairs of his home town, publicly reproaching her son at a dinner party on such a ground as this, he may get some idea of the mixture of amusement and interest we took in this situation.

The young man began to make lame excuses. It was clear that he felt himself very much in the wrong. There wasn't a doubt that he had been neglecting Annette.

"Oui," his sister put in indignantly, "you haven't been near her for months."

"It is not right," put in the mother. "When we return home you must not neglect her so, Henri. She has been so good to you—always. That is the way with Henri," she added, turning to me, "always careless and irresponsible." And turning up her eyes, she shrugged in the inimitable French manner.

"Ever so careless about much," said the little bride, shaking her head sternly at her husband, and yet smiling. "I have told him he must think of her, and not neglect her; but will he listen? Non!"

Utterly bewildered by all this, I turned to my English friend for help. "Am I getting this straight?" I asked under my breath.

He nodded. "It's one of their little ways," he said. "He has kept Annette for years, with money furnished, of course, by his Mama. The girl is below him in station. A Frenchman of position picks for his mistress a girl who is not his social equal. You can see for yourself that his wife is not jealous. But let him choose a woman of his own social rank—then you'd see the fur fly; and they wouldn't be talking and shrugging about it as if they classed it with the weather. As it is, they think a lot of the girl, and they propose to look after her interests."

"Even the bride," I murmured.

He chuckled. "Even the bride! Charming, eh? And no jealousy!"

Later, when we could talk above a whisper, he observed, "Now in England we see these things differently. A high class Englishman regards the psychological satisfactions of sex. As a rule the woman with whom he has an intimacy must be intellectually and spiritually congenial. He would derive little satisfaction from a woman who was merely a body, so to speak. That is why such *liaisons* in England are likely to be between social equals. And of course they are usually secret. And yet I think this English view—which is also your American view—accords a much greater dignity to Sex. We English require more of Sex, spiritually, than does a Frenchman. Perhaps," he added, "there should be a compromise between the two points of view. The French have much to teach us, and we have something to teach them."

In relating this incident, I don't vouch for the interpretation placed upon it by my English friend. Personally I know little about

French customs. I simply record the happening for what it is worth, and for the light it sheds on certain of our own customs. It may have been merely an individual example rather than the custom of the country, as my English friend affirmed. But at all events it happened.

The moral of this little story is plain. What it means, if it means anything, is that custom can make anything "right" in the eyes of society and that it can make anything "wrong," and that the sooner we get over our superstitious reverence for the authority of custom as custom, divinely sanctioned, and established with the beginnings of Time, the better for all of us.

II.

It used to be the custom in the North American colonies in the Seventeenth Century for courting, among perfectly respectable persons, to be carried on in bed. A pair who might or might not contemplate marriage spent the night in bed together partly dressed. This was simple courtship, equivalent to sitting together on a divan now, and it was binding on neither party unless the couple violated the convention under which it was permitted, and the woman became pregnant. In that event marriage was expected, then as now.

This custom was known as "bundling." Other names for it were "tarrying" and "questing." It was practiced as a matter of expediency because of the scarcity of beds and fuel. It made for comfort. Husbands, as a matter of course, permitted travelers, stopping at their homes, to bundle with their wives and daughters; and it was proper to ask for the privilege. Bundling was regarded as innocent and it usually was. Young people, then as now, were supposed to be able to behave responsibly without a chaperone.

Ministers finally began preaching against the custom, but conservative parishioners stoutly resisted all attempts at change. When sofas were introduced, about 1750, after more than a century and a half of bundling, conservative persons pronounced the sofa improper and insisted on their daughters and their suitors retiring to bed instead. Sofas, said they, were an incitement to irresponsible conduct.

My reason for telling of this custom is to demonstrate once

again what custom can do toward legitimizing any practice which society, whether to save firewood and beds, or for whatever other reason, finds expedient.

Such facts contain a wholesome shock for our self-satisfaction and our smugness. They are disillusioning. They demonstrate that, outside the range of genuine ethics, allowable conduct is simply conduct which society, for any reason whatever, chooses to permit, and that unallowable conduct is conduct which, for reasons equally arbitrary, and often irrational, society chooses to forbid. Sometimes allowable conduct is outrageously unethical. It is nevertheless "right" in the eyes of society. Sometimes perfectly ethical conduct is a violation of conventional morality. Such conduct is always "wrong." Bundling was "right" once; it is "wrong" now, and contrary, the average moralizing minister would tell you, to the will of God.

Our present marriage customs are just as much a matter of expediency as was bundling. They have the same degree of divine sanction, and like bundling they may be expected to last so long as they work. When they fail to work a few rebels will start changing them, as some are now doing; then the crowd will follow this lead; and God, somewhat belatedly, will be found by His interpreters to have changed His mind. The new custom will then be the "will of God"—so long as it works. This epitomizes the whole process by which customs come into existence and then give way to other customs. We should do well to rationalize the process. By so doing we might spare ourselves a great deal of needless crime, tragedy, and unhappiness.

In the meantime, we are given to understand that marriages are made in heaven. I admit that some might have been. But as to others—why blame them on heaven? Above all, why blame the jealousy tradition, that curse of matrimony, on heaven? Any custom that gives two free persons the ownership of each other is a device of the devil. Heaven has nothing to do with it. It is a worse offense against ethics than all the "infidelity" in the world, and it destroys more marriages than all the adultery ever committed. The capital crime against marriage is not infidelity, which is the one ground for divorce in some states, but jealousy, which isn't a ground for divorce anywhere.

12.

Among the most interesting confidences I have ever received in connection with my domestic relations work I count the story of a man who had come to see me in behalf of his sister, but wound up by telling me a story about himself. His sister was having trouble with her husband because, to her highly virtuous mind, sex was a thing repulsive and unclean. Her husband had sought consolation elsewhere. However, that is another story.

It happened that I already knew Stanley Hubbell very well; and our consultation about his sister's troubles led us to a discussion of the general problem of possessive jealousy. And presently he began to tell me about himself, and how he had once saved his own home by putting jealousy out of his life.

A few years ago he married a woman whom I have since come to know. She is very lovely—a strong and splendid soul in a beautiful body. He had had to display considerable enterprise to win her; for her suitors had been many.

"I have never been able to understand," Hubbell said to me, "why Alice chose me instead of some one of those men who would have provided her with wealth and comfort beyond anything she could wish. They were many of them fine fellows. She could have had anything. Yet she chose me. I can only wonder, and be thankful that women are not always logical.

"Well, shortly after our marriage, some curious things happened. You can judge their significance for yourself.

"Alice and I were married in Denver, and we went immediately from here to San Francisco, where I had business. My friend, Will Carson, accompanied us on that trip. He had been best man at the wedding; and while I was courting Alice, he had exerted himself —at first—to further my cause. He had shown her many courtesies. I did not learn till later that when he thought she might not accept me, and that my fortunes appeared uncertain, he fell madly in love with her himself.

"With him in Denver was another friend of mine, and his—Tom

Ryan. Tom, as I learned later, fell in love with her too. Neither man admitted his thoughts to the other, but on the theory that all is fair in love and war, each tried to win her favor. Tom was a bachelor, but Will was married, to a very rich girl whom he did not love.

"Such was the situation when Will, and Alice and I took the train to San Francisco. After we had been in San Francisco a few days, I was obliged to make a trip from there which involved an absence of three days. I left Alice at the hotel, where Will also had a suite.

"The next evening he took her out to dinner, during which he made undue use of a hip flask. When they returned to the hotel he paused at the door of his suite and leaned against the wall, saying he felt faint. Alice, much concerned, took him by the arm and helped him into his room—whereupon he whirled about, locked the door, and began to make violent love to her. Violent is the word. He had, as I have said, been drinking. I suppose that accounted for the fact that a terrific physical struggle followed.

"She happened to be very strong, and was able to resist effectively. But even at that, she emerged from the struggle with her hair down, her clothes torn, and a diamond pin she had been wearing broken to bits, with the stones scattered over the floor.

"By some miracle they had not been heard. She finally escaped and went to her room. The next morning she met him at breakfast as if nothing had happened, with a calm 'good morning.' Later he came to her, abjectly apologetic. He wept; he berated and bitterly reproached himself; he begged her pardon, and altogether exhibited the most extreme signs of repentance.

"She forgave him. But—when I returned she told me what had happened.

"Now figure it out for yourself. What was the traditional thing for me to do? Well, I didn't do it. I thought it over, and I never indicated to Will Carson in any way—never have to this day—that I knew a thing about it. I have reason to think that he suspects I know. I also know that he is to-day one of my most devoted friends, and that Alice and I have both his respect and his loyalty. I am sure he still loves her, but I don't blame him for that. I think that is better than shooting him.

"It was not long after this that Tom Ryan came into the picture. When we returned to Denver, Tom was there. He began calling at the house constantly. He came frequently in my absence. Of all this Alice said nothing; but I suddenly began to realize that Tom was mad about her, and that it stood to reason he was not keeping the fact to himself.

"Tom was a fine, big, handsome chap—a fascinating personality. It would not have been strange had he attracted her.

"One evening Alice said to me, 'Tom thinks you are away. He is going to call me by 'phone this evening and ask me to go riding with him in his car. Would you object to my going?'

" 'Not at all, Dear,' I said. 'That's all right with me. You are a free person.'

" 'Tom is in love with me,' she continued, calmly. 'He will want to make love to me, and he will probably want me to run away with him. Suppose, Stanley, I let him make love to me, and suppose I decided to go away with him. What would you do?'

" 'If that suited you, it would be all right with me,' I said. 'I don't own you. I merely love you, and I want you to be happy.'

"Well, Judge, I wish you could have seen her. She sat there with an enigmatic, Mona Lisa smile on her lips. I swear I couldn't make out whether she was tempted by Tom or not, or whether she would go or stay. But I stood by my guns. Whatever else would keep her, I knew no assertion of ownership would. And yet I had doubts. Some women, you know, resent it if a man doesn't show jealousy under such conditions. They interpret it to mean that he doesn't care.

"And sure enough, that was the next thing she shot at me. 'You don't seem to be jealous,' she said. 'Does that mean that you don't care?'

" 'You are too intelligent really to mean that question, Alice,' I said. 'I do care. But my caring has nothing to do with it. My respect for you as a person, with the rights of a person, has everything to do with it.'

"And still she sat with that enigmatic smile on her face; and I watched her and wondered. Pretty soon the telephone rang.

" 'That will be Tom,' she said, glancing at the clock. And she took down the receiver. 'Oh, is that you, Tom? Good evening! So glad you called up. Surely! A drive would be delightful! I have just told Stanley that you had suggested it, and you know how he does love to drive! When will you be over?'

"Tom arrived a half-hour later. He was his usual urbane self, and drove us forty miles before he brought us home—game to the last. He doesn't suspect that I know; but he never tried it again.

"Now how long do you think it would have taken me to have driven her into the arms of a man like that if I had followed the traditional course? She stayed—absolutely of her own will—under no compulsion from me. As for the other men, they had a right to win her if they could, say I. Of course Will Carson's methods were outrageous, but aside from that, I say it's up to me to hold her because I hold her love, and in no other way.

"And if she had yielded to them, and then come back to me, I'd feel the same. To my way of thinking, so long as she loves me, nothing she might give to them would rob me of her. As it happened, she was not tempted. But that was a matter of temperament and inclination. Had she been tempted, it would have been the same. What she wanted to do or wanted not to do lay equally within her rights. I claim nothing, and I have everything. I would still have everything had she seen fit to confer on one or both of those two men what they wanted. And had she gone to one or the other of them and left me, I would have had nothing—which is precisely what I would have had anyway had I held her by possessive jealousy.

"Some would call this a spiritless philosophy, Judge; but I think it takes nerve and courage to put it through. Jealousy is a kind of cowardice. It will go to any extremity in its effort to avoid the truth and pretend that facts are not facts. I refuse to yield to it."

So much for Hubbell's end of the story. A few years after my talk with him I met Will Carson on a train during a trip to Chicago. I knew him fairly well, though not so well as Hubbell; but before the trip was over we were on more or less confidential terms, so much so that he opened up with a tale which, I confess, I more or less paved the way for, and which was substantially in accord with that which Stanley Hubbell had told me.

"You know," said Carson in conclusion, "I think Stanley knows what happened. And yet he has never said a word about it; I am received at their home, and they seem to think a lot of me. Only—Alice never sees me alone. I don't think Stanley holds any grudge or resentment. In fact I sometimes think he sympathizes with and understands the impulse that overwhelmed me. All I can say is that I don't get it. I don't think I would be capable of such conduct if the situation were reversed. He has shown a nobility and a reasonableness in his view of this matter that is beyond me. And it's from no lack of ability to assert himself or put up a fight, either." Later, Carson learned that Hubbell did know. They remain fast friends.

From this double-barreled story the reader may draw his own inferences. To me it means, among other things, that the most important thing about a man is his philosophy.

13.

The reader will, of course, note the significance of certain of these stories in their relation to each other.

The union of Phyllis and Bert was a success before their legal marriage and a failure after it because marriage introduced into their relations with each other restraints which they did not like, and which, in their case, did not make for happiness and contentment. In other words, whatever may be said in favor of the monogamous ideal, it has in this instance, when forced on a couple who find it repugnant and irksome, failed to make marriage either livable or endurable.

The theory on which society maintains monogamy in marriage is *that no other relationship in marriage makes in a like degree for happiness;* but Phyllis and Bert lived together for some time in a non-monogamous relationship, before their legal marriage, and they were happy in it. Apparently, then, there are people so constituted that monogamy does not meet their temperamental needs; and the question is, can society wisely or successfully force such persons to accept the monogamous ideal whether they like it or not? I think it cannot. The effort of society to forbid and prevent outside episodes in all marriages is precisely the thing which seems to have wrecked this particular union—since it was a successful union previous to the time when law and custom introduced that restriction into the relations of this couple with each other. In other words, the marriage of Phyllis and Bert apparently contained elements which were capable of making a success of it under conditions not sanctioned by our conventions.

The marriage of Archie and Esther, on the other hand, lacked the success element. It was no true marriage because Esther did not love her husband. It was not possible to make a real marriage of this union, monogamous or otherwise. In putting an end to it, therefore, Archie made it possible for Esther to find elsewhere the happiness she could not find in her marriage with him. He also left open for himself the possibility that he would later find happiness with some one else; and he provided for Bob's happiness besides. Thus instead of making three people miserable, he made three people happy. He did it, however, by running counter to what society deems "right." According to those who believe in what they call "the sacredness of marriage," Archie should have stood by his guns and made them all miserable. At the most he and his wife should have separated, and then gone on eating their hearts out and denying their sex life a normal activity. I think society is rapidly discarding that cruel doctrine, and I feel sure that if Jesus were among us to-day he would be the first to repudiate some of the people who are teaching such things in His name.

The Hubbell marriage contrasts interestingly with these other two cases in that it has proved on test to be genuinely and voluntarily monogamous. This voluntary monogamy suits the temperament and needs of Mr. and Mrs. Hubbell; it makes them happy. Anything else, if *they* should practice it, would make them unhappy. Their impulses and preferences, in other words, are precisely opposite to those of Phyllis and Bert. But note that it must be a *voluntary* monogamy. Had Hubbell, by showing jealousy, attempted to make of it anything other than a *voluntary* monogamy it would have become what the marriage of Phyllis and Bert is, a fake monogamy. By the same token, if jealousy could be eliminated from the marriage of Phyllis and Bert, it might become, like the Hubbell marriage, a voluntary monogamy. I think it would probably pass through a triangular phase, but I think, in the end, they would tire of it, and find it inadequate, and that they would find a real monogamy better suited to their needs.

Our racial experience seems to show that monogamy is better fitted to the needs of most human beings than any other form of relationship between the sexes. I feel sure it will predominate in marriage by virtue of its own inherent merits—*if given a chance*. Where we make our mistake is in thinking it can be forced, and that any departure from it on the part of any number of individuals will destroy it. What destroys it is our system of forcing it on people whether they think they want it or not.

14.

The evidence before me indicates that triangular relationships in marriage make *some* persons happy, and that such relationships, when the parties mutually consent to them, have put many a marriage on a psychologically stable basis. Such persons would often be unhappy if divorce should separate them. They insist that they love and need each other, in spite of their outside fancies. These, permit me to emphasize, are *facts*. I ask the indignant reader, if he is indignant, not to hold me responsible for them. I record them for his information.

Our social traditions have taught all of us since childhood that the Triangle is intrinsically and unescapably tragic; that it must from its very nature deprive one of its members of his or her rights; and that an absolute monogamy in marriage is, *without exception*, the only basis on which marriage can be made to work. When a marriage fails we never say of it that it failed because it was monogamous, though we wouldn't hesitate to say of a marriage that it failed because it was polygamous. This may be orthodox, but it is not necessarily reasonable. If an unconventional polygamy can ruin this marriage, why should not a forced monogamy ruin that?

Many men may have many minds about most things, but they are not permitted to have them about this one, on which they differ more, perhaps, in taste and natural bent, than about any other thing. Here they must be uniform. Here one man's meat cannot be admitted to be another man's poison, even if it is. There may be diversity of taste, but there must be outward uniformity of response. Differing conditions, differing capacity, differing needs—all met by the same prescription! And this in the most variable and intimate of human relationships! In no other phase of life do we expect this absurd and impossible thing of human beings.

This is in no sense an attack on monogamous marriage. I have said before, and I say it again, that I think the marriage in which one man and one woman fill each other's lives is the ideal marriage. That is the thing to strive for and hope for. But when individuals find themselves so constituted or so matched that they desire in their hearts some variation from this ideal, then I am sure that the restrictions they impose on each other tend to make a tragedy out of conduct which would otherwise be innocuous and often only temporary. The subjective effect on the individual of conduct carried out in secret violation of such restrictions is often devastating to health, morals, and common decency; and the social consequences, if there be no secrecy, are just as bad or worse. Thus the effort to achieve an outward respectability often makes persons who rebel against our social code genuinely immoral; while a courageous sincerity and openness in unconventional conduct makes others *seem* immoral in the eyes of society, and so destroys them by an adverse and hateful social suggestion, which they are constrained subjectively to accept.

Non-monogamic marriages would, I think, usually become monogamous if allowed to work themselves out freely. If they didn't, they would be falling short of the ideal, of course, but they would still usually work out with a reasonable degree of happiness for all concerned. At present they work out in misery, vulgar intrigue, lies, heart-burnings, hatred, cruelty, daily unkindness, neglect, sexual indifference, divorce, and parentless children. This happens in the best regulated families. Having reached the limit of endurance, the bewildered couple finally seek the divorce court, split up their homes on highly triangular charges, wrangle over the possession of their children, and finally leave it to the court to determine that Johnny, aged six, and Sadie, aged five, are to be with their mother so much of the time, and with their father so much of the time, and that they are to have a home, with two parents in it, *none* of the time.

15.

I think that if individual preferences and tastes could be given even a reasonable right of way in marriage society would benefit incalculably by such a change. I think society suffers untellable and unguessable harm from the traditions of marriage which are in the saddle at present, *however fundamentally desirable may be the monogamic ideal back of those traditions.*

I am anxious, in this connection, not to give the impression that I favor the Triangle in marriage. I don't favor it. I think it far better when couples are so matched that they genuinely don't want any outside episodes. I think monogamy is natural, and that marriage in general tends to seek the monogamic status. I think such a status is attainable *on a free will basis* in most marriages, and that it would, under favorable conditions of freedom in marriage, tend to become more so. *But the monogamic preference, when genuinely felt, under the artificial conditions of a civilization that has gotten very far away from nature, and from the jungle, is a product of culture. It involves voluntary self-restraint and voluntary self-discipline. It must be evolved by society on a free will basis, and it can't be legislated or otherwise forced into existence.* At present we are legislating and forcing; and the more legislating and forcing we do the more unmistakable becomes the rebellion on the part of men and women everywhere. And in such rebellion there is great peril for the individuals involved in it.

I feel no alarm about these social tendencies; but I am often keenly alarmed for the welfare of individuals who get themselves so entangled in the machinery of Change that they are in danger of being crushed in the wheels. When I deal with individuals I therefore urge them to abstain, if possible, from monkeying with the buzz saw, to keep away from it, and to leave that diversion to persons whose special talents seem to make it, if not safe, at least less dangerous.

But if they insist on their own way, why, then I do what I can for them and let it go at that. There is no use in trying forcibly to stop either them or the machine. Why waste one's energy trying or one's breath denouncing? Why not give help, guidance, and tolerant sympathy instead?

This can be done. And the doing of it would be easy if society would look to the beam that is in its own eye, and pluck from its heart that darkest of superstitions, the Ultimate Blasphemy, that God is static and Satan progressive.

CHAPTER V

MARRIAGE ON TRIAL

I.

A WOMAN, whom I shall call Mrs. John Smith, sat and looked at me across the long table in my private chambers. She was plainly ill at ease; and she rolled and unrolled a pair of gloves she had drawn from her hands.

They were fine hands, with long tapering fingers, and an expressive way of moving. They went with the sensitive and beautiful face, the blue eyes, the soft brown hair, the sweetly shaped though nervous mouth. She was of a type that would seek a court only in the last extremity. I saw her look about and eye the shut door as if she feared it did not insure the privacy she wanted.

"I have come here, Judge Lindsey," she began, "because I have heard that secrets are safe with you, and that you help people. I have reached a crisis in my life, and help is what I need."

"You shall have all the help I can give," I answered. "And your secret, whatever it is, will be safe."

She smiled. "You seem more like a doctor than the traditional Judge."

"That is a great compliment," I answered. "I do try to deal with sick hearts more or less as a physician deals with sick bodies. I think that is better than punishing people for their sins, though there are times when I do have to punish— What is the trouble?"

Again she looked about her uneasily. "Will there be any record of this?"

"Not a scrap of a record," I said emphatically, "except maybe your name, address and telephone number on this pad."

"So I have heard," she replied. "Otherwise I could not have come here. You see, one thing that made me nervous about coming was that once, before I lived in Denver, I used to know a social

101

worker who told me about her work and her methods. I could never have come to her. She kept what she called case sheets; and she used to put down every detail about the cases she dealt with. She would put down things of the most confidential sort. It makes me shudder to think of it. I don't see how she ever got a word out of anybody."

"She probably got a lot of words and very little truth," I said. "I know her type; but I am glad to be able to add that not all social workers are like that. I suppose she called the stuff she recorded 'scientific data,' didn't she?"

Mrs. Smith laughed and nodded.

"There *is* a certain type of social worker," I went on, "that is long on scientific data. These unfortunate zealots busy themselves to such an extent with surveys and graphs and mathematical computations, that they clean forget that they have to do with people. The shelves of our libraries groan with tons of the dusty junk they write. Most of it is fit only for Ph.D. theses, with footnotes and book references at the bottom of each page."

"She was always talking," put in Mrs. Smith, "about being scientific and having 'the modern technique.'"

"And if she's the type you describe," I added, "I'll warrant she has told you that I'm not scientific."

Mrs. Smith's eyes widened. "How did you know?"

"Oh," I said, "that's easy. I get reports every now and then of what the most scientific of our social workers think about my failure to keep 'scientific data.' They are very amusing. Still, I wouldn't have you think we keep no records. We do. We have case sheets. They have their place in a certain class of cases. We even make surveys. But we also know when not to make them. And, too, you must remember that not all social workers are as absorbed in scientific data as the one you tell of. Every profession has its quota of incompetents, and social work is no exception. However, you may be sure that you are quite safe from the case sheets here."

"But," she said hesitatingly, "if I should be seen coming here, won't some one suspect that I'm in difficulties?"

"People come here for all sorts of reasons," I replied. "They come in behalf of friends who are in trouble, they come looking for jobs, they come looking for babies to adopt; now and then a Ku Klux Klan spy hovers 'round in the hope of digging up something that can be used against me in the next political campaign. Reporters come seeking news; magazine writers come seeking material; story writers come seeking plots and local color; out-of-town lawyers and judges come, some to observe, and others to find out if I violate the legal conventions as much as I'm said to, and they want to know if I really do send kids to reform schools and reformatories with nothing to keep them from running away but their word to me and the railroad ticket to where they're going. You see, if it were to be suspected that all these people come here because they are in trouble, the suspecters would be kept pretty busy. The fact is that the suspecters have long since given it up as a bad job.

"I even manage to take care of the proprieties in a reasonably efficient though probably unscientific manner. Mrs. Lindsey's desk, you will note, is just beyond that door; and the two doors of this room are never locked. Everybody in the court is under instructions to walk in at any time without knocking. So you see, women who want to talk with me confidentially are much better protected against calumny than they would be in the office of the average physician.—And now what is it all about, Mrs. Smith?"

"I am separated from my husband," she began. "We have lived apart for a year, and he is not contributing to the support of our five-year-old son. I live with my mother, and I have some money— so I want no help from him, but he should support his son. He makes a good income, and is well able to. I wish you would take the matter up with him."

"I'll be glad to," I said, looking at her attentively. "But tell me, Mrs. Smith, what is your *real* reason for coming to see me?"

Again she rolled and unrolled her gloves. She looked down at them in silence, her long lashes sweeping her cheeks. At last she spoke, very low. "I—wish I might be with my husband. You see— I love him. I wish you could find out what is the trouble, and bring us together."

"And you don't know what is the trouble?"

She shook her head. "I never could understand it; never knew why he acted as he did. But he seems to take it for granted that I understand; and he won't believe me when I say I don't. He has a great deal of pride. So have I. And I find it hard to ask questions. He never would say much; never would speak plainly. But once— he said I was cold toward him."

"Were you?"

"I think not."

"Sex misunderstandings," I observed, "are the cause of most divorces and separations—whatever may be the reasons given in public. Usually they result from ignorance, and the failure of the man and woman to understand themselves or each other."

"I suppose this is something of the sort," she replied. "Perhaps you can get to the bottom of it. Things have gotten to a point where I feel I must do something if I am ever to have him back." She paused, a catch in her breath. "One night, a month ago, I saw him at a dance resort with a girl. I have heard that he is attentive to her. I think he is living with her. I don't know her, but she is pretty—though not," she added with a pathetic smile, "as pretty as I am—if you won't misunderstand my saying so."

"This is a good time and place to be frank," I answered. "Beauty, however, is far from being the only factor in these situations."

She nodded. "I am not jealous of her. I would not be greatly disturbed over his relations with her if I knew he loved me, and if I saw any chance of getting him back. If to hold him meant ignoring affairs of that kind I could ignore them and not be so very unhappy about it. I think such affairs are likely to be casual, and that this would mean nothing that could really harm me or deprive me of him—if he loved me."

"You are rather unusually moderate in your views on that subject," I said. "What does that mean? Is it simply that you have worked out a philosophy, or that you are charitable toward him because—excuse me if I speak plainly—you have a similar inclination in that direction that might balance his; an inclination, say that he knows about, or thinks he knows about."

"Not exactly that," she replied. "There is, or was, another man but not in the sense that John thinks there is. I used him to make John jealous after we were married, because the more jealous he is the more I love him."

"Oh," I said, "the more jealous he is the more you love him; and the other man is just a fiction. Is that it?"

She shook her head. "I mean that he isn't real now; though he once was. Judge, I've never told this to a soul; but I'll tell you now. His name was Richard. I—I lived with him for a time before I was married to John. And he was a wonderful lover. It was an exquisite experience. I wish—"

She broke off with a sigh, then after a short silence resumed. "John does not know this. But he does believe, owing to things I have said to tantalize him, that I was once in love with another man—he doesn't know who."

"But why—" I began.

"My reason? Simply to make him jealous. You see, women are not as free as men—at least not yet. I don't think the double standard is just, but I more or less accept it. And so I am willing he should have this girl I saw him with if she makes him happy; but I make no claim to a similar liberty; and I won't be jealous so long as he loves me. If he doesn't, then I just can't help being jealous.

"But he would not stand for similar conduct on my part; and the mere notion that I once loved another man before we were married is enough to upset him. If he knew the real facts it would be still worse. And of course the notion that I may still care for the other man makes him madly jealous. He can't get that idea out of his head. I suppose that is partly my fault, in having started something I couldn't stop. But he is in error there.

"And yet, when I found out how suspicious he was, I couldn't resist the temptation to make him jealous—particularly since I could do it without having a real lover. He calls Richard, whose name he does not know, my 'phantom lover.' He's jealous of a phantom. Do you see?—I may have carried it too far. But—it was the only way I had of getting any satisfaction out of my relations with him. Making him jealous was a way of loving him."

"And your husband's side of it?"

She looked up eagerly. "Oh, how I wish I knew it! That **is** why I have come to you. Perhaps you can get both sides."

"When can I see him?"

"I'll send him to you."

After a few minutes more of talk she left.

The conversation with Mrs. Smith, which I have reported as briefly as possible here, occupied a matter of two hours.

Two days later I was face to face with Mr. Smith.

"I have been anxious to come to you before now, Judge Lindsey," he said as he took the very chair in which Mrs. Smith had sat during her talk with me. "But my wife stole a march on me. I am glad she did; though since she doesn't care for me I am rather at a loss to know why she did it. I suppose she has the welfare of our boy in mind."

"The reason she came to me is that she loves you," I said. "She mentioned your failure to provide money for the support you owe your child, but that was merely an entering wedge. I had a long talk with her. Do you love her?"

"Yes," he said simply. "But actions speak louder than words; and you can discount whatever she may have told you about loving me. She loves some one else better."

"What makes you think that?"

"Well, she has simply shut me out. I can't begin to tell you how miserable it has made me, and how I have fought to hold her. To me she is the most exquisitely beautiful woman in the world. Physically she is perfection; and as for her personality, you have had a chance to judge that for yourself. But she is not for me, apparently. She has a lover."

"I have known a good many women," I replied, "who had lovers, and who yet loved their husbands, and vice versa. Don't let your training and traditions keep you from thinking straight or accepting facts. Do you know the man?"

"That's the funny part of it. She talks about him; he is in her mind constantly; and the horrible part of it is—" Here he drew a long breath and looked me in the face. "Judge, I thank God I'm not talking to a Judge. This is the first time I have fully realized what your methods mean to people. I'll talk frankly to you now. It is because of her coldness and of my utter inability to bring any response from her at times when such a response is imperative that we have had to separate and go our ways. It is partly her coldness, and partly because of an intolerable thing that happens. She has made the situation impossible."

"What about the girl?"

"Oh, she told you of that, did she? Well, *that's* the reason for the girl. She is right if she thinks I'm living with Minnie; and she has herself to thank, because I'd rather a thousand times have her than any other woman in the world. I'm not apologizing. She needn't object, so long as she herself is crazy about that fellow she knew before we were married, whoever he was. Did she tell you about him?"

"She told me a great many things," I answered. "Tell me your side of this. Who is this chap?"

He leaned over and half whispered, "She's actually intimate with him."

"Oh, he's here in Denver, is he?"

"Hell, no—he's never been in Denver. But he's in her mind and heart, damn him, where I can't get my hands on him."

"Isn't your evidence," I suggested, "rather intangible? May he not have his sole existence in your mind and heart rather than in hers?"

He shook his head, and then he told me, in plainer English than I am at liberty to use here, that he had what seemed to him ample evidence that his wife carried the picture and image of the other man in her mind at times when such a substitution was least to be tolerated.

"Even when I kiss her," he growled, "she imagines she's kissing that damn' phantom lover of hers. And that isn't the only time. You can guess how I feel when I'm conscious of such a thing as that. She gets no satisfaction from me," he concluded, "and she makes no bones about it. If she should put it in words, she could not more plainly tell me that as a husband I'm a very inadequate person. And, Judge—" He stopped, laying a shaking hand on my knee, and his face looked gray and tired, "My humiliation doesn't end there. That damn' ghost comes between us. It is he who kisses and caresses her—*after* me, if you'll believe it. . . . If he doesn't, she's so nervous and distraught that there's no living with her. Oh, she's got a way of making it real, believe me. . . . I'm superfluous in her life."

And he explained a number of things in words of one syllable. "How," he finished, "am I to put up with this thing! I can't do it."

"You would, of course, be glad to find out that your inferences concerning her attachment for this other man were wrong," I said.

"Of course."

"And you would be willing to go back to her if I could prove that you were wrong?"

"Yes, but—"

"Leave it to me," I said. "I'll communicate with you later."

Whereupon he took his departure, looking hopeful in spite of himself.

All of which represents one hour with Mr. Smith—presented here, of course, barely in outline.

Soon after he had left, Mrs. Smith hurriedly arrived at the court, without an appointment, and asked to see me. "I knew John was coming," she exclaimed eagerly, "and I just couldn't wait, Judge. I took a chance on getting to you."

"Mrs. Smith," I said, "you are sure, are you, that this phantom lover of yours is merely a device in lieu of a real affair, to excite in your husband the jealousy from which you say you derive so much satisfaction?"

She nodded. "Most assuredly."

"Do you ever permit the image of this phantom to come into your mind, when your husband kisses you, for instance, or at other times?"

She flushed. "Once, Judge, it seemed as though I did. It was merely that there came into my mind a memory of that affair before my marriage, and of how completely Richard satisfied me, and of what a contrast there was between that and what I now had. I have had nothing of that sort in marriage. Well, you see, in a moment of exasperation I said something that indicated what I was

thinking—nothing very specific, but it was quite specific enough
John became furious. And he swore he'd never have anything to
do with me if I would let such a thing happen in my mind."

"But why did you tell him such a thing?"

"I thought it would arouse him. He never makes love to me as I
wish him to. Do you understand?—I become frightfully nervous,
you see."

She bit her lip in an effort at self-control. "Judge, my husband
is this kind of a man. He is always in a hurry about everything he
does. If he goes for a walk—just a pleasure walk, you know—his
impulse is not to stroll and steep himself in beauty and enjoyment as
he goes, but rather to hurry as if he were bent on getting somewhere.
You'd think he was going to catch a train and was late for it. In
going toward his destination he would want to cover in a few minutes a distance for which I, with my temperament, would find a
half-hour none too much; and, of course, if I happened to be with
him, he would forget all about me, in his impatience and nervousness, and would leave me far behind.

"And he has another trait. If we go out together, he has a way
of walking on ahead of me; just as if it didn't matter whether I came
along or not. And so I don't care about taking walks, with only
myself and my own thoughts for company. And yet, if one should
complete such a walk the best way one could, with the aid of crutch,
say—and perhaps not thinking very hard of the person with whom
one was supposed to be walking—why, that would become a cause
for offense. It would imply, to a person who did not understand,
and who was always in a hurry, that one would rather be walking
with some one else. But who would be to blame for such a condition
of things?"

"Nobody in particular," I answered. "Chiefly an educational system that doesn't teach people how to take walks. And then, too,
temperaments differ; and people should be intelligent enough to
compromise and keep step. I think a little of the right kind of
instruction—from a psychiatrist, for instance, might inform you and
your husband of a lot of things which it is the crime of society and
convention that you didn't know when you were married. The
whole trouble here has been ignorance, not incompatibility. If he

doesn't want you to walk by yourself, let him lend you his arm; and if he doesn't want phantoms around, let him be something less of a phantom himself. I am perfectly sure that he doesn't even dream of the things you have been telling me.

"But there is another side to it, Mrs. Smith. You have been as blind as he. Did you never stop to think of the effect on him of certain things—and of the intense humiliation and chagrin he must have felt? How simple it would have been had you told him what was the matter."

"I have thought of that since," she answered with a rush of tears. "It was pride that kept me silent. I suppose it has kept both of us silent."

"Now," I continued, "I am going to put you and your husband in the hands of a psychiatrist who will tell you some things about yourselves that you don't know. Such instruction will enable you to handle yourselves intelligently in future. I shall have one more talk with Mr. Smith, and then one with the two of you together; and I think that will settle it. Oh, one other thing. Don't try to dictate to him about that girl. Let him alone, and I'm sure he will drop her. But if you *insist* on his dropping her I can't answer for the result."

"He can do as he pleases, so he comes back to me," she said. "But even if I felt differently about it I would see the soundness of your advice."

I got in touch with Mr. Smith the next day, and I gave him a clear account in plain English of what I have had to put down here in English less plain. "She hasn't a phantom lover," I concluded. "She loves you, and she brought in the phantom not because she cared about any one else in her mind, but simply to make you jealous and stir you up. Also, what you don't know about making love to your wife would apparently fill a book. I don't wonder you've had trouble. It's a wonder to me she ever stood by you as long as she has. Now all you've got to do is go back to her and use some common sense. Above all, quit working at the office till there's nothing left of you at the end of the day. You may be a pretty fair business man under those conditions, but as a husband you become a candidate for the divorce court. In the meantime, you can take my word for it that your wife loves you and wants you back."

Then I told him what she had said of his habit of walking on ahead when they were out together.

"God," he exclaimed. "Is that it? Do you think so? Just that she wanted me *with* her?"

"Yes," I said, "it's as simple as that. And you didn't see it. Lots of men are just as blind—and lots of women, too, when the shoe is on the other foot."

"I'm going to her right now," he cried.

"Hold hard," I said. "You'll do nothing of the kind. First you'll have a talk with the medicine man, and learn how to exorcise this demon lover, or whatever he is. And if you can't do it by the time he gets through telling you things you've never learned before, why you're less worth helping than I thought."

"All right," he laughed. "Make an appointment for me right away."

"What about that girl?" I asked.

"That's over with," he said emphatically.

So I turned to the telephone, found my medicine man at leisure, and presently set Mr. Smith on his way. Of course I had previously prepared the way by a conference with the physician. He knew all about it.

Later I sent for Mrs. Smith, told her as much of my talk with her husband as I thought best, and sent her to the psychiatrist that afternoon. Apparently the Smith case is settled. I shall be much surprised if they ever have another serious misunderstanding. Their marriage is now grounded as every marriage should be grounded. They have enough money for their needs, they are intellectually and temperamentally congenial, they have good health, and they have an intelligent sex life based on a thorough mutual understanding of what they are about, and on the mutual confidence which such an understanding begets.

On this matter they have no reservations, silences, and secret thoughts any longer. The light has been let in, and they have mental and spiritual health where there were formerly doubt, fear, suspicion, and tension of the nerves. Where the whole stream of their life was formerly polluted by these things, so that all their relations with each other were distorted and strained, it now flows clean, clear, and quiet, with only such disturbances of its calm as are to be expected in all human relationships.   Marriage has become, for them, the success it is capable of being in all cases where the conditions are such that it has a reasonable chance.   *Given a chance, marriage is a sound institution.*   This case is one of the many proofs I have of its possibilities.

Yesterday while I was on my way to lunch the Smiths passed me in their car, with their boy between them.   They waved a delighted salutation.

"Those people seem to be good friends of yours," said a visiting lawyer who was with me.

"Pretty good," I answered.   "They have watched the workings of my court rather closely and are quite enthusiastic about it."

2.

My reason for telling the story of the Smiths, and others like it, is that such happenings—and they are happening all the time—illustrate better than any amount of expository argument how ignorance, second hand, traditional thinking, and our sedulous censorship on books that give any genuine information on sex, can turn the splendid possibilities of the most promising marriage into a miserable failure, unless experience and knowledge from some source can intervene.

It seems incredible, when one considers this story of the Smiths, that two intelligent and cultured persons, both of them adepts in the uses of the mind and the handling of ideas, could have been so completely confused by facts which ought to be commonplaces to any mature person.

From start to finish the whole difficulty was needless.   Three things caused it: First, ignorance; second, traditional and irrational jealousy, based on the property notion as applied to women; and, third, pride, which prevented frank speech on either side.   These three things are at the root of most marital unhappiness; and they can often be removed with the aid of a third person, qualified by training and experience and an educated sympathy to diagnose such difficulties.   Of course where the marriage is between incompatibles, that is different. For such marriages there is usually no solution but separation, divorce, or intelligent compromise in the interest of the children, if there are children.

There is one other factor in unsuccessful marriages, however, which is not so easily disposed of: I mean *poverty—plus too many children*. Poverty alone does not necessarily make trouble in marriage, for a husband and wife free from encumbrances can, if need be, both work, and so be self-supporting. This is an excellent solution, particularly in the case of young couples who need and want each other, and who are not financially able to afford marriage on the usual basis.

But when children come in such marriages, the poverty which prior to their coming was merely an inconvenience which youth puts up with light-heartedly, often becomes a tragedy.

Birth Control and the free dissemination of contraceptive information is the best solution here; but most young people marry with very hazy and inadequate notions along that line, and they "get caught." If methods of contraception that have lately been worked out by the Birth Control League could legally be given general circulation, the business transacted by our divorce courts as a result of poverty plus too many children, would drop off enormously.

3.

Nearly all the annulment and separation cases, in behalf of minors, that come before me involve, first, poverty and economic incompetence on the part of the husband—often by reason of his youth; secondly, an accidental baby, born, owing to ignorance of adequate contraceptive measures, *within a year after marriage*, or even within a few months, where there have been prenuptial relations.

There are people who hold that the possession of such contraceptive knowledge on the part of the unmarried would make for "immorality." But I should like some of these moralists to demonstrate in what respect unwanted pregnancies improve the morals of the situation. The lack of contraceptive information does not act as a restraint on the unmarried; it merely results in a kind of trouble which helps nobody and does no good. Illegitimacy, social disgrace, abortion, and even suicide, are among the fruits of such ignorance.

The type of mind that thinks that the way to save the world is to keep it ignorant, is the type that is also' willing to put deadly poisons into alcohol in order to prevent people from drinking it. The fact is that the poisoning of the alcohol does not prevent people from taking a chance on it, and that it kills quite a number of those who do so. Certain of the moral savages running around loose in this country apparently think the death of these people a fair penalty for their transgression of the law and for their failure to do as the moralists tell them. There might be some equity in the situation if that poisoned alcohol could be fed to the persons who are willing to feed it to other people.

It is the same with the use of contraceptives in illicit sex relations. Withholding the information does not act as a restraint; it merely causes needless tragedies. And in marriage the same thing is true in a different way; for in marriages where the parents are financially incompetent to support children, the birth of children is worse than an inconvenience; it is likely to wreck the marriage.

I don't mean such a couple will necessarily seek divorce, but I do mean that however well they may stick together for the sake of the children, they will not be happy. The fear and anxiety and worry caused by the bite of poverty and debt, make happiness or kindly human relationships nearly impossible. And, of course, such homes are not fit places for children to be living in.

On the other hand, put off birth of children till the parents are on their feet financially, and then a few babies will help rather than hinder, and unite rather than estrange, their parents.

4.

I think there is little comprehension in the public mind of how easily most divorces, save those genuinely due to incompatibility, could be avoided if men and women understood sex better than they do, and if certain of them also understood what a disaster children are to a couple who are unable to provide for their support without undue hardship and deprivation for all concerned. I am not talking of sane economy and self-sacrifice, or of making ends meet, understand. I am talking of unwise debt, and not enough to eat, and of the rent overdue, and of things like that. These are the things that wreck lives, that poison happiness, that make sex a source of misery, and that sow the seeds of divorce.

Young couples who marry usually do so primarily because they love each other and want to live together and gratify their desire for each other without opposition and persecution from society, such as they would incur if they followed their natural inclinations outside of marriage. If they are really intelligent in these matters, and if they are informed, and if they know what they are about, they marry with the thought that this marriage relationship will in due time, and with the help of the sex impulse, strengthen into an intimate comradeship, at once physical and spiritual—a comradeship which is not attainable without the tremendous emotional momentum of sex behind it—a comradeship which is capable at its best of making a man and woman genuinely one. Later, sex begins to fade out of the picture; it becomes less important, less central, after middle life; but by then it has done its work.

Having thus grounded their marriage on what is most true and permanent in their natures, and having likewise gotten themselves into a reasonably secure economic position, they may have children with some assurance that they are not thereby sounding the knell of their own happiness.

In the case of the Smiths, of course, there was plenty of money; but the sex impulse, which would normally have made this couple one, merely served as a wedge to separate them—because they used it ignorantly. It will not have that effect now.

5.

Another, somewhat similar case of the fruits of ignorance that I have lately had to deal with is that of a couple whom I will label Mr. and Mrs. Charles Hill—that being as far from the real name as I can get. (Please understand that in all these stories I make radical alterations in all facts that might serve to identify or direct suspicion toward the persons I tell of.)

Mr. and Mrs. Hill were aged forty-four and forty-two respectively. They had married in their early twenties. They were good conventional church people. They went to church on Sunday, and they had always taken great pains to see that their children received what they called a "religious education." They had brought their family up straightly in the way it should go, and so far as outward seeming went, the Hill family always behaved conventionally, and correctly, to the last degree. Outwardly they played safe and they stood pat. Their neighbors didn't remotely suspect that there was anything more exciting in the life of the Hill family than that.

Then one day Mr. and Mrs. Hill got a divorce. The real facts never came out in the divorce court. What they wanted was a divorce, not notoriety and scandal. But I learned the real truth because Mr. and Mrs. Hill came to me with their troubles before taking formal action, and because I was also on confidential terms with their seventeen-year-old daughter. As an example of the collisions that are constantly taking place between the old order of things in sex conduct, and the new, it is perfect. The husband and the wife talked different languages, and the daughter talked a third.

As Mr. Hill is a successful lawyer in Denver, and as his wife and daughter move in a social set whose names and pictures appear frequently in the society columns of the press, I knew of the Hill family in a general way. I was interested, therefore, when Mrs. Hill called me one day by telephone, and asked for an appointment—which I arranged for the next day.

In the long conference which I had with her I listened to the old, old story: a puritanical attitude on the part of the wife toward sex, a husband powerfully sexed, and yet utterly dense and inhuman in his sex relations with his wife, a long ordeal of grinding poverty through the first years of marriage, many babies, averaging seventeen months apart. Life for the Hills had been a drab affair, largely devoid of color, charm, beauty, life, and joy. They had more money and more leisure now, but it had come too late. It had merely made Mr. Hill unruly and restive, and Mrs. Hill had become more prim, more drab, more set in what she regards as her righteous way of living, than ever.

"I don't know that you can do much to help my relations with my husband," said Mrs. Hill to me; "but perhaps you can do something about my daughter Millie. She is with her father and under his influence. He is letting her go to late parties; he buys her elaborate clothes—in extreme styles—hardly decent; in fact, she gets anything she wants. He never spent money on me that way. He never used to spend it so on her. He began it all of a sudden, some months ago. Apparently they understand each other perfectly. Millie's tendency is to take sides with him. She thinks I am old fashioned and out of date.

"Mr. Hill and I have separated. He has taken an apartment, and has left me the house. Millie is with him. The younger children are away in boarding school, except the two youngest."

"Why did you and your husband separate?" I asked. "Please tell me the exact truth about it, Mrs. Hill."

"He does not respect me and my rights," she said with sudden vehemence. "He expects me to be as beastly as he is."

"You mean you don't agree about your sex life?"

"I suppose so."

"And it's all his fault?"

She hesitated. "I don't want to be unfair to him. It is just that I have had a different upbringing. I know there are lots of people who find nothing repulsive in things I can't for the life of me help detesting. Sex seems to me a horrible thing. It seemed so to my mother before me. She said the Bible teaches that it is evil, and that its only excuse is for propagating the race. That's true, isn't it? I always thought that after we were through having children we'd be done with it; but we weren't."

"And you knew nothing of it when you were married?"

"Nothing! And when I told him that I knew nothing of such things he passed it off. Said he would take care of all that. So I always depended on him. And I comforted myself with the thought that we had to go through this so we could have children, and that that justified our sin. It wasn't till later that I realized that he actually enjoyed it. It didn't shock him, and he had no notion that it shocked me. It was perfectly incomprehensible to me that any decent person could feel about it as he did. And when I understood what he expected of me, I came to hate living with him. And how I dreaded the coming of night!

"We had our first child," she continued with mounting indignation, "nine months after we were married. That mortified me. I'll never forget how a girl I knew well—she was engaged to be married to a man I had refused, though she didn't know that— smiled significantly and said, 'My dear, you and Charlie didn't lose any time, did you!' Ugh! I could have slapped her—with her dirty jokes. And she engaged to be married! But she has no sense of shame. Apparently nobody has, any more. She has two children, and openly says she knows how not to have any more.

"Well, Mr. Hill and I might have gotten along better together if we had not been desperately poor. Mr. Hill decided after we were married that he wanted to go into law. He was teaching at the time. So he took that up—and I'll have to say for him that he has made a success of it. But for long years, while he was studying and going to lectures at night, paying out money for his training and for costly books, how we did have to stretch a dollar, and how I did slave! He forgot all about me, so far as I could see, except"—laughing bitterly—"when he wanted the use of me. And believe me, the babies came and kept on coming, one every year and a half, and sometimes closer together than that."

"Why didn't you use contraceptives?" I asked.

She looked at me as if I had made an immoral suggestion. "Why, that wouldn't have been right, would it? It seems to me that *abstinence* is the only moral way. Probably that is why God has made the—the act so repulsive, to teach us what the lusts of the flesh are really like—sinful except for one purpose. Besides, we must not try to frustrate God's purposes. And in this matter His purposes are *perfectly clear!* It's all in the Bible. There are other natural functions, you know, which are also repulsive, but necessary. But what decent person— Well, you see, it's all the same. Sex is repulsive but necessary, and it's a sin to take pleasure in such a thing.—Don't you think so, Judge?" she added, with a pathetic appeal in her eyes, as if she hoped not everybody in this puzzling and unregenerate world was siding against her. "And besides, what pleasure can there be in it? People seem so— perverted about it. It has never even tempted me," she finished, with a touch of pride.

"There is a side of sex," I answered, "with which you have evidently had no experience—probably it is your husband's fault that you haven't. I mean the emotional side. That is what exalts and purifies what might otherwise be regarded as a physically repulsive thing. Do you remember when he first kissed you? Did you find any emotional exultation in that?"

She gasped and the tears rushed to her eyes. "Oh, Judge— yes—yes. But it never came again. Never! Is it like that? Oh— oh." And with a little moan she sunk her face in her hands. Then she looked up. "I guess I'm too old to learn," she said. "But I'm ready to admit that there may be another side."

"You see," I explained, "this marriage has been a failure, has wound up in failure, because of the ignorance of both of you. He was so eager that he could not understand your language of reluctance and false delicacy, instilled into you by your training. You, on your part, knew nothing of the forces you were trying to oppose and shut out, not only from your own life, but from his. You didn't know his language. A little more sympathy and wisdom on his part, and he might have educated you. There are many men like that, well meaning but obtuse. They think their wives are frigid. They don't know that a really frigid woman is very rare, indeed. I think you are like other women, Mrs. Hill. Remember that first kiss. Perhaps he would have known how to make love effectively to a woman more like himself, but he didn't know how to adapt himself to you. Any psychiatrist could have told him things that would have enabled him effectually to bring about a change in your views about sex."

She had been listening with a look of keen interest. But now suddenly she eluded me; and the old look came into her eyes. "I don't think I would want them changed," she said with a touch of resentment. "There was more that he did. He insisted on having relations with me even when I was pregnant. Why, even animals don't permit that. It is one more evidence that we are a fallen race, given to unnatural practices."

"There are differences of opinion about that," I answered; "but the weight of scientific opinion seems just now to be against you.

Of course, you understand, or should, that sex plays a different part in human life from what it does among animals. Animals, apparently, have much less imagination than we have. They have no art, no music, no sculpture, no hands to do things with, no finely articulate language. You make a mistake in judging human conduct too confidently by the measure of animal conduct."

"You're against me," she flared.

"I'm merely telling you some things you don't know," I answered. "Don't resent it. Let's go on with your story. You denied him, you say. And you have already shown that you have no knowledge of what that deprivation of a thing he normally craved must have meant to him."

"Judge," she said earnestly. "There is one thing I have not made clear. I want to give him his due. My husband is a good Christian man; and I have such faith in him that I have felt that he could not *really* want a thing like that unless I did. I think you attach too much importance to it. I am sure it couldn't have been much of a deprivation."

"Oh, you are!" I exclaimed. "Suppose he should deprive you of food because he was not hungry himself. Would you get along with him very well? Sex is a hunger; and it can be an imperative hunger, capable of wrecking lives. Well, we can go into that again if necessary. Let's go on with the story."

"It was several years," she continued, "before Mr. Hill became a practicing lawyer. It was longer still before he could make a decent living. During that time I stood by and did my best and never complained, except that I never would give in about this thing we have been talking of. I had to work very hard, and what with that and repeated pregnancies, I soon lost what good looks I had—long before the struggle was over."

"How long has it been," I asked, "since you and your husband have had relations?"

"It happens about once a year. The last time was six months ago."

"Suppose your husband had done what some husbands do under like conditions. Suppose he had found him a 'sweetie.' "

"What is a 'sweetie'?" she asked innocently.

"Suppose he found him a sweetheart; what would you do?"

"Oh," she exclaimed. "I know it would be *impossible* for him to do anything like that. He is a good Christian man. But if I ever thought he would or that he did, I would divorce him in a minute."

"Then you don't think you have deprived him of anything he has a right to?"

She shook her head. "I still don't see how he could have a right to a thing so repulsive to me, since I am involved in it. I am sorry we should care for different things; but he married me for better or worse." Here her mouth set firmly. Then she went on, "Besides, we have our children; and neither of us wants any more babies. So why should there be any further sex life between us? It is carnal appetite. Why should I degrade him, and myself along with him, by letting him indulge it?"

I looked at her—tried to read in her face some clue to her state of mind. In spite of all I had said—in spite of that one moment of insight that had come to her like a brief lightning flash, as she remembered her first kiss, her mind had gone back to its habitual channel as the needle toward the pole.

This woman had gone to school, Sunday school, and Church. She had been "educated" rather beyond the ordinary run. She was a perfected product of the puritanism that had made her. I had met hundreds like her, all fruit of the same training. Our civilization had produced this warped and twisted thing. Such was the preparation with which she had been permitted by state and church to marry, bear children, and, if possible, make them as idiotically immoral as herself.

Questioning her further, I found that she disapproved of the new modes in music as being immoral. She didn't want them utilized and made better. She wanted them abolished. She disapproved of dancing, particularly the new dancing. She wanted that rooted out also. She thought the ways of young people shocking, and prided herself on having kept her own children apart from the dangerous currents around them.

In short, she was perfect and complete. She was the staunchest, the most unalterable, that the old order could show. She was righteous, virtuous and good according to orthodox definitions of righteousness, virtue, and goodness and according to no other definition. So far as human relationships went she was an intolerable prig and an impossible person. What her code amounted to in terms of practice could be seen in the fact that she could not live with her husband, or make him happy or herself happy in a marriage which, according to her, was recorded in Heaven, and as fixed by the decree and sponsorship of God as the course of the stars.

Happiness or no happiness, she was hell-bent for heaven. There could be no question that she would probably get to "heaven" if she kept on, and sprout wings, and decorously play a harp, with some millions of others just like herself. There could also be no question that they would make the place uninhabitable for the rest of the human race.

What I am interested in is a heaven for humanity—sweating, swearing, toiling, loving, lusting, hating, worshiping, wonderful humanity—unregenerate yet lovable.

These thoughts flew through my head for an impatient moment; then they passed, and I found myself pitying her—pitying her and wanting to help her if I could.

We talked further about what might be done. What she chiefly wanted was that I get hold of her daughter Millie, and arrange for her to see the girl oftener so she might regain her hold upon her, and wean her if possible from what she regarded as the hostile and unsafe influence of her father.

My next conference was with Mr. Hill. Here I found myself dealing with a thoroughly sophisticated man. In fact, what surprised me when I had talked with him a few minutes was that he had handled his relations with his wife so unskillfully. I told him so—privately thinking, as I still think, that he was the type of man who would be more or less wanting where tact and sympathy were necessary, though he would get on perfectly with a woman of his own temperament, whose desires were so like his as to need no difficult interpreting.

"Oh," he said with a shrug. "I had it all to learn. Like her I was brought up in an overprotected home. Of course in those first years of our marriage I made mistakes. I can see now how I might have made a different thing of it if I had known what I know now. But it's too late now; much too late. That side of her has atrophied. Sex is her blind spot. It would be wasting your time to try to bring us together, Judge. I want a divorce and she knows it. I think we had better arrange the terms of the settlement through you. After I get the divorce I'm going to marry the woman I love; but Mrs. Hill doesn't know that yet.— Of course, this divorce, if she consents to it, will hurt me some socially and professionally; but I'm willing to pay that price for my freedom and happiness. And my wife will be happier without me. She knows she's cheated me out of something; or she ought to know it."

"She's alarmed about Millie," I said, "and she thinks you have alienated the girl from her."

"She's done that herself," he answered. "If you don't believe me, talk with Millie. I'll send her around." As he spoke, he smiled a peculiar smile. "Millie used to worry me a bit," he added. "I thought she might run wild and get into trouble. But I've quit all that. When you see her and talk with her you'll understand why. She's one of that Younger Generation you've been doing a book about. You'll find Millie an unusual kid for her age. She and I are very sympathetic, and we have talked a lot together. Ideas to which most kids are strangers are an old story to her."

But before he could send Millie a curious thing happened. Mr. Hill had indiscreetly confided to a colleague the fact, which he also confided to me in the course of our interview, that he was having a *liaison* with the woman he hoped to marry when he could get a divorce. The colleague still more indiscreetly confided this news to his wife, as colleagues will. And the colleague's wife, as soon as she was up the next morning and had the breakfast things cleared up, hied straight to Mrs. Hill and told her all about it.

I suppose she wanted to stir up the puddle. She succeeded. Mrs. Hill came flying furiously to me with the facts. "And now," she concluded angrily, "he can whistle for his divorce. I won't let him have it. He thinks he can pick up with this hussy and marry her. I'll show him.—And you must make him give up Millie. He is no fit company for an innocent young girl—even if she is his own daughter. Why, Millie still thinks the doctor brought her in a satchel. There never was a girl more completely protected from every degrading thing—while I had her. I've questioned her to see if she has been contaminated at school, and it is astonishing how everything I don't want her to know has passed right over her head. She is still a child—though a lively and high-spirited one. I wish she wouldn't wear her skirts so short," she added with a sigh. "And she got her hair bobbed before I knew about it— but it does make her look pretty."

I passed over the comments on Millie, and came to the point, by observing, "You said you'd divorce Mr. Hill if you discovered him in an infidelity."

"Yes, but he *wants* a divorce. I didn't say I'd divorce him if he wanted it. Just wait till he tells *me* he wants a divorce."

Mrs. Hill was plainly in no state of mind to listen to arguments just then. I did the best I could, proposed that she see me later, and then let her go. Having done that, I sent for Millie. I thought Millie might help. Besides, the contrast between the mother's and the father's account of the girl interested me. I wondered what she was really like.

The next day, at the appointed hour, there walked into my chambers one of the most completely fascinating little personalities it has been my fortune to meet with in the flapper world. Millie, to my fairly experienced eye, was clearly of her own generation. Incidentally, her resemblance to her highly sexed father was striking. She was the type that matures early. Her body was finely developed, straight and lovely. She had escaped the débutante slouch, and carried herself with strength and poise. Her face coincided with her mother's account of her, and it in no way prepared me for her conversation. It was appealingly childlike and delicate; and her eyes were wide open, steady, guileless, and direct in their gaze.

I told Millie as much as I thought best concerning my talks with her parents. She sat back and listened with a comically judicial air, her knees crossed, her short skirt carelessly drawn back exposing her bare knees, and legs ditto half way from knee to hip. She was apparently unconscious of any impropriety in her pose. Seemingly the added display had become as much a convention in her world as the very shortness of her skirts. I made no comment. I reflected, however, on the fact that a few minutes earlier another girl had sat in that chair, who was a very wild specimen, indeed; and that she had been garbed precisely as Millie was garbed, and had displayed her person with the same apparent unconsciousness of doing it. Was the unconsciousness apparent or put on? The first girl had had affairs with a number of boys, and it was taking all my ingenuity to get her straightened out. I made up my mind to find out about Millie before I was through.

"Dad and Mother," she said, when I had finished, "ought to get a divorce. The present plan's no good. I don't know what Dad told you, but he's in love with a woman Mother's never even heard of.—Ah, he's a sweet one to be getting after me for coming in late from parties. But after I found out about his affair, he didn't try to pull any more preaching on me.

"You see," she continued, leaning forward confidentially, "I came to the office late one afternoon, after five o'clock. It happens I've got a latch-key. I guess Dad had forgotten that. Anyway, I walked right in on them. What's that Latin phrase Dad uses in divorce cases? *In—in flagrante—delictor—delicto*—that's it!

"Well, Judge, I guess you'll think I'm pretty hard-boiled for a girl that's never let a boy do more than kiss her; but I know all about these things. You see Dad shot the whole works at me a couple of years ago. Told me he hoped I'd go straight, but that if I didn't, he wanted me to know the ropes—*all* about it; how to take care of yourself and all that. So I was wise. And when I saw them—well, I just leaned against the door and laughed and laughed, with Dad looking at me with his face red as a boiled lobster.

" 'Dad,' I said, 'don't let it worry you. I won't say a word.

But you've sure got to give me a hat and a gown and some silk stockings—and good ones!' And believe me he did. And he still does. He calls me 'the beloved blackmailer.' Look at this hat, Judge. Isn't it a peach?—Mother can't make out what's come over him, giving me all these things. Poor Mother—what she needs is to cut loose and have some fun. She's *too* good. There's no living with her. She makes every one miserable.

"Well, that made me see where Mother stood. I already knew, but that made it plain. I had a talk with Dad that night, and he told me the story. Poor Dad and poor Mother! But there's nothing to do about it. Mother doesn't know a thing that's going on. She thinks Dad is a 'good Christian gentleman,' *and that she's got him by the throat because he is*. As for her, she's up to the neck in two or three religious societies and her church; and outside of that and us kids, she isn't interested in anything, and doesn't know anything. If she knew all that's packed away in my head, she'd think *she* was the Scarlet Woman for even knowing that I knew it. Of course she can't understand why Dad should care anything about—well, you know what I mean—life, and all that. And if she knew about the thing I caught him at she would never understand that it was her doing, and that it served her right. Now that he's made the break I hope he has a good time—and I told him so."

This, I thought, from a seventeen-year-old girl!

Aloud I said, "Millie, your mother does know. Your father told Mr. Herbert, and he told his wife, and she tipped your mother off. And now your mother says she won't give him a divorce, since he wants to marry another woman. She's angry for one thing, and she doesn't think it would be moral for another."

"What!" gasped Millie. "She knows? Say, Judge, that's awful. Poor, poor Mother! I'll have to go to her this evening. She just can't get that sort of thing. I don't know what I'll say, because I've kidded her no end into thinking I'm as innocent as a baby. I'll have to come across with the stuff now, all right. But I think I can manage her; and I'll bring her around to talk things over. Dad's just got to have that divorce, you know, and marry and settle down."

"Bring her," I said.

"Poor Mother," she sighed. "So damn' good—and so dumb!"

Then she stopped and I saw her lift her head like a little war-horse. "That cat that told her," she flared. "Ah—wait till I meet her. I could tell her something, but she'll find it out quick enough. Her husband hates her, and he's got a love affair, and he's going to divorce her and marry his sweetheart. Dad told me so. That's where *she* gets off."—It has since happened as Millie predicted.

"Tell me, Millie," I said, switching the subject to herself. "You meant it, did you, when you said you had never had sex relations with any boy?"

She looked up frankly. "Sure I did. A lot of girls think that, and petting, are the only way to hold boys; but Dad and I talked all that over. He's been a boy himself, you know. And we figured there was nothing to it. Boys are keener about what they can't have than about what they can have; and so a lot of them are keen about me. I never have any trouble with familiarities and petting and all that. Oh, yes, I've been kissed. I wanted to know what it was like. It doesn't amount to anything unless you like the person you kiss, Dad says; and if it doesn't amount to anything, why do it? It's just silly and slobbery. I won't have those half-grown kids that couldn't raise a mustache if they died for it, and that I don't care beans about, pawing me over and kissing me and—all that, much less going the limit. There's no kick in it if you've got any judgment, Dad says.

"Now some day I'm going to meet a fellow I really like—you know what I mean. He'll be big and tall, and I'll look up to him. That's the sort I want. And when I meet him, I'll fall in love with him. And if he wants to kiss me, there'll be some thrill in that. And believe me, when I fall in love I'm not going to be stingy.

"Then, if we cared for each other enough to want to stick, we'd get married and have some babies; only he'd have to have enough money to support them. I'm crazy about babies, Judge. I'm going to have a lot of them. I suppose it will hurt, but I don't care."

"Let me get this straight," I put in. "Do you mean that you would have what your generation calls prenuptial relations with this hypothetical man?"'

"Now, Judge—don't tell me I'm shocking you."

"Not at all. I'm interested. Did you and your father work this out together in your talks?"

"Yes—you know Dad is pretty broad-minded. Dad said, 'Millie, I'd rather you didn't have anything of that sort happen till you're married to the man it happens with. It's always likely to make trouble between you and society. But it's up to you. I've told you all I know. Don't have anything to do with any fellow that you don't like an awful lot and that isn't clean-minded and clean-bodied. Be darned particular.' And another thing he said was that it's better to live together unmarried than it is to marry in a hurry just because you happen to want each other just then. 'Take each other without marriage if you have to,' he said; 'but don't tie up in legal marriage unless you're sure what you're about. Take each other if you have to,' he said, 'but whatever you do, take your time.'"

"Do you find this idea being practiced by people you know?" I asked.

"Do I! Why, Judge, nobody really thinks it wrong any more to give a person you love everything you've got, whether you can afford to marry or not. Of course I suppose there are mighty few that would say it right out loud in public, but that's what they think. Dad says so, and I know that's the way with my crowd."

"And your father actually taught you these things? Of course, you know, Millie, that there are mighty few parents who would take such a responsibility as that, even if they thought as he does."

"I'd have learned it from my crowd, even if he hadn't said anything," she answered. "Only I wouldn't have learned so well; and I wouldn't have learned what to look out for. And I'd have been letting a lot of boys kiss me and handle me, the way the other girls do. You see, Dad and I have talked this thing over—simply for hours. We've got the same problem in a way."

"Your mother has suggested that I take you away from him and turn you over to her," I remarked. "If she knew what you have been telling me of his influence on you and his ideas, she would be still more set on it. What's your honest opinion, Millie? Would you have been likely to have gotten into trouble, and would you have been letting boys pet you and all that, if he hadn't taught you these ideas, which by society are considered thoroughly immoral?"

"Of course I would. I wanted to. I thought I'd like it. In fact, I tried it a few times. Now I see how silly it was. None of that for me. Dad's got the straight of it. A little love-making goes a long way."

"Well, Millie," I said, "I'm much interested. I'm particularly interested in the way you and your father have hitched up. Now, one other thing. A few minutes before you came in there was another girl, about your age, sitting in the chair you are in. She has had intimate affairs with several boys, and has at last gotten into trouble. I have to provide a secret confinement for her and arrange later for the adoption of the baby."

"Little fool," remarked Millie. "But I suppose nobody ever told her how to take care of herself.—I've got some Dad," she added, with a sage nod.

"No," I agreed. "Nobody told her. She just plunged in the dark. Well, Millie, I hope you won't misunderstand me, because it is merely that I'm curious about your point of view. That other girl, who is a pretty wild one, sat in that chair—just the way you do."

Millie looked down carelessly. What I meant was plain to the eye; some would have said shockingly plain—but evil be to him who evil thinks. As for my opinions about the use of clothing for the concealing of the body, or for any purpose save ornamentation and protection from the elements, I have already expressed them. Clothing used for concealment is a breeder of immodesty, not a conserver of modesty. When in ancient Greece youths and maidens joined in games stark naked, as the climate permitted, they demonstrated a moral health not attainable by the use of clothing or by what we call decency. When men and women bathe naked together in swimming places in Japan, they prove that the Japanese, also, have something to teach us about morals.

Millie was plainly not disturbed by my remark. "This doesn't mean a darned thing," she said, coolly pulling her short skirt an inch higher and placidly eyeing her comely leg. "It's more comfortable and freer, that's all. It's like the short skirts. *Good* people finally got used to them, and even took to wearing them, after they had talked themselves to death against the 'bad' people who started them. Then they bobbed their hair—after saying that bobbed hair was unwomanly. After awhile these birds will learn not to undress in the dark." Here she threw back her head and laughed. Then added, "I suppose this short skirt of mine set you to wondering if I was as wild as that wild one, eh?"

"I wondered if she was conscious of it," I acknowledged, "and just what purpose lay behind it."

"And then you wondered the same thing about me," she put in. "Well, Judge, take it from me that with nearly all girls it doesn't mean a thing. Nothing at all. We all do it. She's wild and she does it; I'm—um—tame, and I do it." She paused and watched me like a bird, head to one side. "I'm all right, really, Judge. Mother's the immoral one in our family, only the old dear doesn't know it.

"I'll see her to-night, and then talk with you later. May I go? Is there anything more? I've got a date for a movie. It's been awfully interesting to talk with you, Judge. With most people I have to shut up about what I think. Good-by, Judge." And away she went.

Millie talked with her mother as she promised. Later I had a conference with the three of them. Mrs. Hill finally came to take a less resentful view of her husband's infidelity, admitted that she was herself not blameless, and finally consented to the divorce, which certain clever lawyers later worked out, with Mr. Hill's canny assistance, by means of a certain amount of collusion and perjury, along lines thoroughly non-committal, so far as the court proceedings were concerned.

This story of the Hill family seems to me to teach several important lessons. It reveals in a typical way what is wrong with many marriages in which either the husband or the wife or both have been infected with Puritanism in their attitude toward sex. In addition, it brings into startling relief a fact to which I have referred in earlier chapters of this book, namely, that the older generation is, in many instances, taking its cue from youth. It is swinging around to a view of sex conduct very similar to that of the Younger Generation, with this difference—that adult wisdom and worldly experience modify the result.

6.

The case of Millie and her father is typical of what I think is going to happen more and more. At least my experience with a large variety of people convinces me that it will happen more and more, and I simply record the fact here for what it is worth.

In this instance, the Older Generation and the Younger put their heads together, with certain clear-cut consequences. Those consequences will shock some of my readers, but they have to be reckoned with. Let's consider them.

For one thing the Younger Generation, in the person of Millie, accepted from the Older, with the utmost eagerness, an adult revision of its own wild code. That revision was a kind of compromise. It did not go as far as conventional persons would demand, but it went a long way, and it produced a great improvement in the code which Millie would have adopted had she been left, like her companions, without adult guidance, sympathy, and counsel.

Note what this revision of Millie's flapper code involved. It involved voluntary and convinced restrictions, genuine restrictions, on indiscriminate petting and promiscuous intimacies. Petting, promiscuity, and a crude and sickening willingness to be intimate with *anybody* that might come along, these were and are characteristic of the raw, and half-baked code of Millie's friends. The utter want of niceness, of discrimination, of taste that is involved in a girl consenting to kisses, fondling, and often outrageous physical

liberties from boys in general, any boy that happens along, seems
logically the first thing from which a girl of Millie's type would
naturally rebel. And she would naturally and easily substitute the
thought that it is well to be finicky and particular about such
relationships, to say the least. Her father had the wisdom to see
that, and he had no difficulty in making her see it. Instead of
saying, "Never do it!" he said, "Be sure you care a very great
deal for any person you admit to such intimacy."

Working this new, raw code over in his maturer mind, he turned
it into something more canny and less dangerous. I think this was
no mean service. Of course many of my readers will complain that
he was no fit guide, that he was an adulterer, and that he gave her
a hard-boiled code at that. Perhaps he did. He was rather
hard-boiled himself. Also it is quite true that Millie's present code
is still widely at variance with the conventional code of society;
but she has, at least, cut loose from the demoralized, witless and
intolerable cheapness of which others like her, having no adult
guidance and no tradition of culture behind them, become the
victims. If it were a choice between changing Millie's attitude
toward *promiscuous* intimacies on the one hand, and toward unconventional but *discriminating liaisons,* which she thinks perfectly all
right, on the other, I can't see how it is possible to hesitate an
instant in preferring the latter to the former.

7.

Millie's father made clear to her the very fundamental difference
that exists between sexual promiscuity and unions which, though
irregular, are founded on the spiritual union, sympathy, and congeniality of two personalities. He made it clear to her *that Sex
divorced from affection does not find the satisfaction and contentment and fulfillment that it seeks.* He showed her that, lacking such
fulfillment of the affections, Sex tends to go on and on, automatically, forever hungry, forever athirst, like a castaway at sea, who
has drunk salt water because he lacks fresh. She understood that
excesses come from that.

Millie, in short, had arrived at a sound evaluation of love. Her
conflict with society was now a question, not of promiscuity, but

of conformity to convention. The two things are very different. I know many persons who do not conform to convention in their sex life, but who are moral; and I know others who conform meticulously, but who remain grossly immoral. Millie, then, is not *immoral*. Her father had seen to that.

Now the thing about this that most interests me is that the unconventional advice which Mr. Hill gave his daughter could, by means of a little sane legislation, readily be translated into a prescription for *two kinds of marriage,* or rather two stages of marriage, in his daughter's life. In other words, suppose that Millie, when she falls in love with the Prince Charming she dreams of, could *marry him forthwith,* instead of having with him an affair which, however sincere, would be outside of social control.

Millie made a sharp distinction, in talking of this possible union, saying that when the permanence of the union became a reasonably assured thing, she and the man of her choice would marry and have children.

Millie didn't want babies till she could be fairly sure of the *stability* of the home in which they would be born. She instinctively realized that such stability would involve two things: first, an enduring and substantial congeniality of taste and temperament between her and the man she chose for a husband; and, secondly, a sound economic basis for the maintenance of a Family.

When young persons marry, they often mistake their condition of emotional tension for the congeniality of taste and temperament which alone can form an enduring basis for marriage, particularly a marriage which involves children. When this mistake is made, it is highly desirable that there be some opportunity for discovering it before the birth of children can complicate the situation, and force the hapless pair into a life companionship for which they have no taste.

Again, when young persons marry, they often get along very well, in spite of poverty, because they have only themselves to maintain. It often happens that both of them will keep on working, as they did before marriage; and this arrangement works very well in such cases, *till a baby comes.* When that happens the woman stops working. Thus, the family income, which was large enough to support two persons in comfort, is cut in two; and at the same time there is an increase in the number of persons to be maintained. And if other children follow before the man can have time to improve his economic position, such a situation grows progressively worse.

8.

On questioning Millie, I found that she was fully aware that marriage, as we have it, involves these complications and risks for young people who marry on a romantic impulse which they honestly think as permanent as the everlasting hills, and who marry, besides, on incomes inadequate for the support of a Family. She realized, too, that many such romantic attachments are perfectly capable of growing into the lifetime permanence of "until death do us part" if given an economic chance—that is to say, by putting off the birth of children 'till provision could be made for their support.

It was clear to Millie, therefore, that she wanted *first* some kind of union, a childless union, which could be ended without inconvenience or disaster to anybody if it should prove to lack the qualities which make for permanence; and that she wanted *second* to have children as soon as a real home could be created for them.

Now here is the point. If Millie could have a *marriage* which would enable her to retain this freedom of choice, and these essential safeguards, till the birth of children, she would take it in preference to the unmarried union which she had in mind. In other words, if she could begin with a regular legal marriage which would involve the practice of Birth Control for as long a period as might seem wise to her; and if such a marriage could also carry with it the right to divorce by mutual consent so long as it remained childless, she would choose that marriage in preference to a secret, irregular union that would be frowned on by society if it were discovered.

Such a marriage would be more convenient than a *liaison,* and it would be free from social fear and anxiety. It would be entered on by lovers who seek, not promiscuity, but a safe and permanent joining of their lives, with a safe line of retreat available in case of a mistake. For people *do* make mistaken choices in marriage; and since they do, it seems silly not to reduce to a minimum the tragedies that often result from such mistakes.

This form of marriage would offer few attractions to persons who wanted promiscuity rather than real marriage. For such persons it would be a nuisance because it would be under social control and under social observation. Promiscuity, or a series of short-time unions, if such were the aim, would be more conveniently achieved, as it is to-day, independently of legal sanctions. I emphasize the point here because the fear that such a form of marriage would become a cloak for legalized short-time *liaisons* is one of the first objections I encounter from persons to whom I have talked of this idea. Such short-time unions would retain the same status that they have now. They would naturally and by preference remain outside the law.

Even under our present system there are a few persons who defy convention, by taking advantage of our present divorce laws for discarding old mates and taking on new ones; and doubtless there will always be such persons. But most persons are more stable in their attachments, and more regardful of social censure than that.

9.

It seems to me, therefore, that this fear of legalized promiscuity under such an alteration in the marriage code as I am suggesting is based on an estimate of human nature which is as low as it is false. My experience with men and women tells me that most of them seek divorce only as a last resort. The same is true even of unmarried lovers. When an unmarried union ends, it ends usually with difficulty. Few persons find it easy to break the emotional ties that grow up from long and close contact with another human being. I think human nature can be trusted on this point.

The tendency of this type of marriage would be toward permanence. Certainly its urge toward permanence would be much greater than that of the unmarried union, if only because the eyes of society and the weight and compulsions of custom would rest upon it. The unmarried union is subject to no such pressure; and any unmarried union that can be converted into a legal marriage, thereby instantly takes on a *tendency* to permanence much greater than what it had before. Hence, if Millie's hypothetical unmarried union could be converted into legal marriage, its inherent stability would by that very fact be enormously increased.

Suppose now, that Millie falls in love with her hypothetical young man, whom we will call John. Let us suppose, just to get down to cases, that Millie and John are college students in some state university, neither of them making a living; or suppose she is working in some office, and that he has a job somewhere else, or in the same office; and that they are each of them making just enough to live on, individually. This situation obtains in thousands and thousands of cases. The country is full of fine young people who, under just such conditions as these, are in love with each other and want to get married, and *can't afford it.*

As things stand, the chief reason they can't afford marriage is that it would halve their income.—But why not marry and then both of them go on working? Fine! There would be no reason against that at all. Even under our present code it would be perfectly moral and respectable, and lots of people do it. But the trouble with such a plan for Millie and John is that they might have a baby. Millie would then have to stop working; and then where would their little income be?

But why have a baby? Why not delay all that?—Precisely; why not! Some do just that, by Birth Control. Others make the same attempt and fail to avoid early parenthood. Why do they fail? Is there no sufficiently certain method of contraception known? Certainly there is; an effective contraceptive technique has been worked out, for instance, by the Birth Control League.

But the late Anthony Comstock persuaded Congress and many of the states to pass what is known as the Obscenity Law; and this law forbids the imparting of Birth Control information and the sale of contraceptive devices. Hence, if Millie and John marry, they are deprived *by law* of the knowledge which would enable them both to go on working after marriage.

Moreover, if they do obtain contraceptive information, it is likely to be a bootleg product, inadequate and unscientific; and thus the Obscenity Law provides them with a baby anyway. Since the contraceptive technique worked out by the Birth Control League is almost 100 per cent successful when intelligently used, it seems nothing short of imbecile that society should thus mischievously defer the marriage of Millie and John when they might as well be married as not.

10.

What usually happens in these cases is that Millie and John become engaged—perhaps secretly engaged. But whether they become engaged or not, they are likely to become "sweethearts." In constant daily association, they resist their natural impulses for some time, and then perhaps yield. I am not talking of what our loud-mouthed moralists say they *ought* to do; I am talking about what they *do,* in thousands of cases. The result is a secret sex affair, that is shot through, very often, with constant terror of pregnancy—because the contraceptive methods used are likely to be inadequate, regardless of whether they are used in marriage or outside of it. The married and the unmarried are on exactly the same footing in this respect, be it remembered—with the advantage, perhaps, on the side of the as yet unmarried younger generation.

Such pregnancy results, usually, in one of two things,—abortion or marriage. Sometimes it is hard to decide which is the lesser of the two evils in such cases. On the other hand, if Millie has her baby without marriage, she confronts the superstitious savagery with which society regards unmarried motherhood; and if she keeps the birth of the child a secret, then how can she provide for it? The laws of most states make no provision, such as we have in Colorado, for the care of such children or for secrecy in the handling of such cases.

Thus, the most dangerous thing faced by Millie and John, whether they marry or whether they don't, is *unwanted pregnancy.* The contraceptive technique available to them via the drugstores, and without medical advice, is usually crude and inadequate. Not only is it often unsafe and unscientific, but it is so unsatisfactory psychologically that many lose patience with the whole business and "take a chance." A large portion of the unmarried girls who have come to me in trouble have gotten into it that way—through their ignorance, and through the use of a contraceptive technique obtained from some drug clerk.

I don't say that such technique doesn't work. It does work in most cases when intelligently used. But it is risky, and it is, as I have said, so unsatisfactory in a psychological way, that disaster often follows.

But suppose the legislature of the State of Colorado, where Millie lives, should pass a law that would place *scientific Birth Control information* easily within Millie's reach; and suppose it should pass another law which would permit divorce by mutual consent, without red tape or difficulty, to childless couples; and suppose it should pass another law that would make it out of the question for Millie to extract alimony from John indefinitely in the event of divorce—*a law that would give them no financial or economic hold on each other while childless, and that would leave them, while childless, legally as independent of each other as they were before marriage.* What would happen then?

It is very simple. Millie and John would marry, just as thousands like them do right now, with the *intention* to delay the birth of children, and also with the *knowledge* that would enable them to make good on that intention.

They would each go on working exactly as if they were still unmarried, till John's income was large enough to support a family. They would remain childless till they were ready for children. They would have an opportunity, over a course of years perhaps, to make sure of the permanence of their attachment for each other, and to develop such permanence under conditions favorable to its growth. And when they finally did have a family, the chance of that home breaking up would be very slight indeed. Thus the number of marriages would *increase;* and the number of divorces and broken homes would *decrease.* At present divorces are increasing. Here is a way to stop it.

II.

Sociologists have had much to say about the possibilities of such a form of marriage as this. They call it *Companionate Marriage,* in distinction from procreative marriage, which they know as *The*

Family. Millie and John would begin with *the Companionate,* and they would ordinarily end with *the Family.*

Every young couple that marries to-day, indeed, begins with the Companionate and ends, usually, in the Family. But some do not. There are thousands of couples who remain childless, deliberately childless. In other words, they prefer to continue in Companionate Marriage, and do so. It is perfectly respectable, and Companionate Marriage is to-day one of our most firmly established institutions.

The reason this Companionate is not uniformly within the reach of all who desire it to-day is that it requires some ingenuity to obtain really adequate Birth Control information, and that the obtaining of a divorce is, under our laws, made a needlessly long and expensive process, which usually obligates the man to the payment of alimony, whether there are children or not. The Companionate, as I conceive it, would not legally obligate the husband to support his wife till pregnancy. Financially the two would be as much on their own as they would be now in an unmarried union.

What I am proposing is that society place this already widely practiced Companionate Marriage within the reach of all, including the thousands of fine young people who would marry in a minute if they could see their way to it. And the reason I propose it is that I think it would convert to social uses a flood of wholesome and natural emotional power which is now going to waste, spending itself in folly and frustration, and getting more and more beyond the bounds either of social control or of self-control,—all for want of scientific, legalized Birth Control and some social common sense.

12.

Let me add that what I am suggesting is quite different from Trial Marriage. When I first discussed the Companionate, the sensational report went forth, through the newspapers, that I advocated "Trial Marriage," with the result that there was a widespread misconception in the public mind of what I was really driving at.

Of course it comes down to a question of definition. The public has a certain conception of Trial Marriage which in no way corresponds to my notion of the Companionate. I therefore object to this sensational and inexact confusion of the two ideas.

There is a sense in which every marriage is a Trial Marriage; for obviously nobody can certainly predict the outcome of any union. It may fail. But "Trial Marriage" in the ordinary acceptation of the term implies something which is frankly tentative, provisional, and experimental. It has a psychology of uncertainty and hesitation which is not true of ordinary marriage. In Trial Marriage the whole thing is usually undertaken with a candid recognition that it will probably be a temporary episode. Thus it does not materially differ from the ordinary unmarried union, except that it takes the name of marriage, and may even resort to the legal form of marriage. You see there is a shift of emphasis here which makes Trial Marriage psychologically different from marriage as most of us undertake marriage.

Now the psychology of a marriage *is* the marriage. Change the psychology and inner intent of the union, and you get a totally different kind of union—not to be called by the same name at all. The one sort of union is Marriage; the other is a free love union to which the name "Trial Marriage" is often given.

I know many very fine persons who have entered such free love unions. I have known some who went their ways after a short period of this; I have known others who finally changed from their Trial Marriage over to regular marriage.

Now I am not concerned here either to attack or defend this kind of union. The thing that makes it often dangerous for the people who enter it is the lack of social safeguards, the risk of encountering social disapproval and possible persecution, and the danger of unwanted pregnancy without legal safeguards either for the mother or the child. Such unions, under the present organization of society, are inexpedient. I do not say they are necessarily immoral; I say they are usually unwise. For most of the human race Trial Marriage, as here defined, is unsatisfying because it is psychologically inadequate. People want permanence if they want marriage. If they don't want permanence then there is no reason for getting married and an unmarried union will be preferred.

I trust I make it clear why I object to having the Companionate confused with this kind of thing. *The Companionate is legal marriage; and every childless marriage wherein, by mutual agreement, the parties can obtain a divorce if they want it, is a Companionate.* In other words, the Companionate is a firmly established, perfectly respectable institution among us right now. Childless couples are socially respectable, and they are as much married as any one else. There is no "trial marriage" about it. It is simply that they are forced to practice bootleg contraception instead of legal contraception, and that if they want a divorce by mutual consent, it is a bootleg affair, since they can and do get it by collusion and perjury instead of under the law. Also the woman has a hold on the man for alimony which she would not have under the Companionate if the Companionate were regulated by law.

The point, then, is this: Under the Companionate, with Birth Control legalized and more generally understood, most persons would marry as they marry now, in the belief that their union would prove permanent. They would merely be provided with a way out in the event that it didn't. It would be an honest way out and not a bootleg way out, as under the present system of fraud and hypocrisy.

As for couples who married with no belief in the permanence of their love, I hold that such people would prefer the unmarried union as more convenient for their purposes and fraught with less social responsibility, and that many of them would probably be much better off outside of marriage.

I have no wish to stir up mere controversy. I prefer that sober citizens should feel that I am proposing a conservative and practicable remedy for certain grave social ills. It is an issue that affects millions of people, particularly millions of our young people; and it vitally concerns the parents of those young people who are desirous to see them happily and permanently married. Many a worried parent, I think, would draw a long breath of relief if a beloved son or daughter having chosen a mate with, perhaps, doubtful wisdom, and with insufficient knowledge of life, as often happens, could marry with such safeguards as the Companionate would give through the early years of marriage.

Such is my thesis. If its implications are not immediately clear to the reader, I ask him to read further, while I unfold the theme as it presents itself to me.

CHAPTER VI

THE CHEMISTRY OF LOVE

I.

INEZ, aged seventeen, and Fred, aged twenty, having married in haste were repenting at leisure. They were pained and surprised to find that Marriage had not married them. Apparently some one had blundered. The marriage ceremony was not a fool-proof, magic formula after all. God, they were told, had joined them together; let no man put them asunder. But it would not take Man to do it now. Marriage itself had effectively taken care of that by becoming unendurable to both of them. All they wanted now was legal recognition of a separation which already existed in fact; Inez had gone back to her parents, and Fred had moved to a single room after selling their furniture and giving what money the sale yielded to his wife.

They had spent several months in an unsuccessful effort to adjust their relations, but finally gave it up; and now they appeared before me to ask that I annul their marriage.

There were no hard feelings, they said. Inez demonstrated this by beginning to weep dolefully, while Fred, who had a red, round, good-natured face and a hand like a ham, clumsily patted her shoulder. Their desire for release, they said, was mutual. They had tried hard, and they were satisfied that marriage was a failure.

"Why did you get married in the first place?" I asked.

Here Inez began to weep afresh. I finally gathered that they had had prenuptial relations, and had even lived together on the quiet for days at a time in a little room Fred had strained his purse to rent; and they had found this sample of heaven so delectable that they wanted more than a sample. And marriage, of course, was the logical way to get what they wanted—which was nothing short of love in a cottage, with golden happiness together forever and ever.

142

I have many of these cases. This one troubled me more than most. It did seem as if it should be possible to make a success of this marriage. So I talked with them together and I talked with them separately, in a vain effort to reconcile their differences. Many of these differences were childish, but they were sufficiently real to them. The root of the trouble was poverty. Fred didn't make enough for two, and they had painfully found out that two cannot live as cheaply as one. Poverty had come in at the door and Love had made for the window. A very old story. Another phase of their trouble was the sense of ownership and possessive jealousy which they had both acquired as a foregone conclusion when they married. To their way of thinking that was an essential part of marriage.

After putting them off for many weeks, and after consultations with their parents, I finally decided that an annulment would be the best solution. So I called in Inez and Fred, and had them sign certain preliminary papers. I could have given them the annulment out of hand; but I wanted to gain time because I still hoped against hope that there would be a way out.

Having signed the preliminary papers, the two went off, apparently happy and relieved.

Several weeks elapsed. I was about to conclude the matter, when a report reached me that Inez and Fred had gone back to living together. I immediately sent for them. Fred was not available just then, but Inez came promptly.

"Inez," I began severely, "what is this I hear about your living with Fred? Don't you know that we can't have that? How can I give you an annulment if you go on living with him, and apparently making a success of marriage after all? Judging by what I hear, you and Fred are getting on all right, and don't need an annulment anyway."

The effect of this on Inez was electrical. As she listened, her jaw fell. When I finished she sprang from her chair as if it had been hot. "What?" she gasped. "Aren't we annulled? Why, Judge, we signed the papers. We thought we were annulled! That's why we're living together!"

"Oh," I said, "that's why you're living together! Well, that wasn't an annulment. Those were merely the preliminaries—so you're just as pure as ever, Inez. You are still a pure, married woman, Inez. Do you realize that?"

"I don't want to be pure," she wailed. "I want to live with Fred and be his sweetheart. I couldn't have lived with him a day if I hadn't thought we were annulled. If we had known we were still married—why—why—" Here she stopped short, an odd look of panic and bewilderment on her face.

"Yes?" I put in.

"I couldn't have lived with him," she repeated vehemently.

"But you did," I retorted. "And you've apparently gotten along fine, judging by the look on your face when you came in here."

Inez sat down dejectedly. "Sure we have," she lamented, like one looking back on happy days irrevocably gone. "We've gotten along just as well as we used to before we went and got married. And now you've gone and spoiled it all by not annulling us. And we're still married. I'm his ball-and-chain and he's mine; and we'll never, never be able to live together any more unless you annul us. Judge, you've got to annul us. Judge, dear, you'll annul us, won't you?—— If you don't," she finished with a flash of defiance, "we'll wait till we're twenty-one, and then we'll get a divorce."

"So that you can live together?" I asked—for I found this twist in her thought most engaging. I was sorry some of the anti-divorce fanatics could not be there to take it all in. Seldom, it seemed to me, had a finer bit of comedy come my way.

But it was no comedy to Inez. She shook her little bobbed head fiercely. "Yes—but what'll become of us in the meantime? Oh, Judge—we just *can't* make a go of it married. We've tried and tried. But if we just live together because we love each other, why— that's just heavenly. And, oh, we've got the sweetest room; and yesterday I put up chintz curtains, and—and—" And from there on she poured forth a lyric tale that was everything the story of their marriage, as they had formerly told it to me, ought to have been. She talked and talked, entirely unaware that her tale counted as one of the most sardonic commentaries on our present code of marriage, and on our current notions of chastity that I had ever listened to.

2.

Psychologically Inez and Fred had sinned a deadly sin. Psychologically they had lived together unmarried. According to the prevailing hypocrisy and cant, they were no longer respectable or pure— since we all profess to believe that sin consists in the mental and spiritual condition of the sinner in his attitude toward what are supposed to be the laws of God. By all that society professes, Inez and Fred were in precisely the position of any man and woman who choose to defy God and Man, and "flout all that is most sacred in human life" by living together out of wedlock. But in point of fact they were socially just as respectable and sinless as ever. Their social status was in no way jeopardized by the "sin" they had thought they were committing. The thing could be known, and published from the housetops, and yet society, the church, professing to have a sense of moral values dependent on people's spiritual condition, would pass the whole thing by with perfect complaisance, on the ground presumably that these two had been saved from sin in spite of themselves. For a man and his wife to live together is pure and proper. Nay, it is commanded by God for the propagation of the race. Ergo, these two, in living together were pure and proper, though they hadn't the slightest intention of being so. To any who deny that the church and society take this attitude in the matter, I ask where is the punishment, where the stigma, that would be visited on Inez and Fred if their identities were known by every person in Denver—by their friends, by the minister of their church, by whom you like? The stigma and the punishment would have been forthcoming fast enough had their annulment been an accomplished fact, and had the news of their subsequent *liaison* gotten abroad. And yet they were the same identical persons, with the same way of thought and behavior in the one case as in the other; and their deserts were the same, annulment or no annulment. If they deserved censure and punishment and social ostracism in the one case they deserved it in the other. Why would society and the church fail to attach such stigma and punishment in the absence of the annulment of the marriage? Simply because our ethic in these matters is a superstitious fake, a hypocritical pretense, a lie which has been told so long and so often that we believe it ourselves, even when we don't even pretend to carry it out.

It simply proves once more that the real reason why society is concerned with marriage is to provide for the protection and care of children; that chastity hasn't a thing to do with it save as it bears on the conception and the care of children, and that when we re-enforce these considerations with so-called divine commands, purity myths, and the like, we are hypnotizing ourselves with our own hypocrisy and living in a fool's paradise. It is a very dangerous state of mind for any civilization to be in. Dishonest thinking is the most dishonest and most dangerous thing in the world.

This is not a thrust at purity or chastity, though I suppose some will jump at the conclusion that it is. It is a thrust at a vicious social lie. The cant and sanctimony that finds expression in blather about the "sacredness of the home" and the "foundations of society" and what some persons are perfectly sure is the "Will of God," and other fictions and myths that form no practicable rule of conduct, nauseates me. Until we learn to think from the facts we can't expect to know what is the Will of God, or to do it. At present we know precisely as little about God's Will as we do about common sense and honest thinking! The two kinds of knowledge maintain a constant ratio. Wisdom is Virtue. At present we act by one code and we pretend to another; and a heaped-up mountain of human misery is the result. We had better make sure the mountain isn't a volcano.

But to come back to Inez. The conversation that followed was so extensive that I can't attempt to give it all here. The upshot was that I persuaded Inez that since the preliminary papers had been quite effective in her case as a full annulment, we had better let well enough alone.

I pointed out that society would not have the slightest objection to her and Fred continuing to pretend to themselves that they were annulled, if that gave them comfort. Furthermore, she could keep on with the new job she had just gotten; and Fred could keep his. Thus they would have enough to live on—which they didn't before.

Also, they could continue to occupy their one bit of a room together, and go on being as secret and wicked about it as they pleased,—with a marriage certificate to fall back on in case of emergencies. Besides, the room would be within their means, while a flat wouldn't leave them enough to buy shoe strings. In short, she could go right on being Fred's sweetheart. The fact that he was her husband needn't prevent that. And if they loved each other and were legally married to boot, everything was provided for; and what more could they want?

Society, I explained, whatever it might say about the matter, really intended legal marriage for the protection of children. She and Fred were not financially ready for babies yet; but I hoped they would be later. In the meantime, they could live together; and they didn't have to rattle the legal skeleton that so terrified them unless they wanted to. Incidentally they could thank their stars that their marriage certificate would serve to keep them out of trouble with their relatives, their friends, and society at large, in the event of their present line of wickedness becoming known.

In the end Inez departed, quite happy over being able to eat her cake and have it too. She and Fred are still playing at being lovers; and so long as they see it that way I think it would take something more than a court of law to divorce them.

Society should have been honest with those two youngsters in the first place. They should have been educated to know what seems already so well known to the clever and educated sons and daughters of some of our leading clergymen, doctors, lawyers, teachers, merchants, bankers, and other sophisticated members of the community —*namely, that our present legal marriage can readily be adapted to their condition and their needs.*

Our thousands of Inezes and Freds, though hampered by their lesser education, should also know that *they too,* with just as much right as the sons and daughters of our clergy and other members of the "upper classes," can legally marry on the understanding that they can practice scientific Birth Control, and delay the coming of children till they are ready for them; and that while practicing such birth control, *they too* are as much at liberty as are their educated and sophisticated contemporaries to live together in legal, though childless, marriage; and to enjoy each other in the intimacy and human companionship which such childless cohabitation would make possible, regardless of whether their financial status justifies them in raising a family or not.

Society should further frankly inform these young people that so long as their marriage remained childless, it would leave them as free of financial obligations toward each other as would an unmarried union. One consequence of this would be that unmarried unions would no longer offer any attraction to couples who at present seek them because they think marriage would be impracticable for them.

It is time for Society to admit the truth—that the enormous increase in the number of unmarried unions is due, not to profligacy, nor to a desire for promiscuous relations, nor to a wish to be off with a new love and on with a new every few months, but to our reluctance to *stop lying* to youth, and to our refusal to tell them the truth about modern marriage as, *with the tacit consent and connivance of practically every church except the Roman Catholic,* IT REALLY IS.

Let certain of the clergy denounce and deride and vilify and predict hell and damnation for me and my ideas all they like; the fact stands that they, themselves, are tacitly, and hypocritically, supporting marriage *with Birth Control;* that they, themselves, are practicing Birth Control; that many of them are deliberately childless by this means; and that they are therefore themselves living in a form of marriage which in every essential respect conforms to what sociologists know as Companionate Marriage.

But to come back to the Inezes and the Freds.—Not only should society give them Birth Control information and instruction freely and openly, and pronounce them as financially independent, while childless, as if they were not married at all, but it should further educate them to a firm, courageous, and whole-hearted acceptance of the fact that in the event, either of deliberate pregnancy, *or of accidental pregnancy,* they are expected by society, and by their own sense of what is right, to accept the responsibility that such pregnancy involves. Also that abortion or shirking in such cases—now so common under our present legal marriage code—is detestable and abhorrent; and that since abortion means the ending of a life process which has definitely started, it seems morally justified only for the very gravest reasons, as when the life or health of the mother would be jeopardized by the bearing of a child. At present society itself is to blame for most of the abortions performed on unmarried women in this country, partly because the dissemination of Birth Control knowledge is prohibited by law, with a consequent increase of unwanted pregnancy; and partly because any unmarried girl who has the courage to do right and bear her child, is stigmatized and disgraced—while if she resorts to the abortionist she is rewarded with social approval, and with complete escape from disgrace.

Another matter in which society should honestly instruct Inez and Fred is that it is now the *prevalent and respectable custom* that childless couples who find that they desire a divorce may obtain it by asking for it in a designated court of law; and that among self-respecting people, such divorce involves no demand for alimony on the part of the woman, *save when there is clear justification for such a demand*—a matter to be decided by the court if the issue is raised.

It is true that the letter of the present law is such that it has to be evaded by various legal tricks; by collusion, which is legally forbidden; and by perjury, which is also forbidden. But since the law on this subject is obviously inadequate, it has become, by common consent, a dead letter. Lawyers, courts, and the people have co-operated in nullifying every divorce law that forbids divorce by mutual consent—especially in the case of childless couples. It remains only to recognize this, admit it, and give Inez and Fred the full benefit of the admission by frankly changing the law.

In short, Inez and Fred should be told the truth; namely—that the system of law and custom which upheld the old theological conception of marriage is to-day a crumbling, worm-eaten, dangerously toppling ruin which has served its purpose and now needs to be junked; that something far better, more sane, more rational, more scientific, and more *durable* and *authentic* in the way of monogamous, lifetime, permanent marriage is taking its place; that the new order will *reduce divorce* and insure a larger proportion of marriages that will endure; and that they are now at liberty to practice marriage with Birth Control and divorce by mutual consent for childless couples, if they wish.

I am not interested in what the theological notion of marriage *intends;* I am interested in the disastrous failure of its good intentions, and on the number of new paving blocks that hell has acquired through the operation of this so-called religious system. It must be judged by its results. And to hear some eloquent minister get up and declare that marriage as we have it is practicable and a success is to wonder at the ability of some persons to believe themselves,— especially when, in the next breath, these same exhorters bewail the increase of divorce, and want to know what we are coming to. Let them not fool themselves into the belief that their hypocrisies, and their evasion of patent facts, are escaping the keen judgment and the discerning eyes of the more intelligent element among our modern youth.

I want to drive it home to the reader's mind that it is a *fact,* even among the denouncers of the ideas I am here expounding, that under present marriage contracts, it is everywhere assumed and taken for granted that the majority of intelligent couples will make consistent and careful use of contraceptives—not that they may forever avoid having children, but that they may have only as many as they can properly care for, and that they may have them when they are ready for them, and not before. And since this is a fact, a very important fact for human welfare, a fact of stupendous importance to the race, think of the incredible, the amazing stupidity of the conservative forces that are straining every nerve to prevent as many persons as possible from finding out the truth, or from obtaining such scientific information as will make the practice of Birth Control effective to a maximum degree. The very least the state should do in this connection is to see that ALL are duly instructed before marriage in the most scientific and practicable methods of contraception known. And the purpose, with normal persons, in the utilizing of such knowledge would be, and *is,* to have a reasonable number of children under conditions that will insure their welfare. The notion that people would not have children if they had contraceptive knowledge is belied by the fact that people with such knowledge do have children, and that the waiting line of involuntarily childless couples wanting to adopt children is so long that I have never been able to supply the demand from the list of "illegitimate" or other babies born under my protection in Denver.

3.

To enter any marriage contract, companionate or procreative, it might well be made necessary for the couple to show, to the satisfaction of a magistrate, that they were physically, mentally, and economically fit to enter on the responsibilities involved in the special kind of marriage they were undertaking. Obviously requirements for procreative marriage would be of a graver sort, since the welfare of children would be involved. It would thus be possible to make it somewhat more difficult than it is at present for people to enter on procreative marriage. But of course the real way to regulate procreative marriage is to educate people to a sense of the grave responsibilities it entails, while at the same time giving them the outlet of the Companionate so long as they are unfitted for procreation and its consequences.

Having, with due thought and consideration, entered on the procreative marriage, a couple would be expected to carry on; and only for the gravest reasons would any court later permit them to abrogate the contract and go their ways, leaving behind them a broken home and children deprived of one or both their parents.

In all forms of marriage, physical examination might be required, to show freedom from acutely infectious or transmissible diseases, such as syphilis, epilepsy, or insanity. In many such cases the couple might be urged voluntarily to accept sterilization as an insurance that their companionate would remain companionate. Such restrictions need not be oppressive, offensive, or objectionable; and wisely used they would be a safeguard and protection to all concerned. I think this should include society as a whole as well as the individuals themselves. In the end it would make for health and happiness. And happiness is best insured by health. Consistently practiced it would mean that in time there would be few defectives left to apply for permission to marry, companionately or otherwise.

Suppose we had such a marriage code as this, *frankly acknowledged and openly taught!* What would happen? Why, thousands of young people who can't think of marriage at present would *get married*. If they did, that would be a great safeguard, both for them and for society, since it would bring their union under adequate social control. Their lives would be normalized. They would become more happy and competent in the business of living than would otherwise be possible.

The problem is really quite simple. *All we need do is honestly acknowledge and better regulate Companionate Marriage as it is now being practiced by our leading church and university people, and in our higher professional and business circles.* For they have it,— though many who are practicing it denounce me for commending them for doing so.

The solution of this problem by the *open* adoption of Companionate Marriage would have a specially profound effect on American life and American morals. It would put an end to one paramount evil in American civilization. It would rescue this nation from a spell that now holds it bound. I mean obsession with sex. Our present conventional concealments and restrictions have produced such an obsession. By means of irrational taboos, we have made sex difficult of access; we have therefore made it an object of continual attention, thought, and baffled desire.

The effect of the liberalized morality possible under Companionate Marriage would be to remove this obsession, or to lessen it. The effect of the change on our national morals, our national nerves, our national character, and our national divorce statistics, and even on our national crime records, would thus be beyond calculation. If one tried to figure such a change in economic terms, it would be necessary to put the saving in tens of billions of dollars. This is no exaggeration. Sex and Money are the two big mainsprings of ordinary human action. Change a sex code and you change everything— even money. Yes, even Art, and Religion, and Literature, and everything else fundamental that you may care to name, except the fundamentalist theology. And for all I know even that would yield to the spell.

The effect on procreative or family marriage alone would be a thing beyond calculation and beyond price. People would not enter such marriage hastily because they would not need to—since their sex lives would find normal expression by another recognized social channel in childless marriage. Most procreative marriages would grow out of companionate marriages that had already had a chance to prove their physical and psychological permanence.

Much of the marital troubles among young people that I deal with involve the birth of a baby in the first year. It is a headlong, ill-considered, dangerous business as we have it. But more education for a wider use of our well-established institution of Companionate Marriage would put off the birth of babies until the groundwork of a home had been laid. Under such a system, domestic relations courts would run one hour where they now run ten.

Finally, it would be the salvation of thousands of young people who at present are given their choice between an abstinence which is against nature, but which our ancient ecclesiastical code, nevertheless, demands of them—with "threats of Hell and hopes of Paradise" held like a club over their heads—and a form of marriage economically impossible for so many of them, a form which, as I have said, thousands are to-day avoiding by means of the "unmarried union." Thus it is that a tyrannical, unyielding orthodoxy of the dark ages, in seeking to impose its sacrilegious hand upon the private lives of the people of the Twentieth Century, is the chief contributing cause to a growing number of unmarried unions and whatever immorality there may be involved in them. How strange that they should be the loudest in protesting against what they are doing most to promote.

The unmarried union is dangerous because it is subject to no recognized control; and because, being secret, it has no inducements and no social helps toward moderation, and toward reasonable stability and restraint. The inducements, indeed, are quite the other way. It is like a balloon without ballast. Since it specializes in evasion and defiance of present public opinion, it tends to go to extremes of license. In our society as now constituted it evades and defies *all* restraint, the good with the bad. It throws out the baby with the bath—sometimes all too literally.

I hope those of my friends who reproach me for "encouraging immorality" will find some consolation and hope for my immortal soul

in the above passage. I hope too that when they quote me by lifting passages from the context in such a way as to twist my meaning,
they will be sure and lift this one. Let them note, however, that I
have nowhere said that persons who indulge in these unions are
impure, immoral, lost, ruined, damned, or otherwise theologically
destroyed. Many of them seem to me to have a much better
chance of making the grade into Heaven than a certain witch-hunting
portion of our population. I am for the Ten Commandments as
much as any of the brethren; but I mix them with Common Sense.

4.

The non-procreative marriage, then, would be at least a partial
solution of our present sex problem, and would restore sex in this
country to wholesome sense and sanity. It would reduce to a minimum illicit sex relationships, promiscuity, demoralization, and lack
of effective legal and social guidance and control in a department of
life where such guidance and control, at the present stage of social
evolution, are imperatively needed—and, as I think I have shown,
conspicuously lacking. The present well-established, though legally
unrecognized, institution Companionate Marriage is clearly not a
disguised form of promiscuity; it is simply bringing under social
control a situation that is to-day largely beyond the control of such
laws and customs as we have. It is slowly but surely establishing
new customs and therefore eventually new codes in the interest of
happiness and real morality. In time we shall cease our present
imbecile practice of blushingly denying the very existence of a custom
that most of us are practicing; and when that happens, the law will
recognize and sanction Companionate Marriage.

Present methods and present codes are the main cause of sexual
lawlessness. I can't understand the point of view of persons who
insist on a return to former standards when those standards have so
clearly failed to produce the restraint and sanity in sex conduct which
they were intended to produce. Why not use more sense and less
superstition? Why not intelligently guide these social tendencies
into channels where society can benefit by this huge Niagara of
emotional power which is now running to waste?

And now to come back to Inez and Fred.—Annulment? Inez

didn't want an annulment. What she wanted was Fred. She and Fred alike wanted each other for two good and proper reasons: First, they wanted the satisfactions of sex; and secondly, they wanted intimate companionship with another human being, the sort of spiritual intimacy which the generous emotional power of sex makes so readily and so normally possible in successful marriage. That is why it is not good for man to live alone. Inez therefore took the only thing she thought she could get, illicit union with the man she loved.

In their case both the economics and the psychology of marriage were involved. Their situation irked them. To this some one might retort that in that event they should not marry.—I answer that in that event about 97 per cent of married persons should not have married—which is nonsense. It isn't that people should not marry, but that they should have a different conception of marriage from anything ever before known in our civilization.

It is orthodox marriage as we have it that is at fault, not the people who marry. They take what they can get. They enter marriage full of hope, their vision misted by emotion, and it isn't till later that they find society grinning in at them through the bars of a steel cage. And when they see it is a cage, do they want to get out— even the thousands who are too proper or too faithful to say so? They do. Don't ask anything else of human nature when it is unfairly taken advantage of. It's that way.

5.

I am aware that many good persons who consider sex intrinsically sinful—largely because they are very uncritical readers of Scripture, —would argue that this would simply let down the bars to a saturnalia of lust. I answer that what is creating and magnifying lust to-day is the very system of repressions and needless restraint which these people advocate. Restrictions? Yes! Let us have them! But not that kind. Sex is as moderate, normal, and moral a thing as the desire for food. To damn it by calling it "an animal passion" by no means disposes of the matter. Psychologists now know the close relationship that exists between the sex instinct and religious emotion. I shan't argue this point here. It is an old story, and the facts are well established.   What it means is not that religious emotion is a degraded or animal thing, but rather that sex emotion, being in a degree identical with the emotions of religion, is an exalted and spiritual thing.   It is simply a question of where you prefer to put the emphasis.

I repeat then, Sex is a spiritual thing; moreover, it is as natural and right as the desire for food—provided you give it normal expression and don't make universal famine a part of your method of guarding people from the sin of gluttony.   You can make any man a glutton by making it exceedingly hard for him to obtain food, or by forcing him to steal food, or to eat it only in secret for fear he will be accused of gluttony and grossness.   Such an attitude toward food hunger has been taken by some fanatics.

The traditional Puritan attitude toward the sex hunger is just as insane and baseless.   Sex is a hunger, a spiritual hunger, healthful to feel and healthful to gratify.   It is simply idiotic for society not to recognize this and provide adequate social regulations for its healthful, fearless, unashamed expression.   We *have,* in many quarters, the orgy of sex that these Puritans fear; and *they* are the people who have created it.   What *I* want to do is to end it.

6.

I recall another annulment case that came before me practically coincident with that of Inez and Fred.   Another young couple, whom I will label Katherine and George, both of them under age, had married in similar circumstances.   They had tried illicit relations, they grew tired of having to live together on the sly, and they therefore got married in order that they might live together openly and keep out of trouble.   As is the case in nearly all affairs of this kind, they had no qualms of conscience in the matter.   They considered that they were being unconventional but not immoral; and they married because they considered marriage expedient.

Trouble began right away.   They rented an apartment and started a home.   Katherine gave up her job.   This cut their joint income to one-half.   They did all this because they had the traditional notion that since they were married it was up to them to put together the machinery of a home where children could be raised.   Katherine married, looked on herself as a potential mother. They were potential parents whether they were competent to undertake parenthood or not. Otherwise, according to society, they should not have married.

Moreover, Katherine gave up all her boy friends, and George looked no more upon other girls. The old story. Restrictions right and left which they took it for granted they must impose upon each other—marital jealousy being, as we all know, a cardinal virtue in our present marriage code, though jealousy, in any form, and under any conditions, is demonstrably one of the most hideous vices of which the human heart is capable.

Something other than their own will, in short, had entered into the union, and it pushed them apart. By the time the case reached me it was hopeless. I put them off, I cajoled and persuaded. Nothing worked. After taking counsel with their parents I gave them the annulment they wanted.

The moment I consented to do this the atmosphere began to clear. I saw them look at each other—at first with mutual congratulation, and then apparently in a kind of panic, as if something were forcibly depriving them of each other.

While at the court they withdrew into a corner where they talked together earnestly, holding each other's hands, and clinging to each other as if afraid of what was to follow. There chanced to be present a middle-aged unmarried woman, as noted for her scorn of men as for her moral rectitude. She reminds me every time I see her of a certain other woman in Denver just like her, who was once told by an exasperated Judge to whom she was furiously protesting about the immorality of some girl, "Miss S——, the trouble with you is that you've never been raped."

The lady in question came rushing up to one of the court officers in great indignation, protesting because this young couple were permitted to sit and talk together, and even hold hands.

"Why," she cried angrily, "these people are having their marriage annulled. And yet Judge Lindsey permits them to hobnob as if there were nothing the matter. It's perfectly disgraceful. They should be kept apart. They have no business to be friendly."

Well, later, on another day, when the annulment was granted,

Katherine and George left the court together, no longer married now; and Katherine, realizing her loss, suddenly began to weep.

"Never mind, Honey," said her former husband, slipping his arm protectingly about her. "If we can't make out better unmarried, we'll get married again."

Fortunately the ill-omened old witch who had objected to their hobnobbing before the annulment was not present. I think she would have thrown a fit on the spot if she had been.

7.

I haven't a doubt that that couple, when things had quieted down in their respective families, went back to living together *sub rosa*. For my part I don't see why society should not have frankly and honestly provided them a legal and respectable way to do it, by means of a scientifically assisted non-procreative marriage suited to their needs, which are the need of thousands like them.

They loved each other; it was natural and normal that they should want each other, in a relationship that would give them the physical and spiritual union they had sought in marriage. They had desired this before, and they still desired it. It was the same mental state after the annulment as it was before. Why demand that they choke and kill it? Why not give them a way of expressing it that would be, not merely socially harmless, but even socially beneficial? I don't see what society would gain by forbidding them what their natures craved, but which they could not maintain under the conditions of a marriage code such as they had been educated to believe in. Their education had taught them that marriage is something which, in the eyes of better educated and more sophisticated people, it certainly is not. They therefore found it needlessly formidable and unlovely. And so unbearable became their lives under it that they were glad of a chance to reject it altogether. I am satisfied that these two were capable of working a huge benefit in each other's lives, and that society loses by the insane and ignoble taboos which would prevent their further union and frustrate their future happiness. George and Katherine are more normal, more productive members of society together than apart, provided they can be happy together. They should have some legally sanctioned means of being together.

This would make law and reasonable responsibility before society a factor in unions where there is at present no law and frequently no social responsibility or restraint; but only destructive suggestions of sin, the sense of guilt and fear, the inducement to excess, and the urge toward an undiscriminating promiscuity.

Above all it would tend to keep young people from placing on sex a greater emphasis than sex should have in their lives. There are other things in life than sex; but they don't seem to know it. The reason is that this damnable condition in our sex code crowds other things off the stage and makes sex the whole object of their thought and attention. Under such conditions, sex readily becomes a destructive force.

The assertion that Marriage is adequate as we have it is poppy-cock. The fruits of our Marriage code speak for themselves; and the protests and denials that have been made by some of the Clergy and the Bench as a result of the assertions in this book are in themselves a proof that I speak the truth.

Marriage is capable of taking care of itself if we will but give it a chance, and make of it something other than a travesty of what it might be. Consider, for instance, the way that young couple clung to each other; how they were trying to find a way to be really married; and how difficult society makes it for them by having one unvarying, rigid marriage formula for every type and every taste. Think of the incredible folly of a social order that would throw such loyalty and love as theirs on the scrap heap rather than give it the conditions under which it might thrive and find itself!

8.

Hortense had "hired a detectuff" to watch Herbert, her nineteen-year-old husband, to whom she had been married four months.

She had paid the detectuff five dollars. To prove it, she pulled from her vanity case a much-folded bit of pasteboard that bore the name of a local agency.

And the detectuff had made good; he had delivered by detecting something, to wit: Herbert, on a public street, being hugged and kissed by "Hattie the Home Breaker," formerly soda jerk in one of our leading Denver drug stores, and now usherette in a leading Denver movie theater.

Hortense, having acquired a hundred dollars' worth of jealousy from her five-dollar investment with the detectuff, had come to see me about it. Herbert must not step out. Would I please take him in hand and, by whatever magic I might have in my judicial bag, make him behave as a husband should?

Hortense, it appeared, was sixteen. So was Hattie the Home Breaker. But there, according to Hortense, the resemblance ceased; for Hortense was a genuine blonde, whereas Hattie the Home Breaker, was notoriously a peroxide; and besides, though Hattie was only sixteen, "she didn't look it" because she had aged rapidly.

Hattie the Home Breaker had won her moniker in their high school set not merely by having vamped innumerable unattached males, but by having broken up at least four homes; and Hortense would be darned if she was going to let her bust hers.

Hortense had tripped into my chambers after assuring all who offered their services that she would talk with nobody but the Judge. The series of interesting little conferences that followed were among the most diverting that had come my way for a long time, for the child was a strange mixture of childish naïveté and adult sophistication. She admitted that she had gone quite a pace, but affirmed that now that she had settled down with Herbert, she proposed that there should be no more nonsense, from Herbert, at any rate.

Yes, she and Herbert had had prenuptial relations. That was what had led to their getting married. She had thought she was pregnant, as the result of some adolescent petting affairs into which Herbert had entered rather too enthusiastically; and she had convinced Herbert that such was her condition; whereupon Herbert, like a good sport, had promptly married her. That was four months ago; and she had since discovered that her supposed pregnancy was a mistake.

That, however, would have made no difference, because they loved each other, and had been very happy with hardly a quarrel through almost the whole four months, till Hattie the Home Breaker had tried to bust in and wreck one more home. "She wanted another scalp," said Hortense. This had led to the hiring of the detectuff, and finally to this visit to my chambers. Wouldn't I have Herbert up for a hearing, give him a dressing down, read him the riot act, and make him live with his wife and support her "like a husband should"?—One of the many rifts in the domestic lute, it seemed, was that Herbert was not working.

So I arranged a session for them, and in due course, Herbert, Hortense, Hattie the Home Breaker, and a cloud of witnesses, many of them high school girls and boys, appeared in my chambers.

I had, in the meantime, had some private sessions with Herbert and Hortense, and found it a simple case of jealousy. Hortense was like a pretty and very angry little cat who wanted to do some scratching. She now demanded that I put Herbert in jail for non-support, just as she had heard I sometimes did to assuage the injured feelings of other wives; and when I pointed out that if I did that Herbert would not be able to make any money for her support, it merely convinced her that in this world the wicked prosper.

In the course of the hearing their high school witnesses, some of whom were there for Herbert and others for Hortense, joined in the discussion freely, both with me and among themselves. Their chatter and talk, with its curious blend of youth and maturity, literally amazing feats in new and strange slang, some of it apparently invented on the spot in a reach for vivid metaphor, made it an occasion that will always stick in my memory as bringing to the surface an atmosphere, a way of thought, and a way of life that are simply not known by most middle-aged persons even to exist.

I am amused after such experiences, when I hear pompous "authorities" say in print, and from rostrum and pulpit, "These things don't happen. Judge Lindsey should be refuted. We never come upon anything like this."

Of course they don't. Youngsters like that don't voluntarily walk into the ordinary court, where nobody ever goes save under the escort of a police officer, and open up in that fashion; nor do they go to teachers whose function, under the rules of the average school board, would be to punish and disgrace them when they had acknowledged this or that form of sexual misconduct.

Here they said what they thought. As for Herbert, he was unterrified and thoroughly aroused at Hortense's threat of a jail sentence, which she pronounced forthwith, apparently confident that I would make good in a pinch. Glaring at her fiercely, he said, "All you need to know is your onions, for I can get out of town."

"Yes," she retorted; "you bet I know my onions and my cucumbers and tomatoes; and you needn't think I don't, and you will just stay right here or I'll know the reason why."

I don't pretend to interpret this lingo. It was a new kind of chatter to me at that time, and the air was full of it throughout the hearings—much of it impossible to reproduce effectively when lifted out of its setting.

The conclusion of the affair, at a later session, was as good as a third act. Hortense had plumped herself down on a chair, her little short skirt above her knees, flopping half way up to her hips; her looks of scorn darting out in the direction of Herbert. She yanked her skirts down when she thought they were showing too much of her bare legs; and then proceeded to announce that she had just met "the cutest, darlingest boy"; and that he had dated her up the first night they met; and they had danced— "oh, the loveliest dance" she had ever had! He was going to take her out every night, she announced; in fact, he was going to take her to supper that very evening, and then to the theater. "And that," she added, with a waspish look at Herbert, "is more than Herbert has ever done for me. Herbert's short, he is."

"Aw, dry up," cut in Herbert; "you know I said I was willing to live with and support you; and that all I wanted was for you to stop lying about me and laying for me every time I looked at another girl. You know I didn't mean nothing by looking at those other girls and going out that night with Hattie."

"Oh," snapped Hortense, as she threw back her pretty head and looked contemptuously at Herbert; "I don't care how much you go with Hattie now; I'm done with you. This is a keen guy I'm going with now, some boy, believe me, kid—and certainly better to me than you ever were." And here she wound up with a string of strange slang and flapper idiom different from anything I had ever heard before. Most of it escapes my memory.

Having finished her pronouncement, Hortense looked triumphantly in the direction of Hattie the Home Breaker. "You can have him," she said, with the air of one tossing a bit of coin to a beggar. "You're welcome, I'm sure. Don't mention it."

Then Hortense began to rub it in. Peter, her new flame, it appeared, had other qualities in which Herbert was conspicuously lacking. She had not gotten far with her catalogue of Peter's excellencies before the entire collection of witnesses, on both sides, suddenly launched into a gale of handclapping, to signify apparently that Hortense had put one over; and above all that she had sounded the proper note of triumph in making Herbert jealous. For jealous he undoubtedly was; and there was every evidence that he was now overwhelmingly anxious to crawl back into Hortense's affections.

Herbert began to explain how it all happened. He was willing to support his wife, but he had lost one job after another. "Why," he said, "I had a good job as a soda jerk in Blake's Drug Store. Suddenly the management canned all the boys and put in girls. Just think of it," he added, with derisive scorn, much as men used to do when talking of a possible woman congressman, or as they still do when talking of a possible woman president, "just think of it—girl soda jerks! What d'ye think of that, Judge! And that ain't the worst of it. I was promised a job in a Curtis Street Theater, as an usher. A kid friend of mine was working there, and had it all fixed for me. When I went over to get the job, the management said they had canned all the boys and put in girls— fifteen or twenty of them. Just think of that—girl ushers, girl soda jerks, girl telephone operators, girl bell hops, girl hash slingers, girl biscuit shooters, girl elevator pilots, girl everything, darn it— except to settle down and stop jawing and chewing the rag at you and talkin' and raising the devil every time you look at another girl; and then she has me arrested and wants me put in jail because I don't support her; and what's a fellow to do," he finished tearfully, "when the girls get all the jobs! It's a hell of a world, it is."

Hattie the Home Breaker then entered a vigorous disavowal of her moniker, which she protested was totally undeserved. "I never take up with no married boy," averred Hattie, "till I've found out he ain't living with his wife, or that his wife has canned him. And when a fellow's wife cans him, why, he wants sympathy, don't he? I don't know why they come to me, but they do. I don't care nothing about them, but I don't want to be hard on them either. And so I get all the blame when I don't love 'em at all."

Then she added with a toss of her head, "I guess I can get plenty of boys that ain't married; and when I get me a real sweetie, it'll be like that, so I won't have a lot of dames talkin' about me and callin' me Hattie the Home Breaker. I'm good and sick of it. Why, one of these dames that calls me Hattie the Home Breaker was sayin' she'd sue me for alternation of affections; and she went to a lawyer about it; but he says to her, 'You'd better drop it; there ain't no money in it for either one of us because she ain't got nothin'. You can't squeeze blood out of a turnip,' he says. And he was right, because I ain't never been anything but a soda jerk, and an usherette."

At the last meeting of the whole gang the three members of the triangle reconciled their differences and shook hands all around. They promised to be good friends. Hortense declared that she was perfectly satisfied with her new fellow, and that she no longer had a thing against Herbert since his conduct had caused her to find a more satisfactory attachment. Herbert said that he thought that as soon as he was making some money he would try to win Hortense back; but that if he couldn't, why, he guessed he'd leave her to the other guy, because the other guy had a real car, and the most he, Herbert, had ever been able to do for Hortense had been to take her out in an old tin Lizzie that wouldn't run, and had old tires, continual blow-outs, the heaves and everything else. It had cost him thirty dollars at a junk place, and it wasn't paid for yet.

Of course, there was only one thing to do with this marriage, and that was annul it, which I did. It should never have been contracted in the first place.

9.

Oh, the scores, the hundreds, of marriages that ought never to have been contracted—marriages made in the heat of passion; marriages made with the reason gone blind and dizzy from an outpouring into the blood of sex hormones more paralyzing to the reasoning faculty than unlimited gin; marriages contracted in fear of real or fancied pregnancy; marriages made out of a whim of the moment—marriages which do society no good, which safeguard no homes, and which are founded on blather, bunk and convention applied with an utter want of discrimination or practical sense, but forced to continue at the behest of some theological leaders who apparently know as much about sociology as they do about the date of the Day of Judgment! The "sanctity of marriage" indeed!

I wish some of the people who allege that I am attacking "the sanctity of marriage" and "the foundations of the Ho-o-ome" could be made to come to my chambers and listen in on a sufficient and representative number of these cases of "marriage"—mockeries against every rule of decency and common sense—such as the one I have just cited.

That case had the merit of having some humor to leaven its sogginess; but in most of them there is little humor. There is a superfluous, unwanted, badly-cared-for baby instead.

It is exactly as I have said in previous chapters of this book, and as I have said at length in "The Revolt of Modern Youth," you can't put Nature in a strait-jacket. If you do, Nature snaps it like a strand of thread.

These children of whom I have been telling are confronted with a social system which, with respect to their love-life, gives them their choice between two things: sex satisfaction in marriage and sex satisfaction outside of marriage. They are on the horns of a dilemma, and it is hard to say which horn is the worse. In both courses there is much that is objectionable. As society is now constituted, if they seek sex satisfaction outside of marriage, the whole business gets beyond control and wrecks lives. Girls become pregnant, venereal disease gets an added chance to spread, and at the best their lives become furtive with concealments and fear of social penalties. On the other hand, suppose they marry. Such marriages are simply erotic projects that carry with them irrevocable obligations which these children are not fitted to assume. I don't mean that this is invariably the case with these marriages; but it is with a desperately large number of them, as I am daily finding out in my court. Such marriages are literally "the easiest way"; and they are more fundamentally immoral, and uncontrollable, and lacking in ethical responsibility, in spite of any sanctions of church or state, than any ordinary resort to illicit sex indulgence outside of marriage.

10.

Society tells these children that they have their choice, under the dictum of St. Paul, that it is "better to marry than to burn"; and that they may marry if they choose, but that if they don't they must burn, and make the best of it, and may the Lord have mercy on their souls.

Well, they refuse that alternative. They will marry, perhaps— though they have no business with marriage, and should not be permitted to assume its obligations; but if they don't marry, then, by thousands, they refuse the alternative of abstinence outside of marriage. This is the fact—a dangerous fact. Why not face it?

The story I have just related, and there are thousands like it, is one more clincher for my contention that we must finally learn to face things as they are, and that, by means of scientific Birth Control, we must provide a legally recognized form of childless marriage for persons who are unready, or else permanently unfit, for procreative or Family Marriage.

Facing the penalties of heresy, Jesus, defying the conventions of his time, said that the Sabbath was made for man and not man for the Sabbath. By the same token, it is now incumbent on those who have the interest of society at heart to take their stand, even under the charge of heresy, and insist that marriage was made for man and not man for marriage. The plain implication of such a

view is that marriage must be made so flexible that persons who
are virtually excluded from wedlock under the present code can
have a form of marriage suited to their special needs.

II.

Here is another story: The boy and girl involved this time
were not married, but their relations had reached a stage where they
were on the point either of marriage or near-marriage. The girl
was sixteen and the boy about eighteen.

I will call the girl Madge and the boy Carl. Madge came to
me in great indignation and said that Carl had driven her in his
car out to Morrison, and then ditched her, refusing to bring her
home. Madge's mother, with whom I also talked privately, suspected that the boy had insulted Madge, and that it was one of
those "come through or walk home" affairs. She was, therefore,
anxious that I should have Carl up on the carpet and get at the
truth of it. When I questioned Madge on this point I found her
rather vague. She made no specific accusations, and merely stuck
to it that Carl had been mean.

When Carl arrived in my chambers he proved to be anything
but repentant or apologetic. He was all but frothing at the mouth
and fuming with rage when I confronted him with the equally
indignant Madge.

"A lot she's got to kick about," he said bitterly. "Judge, I fell
dead in love with that girl because I like brunettes."

At this Madge dabbed her eyes with her handkerchief and I
saw her peek out from behind it apprehensively at Carl. She had
suddenly blushed a fiery red. I looked at her carefully—particularly at her hair.

"I don't think I quite get you, Carl," I said at last. "You say
you prefer brunettes. Then why fall in love with a blonde?"

"Aw, I fell in love with her when she was a brunette. I told her
I didn't have a bit of use for blondes because I was a blond myself
and that was enough. And then she went and read that darn' fool
book 'Gentlemen Prefer Blondes.' I've never read it myself because
I don't prefer them.—Well, after that she didn't do a thing but
go and get some gold hair wash or something and gild her head

with it. That night I took her to Morrison to that dance. I didn't
know what had happened because she wore a hat that covered it
all up. But when we got to the dance she took off her hat; and
say, Judge, I hardly knew her. She was just the way you see her
now."—This, with a mixture of scorn, rage, and grief that I can't
convey in the mere words he spoke. His voice almost rose to a
wail as he tried to express his unutterable thoughts.

"She doesn't look so bad," I said. "What about it, Madge? Did
you gild it?"

Madge nodded and blushed some more, evidently embarrassed by
the turn Carl had given to the tables.

"I says to her," Carl continued, "I says, 'Madge, that's a dirty
mean trick to play on a kid that's been crazy about you, to go
and change from a brunette to a blonde and without telling me
about it."

"And she says, 'My head's my own.'

" 'You can keep it,' I says. 'So's your legs. Walk.'

"And with that I lit out for home in my car.—And I had a right
to; because when I took her to the dance she was one girl, and
when she pulled her hat off she was another.—And so I lit out—
and that's all I done."

12.

Oh, yes, I found it amusing. In fact, the hearing became a
roaring farce before it was over, for it was too much for the
discipline of any courtroom to listen to such testimony without a
laugh. No harm was done. Madge and Carl went their ways.—
But for all I know they will be reconciling their difference a month
from now, getting married a month later, and coming to me for an
annulment a year from now, or with a petition asking that Carl
be required to support his wife and baby. This is the outcome
in literally hundreds of cases. It may not seem real and actual
to persons who do not personally come into intimate daily contact
with this side of life; but it is tragically and terribly real to me.

Crazy kids! How I do love them! But, oh, how utterly without
any sound basis for marriage they are! They should not be permitted to marry. It is a terrible immorality on the part of the

church and of society that they are so permitted. But there is no escape from the necessity of granting them such permission so long as our notion of sex ethics is what it is. If marriage be not permitted them, they simply resort to the *liaison;* and an enormous number prefer the *liaison* to the marriage because they recognize their unfitness for marital responsibilities.

Such marriages and such *liaisons* are, by all conventions, each in their way, equally immoral and equally dangerous. It is a choice of evils. But if there be any choice as to the amount of harm worked upon the social fabric by these two things, I should say that entrance by unfit persons upon procreative marriage, and the bringing into the world of children by persons who have no sound foundation in maturity and character and social competence for the founding of a home, is the more immoral, the more disastrous, the more dangerous of the two courses. Both are wrong, and unfit and immature procreative marriage is the worse of the two. But with the legalization of Birth Control, more education, and a wider knowledge, the now generally accepted non-procreative or Companionate Marriage would resolve such disastrous dilemmas into something that would prove an asset to society.

One of the worst things about these immature and unfit marriages which lack the seeds of permanence is that they disrupt monogamy and lead in many instances to divorce and the breaking up of homes that ought to be held together if only because of the children. What we need is not so much an increase in the number of marriages nor yet a decrease in divorces, but a change for the better in the quality of those marriages. They ought to be contracted so carefully, and under conditions so free from the confusion and blindness of mere eroticism and romantic love, that their permanence would be reasonably assured.

CHAPTER VII

THE COMPANIONATE: WHAT IT IS

1.

THE doorbell of my home rang loud and long one evening when I was congratulating myself on a day's work well done, and on the opportunity for a needed rest by my own fireside. There was emphasis and urgency in that ring; and I answered it with the feeling that my day was by no means over.

My visitor was an old friend—I shall call him John Comstock. He had backed me, in the past, through many a lively political fight; and he had a right to call for aid out of office hours if anybody had it—for that he had something heavy on his mind was instantly apparent.

"Ben," he said abruptly, "Agnes has gotten married, and without my consent or knowledge. I want to talk it over and see what's to be done."

Agnes was his seventeen-year-old daughter. She was in her freshman year at a co-educational college in a neighboring state. I had known her since childhood. She had frequently visited my court, as many young people do, because of her interest in the work being done there. She was a wholesome, attractive girl, well balanced and yet high spirited. Knowing her as I did, I was not surprised at the news.

"She called by telephone an hour ago," continued John Comstock as we made our way to my library. "They got married this afternoon. I don't even know where they are just now. She said they had gotten married in another town."

"And what did you say?" I asked.

He shrugged. "What could I say? I couldn't express disapproval; I didn't have the heart. I made the best of it; confined myself to saying that I was sorry she hadn't let us know, but that of course we would be happy in her happiness. She was happy all right. You ought to have heard her voice—especially when I bucked up and tried to sound glad.

"But, Ben, she's gone and married a fellow two classes ahead of her in college. They are just two kids. And for all I know he may be some rotter. What does she know about men? How can she judge?—You can annul this marriage, can't you, at my request, if this fellow doesn't measure up to specifications?"

"Yes, it can be done," I said. "But let's not jump too quick. I have more faith in your daughter's judgment than you seem to have. Maybe this is the wisest possible arrangement. Agnes is strongly sexed; I can tell that from looking at her; and when the mating instinct is aroused, you've got to reckon with it. I don't think much of celibacy as a remedy for it. Celibacy often plays hob with people, and it tends, in this day and age, to become a fake chastity.

"I was talking the other day with the dean of women of a co-education college," I continued. "She told me she had observed that the young couples in college who were married were under less strain than other students, and that they were far more successful and contented in their work after marriage than before. She said they had an increasing number of marriages between students and that she considered it an excellent thing. She thought it a fine solution for some of the sex repressions and obsessions which are much too common among students in co-educational institutions— thrown constantly together as they are.

"So maybe Agnes is right. Certainly it is better, other things being equal, if they can marry young; and our modern civilization is doing a mischief to young people by making it almost necessary for them to put off marriage over an unreasonably long period. Some have suggested that the educational process takes too long; but merely to shorten it a few years would not materially alter the situation. Early marriage is possible to a ditch digger because he makes as much almost at the start as he will ever make; but it's a very different matter as you go up the rungs of the social ladder.

"Suppose, for instance, that this young man plans to enter a profession. That means that they would have to endure an engagement of from five to seven years before they could get married by the usual route, which you apparently feel they should have taken.

"If they are in love with each other, and in daily contact, is that a reasonable demand to make on them? Would so long an ordeal of waiting be good for them? I think it would be quite the reverse. They will have better health, better nerves, and greater capacity to work if they are married. Assuming that Agnes has chosen a man built after what the psycho-analysts call the 'father image,' I judge that she has probably picked a winner. Let's assume that till there is evidence to the contrary. If she has used you for a standard you can depend on it that she hasn't gone far wrong."

"What I'm afraid of," he said gloomily, "is that he's some reckless young pup who would have liked to seduce her and couldn't. He may have simply taken advantage of her youth and inexperience and pulled her into this. It's taking a long chance on her judgment; the whole thing is so ghastly irrevocable. To think of her being tied up for life on a chance like that!"

"There is divorce," I suggested; "and till she is twenty-one, the marriage can be annulled if annulment is indicated. So don't worry on that score. How does your wife feel about it?"

"How does she feel? She's about prostrated. I may as well tell you, Ben, that she refused to come over here with me to-night because of your Companionate Marriage doctrines. I don't exactly get you on this free love and trial marriage stuff myself; but it has put my wife regularly on a war path. She belongs to a bunch of women's clubs, and she's helping out in the good work of censuring you."

"I'm used to that," I said.

"It doesn't matter with me," he went on. "What I'm concerned with now is not your theories, but my facts. I'd feel easier if you'd talk with Agnes and this fellow, and size things up. I want to know what she's in for. If I send for them, will you talk with them?"

"Certainly."

"All right," he said with satisfaction. "That's that. Now here's another angle. I asked her how this boy is to make a living if he is a student. It seems he is doing some work and partly making his way; and that he gets a little money from home. His folks haven't got much. In other words, he can't support a wife, and doesn't pretend to. Agnes wants me to go on sending her the allowance she has been getting so she can live on that. She says they will live just as they did before except that they'll live together. Did you ever hear the beat of that? Think of that young pup marrying my girl and then coolly disclaiming all intention of supporting her. That was what made me maddest, I think. He must be a fool or a nut. Of course I didn't argue with her over the telephone; and I said I would keep on with the allowance."

"That was wise," I commented.

"Wise," he snorted. "It was the only thing I could do. Of course she's got to have money. But that's not the worst of it. What's going to happen in another year—that's what I want to know! Suppose these two young fools have a baby. Then what? I suppose I'll have to support the kid, while its papa pursues knowledge and prepares to make a living!"

"Well," I said slowly, "if I were you I wouldn't worry too hard about that either. I know the crowd Agnes traveled with in high school, and if there was a girl among them that didn't have a pretty good knowledge of birth control—drug-store birth control at least— I'll eat my hat. I don't mean that Agnes had sex relations with boys, but simply that she probably knows the ropes.

"What you had better do when she gets home is take her to a physician and have her definitely instructed. I know parents who have done this before their daughters have married. If Agnes can avoid babies till she and her husband are ready for them, I see no reason why this marriage should not be a very great success. Unless you want to pay the cost of supporting a few grandchildren before they are financially ready. That might be even better, after a year or two. Think of having Santa Claus back at Christmas time!

"But you can think that over. In the meantime, you can provide these youngsters with knowledge of scientific birth control. They ought to have that whether or no. And in a marriage like this there is one other safeguard that I'd like to see added. I'd like for such a couple to be able to come to me, or to some other judge designated by law, and say—in the event that they didn't make a go of their life together, 'Judge, we find we have made a mistake. We'd like to get a divorce.'

"Now wouldn't you feel safer if the step Agnes has taken were less irrevocable? You just said so, didn't you? Don't you feel that some easy and simple means of divorce would be a great safeguard for the happiness of these two people?"

"I certainly do," he said. "That's the trouble with the whole confounded mess. They can't back out if they've made a mistake— or rather they couldn't if we didn't have you to fall back on in this instance."

"You see," I continued, "if they came to me under such conditions, and there were no children to complicate the situation, I could talk to them and question them, and reason with them; and perhaps I could give them such an understanding of each other that they could make a go of their marriage after all; and if I couldn't accomplish that, why, I could give them their freedom; and they would really be none the worse off for their mistaken belief that they could make a go of a life-partnership. Usually, I think, people entering marriage on such terms would find that they had made no mistake."

He struck his fist into his palm. "By Jove," he exclaimed, "that would certainly fix it. Why on earth doesn't society have a marriage law like that?"

"I am glad," I said, "that you don't find the idea as shocking as you thought it. The thing I have just outlined to you is the Companionate Marriage to which you and your wife are objecting."

"Is *that* it!" he exclaimed in astonishment. "Oh—that's different. I thought it was trial marriage."

"You can take comfort then," I answered, "for Companionate Marriage is practically what Agnes has. This marriage of hers will, for the present, be companionate in the sense that it will be childless. The only difference is that it lacks the safeguard of divorce by mutual consent, and that it has bootleg Birth Control instead of legalized and scientific birth control. It also lacks the medical examination to which I would submit all candidates for marriage.

"You see I am not suggesting that society should establish Companionate Marriage, but merely that it recognize it—since we already practice it. We already have it; and we ought to recognize the childless marriage as a separate thing from procreative marriage, instead of stupidly treating them as if they were one and the same thing. We ought to recognize that regulations which are perfectly reasonable in the one are absurd and irrational in the other.

"In primitive society, of course, there was no such thing as a deliberately non-procreative marriage. But civilization, and our growing knowledge of physiology, has changed all that. Childless marriages are now as much a part of our system as are procreative marriages; but we still refuse to recognize this openly. It is new, and therefore in some way sinful. In practice it is respectable; but to acknowledge it would not be respectable.—I repeat—we already have it."

"This is astounding," he exclaimed. "Why, I never thought of that before. My wife and I couldn't afford a family till three years after our marriage. That was Companionate Marriage for three years—according to you; and then we changed over to the family basis. Of course. I see it now."

"And so you see," I continued, "Companionate Marriage, as I conceive it, as it has been explained time and time again by sociologists, and as it has been discussed for years in the pages of the *Journal of Social Hygiene,* one of our outstanding sociological publications, is a state of lawful wedlock, entered into for love, companionship, and coöperation by persons who, for reasons of health, finances, temperament, etc., are not prepared at the time of their marriage to undertake the care of a family.

"If this form of marriage were recognized in law, people who entered it would *openly* profess their intention not to have children without special license from the state; and the state would instruct them in scientific birth control, to that end. It would also instruct them, in a House of Human Welfare, about the meaning and significance of sex, and in the art of love, to the end that they might enter marriage with some knowledge of how to avoid the pitfalls of ignorance, prudery, and other things which wreck many a marriage."

"What you've called the Temple of Venus," he put in. "A sensational name, that."

"I don't apologize for it," I answered. "It strikes the imagination. The ancients had an idea there which was fundamentally sound; and if they applied it along pagan lines, we can apply it along modern, scientific lines in houses of human welfare, and so teach people how to live.

"One other thing such a law would do, as I have indicated, would be to provide an easier form of divorce in Companionate Marriage than can well be allowed to people with children. That sounds simple and sensible, doesn't it?"

"Just wait till I tell my wife that we lived in Companionate Marriage for three years," he chuckled.

Some days after this discussion I had an interesting conference with Agnes and her husband.

Their marriage is now established on a frankly companionate basis. It promises to be a success. My friend John Comstock is delighted, and even Mrs. Comstock has ceased drafting resolutions censuring my views. Apparently we shall all live happily ever after.

2.

Soon after this incident I had a talk with a young woman whom I had known since her school days. She holds a responsible executive position in a Denver department store. She has been married for a few years, has continued her work, and has no children.

She immediately opened a vigorous attack on my Companionate Marriage views. "I've always stood by you, Judge Lindsey," she said; "and I've been one of your staunch supporters against the attacks and misunderstandings of my friends. But I confess I can't follow you on this Companionate Marriage. How in the world can people be permitted to marry and unmarry in that fashion without the danger that they will use marriage as a means to legalize promiscuity, living together till they change their minds, and then going on to new unions? Or have I a wrong conception of what you really think about it? I've come to find out."

"By the way, Edna," I said, "how many children have you?"

She looked up in surprise. "What makes you ask that? Of course you know I haven't any."

"Such was my impression," I answered, "but I wasn't quite sure. How long have you been married?"

"Four years."

"No babies—in four years?"

"We couldn't afford them," she said defensively. "Larry was making just about enough to live on in comfort by himself. So was I. If we married, and I gave up my position, it meant that his income would have to support the two of us; and it couldn't be done in comfort. So we decided that we would both go on working till he was making more money. Another consideration was that my health was not quite up to par. It is all right now, however; and so is Larry's income."

"Oh—then you haven't given up the babies?"

"No, indeed. There will be some before long, I hope."

"Let me get this clear—for I am much interested. Did you and Larry talk this all over before you got married, or did you wait till after you were married?"

"Before—of course."

"In other words, you chose the kind of marriage you were to enter, didn't you? And then by previous agreement, the two of you continued to live after marriage much as you had before marriage— except that you moved into his apartment, and that you made a home together, and lived henceforth together in sexual and social companionship. Am I right?"

She laughed. "I see what you are driving at, Judge. But that was real marriage. We loved each other, and we proposed to stick, and see it through."

"Precisely," I said. "You proposed to stick. Most young people who fall in love with each other propose to stick. They have a similar vision of permanence in their relationship. Some guess wrong, and some guess right. But for those who guess wrong, marriage as we have it is a terribly irrevocable step. For such persons, it would be fortunate if there were a way of backing out. It would prevent many a tragedy.

"One trouble is that many of these young people are much more headlong than you have been. They don't use their heads. They acquire a baby just about the time they come to the realization that they have made a mistake—a sincere mistake—but nevertheless a mistake.

"Now if *you* had made a mistake, and guessed wrong, you would have discovered it while you were still childless and footloose; and divorce would have been a relatively simple matter. A few years of childlessness have greatly reduced your risk in marriage. Moreover, in the absence of children you and Larry have had a very fine chance to get thoroughly adjusted to each other. You will make all the better parents on that account.

"But tell me this, Edna—why did you and Larry get married? Why didn't you just go on living in single blessedness? I suppose you know that according to orthodox beliefs, marriage is a religious state, a sacramental thing, ordained by God for the procreation of children. Since you and Larry were leaving out the children, why did you marry?"

"You know the answer to that as well as I do," she said.

"Of course I do. The answer—correct me if I am wrong—is that you wanted to be together; that you could not find the happiness you wanted in being merely engaged; that you endured just as long as you could the strain of resisting the force that was drawing you together—and then, since a *liaison* didn't fit with your notion of what was right and moral, and socially safe, you married. And you benefited very greatly by so doing, both in happiness and health. Isn't that it?"

"With us," she said gravely, "it had become a choice between marriage and a *liaison*. Many choose the *liaison*. Many of our friends had done so and made no secret of it in their own set. But we couldn't make up our minds to it—at least I couldn't. It was against my training, it was dangerous, we might have been found out. And besides, the anxiety and fear and sense of social guilt would all have combined to mar our happiness. I don't mean that

I had any religious scruples. I honestly don't think society had any right to keep us apart. We really loved each other, you see. But that is why I mark it off from your Companionate Marriage. We turned to real marriage, and we intended to stay put. It wasn't just an affair."

"Very interesting," I said. "Most young people who fall in love intend to stay put. But you are living in deliberately childless marriage—like many other conventional people who join you in denouncing my views on Companionate Marriage. Don't you realize that *this* is Companionate Marriage; that you are living in Companionate Marriage right now, and have been for four years?—My dear Edna, I hope this news doesn't shock you; and I hope you don't feel *too* immoral and promiscuous. But perhaps you will now tell me when you propose to discard your present husband and try another—since that, according to you, would be one necessary consequence of Companionate Marriage. In short, when are you and Larry going to make good on all these dire predictions of free love, trial marriage, and anarchy?"

"But," she gasped, "it isn't. It's marriage—not a companionate thing at all."

"It is marriage," I retorted; "and it conforms in its physical and psychological essentials to what sociologists call Companionate Marriage. There isn't a jot of difference between legal Companionate Marriage and the deliberately childless union of sexual and social companionship which you have preferred to a secret *liaison* or a long engagement, except that your Companionate is illegal in the sense that it involves the illegal use of Birth Control, and would involve divorce by illegal collusion if you wanted a divorce by mutual consent. I'm proposing to legalize what you now have illegally.

"If you had had a *liaison*, you would, as you yourself admit, have been undertaking the same childless union, but at the risk of social stigma if you got found out. And if you had chosen a long engagement, with the celibacy required by convention, you would have had four years of waiting. Either would have brought you less happiness and benefit than you have gotten by your companionate arrangement, in legal wedlock.

"The Companionate Marriage you are now living in is widely practiced by thousands of perfectly respectable, legally married people to-day. You and I both know scores of childless couples. They have most of them decided not to have children, and they have a perfect right so to decide. It is a personal matter. No stigma of immorality attaches to these marriages or to yours. Society recognizes them as moral and permissible. But the recognition is tacit. Society thinks it shocking if anybody suggests that the regulations governing this kind of marriage be adapted to the practical necessities of such unions, and that if this were done the Companionate Marriage could be made a powerful instrument, both for social reform and for human happiness.

"Now let me point out to you one thing about these childless marriages that you may not have thought of. Deliberately childless marriages involve, in ninety-nine cases out of a hundred, the use of contraceptives. But this involves a violation of the law that forbids the manufacture and sale of contraceptives and the imparting of contraceptive information. Since this use of contraceptives is against the law, deliberate childlessness is also against the law whenever it involves the use of these illegal contraceptives. This is a form of law-violation which people practice as a matter of course, without scruple. It is winked at by the authorities; and it amounts to a nullification of one of the craziest pieces of freak legislation ever put over in this country. This is a fact. Childless marriage usually involves bootleg Birth Control. And *yet* these marriages, childless by means of utterly illegal agencies, and by a technically felonious breaking of the law, are recognized by church, state, and society as perfectly respectable; and no stigma attaches to persons who so marry and so conduct themselves in marriage.

"But the minute I come along with the suggestion that we put an end to this hypocritical farce of pretending to one thing and doing another, I am set upon by all and sundry—even by you—as a disciple of free love. And when I suggest that we make sane use of this already existent condition, I am accused of trying to bring into existence a thing we already have And the very people who are living in Companionate Marriage themselves have the effrontery to accuse me of promulgating immoral doctrines, and of not being

'100 per cent American.' I thank heaven daily that I'm not '100 per cent American'; and I'd walk around the world to avoid having that label pinned to me. I leave it entirely to the Ku Klux Klan. I prefer to be a thinking being with a mind of my own."

I had gotten so heated in my discourse that she laughed. "I'll never call you that," she promised. "And you know that I accept the Birth Control part of your companionate idea without reservations. What bothers me is the easy divorce part of it. Divorce is one thing; but divorce by mutual consent is quite another."

"We'll come to that in a minute," I said. "Let me finish with bootleg Birth Control first. I want you to realize what a hideous thing it is that the law of this land should virtually require of you that you either abstain from sex relations in marriage, or that you let nature take its course, and bear children year after year whether you want them or not.

"Get this clear in your mind. It is important. The law of the land forbids anybody to impart contraceptive information to you or to sell you contraceptives. It thereby seeks, forcibly and by statute, to impose ignorance on you, and to prevent you from acquiring information you have a right to as much as anybody in the world, including the fools that made that law.

"The law has no more right to forbid science to instruct you in these matters of scientific knowledge and practice than it has to forbid you to read your Bible, or Darwin's 'Origin of Species,' or 'Einstein on Relativity.' It goes to these outrageous and unconstitutional lengths for a purpose; and that purpose is, by keeping you ignorant, *to trick you into making a contribution to the population whether you want to make it or not.* Ignorance imposed by law! What do you think of that? You must not be left to judge as to when you will have children or how often. The late Anthony Comstock, and his unclean legions, will take care of that for you in the name of holy chastity. They have rightly named it the Obscenity Law. They put into it all the obscenity they had—but they had as much left as ever when they were through; and they spewed it out into every home in this land. As apostles of prurience and lies the world has seldom seen their like."

"Still," she said, "I don't see that what you propose would make much difference. You would merely make Birth Control a little easier to know about and effectively practice, and you would make divorce for childless people easier to get. Isn't that it?"

"You speak," I answered, "as if you didn't think that was very much. But I assure you if you had seen as much as I have of the misery that springs on the one hand from total ignorance of Birth Control or from a half knowledge of it; and on the other hand from the difficulties the law places in the way of divorce when two persons want it, you would not see it as a slight matter.

"Yes, we do have, in a grudging, half-way, hypocritical fashion, the thing I am proposing. We have it in this degree because we absolutely have to have it, and because without it we would be courting a social upheaval that would rock this nation.

"I tell you if the religious fanatics in this country should ever really succeed in imposing on our population the sex prohibitions in the way of birth control ignorance and no divorce, which they allege to be pleasing to God, we would have a mountain of crime, cruelty, misery, unhappiness, degeneration, perversion, and disease such as has never been seen in the history of the world. It is bad enough as it is; but just you try sealing the spout and cover of a boiling teakettle sometime if you want to learn that there is a point at which prohibitions must give way, and that there is always a limit beyond which they are dangerous and disastrous in their effect on human beings. We were intended to make our own moral decisions, not to have them prescribed for us by law.

"And so we wink at bootleg contraception and at divorce by collusion that involves perjury, trumped-up charges, and faked adulteries. Why do we wink at these things? Because some relief is necessary. And why don't we frankly acknowledge this? Because we think society could not continue to exist if we didn't practice with grave faces a lot of silly hypocrisies that could deceive no thinking person."

Then I invited her to consider the annulments granted recently by the Holy Rota of the Roman Catholic Church. I dug up a newspaper clipping sent by the United Press from Rome, to the effect that twenty-two out of forty-five applicants were granted annulments of their marriages by the Holy Rota during 1926. Of the refusals twenty-one were rejected outright, while two were granted decrees to the effect that their marriage had not been consummated. In the latter cases the parties were prohibited from marrying again. Annulments were granted on the following grounds: lack of consent, pretense of consent, violence and fear, "defeat of the exact valuation of the meaning of marriage," "condition imposed that there should be no children," insanity, and lack of dispensation from the impediment of consanguinity.

The Roman Catholic Church does not grant or sanction divorce. But if a couple agree when they marry not to have children, the church will annul such a marriage on the ground that it never even existed. It is a question of names. Nobody must *call* it divorce. That would candidly be calling it what it is. Nor must one admit that the couple were married, though society considers them married, and though they are, in point of fact, legally and socially *married*, call it what you like. The rose by any other name would smell as sweet; and an annulment does just as well as a divorce, for all practical purposes, even if you insist on calling it an annulment, and say that the marriage never existed.

When a couple agrees secretly at the time of marriage to dissolve the marriage if they find they don't like it, that marriage never existed either. It is and always was non-existent; and the Rota will pronounce it so, thereby "annulling" it. But don't call it a divorce. By no means! This is tweedledum, not tweedledee.

Under this system of theological hair splitting think how much easier it might well become to get what amounts to a divorce by mutual consent than even under our rather liberal divorce laws, which, though they do grant divorce on occasion, are far from handing it out on such liberal grounds as those on which the Roman Catholic Church grants "annulments."

Agree when you marry, for instance, that you will quit *by mutual consent* if you can't make a go of it, and apparently you can, so far as the Roman Catholic Church is concerned, convert that marriage into an "annulment" by mutual consent *merely by making known to the Rota the existence of such an agreement.* It has been done. It was done very recently, for instance, in the case of the eminent Italian scientist, Marconi.

Now, I am not reproaching the Roman Catholic Church for all this. I say it is all very sensible and liberal so far as it goes—and it goes a long way. I wish our laws provided for "annulment" on grounds as easy. It confirms me in a conviction I have always had about that amazing institution, the Church of Rome—that there is no human institution that sees with deeper wisdom, shrewdness, psychological penetration into human need, nor that on the whole so tolerantly and consistently takes human nature as it is; and yet there is no institution less inclined to admit its own common sense in these matters.

Let me hasten to add that I am not accusing the Roman Catholic Church of intentionally granting divorce under another name. I am sure that the Holy Rota really has reasoned itself into the view that its annulments are not divorces. I merely want to point out that the Holy Rota is deluding itself by theological casuistry and sophistical subtleties which in no way alter the facts. The reality of this thing is what interests me; and when two people marry and then are permitted to separate and go their ways after they have expressed the wish so to do, the facts are adequately covered by the phrase "divorce by mutual consent." In the world of spiritual reality and fact, that is what it is—*Divorce!* the destruction of what is, in law and in fact, a marriage.

"Well," said Edna, after we had discussed this, "let's come back to my case. What difference would Companionate Marriage, as you picture it, have made to me, save that it would now give me easier divorce if I should need it. How do you visualize the thing? What steps would Larry and I have had to take if we had married that way? And how would we and society have been any better off?"

"You and society would have been better off in the sense that there would be safeguards against mishaps, and that you could have made your venture more easily and safely," I said. "In the first place, you would both of you have had to pass a medical examination before marriage to make sure that you had no infectious disease or taint that you could transmit to one another.

That examination would also determine your physical fitness for procreative marriage. Suppose there were insanity in your family, or that one of you were epileptic, or that you had some other inheritable weakness. The verdict in such a case might be that while Companionate Marriage would be perfectly permissible, you two could never be licensed by the state to attempt procreative marriage.

"Thus you would know your limitation, then and there; and if you entered Companionate Marriage, you would be doing it with your eyes open, and with the knowledge that you must never have children of your own—though you might adopt children if a court so permitted.

"And later, assuming that there were no impediment of health in the way of your entering procreative marriage, you would have to show when that time came that you would not merely be able to produce healthy children, but also that you could care for them properly, and that your economic status reasonably insured that those children would probably never want for essentials.

"I think it even possible that the day may come when the state will provide money for the support of children in such marriages when financial means are limited, but the stock is sound. And childless people, married or unmarried, might well be taxed for such a purpose. At present we practically subsidize sterility, by permitting a tremendous financial burden to fall on the shoulders of people who add to the population.

"You can see that all this would be quite different from present conditions. As things stand, you and Larry can go ahead and have children whether you ought to or not. You married in the first place without any one making the slightest inquiry as to whether you would transmit disease to each other, or insanity and infectious disease to your possible children. Nobody was in the least concerned with the fact that you might be of degenerate stock; and even if it were known that you were of such stock, the law in most states would nevertheless permit you to go ahead and have children without let or hindrance.

"Because of this condition, we continue to build more and more insane asylums, homes for the feebleminded, hospitals for congenital human wrecks, and prisons for the housing of criminals and other social incompetents. It has been estimated that America is losing at least 16 billion dollars yearly by the economic and social incompetence of thousands of weaklings and criminals, many of whom should never have been born; and these teeming masses go on reproducing their kind without stint or limit under laws that are designed to prevent them from practicing contraception by keeping them even more ignorant than they need to be.

"There was a time, before the coming of modern science, when natural selection took care of the quality of our human stock and kept it reasonably near par. Only the strongest infants survived babyhood. Weak adults died early. Now we save these weaklings and then breed from them. I maintain that it is all right to save them. But I also maintain that since we have meddled with natural selection, it is up to us to put something effective in its place. Birth Control and medical examination and education before marriage are three obviously needed substitutes. They could all of them be introduced in connection with legally recognized Companionate Marriage.

"I don't say this would produce a Utopia; but I do hold that it is of first importance that we educate the American people to breed for quality, and that a non-coercive, human regulation of procreation, managed largely by education in such a way as not to interfere with the love-life of the average man and woman, is the way to get such a result. At present we force the unfit, by means of legally imposed ignorance, to procreate *ad libitum* while the intelligent portion of the population by means of an illegal and contraband knowledge are practicing birth control. It tips the balance in the wrong direction. The way to restore a normal balance is to teach and encourage the unfit to have fewer children."

"But isn't it a bad thing that the intelligent people are practicing Birth Control?" she suggested.

"That doesn't mean that they remain childless," I said. "It means that they have a few children and raise them right. A stationary population is more to be desired just now than a rapidly growing population. It is desirable that we keep the population at its present level and better its quality. Many sociologists are agreed that the time has come for that. Birth Control of some sort has always been necessary to prevent population growth from outstripping the food supply. It used to take the form of abortion, and it still does. There are rural districts to-day where self-performed abortion is practically the only method of birth control. Read your Malthus. We've *got* to practice *some* sort of Birth Control if we don't want to spawn like herring and perish as inconsequently.

"Now Companionate Marriage, as I picture it, would forbid the kind of crimes against humanity and common sense that we have been discussing; and yet it would at the same time be so humane and flexible that it would permit persons unfitted to have children to *marry* without producing children.

"Such persons would benefit themselves and society by such marriages, provided only that their childlessness could be reasonably well made sure of. For marriage is normal. Men and women crave the love and companionship it gives. Deprive them of such love and companionship, and you either impose on them a celibacy which warps the soul and twists the inner nature, or you drive them to sexual lawlessness of the kind that is working such havoc and destruction in society to-day, particularly in the ranks of the younger generation—who go to such reckless extremes because they are ignorant, unguided, and uneducated in these great matters.—Of course you know that celibacy among unmarried men is in most cases a myth; and that an increasing number of unmarried women are disregarding this conventional requirement also—just as you tell me you seriously thought of doing.

"Another point you should note is that this system, linked as it would be with medical examination, would go far to blot out venereal disease. About one-half of men are estimated to contract venereal disease at some time or other in their lives; and the proportion among women is also astounding. Dr. Bundesen, State Health Commissioner of Illinois, reported to a recent Illinois Legislature that 'each year 1,087,872 of our boys reach the age of twenty-one, and that before they reach thirty, at least one-half of all of them have become infected.' How many of the others have promiscuous sex relations and yet escape infection? Figure that out for yourself and then judge how much 'celibacy' exists among our unmarried males.

"There are about 9,700,000 unmarried males between fifteen and thirty years of age in this country; and there are about 7,638,000 unmarried females of the same range of ages. Of the total number of our youth within these age limits, fifteen to thirty, only about one-third are married. The other two-thirds, with the mating instinct alive within them—the most powerful of all instincts save that of hunger, and indeed it is a form of hunger—are unmarried and theoretically celibate. And yet the American people is placidly assuming that our marriage code is adequate to meet this situation."

"But you still haven't met my question about divorce by mutual consent," she said. "That still seems to me the weak spot in this idea. I can see the rest of it; but I don't see how divorce obtained so easily could fail to lead people to marry and unmarry as fast and as often as they chose. They would quit their marriages whenever they got ready, wouldn't they, if there were no pressure put upon them to stay put? And wouldn't that make a bad matter worse?"

"They could quit when they got ready," I conceded; "but when would they get ready? Would divorce by mutual consent lead you to parting from Larry as soon as you got ready? Certainly it would—but when would you get ready?"

"Never," she said positively. "You have me there; but would you have others?"

"Are you such an exception in human nature?" I asked. "No— what you call the weak spot in Companionate Marriage is one of the strong spots. The really weak spot in your marriage was the fact that the step when you took it was too nearly irrevocable. You had to take a needlessly big chance; you had to stake everything on one cast. You knew there was no way of retreat. You were being forced into assuming social responsibilities which, in a childless marriage, were needlessly rigid, and dangerous to your happiness and best interests.

"That was why you hesitated before taking the step; that was why you dallied with the idea of a *liaison*. It was, in a way, so much less dangerous. That is why thousands shrink from childless marriage to-day. It involves putting their lives and fortunes in pawn, and staking everything on that one move. It is not reasonable that they should have to involve themselves so deep in this venture when the fortunes of children are not involved. Obviously, the two kinds of union have not the same social significance.

"Now you took your chance—you and Larry; and you won. But there are many who make honest mistakes in their first choice of a mate; and there is no reason why they should not be allowed a line of retreat—if they are childless—far easier than the one now permitted."

"Still," she insisted, "people might take advantage of such liberality."

"Some would," I admitted. "But most wouldn't. You are forgetting the emotional ties that grow up between people when they are in close daily association, especially in the intimacy of married life. Such a relationship sends out roots, like a growing tree; and it resists being torn up and transplanted. Nearly everybody genuinely prefers to find a stable relationship in marriage. Even married people who 'step out' occasionally cling to their marriage tie and to a common destiny in life with their respective mates. In nearly all cases people seek divorce only when they find anything else unendurable. It is the least of the evils confronting them; it is a last resort. The presence in society of a few polygamous freaks does not alter this essential fact *that human beings are normally monogamous;* and that this passion for monogamy is predominant even in men and women who are physically 'unfaithful' to their mates.

"Most persons, as I say, get divorces because they really need them, or really think they do. Cases of people getting more than one divorce are rare. Now notice how it works out in our social conventions. A divorced man or woman to-day is in perfectly good social standing, and has a sound claim to social respectability. You doubtless know many divorced persons. You think none the less of them because they are divorced. You merely regret that, unlike you, they have made a bad guess in choosing a mate, and you wish them better luck next time. You don't attribute their divorce to wantonness or irresponsibility or a desire to go on madly from one union to another. Divorced persons are in good standing, even with people who strongly disapprove of divorce as an institution, or as part of the institution of marriage.

"Nor do you question the personal morals of a divorced woman by reason of her being divorced—though thirty or forty years ago her neighbors would have regarded her as little better than a harlot, and would have found it unthinkable had it been suggested to them that custom might change in this respect.

"But what would be your attitude toward a man or woman who has been divorced four or five times? Such persons come in for social censure, do they not?

"Thus you see that when people make divorce a cloak for mere promiscuity, our conventions step in, in the form of public opinion, and restrain people from acts which may be entirely legal, but which are not socially respectable. These verdicts of society—and sometimes they are very stupid and cruel verdicts—act as a powerful deterrent; they restrain people who might otherwise be disposed to take unlimited advantage of the divorce laws. Only a few have the temerity wholly to disregard these social judgments. The fact that a few do so would be no just reason for abolishing divorce."

"Then you mean that the same social restraints would operate in Companionate Marriage?" she asked. "Well, that's a good point. I can see that it might be so. I had not thought of it."

"It is inevitable," I replied. "Society shows, and always has shown, active hostility toward persons who plainly overstep conventional bounds, especially when they are brazenly defiant or unreasonable about it. It would be no more disposed to look with favor on persons who divorced and remarried recklessly under the Companionate than it is now.

"*The fact is that Companionate Marriage, with divorce by mutual consent, would prove no more attractive to people bent on extremes of sex license than is marriage to-day. A few of these reckless ones might use it as a cloak for license, just as a few use marriage and divorce to-day; but they would be an insignificant handful. It would be so much easier for such persons to seek what they want in liaisons, just as they do now, that they would want no kind of marriage whatever. If promiscuity is one's object, why bother with the red tape and publicity of marriage, be it Companionate or otherwise. If one wishes to be lawless in one's sex relations, why seek them under such legal and social supervision?*

"On the other hand, men and women who sincerely loved each other would gladly abandon all thought of the *liaison* because here would be a type of marriage suited to their needs; a marriage sufficiently stable, and yet not too dangerously irrevocable.

"Now suppose you combine with this deterrent and controlling power of public opinion, the restraints imposed on people by their own sense of personal decency and social responsibility; and add, besides, the restraining power exerted on most persons by the emotional ties that tend to grow out of the intimate contacts of marriage—even childless marriages, like yours—and you have an almost overwhelming evidence that the tendency of Companionate Marriage would be toward stable relationships rather than toward reckless promiscuity. And yet it would have the saving grace of not being as rigid, unreasonable, and irrational in its demands on human beings as is our present code. It would be elastic enough to make human happiness and *reasonable* human adjustments possible, in a way that is now too often impossible.

"Now suppose you and Larry wanted a divorce, either at this time or later, when you have had children. How would you size that up? Would you have a right to it? Would you resent any social regulation that hindered it?"

"I should say that if we wanted it now, for good reasons, we ought to have it," she replied. "If there were children, then we might reasonably be expected to stick—provided our differences were not of a kind that would make our home a place where children could not be happy or rightly cared for."

"Exactly," I said. "There are cases where it is better for the children that the parents should separate; but ordinarily it is better that they should stick. But suppose you and Larry wanted a divorce now. Have you any notion of what you would have to do in order to get it?"

For a moment she did not answer. Presently she said, "I don't suppose you recall it; but my father and mother were divorced when I was twelve. I was old enough to realize very keenly what was happening; and I was old enough to read the newspapers, which I bought at a newsstand and smuggled into my room. I cried over them there; but Mother didn't know it. She thought I knew only what she told me. Yes, I think I know a *little* about what it means. I remember the things that came out—Father found in a hotel room with a woman, she in her underclothes when the detectives entered. I had always loved and worshiped my father; and I know that thing, so contrary to all I had been taught, wrenched me about inside to such a degree that in some ways I've never gotten straightened out since. Oh—it was horrible, horrible.

"It wasn't till years later that I told Mother what I knew, and learned from her that there hadn't been a word of truth in it all; that they had to slander and lie and commit perjury to get their divorce. They had intended to keep the thing more or less secret— the scandal part, I mean; but some reporter got onto it by accident.

"It was all planned in advance. They met with their lawyers and the lawyers planned the whole thing for them; and Father hired a woman to play the part—a woman he wouldn't have so much as looked at. And Mother had to tell an outrageous story about how cruel Father had been—mental cruelty they called it; but it was as absurd as if she had said he had beaten her. Father didn't defend himself."

"Then I don't need to urge on you," I suggested, "that a condition wherein people have to slander and lie to get the divorce they have to have, is wrong. Like Birth Control, and other things in marriage, we have made divorce contraband by making decent divorce difficult to obtain without indecent measures. You see what it amounts to is this: we have injected into our law books a theological-sacramental conception of marriage, a thoroughly mythical conception, having no relation to the sociological reality we are dealing with. We have read a pseudo-religious meaning into a civil contract, which we significantly call 'holy' matrimony. It is no *holier* than any other contract! Thus for fundamentally theological reasons, which are in no way related to rational sociology, our laws in effect forbid the courts to give two persons a divorce *unless one of them wants it and the other doesn't*. Such is the effect of it since divorce in the open by the admitted mutual consent of the parties is not allowed.

"And so it comes about that if you and Larry should to-day want a divorce, and should mutually and openly avow in court that for such cause you wanted it, the court would not grant it. For both of you thus to want it and to allege some faked-up cause, permitted by statute, as so many do, would be collusion. For your parents to fix things the way they did involved perjury, a penitentiary offense. And yet that is the way thousands of divorces are obtained, particularly in states that allow divorce only on grounds of adultery.

"The law picks this silly, traditional reason, based on jealousy; and it forces people to pretend to have done what in many cases they haven't done. It is all taken as a matter of course. The lawyers know the whole business is a farce; the judges know it; and the juries suspect it; and they all wink at it because it is easier to obey the absurd letter of the law than it is to attack the dragon of 'Christian' theology in his lair, and get your head snapped off. We claim in this country that there is no connection between Church and State. I don't know what humorist started that story; but I know it has ceased to be humorous, and is far too much like a practical joke.

"Suppose you and Larry wanted a divorce. Think how much better it would be if, instead of following out this disgraceful program of lies, hypocrisy, and deceit, you and he could come to some such person as myself, and say, 'Judge, we want a divorce.'

"What would I do? Would I give you your divorce by mutual consent right off the bat, and ask no questions? Not at all. It would be no such offhand proceeding. I would question you both, together and apart; and I'd get all the facts in confidence. The circumstances would be such that you would have none of the present inducements to conceal every vital fact from the judge. I am getting the truth from people all the time by just such methods. In many cases I find some trifling misunderstanding, easily straightened out, is the cause of all the mischief, and am able to start the couple off again, satisfied that they don't need a divorce after all.

"Many times—most times, in fact, some sex misunderstanding is back of the difficulty. Perhaps one or the other had had a puritanical attitude toward sex. There are a score of possible reasons. Often all that can be straightened out, with the help of a psychiatrist, if need be. Under Companionate Marriage these sex misunderstandings would, of course, be less frequent, because we would have a system for training and teaching people about love and marriage.

"But suppose when you come to me, I find that I can't do anything to make you happy together. Why then, and then only, I would grant your petition for a divorce. There would be no lawyers, no alimony, no scandals aired in open court, no newspaper gossip, no purse-breaking expense. You could part without bitterness; you would be little the worse off; and you would both be free to seek happiness further on. Wouldn't that be better? Would it savor of the corruption and hypocrisy and fraud and collusion and lying and lust and real cruelty in which the institution of divorce is steeped at present?"

"There is one other thing I want to ask," she said after a thoughtful pause. "These members of the younger generation, mere boys and girls, who at present have secret sex affairs—wouldn't they take advantage of the Companionate Marriage as a way of carrying on their affairs in the open, under the protection of the law? You know how freely they disregard the restraints of public opinion even now. They have their own code, and they don't much care what their elders think so long as they have the approval of their own set. Isn't that so?"

"Undoubtedly," I answered. "But has it occurred to you that the reason why they are so defiant and reckless is that society is providing them with no reasonable and respectable way of getting what they feel they have a right to? They resort to *liaisons*, which are necessarily lawless. This puts them needlessly at odds with society; and lawlessness breeds more lawlessness. But believe me, they are not nearly so reckless as they seem. They conform very strictly to their own code, and most of them, when they marry, make perfectly dependable husbands, wives, and parents. The notion that they don't is largely a myth. Companionate Marriage would prove, for most of them, a base for rational, responsible and sanely social conduct in matters of sex."

"But they are so young."

"Nature doesn't think so," I replied. "That's what is making most of the trouble. Our economic conditions amount to a demand on young people that they shall restrain their impulse to mate—putting it off for a long period. It is a bad thing. Give them a way to marry—a way that would be feasible economically, and they will come out all right.

"Note that what I am advocating as immediately practicable is something which we *already substantially have,* but do not acknowledge that we have it—*a childless, Companionate Marriage entered into with the expectation on the part of society, and of the persons marrying, that it will be permanent, and that it will probably change over to the procreative or Family Marriage later, as most of them coming under my observation have done.*

"I stand on that; and I refuse to be held responsible for any further changes in this plan that the society of the future *might* make. Hypothetical future developments have nothing to do with the question of what we are to do with this thing we already have.

"But I will add this: *If* some of these youngsters *did* substitute the companionate for their secret *liaisons,* and thus put themselves under the control of law and order, that would be gain, regardless of whether they divorced and experimentally remarried repeatedly or not. On such terms, there would be less danger in their conduct than in the present system of *liaisons* in which they indulge so recklessly, and so promiscuously. Fine types of girls from some of our best homes have confessed to me a dozen or a score of sex experiences with a dozen or a score of boys. Boys make the same confessions. The Companionate would be better than that even if they frankly went into it as a temporary thing, and as Trial Marriage instead of Companionate Marriage."

I shall not attempt here to report the rest of my conversation with

Edna. It lasted a long time, and I have already given the essentials of it. It was typical of many discussions on Companionate Marriage which I have had with various men and women who have voiced their doubts to me, and who have expressed regret that though they were my staunch supporters in most things, they could not follow me this far. Usually I have found that their objections were founded on a misconception of my meaning; and usually, as in the case of the young woman I have called Edna, and of the man I have called John Comstock, I have been able to win them over to enthusiastic support of my view. Such has been my experience with the various groups of men and women with whom I have had an equal chance to explain my meaning and my purposes.

3.

A very fine woman recently talked to me confidentially concerning her experiences as dean of women in a certain state university. I have already mentioned her in reporting my conversation with John Comstock. She told me she was convinced that Companionate Marriage, as I had outlined it to her, was bound to be accepted by the coming generation as a solution of the problems that confront many of our young people who are thrown into daily contact with each other in the relations of college life.

She told me she had had the confidences of a very large number of girls, who had confessed sex relationships with their lovers, and who safeguarded themselves by the use of contraceptives, and thus kept out of trouble with society.

Here is substantially what she said to me: "Judge, I am convinced that there would be absolutely nothing wrong in a young couple at college availing themselves of a Companionate Marriage law, if there were one, and at the same time going their respective ways through college and out into the business world—living their lives separately and associating when they cared to, much as if they were merely engaged. I don't see why they should not continue in such a way of life, either till they decided to form a companionate home, or a home with children, or till one or both of them decided to end the union—as would sometimes happen. I think the coming generation will have something of this kind, and that it will be much better than the present suppressions, the present pretenses at celibacy, and the illicit, secret, and lawless relationships which I know exist among the very finest types of our boys and girls from our best homes—and which, because they are beyond control or detection, constitute one of the gravest problems confronting society to-day.

"Under such a plan, which would in no way interfere with their college work, and which would tend to improve its quality rather, nothing would be thought of their having perfectly normal, decently regulated sex relationships in such marriage, with modern birth control devices as a guarantee against parenthood till they were ready for it.

"It would largely put an end to the preoccupation with sex which to-day makes co-education a difficult problem. More time and attention would be given to studies; and sex obsessions and perversions, now all too frequent in college life, would tend to disappear.

"The great majority of such unions would become permanent marriages later, with homes and children—a thing impossible under the present condition of illicit relationships. It would, as you say, amount to substituting the one for the other. I don't think the people who object to this idea have the least notion of what is really going on, or the extent of these *liaisons* in co-educational institutions.

"With such a system there would be for those who followed it few of the tragedies that spring from the present illicit relationships, none of the loss of self-respect, none of the devastating subjective fears which wreck nerves and health, none of the appeals to the abortionist, and none of the infanticides.

"I would not hesitate," she concluded, "to permit my own eighteen-year-old daughter to enter into such a relationship of Companionate Marriage with a man I approved of, where they both believed they loved each other.

"I think it would be an inducement to monogamy, and that it would lessen polygamy—of which just now we have plenty, in marriage and out of it."

If this dean of women should publicly express these views, her job would undoubtedly be in danger. They are significant views.

4.

Among church circles in Denver, where denunciation of my views on Companionate Marriage and my advocacy of Birth Control have been especially violent, I have been interested to compare these outward protestations with certain inside facts.

The daughter of one of my clerical denouncers, for example, married a young man who, to my certain knowledge, had had seven secret, fleeting sex affairs with high school girls, and one "sweetie." Several years ago this boy married the daughter of the minister in question secretly. The parents were informed the next day. The couple are now living in Companionate Marriage, which has put an end to the boy's promiscuities. That is to say, they use contraceptives and they have no children. I know about the contraceptives because they told me the whole story.

I am well acquainted with another young man who married the daughter of another Denver minister not long ago—a minister who has been very hot on my trail, and who has an especial horror of Birth Control and Companionate Marriage. This young man informed me specifically that he and his wife are deliberately childless, and are using Birth Control methods. It is a Companionate Marriage; and it has steadied both of them.

The son of another Denver minister, of the same conservative stripe, has married a girl well known to me. She recently told Mrs. Lindsey and myself that she is using Birth Control methods, and will have no children till she is ready for them. It is a Companionate Marriage. The young man has settled down in a way that would not have been possible to him by any other means.

Companionate Marriages, all of them! And it is to be noted that these couples, being educated and intelligent, do not consult the clerk at the corner drug store for Birth Control information, as do the poor and the ignorant. They go to a physician and get the very latest devices that science has developed along this line—devices that have made contraception ninety-eight per cent certain; and which, in the case of intelligent people, who follow instructions properly, may probably be counted as one hundred per cent safe.

There is a woman in Denver who denounces me and my views on

these matters on every occasion, with the ancient bunk about the "foundations of the home," and other sentimental nonsense having nothing to do with facts. She has freely expressed and repeated the ancient theological quip that the only kind of control she advocates is self-control; and she has freely said that she and her husband themselves practice "self-control." For this reason she "knows it is practicable, and that it can be done."

I am acquainted also with a certain young woman in Denver who is the sweetheart of this lady's husband. The two of them make frequent week-end trips to Colorado Springs and other resorts. On their return he always sends the young woman a profusion of flowers.

I don't wish to seem heartless, or to appear to exult over the silly wife of this man, living in her fool's paradise. I cite the facts merely to show that, like many other loud-mouthed people, she doesn't know what she is talking about. Self-control indeed! With a half-sexed woman for a wife, and a husband in love with some one else, "self-control" would seem a very effective substitute indeed for Birth Control. But that is no evidence that it would work in other cases. And what are the self-controllers going to do about that?

5.

It always interests me to be present on those occasions when some well-intentioned person rises to make his appeal against my "radicalism," and for "heaven, home, mother," and all that. Then comes the appeal to the audience: Do they want *their* daughters to enter Companionate Marriage, and "have their purity and their chastity sullied"? "Would you want your son to marry a girl who had been in the arms of other men?" It never fails to "split the ears of the groundlings"; it never fails to get a rise out of the crowd, and out of all who find it easier to go on an emotional jag than to think. It's as infallible as waving the Flag and appealing to One Hundred Percentism. It never fails to raise a hubbub of hysterical approval from the very people many of whose sons and daughters are running wild for lack of sane safeguards and sex education.

I noticed a woman who was leading the applause against me when this subject was discussed one night in a Denver church. She is a leading club woman in Denver, active in public affairs of every kind. Without any Companionate Marriage or any other kind of marriage, this woman's daughter has had relations with three young men, to my knowledge.

At the time her mother was applauding so violently against me at that meeting, and demanding that I be ousted from the bench for my doctrines, her daughter was having a very hectic love affair with a youth who, as she told me herself, she had had relations with for several months. She sat beside her mother at the meeting, and watched her with a peculiar half smile on her face. She didn't join in the applause on my side for very good reasons, as I know. Her mother would have asked questions.

I had once asked this girl to my Chambers, and she brought her mother with her, as many of these girls do. Her mother assured me that she was on confidential terms with her daughter—on whom she beamed as she said, "Of course, Sallie, you would tell your mother anything you would tell the Judge."

"Oh, of course, Mother," said Sallie dutifully.

I had seen this little farce enacted so often that I didn't even smile.

I explained to the mother that as I was calling Sallie as one of many witnesses in a case I would have to question her alone. When her mother had gone, Sallie breathed a sigh of relief, and then proceeded to tell me things that would utterly have floored her mother had she heard them.

I saw Sallie a few days after the meeting at which her mother had applauded so violently against me. "I think you have straightened things out in my mind, Judge," she said. "Harry and I just couldn't see this marriage idea; but now we see that it would be a lot better than what we've got. We're going to get married; and I'll find out what's what in Birth Control. No more drug-store advice along that line. Harry is different from the other boys I've gone with. We'll see it through. But just suppose I had married one of the others!"

"Yes, but you felt sure about them—at the time, didn't you?" I asked.

"Not sure this way," she said. "Just the same, Judge, I'd feel a lot safer if we could have divorce by mutual consent when and if we want it. However, we're going to take a chance."

They married a week later. A Companionate Marriage. It will end that girl's *liaison*. As it happens in most of the other Companionate Marriages I know of, I fully expect to see her in due time in a happy home, with a group of thriving children about her.

6.

Among the eminent critics of my views on Companionate Marriage is the president of a certain great Eastern university for men. He courteously expressed his dissent recently in a newspaper interview, and incidentally showed, by referring to Companionate Marriage as "trial marriage," that he had not informed himself of my views at first hand.

He would have been interested to know that on the very day that interview appeared in a Denver newspaper, I received a letter from a student in the university of which he is the head. It was a pitiful letter from a boy very badly in need of guidance and help. He was writing me because he had read what I thought about Companionate Marriage, and because there was nobody else, he said, to whom he could confide his problem without being condemned and told to follow a course that was already wrecking his health and happiness.

He was in love with a girl who also loved him. He could not afford to marry. And his principles and those of the girl had so far kept them from entering on a *liaison*, though both of them felt an almost irresistible wish to do so.

One result of this terrific effort at self-control on his part had been that he had sought a kind of appeasement which he was now unable to resist or break away from. It was, he thought, wrecking his health and his nerves. He found himself helpless without marriage—since, as I have said, a *liaison* was against his principles. Here was no reckless specimen, but a fine, upright boy, eager to do right and seeking help. Companionate Marriage would exactly solve his problem.

How would the president of his university meet that problem?

Would he have a single idea to offer that was not part of an outworn code which is demonstrably failing to work in people's lives? If he has something to offer besides moral platitudes about the "sacredness of womanhood" and the "sanctity of the home" and other catchwords that get nobody anywhere, why is he not sought out by this boy? The answer is that the boy knows it all by heart already. He could say it all backward or read it upside down. And he knows it is worthless, and that it doesn't meet the facts.

7.

I have letters from many university students, men and women, telling me their circumstances, and eagerly pointing out how perfectly companionate marriage would solve their personal problems. One letter comes jointly from a young couple who are at Harvard, the girl being a student in Radcliffe. They love each other. They want to marry. And they want both of them to go their ways as before, with the aid of Birth Control. But they hesitate. Marriage is such a long step; society expects so much; their friends wouldn't understand their marrying and yet not living together, but associating only occasionally instead. It would make them conspicuous; it would make their arrangement a source of embarrassing comment. They have no thought of anything other than a permanent union; but they frankly face the fact that they *may* have guessed wrong, because so many people do guess wrong; and why should they assume themselves to be infallible where others fail? What horrifying candor; what an immoral and shocking and shameless honesty! What is the world coming to!

There are many very religious people in Denver, some of them very important and wealthy people, prominently identified with the activities of churches that take a strong stand against Birth Control and divorce. Such persons come to me for counsel in their sex difficulties. I find them as keen on learning how and where they can obtain the latest and best scientific information on Birth Control as anybody; and when I refer them to physicians who are qualified to impart such information, they avail themselves of this channel of knowledge at once. But they don't admit it.

Parenthetically, let me explain that there is a federal law which makes it illegal to use the mails for imparting contraceptive information or for transmitting contraceptive devices; but that physicians practicing within the state where they have their license are governed by the state law. The Colorado law is fairly liberal in this respect, and permits physicians to impart Birth Control information when in their professional judgment it is wise to do so.

8.

I have in mind a recent case that illustrates how ready people are to avail themselves of Birth Control regardless of the stand their special church may take about it. A young man and young woman, both of them from well-known, extremely religious and orthodox families, belonging to one of the churches that oppose Birth Control, were about to be married. The girl's father came to me and asked me to send him to a physician competent to prescribe scientific Birth Control methods. I gave him the name of such a doctor.

Ten days before the marriage the girl's mother took her daughter to this physician, and obtained for the young woman the information that suited her individual case. There is no blanket prescription for contraception; each case is an individual problem, needing scientific examination and diagnosis. The girl's mother gave as her reason for this course that she thought it would be unfortunate if the young couple had children too soon. She thought their marriage would probably be a much greater success if they could defer children for a year or so, till they were temperamentally adjusted to each other, and were sure they could make a go of marriage, and till their finances justified the step. In other words, she recognized that Companionate Marriage would be a great safeguard for her daughter's happiness—while celibacy on the one hand, and immediately procreative marriage on the other, would not. I have known many many parents who have felt the same way about it, though few of them have met the issue so frankly, or so effectively.

A few years before this happened I picked up a bit of information concerning a man who is a near relative of this girl with the wise mother, and who is a very active member of the same church. He was having an affair with a girl who told me the whole story. The girl said they had thought of getting married, but that the man—whom I will call Robert Kay—dreaded being "tied up," because he knew his family, his church associations and his church activities would all combine to make it very difficult for them if they should ever want to separate. He argued that it was much better and wiser and *even more moral,* for them to go on the way they were going, making use of drug-store advice on contraception. And this they had been doing for a considerable period. They married later, when they had lived together long enough to be sure they wanted to stick. What the boy didn't know at the time was that his alert parents knew all about the affair, discreetly said nothing, and gladly welcomed their new daughter-in-law when the time came. This marriage then became a companionate, instead of a secret *liaison.* There are still no babies; but as the young man is steadily improving his economic fortunes, babies will probably be the next step. I suspect that the boy's orthodox parents, when they saw how well the thing was working, decided to see that their daughter obtained her safeguards under their supervision.

If these people had been Roman Catholics—I am not saying what they were—both of these marriages would have been eligible for annulment by the Holy Rota, judging from its decisions in similar cases.

This double-barreled story shows how little theological prohibitions are regarded by people who have practical problems to solve, and who propose to solve them by the use of common sense. It also shows how many a tragedy might be averted if more persons would face facts as courageously as these people faced them. The day of involuntary parenthood, that pedestal of ignorance which upheld the old order of procreative marriage, has gone. It can never return. *In practice, therefore, we have two kinds of marriage to-day.* We shall do well to face this fact frankly, and *use them both.*

9.

A few weeks ago there came to see me a young man who happens to be conspicuously identified with the same church as the people I have just been telling about. He was in a bad way, tied up to a wife he didn't love and who didn't love him. They had married in haste, and they had had two children in two years, by accident—children they didn't want because they were financially unprepared to take care of them, and because their own relationship was badly adjusted, and threatening to go on the rocks.

Poverty and worry and unwanted babies had done their work. There was no love left; only a tension that now made mutual understanding well-nigh impossible.

I said to him, "Why did you marry her?"

"I never really did love her," he answered. "I just thought I did. It wasn't till after we had married, and the first novelty had worn off, that I realized that I had done the thing on impulse, in a moment of desire—largely because I couldn't have her any other way. It would have been a lot better if she had yielded without marriage. Then we'd have discovered our mistake.

"It wouldn't have been so bad if we hadn't been so poor, and had the babies on top of it all. What with worry and debt, the combination has about broken both of us. She'd be as glad to be rid of me as I to be rid of her. She hates me and I hate her, and we're living in hell. I can't work, and I can't eat and I can't sleep. And it isn't her fault and it isn't mine. We just made a mistake.

"And now, Judge, I've met another girl. Her name's Anne. Anne and I have been going together for more than six months. I love her. This time I'm certain of it. I have had nothing to do with Jane for a long time; and so Anne and I have been going the limit. And now Anne is pregnant.

"For God's sake, Judge, can't things be fixed in some way so that I can get a divorce from Jane or she from me? This marriage of ours is a rotten thing. It isn't marriage. Why can't I marry Anne? If this can't be managed I don't know what to do. I know a doctor that would do a job for twenty-five dollars, but Anne and I don't like to do that."

Of course there is really no way out of a mess like that. It is a tragedy by any solution. Divorce would deprive the children of at least one parent, and of a home; and yet for such a couple to remain together may make a home so wretched that no child can be rightly reared in it—so that divorce might well prove the lesser of the two evils. That's the dilemma. So far as Anne is concerned, I can arrange for her confinement, secretly, and have her baby adopted later by some one who will be glad to have it; but that deprives her of her baby, thanks to the wrath society would visit on her if it knew the truth. From start to finish it is a bad business. And it has all come to pass from the attitude of society toward sex and toward marriage. It is all very well to blame the mix-up on these three ignorant young people; but it is perfectly plain that adequate education in matters of sex, plus the safeguard of Companionate Marriage, with Birth Control and divorce by mutual consent, would probably have prevented this tragedy, and would certainly prevent thousands and thousands of others like it. They are not to blame for their ignorance when that ignorance is forced upon them by the society in which they have grown up from babyhood.

10.

"Religious" people may find something holy—some hint of "holy" matrimony—in such a tangle, but I don't. I say that the devil never invented anything worse than this piece of "sacramental" poppycock that has been "sanctified" by the Christian church. I say that back of this hideous thing stands a superstition unworthy of a civilized people. I say that such absurdities are on an intellectual level with devil worship, and that we uphold and perpetuate the thing either because we can't think straight or are afraid to do so.

It is mostly the so-called "religious" people of this country, don't forget, who rise up in arms when anybody proposes that we sweep their theological junk off the map and try to use a little intelligence in ordering our affairs. They appear to me to be in error when they call their system of superstition by the sacred name of Religion. Religion consists in putting oneself in harmony with reality; but they are not interested in that kind of harmony, because they think it a sin. They hate "free thought" far more sincerely than they hate "free love."

Many of these people, moreover, who are talking the loudest about obedience to law and religion, are practicing contraception themselves as a matter of course; as I know from long contact with them and their kind. If they are such sticklers for law and what they call religion, why don't they go on having children year after year, or else abstain from sex relations—the only preventive they outwardly recognize as legitimate?

Obviously, this kind of "religion" is a virulent social disease; for it paralyzes the mind and makes thought impossible. It is out of the question that people should think rationally about anything so long as they ascribe to certain entirely human traditions a divine authority and infallibility which places them beyond candid inspection or honest examination, and which make it a sin to so much as demand of these alleged truths that they prove their validity by producing human happiness instead of human misery.

II.

I recently had a conversation with a Denver minister who had listened to a public talk I had made on Companionate Marriage, wherein I explained my views much as I have done in these pages, emphasizing again and again that companionate marriage is an actual institution, an actual part of our marriage system now.

"Why, Judge," he exclaimed, "I can't see anything wrong with this idea at all. What amazes me is the hullabaloo and fuss that has been kicked up, and the confusion and misunderstanding that has been raging about your head all over the country since you first proposed social and legal recognition of the Companionate. I'm even told that the estimable lady who heads the Federation of Women's Clubs has taken a crack at you and said you are a public menace and ought to be taken off the bench. I don't see where they get it. It's sheer hysteria; they are afraid of something.

"The fact is, Judge, that a lot of them are just waking up, after venting their fury on you, to the fact that you've told the truth, *and that unlegalized but socially recognized Companionate Marriage is going on right in their own churches, right under their own noses, right in their own homes, and that they themselves are, many of them, practicing it.*

"I am sure they never thought of it till you brought it to their attention. But now they can't deny it; they *know* the thing is here, right among them, the minute they stop to think; and it is rather funny to see how dazed they are to discover that they have been violently denouncing you for expressing in plain English a practice which has grown up in their midst, unsensed by them and unsuspected—a thing which they thought they had a holy horror of, but which they have all these years been taking to their bosom as a Godsend that has helped to make their lives tolerable. Don't let them forget that it is their own prescription and their own practice, that you are advocating; and that it is their own unconscious hypocrisy that you are exposing. You have told them the truth."

12.

Soon after this incident, and strikingly in confirmation of it, I received from my friend, J. N. Williams, Professor of Sociology in Hobart College, the following letter:

"DEAR JUDGE LINDSEY:

"You may be interested to know that the State of New York already has a law that goes far beyond the Companionate Marriage law which you have suggested for Colorado." (Professor Williams is here referring to my suggestion that a law legalizing birth control, and permitting divorce by mutual consent to childless couples, would establish companionate marriage in any state that chose to adopt such measures.) "According to the New York law," continues Professor Williams, "two people may legally marry by privately taking each other as husband and wife in the presence of any two witnesses, no minister or civil officer need be present, no license or other document is necessary. According to the law this private contract of marriage must later be acknowledged before a judge of a court of record by the parties and the witnesses. Also it must be recorded within thirty days with the State Department of Health and a copy filed in the clerk's office of the county where solemnized; 'but,' says a distinguished lawyer of the state, 'failure to acknowledge and record the contract does not invalidate the marriage. But it might be voidable.' That, is, one party might claim it was null and void and so dissolve the marriage. That is, here in New York you have a marriage entirely private, and voidable at the wish of either party. *This is not Common Law Marriage.* The statute is found in section eleven of the Domestic

Relations Law of the State of New York. *It is difficult, therefore, for any one who knows about the New York Law to understand the furor created by your proposal in Colorado. Your proposal, compared with our law, is very conservative.*

"Along with the above mentioned law we have, of course, legal marriage by minister or civil officer, with license required. But all this is optional. A couple is just as legally married, in the manner above described, as by a civil or ecclesiastical formality.

"Sincerely yours,

(Signed) "J. N. WILLIAMS."

13.

Among the many illuminating comments that have come to me in connection with my advocacy of Companionate Marriage I especially treasure one from Bertrand Russell, to whose views I have made reference earlier in this book. Here it is:

"Carn Voel
Porthcurno
Penzance.

"MY DEAR JUDGE LINDSEY:

". . . You know, of course, that you have my warmest sympathy in your political fight with the Klan and in your social fight to cause the prevalence of a less vindictive morality than that preached by the old orthodoxies. I must confess that I am not surprised by the vehemence of the opposition you encounter. The churches know that the two great sources of religious feeling are sexual frustration and the sense of sin, the latter being usually due to remorse for acts which a rational man would not regard as sinful; therefore the churches cannot tolerate a rational ethic. And that large part of the elderly and middle-aged population which lived austerely in youth cannot bear to think that the austerity was unnecessary—just as those who lost sons in the war cannot bear pacifists. And on this psychological foundation there is a vast superstructure of financial interests.

"With regard to 'Companionate Marriage,' I think, of course, that the recognition of it would be an advance on the present system. But I go further than you do: the things which your enemies say about you would be largely true of me. My own view is that the state and the law should take no notice of sexual relations apart from children, and that no marriage ceremony should be valid unless accompanied by a medical certificate of the woman's pregnancy. But when once there are children, I think that divorce should be avoided except for very grave cause. I should not regard physical infidelity as a very grave cause and should teach people that it is to be expected and tolerated, but should not involve the begetting of illegitimate children—not because illegitimacy is bad in itself, but because a home with two parents is best for children. I do not feel that the main thing in marriage is the feeling of the parents for each other; the main thing is coöperation in bearing children. . . . The persecution to which you are being subjected is supplying me with evidence for my favorite thesis, that religion is the chief enemy of kindliness and decency in the modern world.

"Yours sincerely,

(Signed)   "BERTRAND RUSSELL."

By "religion" I take it that Mr. Russell means "religion" in the narrower and more restricted usage of the word, as referring to the systems of organized superstition that masquerade under that name.

CHAPTER VIII

BIRTH CONTROL AND THE COMPANIONATE

I.

A DENVER lawyer who is secretly a friend of mine, but who, for bread and butter reasons, remains publicly in the camp of the Philistines, came to me recently. And he opened fire with this:

"Judge, I was with a bunch of fellows the other day, all of them lawyers. We got to discussing you and your views on Companionate Marriage."

"What did they say?" I asked.

He laughed. "First I'll tell you who they were; then I'll give you one guess at what they thought about it."

He named six or eight men, all of whom I knew to be opposed to me on general principles. Several of them had already denounced my views on Companionate Marriage as an attack on the "foundations of the Home."

"It's no trick to guess the verdict of that crowd," I said.

My informant grinned. "Well, you'll be interested to know that every man there admitted that you were right; and that they further agreed they couldn't afford to say so in public because you were trying to wreck the divorce business that most of the fees of so many of us come from."—Whereupon he launched with gusto into an account of the discussion, which I repeat here as fully as I can recall it.

"Of course Lindsey's right about it," said one who had lambasted me a few days before at a public meeting where he hoped to gain favorable newspaper publicity for himself at my expense. "All this Companionate of Lindsey's amounts to is that it would legalize Birth Control and establish divorce by mutual consent for childless couples. Birth control and divorce by mutual consent are illegal, but we've got them. Lindsey wants public and legal ac-

211

knowledgment of the fact so it can be made even more useful than it is.

"Add a few frills about medical examination, the only feature of the scheme that we are not already practicing, and there's your Companionate. Some states like Wisconsin already have the medical examination, even. And so there isn't a new thing about the proposed Companionate except that everybody could have it without confidential and illegal help from a doctor and a lawyer."

"Sure, I put in," continued my friend, "I know Lindsey is not for *easy* divorce; he is for *honest* divorce, and you fellows know it is not that way now. It's *easy* enough already."

"True enough," observed another. "We're all for Birth Control. I'll warrant there isn't a man here that doesn't practice it. And, of course, there isn't a man of us that hasn't handled case after case of divorce by mutual consent—by collusion, that is. In fact, we lawyers invented the thing because it was a necessity and a darned good job, too, I call it.

"Why," he went on, "I'm cooking up a case of that sort in my office right now. When I get it into court it will go through on skids—an evasion of the law from start to finish. That couple are on friendly terms, but they just can't hit it off in marriage. They are extremely conventional, good church members and all that—very moral; and the joke of it is that I heard them discussing Companionate Marriage; and they *didn't believe in it!*—It was rich. I told them I didn't either.—They agreed that Lindsey is a dangerous man; and I didn't dispute that. He is.

"But what those nit-wits didn't see was that if their divorce by mutual consent were legal instead of illegal, they could have had it by simply asking for it, without attorneys, collusion, and red tape, and that they wouldn't have to pay me a fat check for slipping them through the divorce mill."

"Lindsey is going to hurt our business," said another. "The reason this country has divorce by mutual consent to-day is largely due, as Jones just said, simply to the cleverness of us lawyers in working out a technique of artful dodging that would get around the asinine divorce laws. We have created that technique in response to a demand for it, law or no law; and we are entitled to make something out of it. It's been a service to humanity. That's the way I see it.—But so long as this thing is against the law, people have to have us to help them out—and the longer it stays against the law the better for us financially.

"And now along comes this damn' little cuss Lindsey, trying to show it all up; trying to snip the red tape till there's just about enough of it left for us fellows to go hang ourselves with. If Lindsey would stick to his own bailiwick I'd be for him. He's done a lot of good. But I've got to look out for my own interests; and it's perfectly plain that if the general public ever finds out how completely right he is about this companionate stuff, it will go over with a bang. Legislatures will pass bills, and there we'll be. Luckily for us, they have so far misunderstood it."

At this point there spoke up a man who had privately admitted to persons who had promptly brought the news to me that he would like to succeed me as Juvenile Judge. "What I don't get," he remarked, "is why Lindsey didn't say he was for Birth Control and divorce by mutual consent, instead of calling the thing by a fancy name. He sprung his notion in terms that made the ministers and church people think he was preaching trial marriage. In fact, they started out by calling it that. I suppose what set them by the ears was that he pointed out that people could marry young instead of having *liaisons,* and could then get out of the thing if they found they had made a mistake. But why shouldn't they?—Only we can't say so. It sounds a lot too true to be good."

"Huh," snorted some one else. "That Birth Control and divorce by mutual consent idea has been sprung time and again; and it no longer makes a ripple. Suppose he had put it that way. Suppose he had said to the public, 'Let's make Birth Control legal, and let's give divorce to childless people who want it.' Would it have attracted any attention? Not on your life. It's old stuff. The crowd's used to it. Even the ministers are a good many of them won over to that—especially the Birth Control part. Ministers don't have as many kids as they used to, you'll notice.

"Well, Ben sees he can never make a dent that way; so what

does he do? Why, he simply stands on his head, and then describes the same identical thing upside down. Instead of stating it in negatives he states it in positives. Instead of talking of childlessness and easy divorce for the childless, he talks about freedom and happiness in marriage, and about marriage made easy and safe for people who, when they enter it now, find it a trap. He points out that there is a way to get at the bait without springing the trap. That sounds sinful. Everybody's shocked—especially the people who think it's a sin to admit that things are as they are, and who are suspicious of happiness, and who don't like to be stood on their heads anyway—or to be handed a new idea, regardless of whether it's right side up or upside down—

"Honestly, the roar that has gone up about this thing strikes me as one of the jokes of the decade. Trial Marriage! Free Love! Bolshevism! Help! Fire! Murder!—And here the whole conservative pack of them have been doing all that shrieking against a thing they practice themselves, illegally, as a matter of course."

"That's all right," observed the first who had spoken. "But there's a lot of money at stake in this, and Lindsey's got to be snowed under, with the coöperation of the Roman Catholic clergy on the one hand and the invaluable Klan on the other. Queer bedfellows. The Klergy and the Klan!

"Now suppose Lindsey should put his idea over. Suppose he makes such divorce obtainable by childless couples, without red tape, or the services of attorneys. Just figure it out. There were between 1,500 and 2,000 divorce cases filed in Denver last year. If Lindsey had his way, not one in fifty of those cases would have required a lawyer, and this would be true even in cases where there were children involved. That is what is going on in his court now—not one lawyer in fifty cases there. Figuring on the average rate of $300 a case, that means somewhere between $450,000 and $600,000 a year taken right out of the pockets of the legal profession in Denver."

"That isn't half of it," said another. "I'm holding office. Where would I get off? I tell you, you can't mix Lindsey and politics without a row. It takes courts and court machinery to run things

the way they are; and courts and court machinery mean jobs—
my job among them. A court, on Lindsey's plan, can run on a
shoe string. Look what his own court runs on—about $40,000 a
year, as compared with $200,000 for the other courts right in
the same court house; and most of their trial cases are divorce
cases. And he handles as many or more cases than they do. As
for me, I haven't a thing against Lindsey, but I want to keep my
job."

"You bet," came another voice. "Look at the way Lindsey
handles these annulment cases if you want to know what would
happen if the courts could use such informal methods of handling
divorce. I was in his court only the other day, and found him
in the act of annulling the marriage of a boy and girl who couldn't
get along.

"From what he said I gathered that he had talked to them two
or three times without being able to get them together. So now he
gave it up, and granted them what they wanted, as easily as I'd
write a check for five dollars. Why, hang it, there wasn't a lawyer
mixed in that deal from beginning to end. The petition for annulment was made out in Lindsey's court; all the papers were
gotten up on blanks Lindsey had gotten printed; there wasn't a
red cent paid for attorney fees; and the boy had to shell out a
few dollars for court costs. The docket fees and all court costs
for filing the annulment papers totaled $12.50. This covered what
ought to have cost at least $300; and not a cent did the legal pro-
fession get out of it."

"I had an annulment case," put in another; "and I steered it
away from Lindsey and into a regular court where I knew I'd get
mine. The couple didn't know the difference. Of course I put in
everything, typewritten statements and all that. It runs up into
money. Not a bit of it would have been necessary in his court.—
More than that, just think of the number of political jobs involved
in putting a divorce case through a regular court. There's a judge
with a salary of say $4,000; a bailiff with a salary of $2,000; a
court stenographer with a salary of $3,600—not to mention all
the frills and elaborations, and jury costs if there is a jury. So
that it isn't merely the attorney that gets something out of it; it's

everybody connected with the court machinery. It takes some machinery to handle 2,000 divorce cases a year. And the bigger the machinery is the more bread and butter there is in it.

"Well, as I was saying, I got together some witnesses, and after the usual round of explanation, petition, answer, hearing of evidence, and delays, the annulment was granted. It cost the parties $200, most of which went to me. The total overhead cost to the county taxpayers was probably another $200 or more. That went into the pockets of the people who run the court. It's an extravagance—a needless extravagance, of course. I don't say it's the way it ought to be; but I do say that we've got livings to make, and that we've got to stand pat. I can't *afford* Lindsey's brand of idealism."

"Oh, you needn't talk ideals," growled another. "We've got a good enough case against Lindsey even if our incomes weren't involved. He's just plain encouraging immorality. Look at the line of talk he hands out to these people that come to him, and the ideas he puts into their heads. Why, I saw a couple whose marriage he had annulled walk away arm in arm, like good friends. You can't tell me that's moral." (The man who delivered this utterance teaches Sunday school in a Denver church.) "That was nothing in the world but Lindsey's influence. That couple were very sore at each other when they came to him. I saw them. You can bet there'd be nothing of that sort if *I* had his job."

"I was there one day," spoke up another, "when Lindsey was hearing the case of a middle-aged couple—for nothing, of course. The man was charged by his wife with not supporting her and their six kids.

" 'Why don't you support your children?' Lindsey asked.

" 'Too many of them,' said the man.

" 'What did you want when you got married?'

" 'I wanted a woman.'

" 'Then you didn't marry because you wanted kids?'

" 'No,' the fellow repeated. 'I didn't want kids; couldn't afford 'em. An' then came the kids, one after another, steppin' on each other's heels. There was no stoppin' 'em. I wouldn't have minded a few, but I can't handle six. My wife didn't want 'em any more than I did.'

"And then, if you'll believe it, Lindsey had the nerve, in the teeth of the law, to say to that fellow, 'It's a crime against humanity that you've been tricked by society into having children you didn't want and couldn't care for; and that you've been forced by the ignorance legally imposed on you to have so many. You could have raised one or two all right, couldn't you? That would have been fair enough, wouldn't it?'

" 'Yes.'

" 'There was no need for you to have so many,' Lindsey went on. 'If you and your wife had come to me I'd have sent you to a Birth Control specialist. Then you wouldn't have had more than you could handle; and you wouldn't have had this last one, the straw that broke the camel's back.'

"When Lindsey set the amount of support money the man nearly threw a fit. 'I can't pay that,' he shouted.

" 'Why not?'

" 'Why, my wife has brought a divorce suit against me in another court. They sent us down here to settle about the kids.'

" 'I know that,' said Lindsey. 'What about it?'

" 'A lot about it,' said the man. 'The judge told me I'd have to pay $150 cash to my wife's lawyer; and that ain't sayin' what I've got to pay my own lawyer.'

"With that Lindsey cut loose, looking my way every now and then as if to be sure he was aiming straight—for he knew I hadn't much use for his methods. He explained to the couple just what would be the arrangement if he had *his* way. He told them he could have saved them about $300, and that he could have arranged what to do about their children, and would have given a divorce free and clear, so to speak.—His shooting off his mouth in his own court didn't amount to much, of course, because he merely put a few people wise. But now, good heavens!—he's shouting it out so everybody can hear. He's even doing it over the radio."

The conversation went on from this to a further discussion of me and my misdeeds. I have given enough of it here, as it was reported to me, to illustrate what I am up against, and probably always will be up against.

2.

I face two kinds of opposition. One sort comes from persons who have no ax to grind, but who are conservative and unimaginative. These are the type Schopenhauer had in mind when he said, "If we want to take a serious view of any question, we have first of all to consider whether it will not give offense in some way or other to dullards, who generally show alarm or resentment at the mere sign of intelligence."—I think Schopenhauer's word "dullards" is too strong. I don't feel that the people who oppose my views are all of them dullards by any means. But I do feel that many of them are either wanting in imagination, or are too ready to form opinions without a knowledge of the facts involved.

The other sort of opposition comes from sophisticated persons, like those whose talk I have reported above—persons who have an ax to grind, and who want to use it on my head because their interests are identified with the organized political system whose *status quo* is more or less jeopardized by any suggestion for a radical change of law or law administration.

As a matter of fact, the fears of those men were as groundless, economically, as were the fears of workmen a century ago, when they opposed the introduction of labor-saving machinery on the ground that if one machine would do the work of twenty men, it would deprive nineteen of them of their jobs. The cotton gin, for instance, so cheapened the cost of cotton goods that people bought more; and thus jobs were created, and the industry grew apace. If justice were cheap and easy to obtain, there would be more demand for the legitimate and humane services of the courts, and of the legal profession than there is at present. As things stand, the man who seeks justice at the bar of justice too often receives a very inferior, machine-made article for which he pays a ruinous price.

The changes I have already initiated, and the statutes I have written, have saved Colorado many millions of dollars. The further changes I favor would save, in court operations alone, many millions more. A total of at least a million dollars a year is being needlessly paid by the people of Denver alone to lawyers, politicians, court appointees, and judges, and for other court overhead. Of course it is quite natural—though short-sighted—that persons whose immediate financial status is involved in the continued functioning of the present cumbrous and costly system should resent any effort made to simplify it.

In other words, I am experiencing in Denver to-day exactly the thing I encountered when, twenty-eight years ago, I first undertook to fight the old system, which is still operative in some states, of treating young child offenders like adult criminals. In my effort to change that system I nearly destroyed myself. It was a costly victory. I built up enmities then which follow me like furies of revenge even to this day—as some of my recent reverses attest. Merely to remain in office, and obtain reëlection sometimes as an independent candidate in order to carry on my work, I have often had to spend more than the entire amount of my yearly salary of $4,000 in campaign expenses; and I have had to live on what I could make lecturing during my vacations. And, as if that were not enough, those after my scalp have time and again raised the howl that I was neglecting my work "in order to seek publicity and make money."

I have ample reason to know, therefore, that this "System," bent on maintaining itself, is no myth. I have reason to know that its members act in instinctive unison like the individuals of a colony of bees; and that they sting as viciously and as instinctively any one who seems to threaten the hive. I am not blaming them. I am merely stating the situation.

It is the same system that lined up against me in the days when, with Harvey O'Higgins, I wrote "The Beast." That sinuous and graceful animal still works in marvelous ways its wonders to perform; and it can still scratch its right ear with its left hind foot.

A recent spectacle of the miracles it can work is to be found in the alliance now existing in Denver between the Roman Catholic clergy and the Ku Klux Klan, in a united and brotherly effort to oust me from office because of my opinions on Companionate Marriage. I think the Roman Catholic clergy are quite sincere about this. At any rate, they honestly think they are. They really mean what they say. But the righteous indignation of the Klan leaders makes me smile.

However, the Roman Catholic Church is strong; and perhaps it can afford to let itself be tarred by the Klan stick. At any rate I draw a sharp line between my deep respect for my foes among the Roman Catholic clergy and the deep contempt I feel for the conscious hypocrisies and insincerities of the Klan leaders. As for the rank and file of the Klan, I have nothing against them. They excite my pity. They are good average folk who mean well and are easily led around by the nose. Their leaders have found this out.

3.

Most of the clergy, both Protestant and Roman Catholic, uphold the established order. They are part of the System, whether they realize it or not; and if they want to test their independence, let them try speaking the truth and see how long their leading parishioners will let them keep their jobs. The truth about any-thing vital in politics or sociology, I mean. It is easy for people to "believe" what they would get walloped for not "believing." Many of the clergy have kidded themselves into believing things about which, if they would be honest with themselves, they would realize that they have at least an honest doubt.

As a passing example of what I mean when I say that trouble awaits ministers who dare to be open-minded, let me recall the case of a young student pastor who was rash enough to arrange for me to speak on Companionate Marriage before some students in Boulder, Colorado. He innocently assumed that the authorities of an institution of learning, and the leaders of his church, would all of them welcome a public discussion of a matter subject to so many differences of opinion. He found them not at all interested in that—but very vastly interested in the question of what punish-ment should be meted out to him. He was promptly called on the carpet and roundly "scored," though the superiors of the young pastor finally decided to call his lapse from orthodoxy a youthful indiscretion and let it go at that,—which was doing very well for them. I don't doubt that they have acquired merit by it. But the *next* time the young man shows a spark of independence—what then? Don't ask.

I would not mind the opposition of those of the clergy who have denounced me if the criticism which some of these gentlemen have directed at me showed the slightest comprehension of the matters they are talking about, or the least sign of any ability to do anything but mechanically apply their authoritarian prepossessions and their magic formulas to the affairs of an age which these formulas no longer fit. They seem to be in blissful ignorance of this *fact*.

4.

I dined a few nights ago with two eminent Denver men, both of whom are thoroughly conversant with my views on Companionate Marriage. Both of them go about a great deal in society. They told me that everywhere they go they find Companionate Marriage being discussed, and that they have found few who understand it. They commented on the tendency to call it "trial marriage," and to think of it as a union deliberately intended to be impermanent—a system of legalized promiscuity. They found an almost total failure on the part of the average man to understand that human nature normally prefers one union to many. They added that one thing they noted among their friends was that most of them are unhappy and dissatisfied with their married life, hoping to find some remedy, some relief, and if possible some solution without the necessity for divorce.

Both of them had been present at a social function which was also attended by a certain eminent educator and his wife. This educator had publicly criticized my views on the Companionate.

On this occasion the man's wife expressed the emphatic opinion that the best solution for the sex problem in universities, particularly co-educational universities such as the one her husband was connected with, as to certain types of college students would be for them to marry. She said that there was every evidence that such students married did better work, that they were more manageable, that they were in better health, and were obviously leading a more normal life than their unmarried fellows. She thought it very encouraging that the proportion of married students in universities was steadily increasing. She said, however, that there was one grave difficulty involved in such marriages—the birth of children. This, she pointed out, was undesirable because such couples have neither the money nor the time for this responsibility. But she added that fortunately there seemed to be very few children in such marriages.

Now the interesting thing about this was that the lady, after making that statement, side-stepped or ignored the *reason* why there were few children born in these student marriages. Apparently she either did not understand the reason for such sterility, or preferred not to understand it and therefore deliberately ignored an issue which it was plainly up to her to face candidly.

Her final suggestion was that it would be an excellent thing if some philanthropists would provide endowments that could be used to maintain dormitories for married students.

"That would be fine," said some one present. "And of course such dormitories should each be supplied with a nursery."

This suggestion was allowed to pass without comment, though it would have been quite in order to reply that no nursery would be needed, and that the whole success of such an arrangement would be contingent on the deliberate childlessness of these student marriages. A dormitory filled with married students, each couple of them blessed with one or more babies, would be unthinkable and impracticable, nursery or no nursery, if all the occupants were students with classroom schedules.

My two friends added that the lady evidently had not suggested the nursery herself because it was obvious that college students, who marry, and who both of them must carry on college work, and whose earning capacity and time are alike limited, would have no business with babies, even though they would admittedly have business with marriage.

The husband of this lady, let me repeat, had made a statement of dissent from my views which misrepresented me as advocating trial marriage; and this interview had been printed in newspapers from one end of the country to the other. He had been very specific about it; and yet he turned right around, and in company with his wife, advocated the same thing.

What these evasions amounted to was an effort on the part of these two very law-abiding and proper people to avoid going on record about a thing so ticklish as Birth Control, and at the same time advocate a system that would make Birth Control, be it legal or illegal, absolutely necessary. It was a tacit recognition that many students are, as a rule, fit for Companionate Marriage, but not for procreative marriage. It was also the exact and evasively disguised equivalent of the proposals which so shocked them as coming from me. I said that young people who are restive and inclined to get into trouble sexually, and who fall in love, ought to be permitted by society to marry, and to marry under conditions that would exclude procreation. *That is what they say also, in different words*—words less blunt and direct. And if they did not realize that an inevitable corollary of such childless marriage is the privilege of divorce by mutual consent, then they certainly have a very limited understanding of human nature.

5.

Birth Control!—I have before me a report by Katherine Bement Davis, published in the *Journal of Social Hygiene* in 1922. Dr. Davis sent out a questionnaire to one thousand women, inquiring as to their use of contraceptives and their belief in voluntary parenthood. Answers came from 754 of these, and 691 of those who answered were college graduates; 75.11 per cent admitted that they made use of contraceptives. Only 78 of the answers expressed disapproval of the use of birth control methods.

It has been my experience that practically the only women who make no use of birth control are those who are ignorant of it, or who are sterile and don't need it. The practice has become all but universal; and, quite regardless of law, those who don't have the necessary information obtain it if they can.

Incidentally there are fully as many Roman Catholic women coming for help to the Birth Control League in New York City as there are Protestant and Jewish women. The proportion averages a third of each.

I know a wealthy and prominent Roman Catholic in Denver who has offered financial support to the Birth Control Clinic here. This man told me that the prohibition imposed by the clergy on Birth Control for Roman Catholics is having less and less effect, even among the ignorant and superstitious, and that in his opinion opposition to Birth Control in the Roman Catholic Church is breaking down from within the church. He added that such prohibitions had no effect on him at all.

I also know many of the Roman Catholic laity who personally believe in Birth Control, and who have, on occasion, used it, or advised its use. Naturally I don't divulge names; but I may say that Roman Catholic women have reported to me receiving absolution from their priestly confessors after they, in Confession, had admitted that they were making use of contraceptives. Having received absolution, they went right on using contraceptives—which I thought very sensible.

At this point let me explain that in referring to Roman Catholics I am not actuated by the least hostility toward them or their Church. But the fact that that Church has gone so decidedly on record with respect to Birth Control makes reference to Roman Catholics in this connection unavoidable. It should not be overlooked, however, that there are Protestant Churches, and particularly many Protestant ministers, in this country who are also putting up a strong fight against Birth Control. What I have to say concerning the Roman Catholic Church therefore applies with equal force to the much more limited body of Protestant opposition to Birth Control. I believe most of the progressive, intelligent element of the Protestant clergy and laity favor Birth Control.

The Roman Catholic stand in the matter is more clear cut, consistent, and easily defined than the Protestant stand. The theory of the Church is that contraception is "unnatural," and hence injurious, sinful, and against the divine will. I don't know why that word "unnatural" should hold such terror, but it seems to, even in an age when Man has gone rather far in using his brains to improve his lot by "unnatural" devices that range from electric lights to houses, clothes, and cookery. Apparently it is a question of what you happen to be used to.

6.

According to the Roman Catholic Church, as I understand it, the only permissible form of Birth Control is voluntary abstinence from each other on the part of *both* parents. If one parent insists on abstinence against the will of the other, that also is sinful. It is considered moral, however, for the parent who does not want any more children to limit intercourse to that portion of the month which is known as the "safe period," during which time it is supposed that conception is unlikely to take place. But this "safe period" is in many cases a myth; it lacks sound scientific basis. What this rule of the Church amounts to, therefore, is that if the husband insists on marital relations, as he is likely to do, the wife commits a sin in refusing, even though her refusal be based on a desire to avoid further child-bearing by practicing abstinence as the Church commands. Comment on the condition of virtual slavery in which a rigorous application of such beliefs would place American women is, I trust, needless. Such attempts to import medieval codes of living into the Twentieth Century cannot succeed. They can, however, impede the march of progress—and they do.

Both in the Roman Catholic Church, and in many Protestant churches, there seems to be a deep-rooted conviction that sexual indulgence dissociated from procreation is a sin, and spiritually hurtful; that it is somehow sinful to indulge sex for the pleasure, psychological and physical, inherent in it; and that freedom from the possibility of unwanted pregnancy would lead the race to excessive sexual indulgence. That there is no evidence of any such results among the many cultured and excellent people in both the Catholic and Protestant churches who have practiced Birth Control for years without becoming sensualists seems to make no difference in the persistence of this old and utterly unwarranted belief. The younger generation, however, has almost completely gotten rid of it.

The theological view of the matter is that "Sex" is "Sin." The traditions of orthodox Christianity have always upheld the ascetic ideal that sex is essentially a wrong and shameful thing, an evil which we must put up with solely because it is necessary for the propagation of the race. St. Paul's view, which is the orthodox Christian view, was that truly saintly people would abstain from sex entirely, as he himself did, and that people who were merely good in the ordinary sense of the word would restrain themselves as far as possible. The exercise of the sex function, according to Paul and his theological successors, is least offensive to God when practiced in marriage, but it is always offensive. "It is better to marry than to burn." And again, "The flesh lusteth against the spirit, and the spirit against the flesh."

The old notion of the antithesis between flesh and spirit is the source of this view of sex, and of all activities of the "flesh," as evil. Most persons accept uncritically the idea that mind and matter are opposites; the one good, the other evil. That antithesis is the root principle of Christian Science, for instance, which holds that since God is Universal, and since God is Good and God is Mind, there can't be any Matter because Matter, if it existed, would have to be the opposite of Mind and therefore Evil. In short, a Universal God excludes his opposite. Very simple and logical, you see, if you admit the premise that Mind and Matter are opposites, and hold that they are not two aspects of the same reality.

Every religion that holds to the antithesis between Mind and Matter, is forced, logically, to view Sex as essentially an evil, material thing. But if one abandons that notion for the belief that Mind creates and permeates all things, then there is room for the conviction that the Spirit and the Flesh can help each other, affect each other, and interact to produce the Flame we call Life. As between saying that Matter is an aspect of Mind, and saying that Mind is an epiphenomenon of Matter, accompanying it as a sound accompanies the vibration of a harp string, I don't see that there is a particle of difference, save in where you want to put the emphasis. The fact that the two exist together justifies the assumption that it is our business to make them function together harmoniously within us, rather than keep them fighting till, like the mythical gingham dog and calico cat of Eugene Field, they eat each other up.

In taking a stand on the ethics of Birth Control it is rather necessary to decide first what one thinks about this fundamental matter of Flesh and Spirit—whether they are antithetical or not. If they are, then you must follow the Church. If they are not, then the theologians are tilting at windmills.

According to the theologians we are a "fallen race," and one evidence of our fall is to be found in the fact that whereas among animals sex serves only for procreative purposes, the human race indulges in sex primarily for pleasure—which is all wrong. The proof offered is the fact that female animals receive the male only at certain times, when the ovum is in the womb ready for fertilization—and that they refuse intercourse at all other times. It is argued that this is "natural," and that the fact that women differ from the lower animals in this respect is "unnatural." Hence it is contrary to the will of God, and is the direct result of the Fall. Thus we are given to inordinate desires, to beastly appetites, to expressions of our "animal nature." Instead of expressing our "animal nature" in this unbridled way, we ought to express it in moderation the way animals do. Apparently the animals are free from the "animal nature" that plays so much mischief with us. You see the theologians get somewhat confused about this "animal" business.

7.

The fact is that the use of *imagination* in connection with the sex impulse is one thing that has served to raise the human race above the brute level. Such *creative arts* as Music, Painting, Sculpture, Poetry, the Dance, Love, and Religion itself have sprung from this union of sex and imagination. It constitutes one of the great motive powers of life. It is not merely procreative; it is *creative*. It does more than conceive a man; it makes him grow and aspire.

What this means, if it means anything, is that sex fulfills purposes in human life which go far beyond the mere function of procreation which it serves among animals. Among animals it apparently serves no other end, though it would not do to speak too absolutely on that point. It is quiescent save for that. But among human beings it is quite otherwise. To this fact we owe nearly everything that is fine, beautiful and uplifting in human life. That is the biological base from which spring our reachings-out toward the skies. And if some of our theologians want to call this wonderful thing the result of the "Fall," and if they want contemptuously to dub it "Carnal Appetite," they are at liberty to do so. The words no longer mean anything.

Sex plays a part in human life which it apparently does not play— in anything like the same degree, at any rate—among animals. Love, with us, is geared to match our greater capacity. It enriches the emotional life, it is a profound spiritual experience when combined with affection, and it makes it possible for two lives to enrich each other in ways not otherwise possible. Sanely used, without fear, and under conditions that work no social harm, it has in it possibilities for good that are apparently completely overlooked by these fanatics who see in it nothing but ugliness, original sin, and fig leaves.

Now let me say a word as to the actual effects of these ecclesiastical prohibitions against Birth Control. Again I choose my examples from among Roman Catholics because these cases are more clear cut than any others, and are the direct result of such control, consistently and authoritatively maintained.

Many Roman Catholics have brought their difficulties to me. I know many instances, for example, among educated and well-to-do Roman Catholic families in Denver, where the wife has compelled her husband to practice continence as a means of avoiding pregnancy, and where the husband has promptly sought outside relations with other women, particularly younger women.

In these cases, where the wife has found it possible to render such exemplary obedience to the commands of the Church, the real explanation was usually that she was the victim of a system of education that had given her a loathing toward sex from childhood. I am continually coming in contact with such women. Women of this type are usually glad of an excuse to put a stop to marital relations with their husbands. The story is likely to be quite different in the case of those who are strongly sexed. Rather than give up their sex life, these women risk pregnancy, remaining obedient to the command of the Church not to "interfere with nature." I have known women of this type, being convinced that contraception was immoral, to resort to the abortionist when this highly moral and excessively pious line of conduct resulted in pregnancy.

8.

The truth is that this notion that men and women will practice Birth Control by means of *continence* is a sham; and the very people who advocate continence for such a purpose know, if they have the sense they were born with, that such a doctrine is preposterous. Normally sexed people will not practice continence in marriage. They will run all risks rather than practice it. That is the *fact* of the matter.

Continence works with the few—usually with the abnormal and undersexed; but in the case of the vast majority, the measure of its effectiveness may be calculated from the fact that orthodox Roman Catholic families, where no contraception is permitted, tend to be large.

I know what I am talking about. I have in my mind a picture of scores of women, wrecked in health, broken in spirit, bowed down with poverty that has resulted from there being too many mouths to feed, who have come to me with their stories. Their married lives have been one long tragedy of parturition. The Church had forbidden "interference with nature," the husband had insisted on his "rights," and the babies had kept on coming, year after year,—such being the mysterious will of God, which it would have been a sin to evade, and which the Church knows all about.—Does it?

I have in mind a small town, one of many like it in the United States. Let's call it Sleepy Hollow. In this particular district, the Klan is strong, and the Roman Catholic Church is anathema. The people belong mostly to the little Baptist, Methodist, and Presbyterian churches that are in Sleepy Hollow, and if you go into one of those churches of a Sunday you will probably hear a discussion about monkeys that would have warmed the heart of my friend, William Jennings Bryan. It is a thoroughly fundamental region, where Hell is Hell and Heaven is Heaven, and America is for White, Nordic, Blond, Protestant, One Hundred Per Centers—and where Heaven is for such also.

Birth Control is not respectable in Sleepy Hollow. A few radicals make use of clumsy drug-store devices on the sly, but most of them abjure such immoral practices and don't interfere with nature. The result is that some of the families have an excessive number of children; and that in those homes where there are only a few children, there are one or two abortions a year, regularly perpetrated by a couple of local midwives, or by the women on themselves, since medical services in this field come high. You can tell when there has been one of these home-made operations by the sudden, mysterious, and often grave illness of some apparently healthy woman. It is announced as "heart disease" or something similar; but once the woman is up and around she is apparently able to work just as hard as ever, in spite of her heart.

In short, abortion is the secretly accepted method of birth control in Sleepy Hollow.

9.

Not long ago a Mrs. A of my acquaintance who believes in Birth Control, and practices it herself, sympathized with a Mrs. B who lived in Sleepy Hollow, who had a nice little family, and who would be better off if she had no more babies. Mrs. A sent Mrs. B to the nearest Birth Control clinic. The results were entirely satisfactory. Soon after this Mrs. B told Mrs. A that she had a friend whom she thought she should take to the clinic. "She badly needs help," said Mrs. B, "because she had two abortions in the last year, and her health is a wreck in consequence."

Then Mrs. A, who related this to me later, said to her, "Why not spread the idea among all the women you know—all your neighbors?"

"Oh," said the woman, "that wouldn't do at all. Why, if they knew about you and me going to that clinic *we just wouldn't be respectable around here.*"

Such is the hold of "religion" on people who ought to be at liberty to think and act sanely and be free from their superstitions. As a producer of immorality, wretchedness, crime, and black tragedy, I know few anti-social agencies that equal the record in mischief making that can be chalked up against this "religious" notion of birth control by "continence." The record of Alcohol as a wrecker of human happiness is lily-white beside it. Talk about "interfering with nature"! There isn't a more sickening page in our social history than this record of the mischief done by the churches, Catholic and Protestant, in *their* attempt to interfere with nature.

Unhappily, the mischief does not stop with the growth, among "religious" people, of disastrously large families supported by inadequate incomes, in squalor, poverty, and actual want. It extends its curse, through the Comstock Obscenity Law, to people in this country who do want to practice Birth Control, and who are ignorant, because of that law, of how to go about it.

It does not satisfy these clerical fanatics and Bible worshipers that they are bringing down disaster on members of their own churches who choose to submit to such gross superstitions; they must go outside their churches, and impose their ideas on people over whom, by the fundamental law of this land, they have no control whatever. It was such agencies that passed the Obscenity Law in the first place; and it is they who are fighting tooth and nail to-day every effort to repeal or modify that law.

Thus, by means of an organized fanaticism that is vicious in its intolerance and degraded in its superstition, these forces have succeeded in imposing on the American people as a whole an ignorance of Birth Control which is injurious, and which wrecks the health and the morals of thousands. I know women who have been injured for life, not merely by abortion, but by the use, without instruction, of strong chemicals for contraceptive purposes. I know others who have met with the disaster of unwanted pregnancy, through the ineffectiveness of the mechanical devices they have used, when another baby meant nothing short of tragedy.—This in a "free" country!

What is the purpose of it all? How can we tolerate such conditions in a country where people are supposed to be free to order their own lives, and where they are supposed to have no right to impose their private opinions on others?

Every church has a right to forbid its members the use of birth control if it wishes; and its members have a right to submit to such ecclesiastical prohibitions if they wish to do so; but that this thing should reach out and control the lives of persons who accept no such authority, and who yet find themselves ruled by it, through the introduction of ecclesiasticism into the law of the land,—this is an outrage so monstrous that I see red when I think about it.

10.

Birth Control is, of course, intimately linked up with the whole problem of eugenics. I commend, therefore, to the attention of those who think that people can be legislated into heaven, this passage which I find in a recent newspaper interview given by the English scientist, Professor J. B. S. Haldane:

"I should be inclined to regard eugenics itself as an ethical principle—the principle that those likely to produce satisfactory children should recognize it as their duty to have them, while those who, for example, possess an hereditary taint, should regard it as their duty to refrain from reproducing.

"This principle is being gradually recognized, and I look for far more important results from its recognition than from any schemes of eugenics run by the State or any other organization. At present the problem is not so much of any one great discovery relating to eugenics as of the accumulation of a mass of knowledge which will enable people to forecast accurately the probable offspring of a given union, *and thus to bring biological motives into marriage just as economic motives are now brought.*"

Here is a sound ethical principle on which all human affairs should, as far as possible, be ordered. It is strange that such pronouncements should be coming from a great scientist, and that faith in the dignity and possibilities of human nature should be manifested from such a source, when many of the churches, which are supposed beyond all others to uphold the dignity of man, should be proceeding wholly on the theory that we are a fallen race, incapable of ethical conduct into which we are not forced by laws and prohibitions. Which is the more exalted conception?

The question is often asked to-day, why has the Church lost its hold and its authority? The answer is easy. This is one of the most religious ages in the history of the world. Men hunger and thirst for real religion. But the church is much too busy with superstitious poppycock to be interested in religion of any sort.

It is leaving that to scientists, and to other people who are interested in getting at the truth. I speak now of certain churches as organizations, and of the conservative forces that rule them—not of the *individuals* among the clergy and the laity who *are* interested in the truth. I recognize, too, that there are certain churches which do not attempt to interfere with the lives and consciences of their members. But they are still in the minority.

II.

Here is a letter from a woman who wants to know where she can obtain contraceptive information. It is typical of scores of such letters that reach me from every part of the United States, and it tells such a poignant story that I present it here with such alterations in the text and signature as will effectively protect the writer from possible identification:

"DEAR JUDGE LINDSEY:

"It seems to me that you pass too lightly over a very vital point in your plan [of Companionate Marriage]; in fact the whole idea of Companionate Marriage rests on this point, the ability to control conception, to have or not have babies at will.

"You assume that the knowledge of how to do that, without injury to health, or interference with the act of coition and the pleasure and benefit to be derived therefrom, is easily available to all men and women who desire to acquire it. I assure you that it is not so. I know, and of course every one does, that it is possible to prevent babies from being born, and that many people, married and single, employ various means to that end, but I am assured that *there is no means* of preventing conception that does not lay one open to one of three risks: injury to your own health and the vital organs, loss of pleasure in coition, and the various ills consequent on such loss, or the ever-present possibility of murdering an already formed baby.

"I have been to see four competent and reliable physicians on this matter, and my husband has consulted two others, and they all agree. They all said that the fact that many people who practice birth control are in *apparent* good health and living natural, happy lives, means nothing at all, because all members of the medical profession who have to deal with such people know that sooner or later they come to grief, that many an operation that is listed as appendicitis, or gall stones, or some such disease, is really to clean up the damage done by contraceptives. They will cite examples from their own experience until they make you so scared that you go away shaking in your boots.

"Now where is the catch? Are these men all liars? Or don't they *know* their business, which is custody of people's health?

"*I* have had four babies in six years, and am now pregnant again. We are still young enough to have ten or twelve more children if we continue to live 'naturally,' provided I don't die in the meanwhile, and we are both in despair. It is out of the question for us to consider living together as 'sister and brother,' which is what our pastor advises. We are still young, passionate, and too accustomed to seek comfort in each other to change now.

"My husband is as good and kind and considerate as any one in the world could be, and still it taxes him to the limit of his endurance to refrain from intercourse for the few weeks before and after the advent of a baby that are required for my health and comfort; and I could no more refuse him when he does come to me than I could refuse him a drink if he were thirsty, or food if he were hungry. I love him too dearly. Neither of us ever had any sex experience except with each other, and when we married it was because it seemed to be the only simple, easy, thing to do; we never thought of anything else. And then this tidal wave of babies! They are lovely children, healthy, handsome, intelligent. But they are literally consuming their parents alive. We adore them, and would not lift a finger to harm them either before or after they are born, but *we don't want so many,* and particularly I don't want them *so fast.* I am really physically *sick* about two-thirds of the time, so that the tasks that would ordinarily seem easy, the little mishaps that happen now and then, all assume gigantic proportions. It's like swimming against the tide, I strain every nerve and muscle, and still I am slipping back all the time; there are more and more things left undone, and it is more and more of an effort to do what I do. We have no time and not much inclination for reading, recreation, social intercourse, church, politics, or any of the things we used to be so vitally interested in. My husband is a ——. We had great hopes that he would be an independent —— one of these days, but the day seems farther and farther away. He doesn't dare risk a penny, he can't seem to accumulate any capital; every half day he has off is a calamity.

"We built ourselves a lovely home, but with this next baby coming I fear we will have to let it go. Even by renting part of it we cannot meet expenses. We used to study in the evenings together; now we wash didies. That our mutual affection and respect have so far withstood the strain and disillusion seems to me to be really a miracle. But how long can it continue? What will we do if he gets sick, or I get sicker? What will we do when the children get bigger and need so many more things? We are of the great American middle class in which education is considered essential; we *couldn't* put the youngsters to work to help us out. All the men on my side of the family followed professions . . . in which brains and education were first. My husband's family were almost all farmers, with a preacher here and there, but all were as well educated as they could, by effort and perseverance, manage to be. He and I are both college educated. I was a —— before we married and made good money. . . . We have taken courses in —— and ——, and have a natural bent in that direction. We have always felt that we could do much *together*, but with every baby our dream of coöperation and achievement grows more remote.

"Now this letter isn't just an aimless complaint. It presents a problem, in the light of our own personal experience, that directly hinges on birth control. If we *could* know that after this next baby comes there wouldn't be any more, that we could live together lovingly and naturally and be free of the fear of impaired health, frazzled nerves and guilty consciences that are supposed to accompany the use of contraceptives, and that I could get on my feet again, out of this nightmare of nausea, backache, swollen feet, and all the rest of it, and have five years or so of plain sailing, I feel we could make a real success of our marriage, and of parenthood too.

"You are a prominent man. You have already taken a stand on this question that clearly indicates your convictions. *Why don't you challenge the medical profession to come out in the open about this matter?* If *you* know a means of birth control that is perfect, and that is being practiced by hundreds and thousands of couples, as your statements imply that you do, *why don't you proclaim the right of all to the same knowledge?* Why is it criminal in the eyes of the law to impart such information? Why in the name of pity, if such knowledge exists, are desperate women in this enlightened land resorting to abortion? Why, if there is such a means, should knowledge of it be denied to us? Surely we have done our duty and are entitled to a breathing spell in which to catch up with the ever-increasing financial burden, to take care of those babies we already have, to take a little thought for ourselves, to lay up a store against the future.

"Why should some of the doctors and the priests take the stand they do? Every one acknowledges that big families are impracticable now. Every one deplores the propagation of the unfit that goes on around us, and still if you go to the only source of reliable physiological information that most of us have, and ask the family doctor to tell you some way to prevent conception, he will not only refuse you, but will hold over your head the threat and menace of untold horrors to come if you 'meddle' with natural functions, and your pastor will condemn you to everlasting hell for the murder of untold numbers of innocents. Your physician will inform you that some apparently happy neighbor had a malignant tumor from an infection, another is sterile from gonorrhea, another has regular miscarriages due to the use of medicines, another is incapable of coition because the tissues are scarred and ruined by strong drugs and acids —and so on and so on, until, as I said before, you look with suspicion and distrust on all childless people.

"Now I must get back to my work, which has been piling up in an alarming manner while I took time off to write this letter. Among the hundreds that you undoubtedly will receive, kindly consider it seriously, for it seems to me that your whole excellent plan of Companionate Marriages, as well as the solution of many another problem, rests on your ability to present such a means of Birth Control to the world, as will satisfy the most scrupulous, be unassailable by even the doctors and the clergy, and acceptable for publication, and promulgation, even through our most pure United States Mail. . . .

"I have never before written anything of this sort, and such a radical departure from my conventional mode of conduct frightens me a little.

"Very sincerely yours,

"VIRGINIA ELLIS."

12.

My answer to Mrs. Ellis and to every other woman who wants to know what has already been accomplished in the way of scientific contraception is to write to the Birth Control League, at 104 Fifth Avenue, New York City.

This organization, under the leadership of Mrs. Margaret Sanger, has developed methods of contraception which, *when intelligently applied,* are practically one hundred per cent safe. These methods show about 2 per cent of clinical failure; and all of the failures are found among women so ignorant and so lacking in normal intelligence, that they cannot follow effectively even the simple instructions they receive.

I cannot indicate the methods here simply because it is against the law for me to do so. I can say this, however: that the methods recommended by the League as most safe and effective involve a medical examination and the prescription by the physician of a mechanical device adapted to the physiological peculiarities of the individual case. What works perfectly in one case might fail utterly in another. The League employs in its clinics the services of physicians who, by long practice, have become exceedingly expert in this work. Most of the physicians so employed are women.

The methods recommended by the Birth Control League are not harmful or irritant in their effects. This is due largely to the skill of the League physicians in prescribing what is needed. The mishaps with which Mrs. Ellis was threatened by the evidently very conservative physicians she consulted would be impossible under this technique. This is not, of course, to say that the system is fool-proof. Its use assumes that instructions will be followed.

13.

Another point that should be emphasized here is that the psychological disadvantages of this new contraceptive technique are slight, much more so than those of any other known method. It merely means taking a little trouble beforehand; and this inconvenience is offset by entire peace of mind and freedom from anxiety afterward. I know couples who, after years of dissatisfaction with ordinary contraceptive methods, have rehabilitated their love-life together by this new technique. It has thus prevented many a divorce.

On this psychological problem involved in contraception, there are common misunderstandings, even on the part of some physicians. Dr. Morris Fishbein, in his book "The Medical Follies," for example, makes the point that no method of Birth Control has yet been perfected, "that is, physiologically, psychologically, and biologically sound in both principle and practice. . . . The difficulty," he adds, "lies primarily in the imperfection of the devices themselves, and in the peculiar psychology of the lower stratum of society which the birth control enthusiasts insist must be brought to the light, lest its descendants inherit the earth.

"Every practical psychologist," continues Dr. Fishbein, "knows that such folk are not at all interested in the welfare of the United States as it may be one hundred years from now. The desire to plan for posterity—and that posterity not of the next succeeding generation, but of four generations ahead—connotes a high order of intelligence and public spirit. The impulse to sacrifice the pleasure of the moment for the profit of a far-removed future is within the moral scope, and always will be, of very few men, and perhaps of an even smaller number of women. . . .

"Little is said by such propagandists about the psychological aspects of birth control, but this, obviously, is a matter of greatest importance. The psychological factor, indeed, is largely responsible, not only for the frequent failure of all the common devices when applied under even the best of conditions, but also for the reluctance to utilize them, imperfect as they are, in the lower ranks of society. It would be possible here, if it were a popular, rather than a scientific, consideration of the subject, to picture a nocturnal scene between a male of the lower stratum, somewhat stimulated by alcohol, and the feminine partner of his misery, weary after a day at the washtub or scrubbing the halls of an apartment house. The mental status of the two, it must be plain, are hardly such as to lead them to pause for a consideration of their own difficulties, much less of the economic problems of the twenty-first century. The stimulated emotions of the male, coupled with the fatigued inhibitions of the female, are little likely to encourage a recourse to complex mechanisms in the name of humanity."

My comment on this is that Dr. Fishbein appears to have overlooked the fact that people who do practice contraception are not thinking of the twenty-first century but of the immediate, practical contingency of avoiding the birth of children they, for one reason or another, do not want. The assumption that the lower orders of society are supposed to practice Birth Control, if at all, in order to avoid burdening a future civilization with the presence of their descendants, has never been advanced, so far as I know, by any advocate of Birth Control, save as a secondary motive that could have only a minor influence on conduct in this matter. The day will come, doubtless, when we may be able to persuade the really unfit to submit to sterilization which would not interfere with their love-life. In the meantime, the unfit usually have a strong economic reason for wanting few or no children. They will resort to Birth Control because of that.

The point is that women of the type so graphically described by Dr. Fishbein have a very acute and urgent personal interest in avoiding pregnancy. It is an impulse of self-preservation. Such women live in constant terror of more babies, more drudgery, and more mouths to feed out of resources miserably inadequate. Hundreds and hundreds of such women come to the Birth Control clinics for help; they come oftentimes speaking foreign languages among themselves; and one nurse who happened to understand several of these immigrant tongues relates that these women told things to each other that they did not reveal to the doctors; and that some of the experiences they related, not knowing that she understood their language, made her blood run cold. Many of these women have husbands who, at the behest of their clerical advisers, are violently opposed to Birth Control, and will not knowingly permit their wives to use contraceptives.

But the devices given them by the Birth Control League are of such a kind that they can use them, if they wish, without the knowledge of their husbands. Many of them do just that. Thus, they are able to determine, *as they have a right to do,* when, and how often, they are to undertake maternity.

These methods place the whole matter in the hands of women; and by making consistent use of them they can, with very little trouble, and without the knowledge of their husbands, if necessary, have complete control of this whole matter.

The only psychological disadvantage involved in the use of this technique is the fact that in cases where the device was not regularly made use of on retiring, delay and preparation would become necessary at times when such interruption would be least welcome. Aside from that, this technique is psychologically an advantage rather than a disadvantage, since it frees the mind from the fear and anxiety that poison the love-life of so many persons.

The Birth Control League, I am sure, would be the last to claim that its present methods are perfect. It is the hope of all connected with this work that something even better will be discovered in time. Perhaps the day will come when the practice of contraception will involve no more delay and inconvenience than would the swallowing of a pill. But in the meantime, the technique already found constitutes an enormous advance on anything hitherto known; and it would satisfactorily solve the problem presented, both by Mrs. Ellis and by others who are in her position.

It must be remembered that up to the time when the Birth Control League undertook clinical and laboratory research in this field a few years ago, virtually nothing of the kind had ever been attempted. Thus the whole science of contraception is still in its infancy.

The reason no such research had ever been attempted was that Birth Control had been pronounced immoral by the Church. It was, moreover, against the law to impart contraceptive information. More than that, the medical profession, as a whole, took the stand that it was "unethical"—not so bad as abortion, but similar to it—and so most doctors would not impart contraceptive information—though a few did so to patients in their confidence.

But the amazing thing about it is that very few physicians to-day know much more about scientific contraception than the average layman. Students go through our medical colleges without having been taught a thing about this subject, save what they can pick up as any layman would pick it up. I have before me right now a letter from a regular licensed M.D. in a town not far from Denver, who asks me, if you please, for information on this subject, admitting that he knows little or nothing about it. This amply explains the sort of advice given Mrs. Ellis by the physicians she consulted. They evidently had the stock information concerning inadequate methods, and that was all they knew about it. And apparently they hadn't had the energy and enterprise to go to an organization as unorthodox as the Birth Control League for information.

Any physician can obtain that information and specific expert instruction, if he wants it. For many women, who can't get to a Birth Control Clinic, the best course, doubtless, would be to seek out a skilled and progressive physician who would act on the suggestion.

The Birth Control League is establishing clinics in various cities all over the country, as rapidly as means are available, and as local opposition, *both medical and clerical,* can be overcome. The quickest way to overcome such opposition in most communities would be for the intelligent women of the community to demand that the local physicians participate in the formation of a Birth Control Clinic, whether the local self-appointed spokesmen of the Almighty approve of it in behalf of Deity or not.

The League sends its physician to such places on invitation; and thereafter Birth Control becomes available in such communities under medical auspices, and subject of course to State law. We have such a clinic in Denver, for example; and under the Colorado law, physicians are permitted to prescribe contraceptives. Of course the federal law would prevent a Colorado physician from imparting such information outside of the State. Mrs. Ellis wrote from a town which is not far from a city where I think there is a Birth Control Clinic, which she can reach by a short railroad journey.

In New York State the Birth Control League is now able, by virtue of a court decision, to prescribe contraceptives when the health of a woman would be threatened by the birth of another child. "Health" is interpreted in psychological as well as physical terms; and thus the League finds itself able to give help to a large number of women who need such aid.

Such help, given always under conditions that are within the law, is available only to *married* women who may need it, as I have said, for reasons of *"health,"* physical or psychological.

14.

But in my judgment, this help ought to be available to all women who ask for it, married or unmarried, good health or bad health. I do not believe in coercing the unmarried into virtue by keeping them ignorant of scientific facts they have as good a right as anybody to know. There are thousands of persons who think Birth Control should be available to the married but *not* to the unmarried; and I believe the Birth Control League itself accepts that extremely pious theory. I hope, however, since the League is already so enlightened and liberal in many directions, that it will presently outgrow this mid-Victorian limitation. There is no organization in the world that should have less use for censorship or that should be less inclined to supervise the "morals" of other people, or to uphold or advocate such supervision.

I get scores of letters from good people who anxiously express the hope that I am not advocating the imparting of contraceptive information to the unmarried, or the placing of contraceptives within their reach. This interesting tendency to believe that the way to make people "good" is to trick and coerce them into conventionality, by means of enforced ignorance, seems very difficult to eradicate. Such legalized fostering of ignorance promotes the most dangerous kind of bootlegging, and it cannot be justified in a free country, even if it were effective. It acts in the interest of immorality— not of morality. As a matter of fact, it is not effective. I know of no worse tyranny than a censorship on knowledge.

In any event, this attempted censorship does not work. Youth knows about Birth Control anyhow. The more we try deliberately to deprive them of knowledge in such matters the more they are determined to know. And if we persist in such an attitude they will know in spite of us. The unmarried can obtain contraceptive information at any drug store; and since they can, it would be far better for them to have really scientific information rather than the very imperfect and incomplete knowledge which the average drug clerk can impart. Moreover, the proper application of the best contraceptive information requires a medical examination—which is one thing not available at the modern drug store. Of course, I do not mean by this attitude to encourage the improper use of contraceptives any more than certain eminent Catholic clerics mean to encourage the misuse of alcohol because they oppose prohibition laws.

My thought here is that if we would face these facts, and throw this information open to everybody, then thousands of tragedies of disease and unwanted pregnancy could be avoided, both in and out of marriage. The proper—the only proper and effective way to foster morality is, not by enforced ignorance, but by real religion, education and enlightenment, culture and good taste. When will we learn this lesson? The whole of human history proves it, and yet we persist in the other stupid course.

I don't believe in poisoning alcohol to prevent people from drinking it—on pain of probable death or blindness if they do; and no more do I believe in disseminating by law the stupefying and stultifying poison of Ignorance, nor in *blindfolding* people by law with the threat that if they take certain forbidden steps—being blindfolded —they will fall over a precipice they are not permitted to see.—In fact, I believe it would be an excellent thing if the many persons in this country who are looking after the virtue of their neighbors would mind their own business.

CHAPTER IX

LEGISLATING FOR THE COMPANIONATE

I.

I HAVE been asked many times what specific measures I would take if it were in my power, by passing a law or a group of laws, to establish Companionate Marriage in the State of Colorado.

My answer is that there is no need for a Bill to establish Companionate Marriage as a separate thing, either in Colorado or in any other state, because we already have the Companionate as one of the privileges of present-day marriage—a privilege which merely needs to be recognized and made legal. The fact that contraception and divorce by mutual consent (collusion) are illegal does not particularly matter so long as people have the good sense to practice them anyway. But having them illegal does undoubtedly make needless difficulties and tragedies in marriage which could readily be avoided if these two remedies were within the easy reach of all persons. The present prohibitions on Birth Control impose ignorance or *half-knowledge* on thousands; and thus they have the evil effect of leading to the practice of much contraception that is unscientific, ineffective, risky, and often dangerous; and when such contraception fails, then abortion follows, not occasionally but in literally *millions* of cases.

Society *must* find relief from the population problem. The pressure is terrific. And if it cannot find it in humane ways, then it will find it in inhumane ways, and by the murder of unborn children if necessary. I know many very excellent persons who have been driven by their fears to this murderous extreme.—The poor, the ignorant, the economically inefficient—in a word, the very persons who most need to know how to practice Birth Control, are the very ones who find it most difficult to obtain effective scientific knowledge of the subject. Thus they are tricked, as it were, by society into furnishing its unwanted progeny, while the more intelligent regulate their families by their individual preferences and economic necessities.

There is no need, I repeat, for any separate law that would change the present status of marriage or alter its fundamentals. It would not even be necessary to change the method of getting married. Companionate Marriage *is* present marriage. What is needed is a law to legalize the already existing privileges and practices of marriage, and place them and their social benefits within the reach of all—even of the poor and the ignorant, who most need them.

2.

Here is a brief outline of the three essential Legislative enactments or Bills I have in mind:

1. A Bill for an Act to repeal the present stupid laws against Birth Control, and to legalize and regulate the right of Birth Control clinics to carry on and give advice to married women, who might make use of the information or not, as they chose; leaving it to their personal judgment as to whether they should remain childless or not, and if so, how long.

This would not be the grudging permission which at present allows a physician or the Birth Control League to impart Birth Control knowledge to a woman when it would endanger her health, psychologically or physically, to have a child. Such information, imparted under such conditions, is a mere subterfuge which enables the physician to remain safe from prosecution on the charge of breaking the laws against the imparting of contraceptive information. It is an absolutely necessary and justifiable dodge for avoiding persecution by busybodies who are not content to abstain from the use of Birth Control themselves, and who insist on foisting their personal opinions on everybody else.

Let me say again in this connection that I haven't the slightest objection to Roman Catholics and others abstaining from birth control themselves, if they think it sinful. What I cannot understand is their fixed determination to force this fanaticism on the American nation. This government is not a theocracy. They have no right to try to read their theology into laws intended to govern people who do not subscribe to that theology, and who cannot legally—under the Constitution—be forced to do so. These opinions regarding the supposedly evil results of Birth Control are opinions, nothing more; and they are *minority* opinions at that. This country has too long been ruled by organized and fanatical minorities; and it is time to call a halt. It is not so much a question of my being for or against the use of Birth Control as it is the right of people to their freedom of choice as to whether they will or will not use it.

2. A second Bill to Amend the laws relating to Divorce. This bill would add a clause providing that "where couples are childless, and where the efforts of the magistrate to bring about a reconcilement have failed, and where the couple mutually desire a divorce, the divorce shall be granted without further expense or needless delay." This would require no lawyer, any more than getting married requires a lawyer. A Judge can marry people, and by this law he could, under the prescribed conditions, unmarry them.

3. A third Bill to regulate the property status of the divorce. It would deal with the right of the wife to support and alimony. It would withhold or grant such support and alimony according to the conditions of the case. For instance, if a woman were in good health, and able to work, and to support herself, there would ordinarily be no alimony.—*Such a bill might provide that the property rights of childless couples should, at the discretion of the court, ordinarily be the same as the property rights of single persons.*

In this connection let me emphasize what I have already pointed out, that one very common condition in Companionate Marriage would be that both the husband and wife would go on earning a livelihood, exactly as before marriage. Naturally, however, this would not always be the case. It would depend on the inclination and desire of the couple, on the temperament and capabilities of the woman, etc. Some women find their most effective place in life in making a really happy and lovely home for the man they love. Such a home increases the man's economic efficiency and his value to society. The arrangements in marriage must depend on the situation and on the people; and so must the question of property and alimony. Equity and common sense would have to be the determining factor so far as the court decision was concerned. Rigid applications of rigid laws could have no place in such a system—and "legal minded" judges ought to keep out of, or be kept out of, such work. They would merely throw a monkey-wrench into the machine.

3.

The passing of three such bills, as roughly sketched here, would establish the Companionate, *as we now illegally have it,* on a legal basis. It would mark it off sharply from the procreative marriage, and it would justify us in calling childless marriage the "The Companionate" and procreative marriage "The Family." This nomenclature has long been used by sociologists to distinguish the two. *"The Companionate"* and *"The Family."* I suggest these terms for general use.

Since the passage of these bills would in no way change the fundamental status and practice of marriage as we have it, and would merely make the institution flexible and better adapted to the needs of society, the only objections that could be made to these bills would be the already operative objections on the part of a minority of our population, to Birth Control and divorce by mutual consent. If this minority continued not to believe in these two things, they have the inalienable right not to practice them. If it would make them feel any better, we could pass a law giving them that liberty.

I propose that these three laws would be *immediately practicable,* if not in Colorado, then surely in some other state or states. The Legislature of Nevada, for example, has recently passed a law reducing the time necessary for establishing residence in Nevada to three months. Why three months? It's a mere camouflage, in line with other hypocrisies of our marriage code. Why not call it a day? And why not at the same time establish the Companionate in Nevada by passing three such Bills as I am here suggesting. It would be a social experiment of the utmost importance; and it should be undertaken at once by at least three progressive states, one in the Far West, one in the Middle West and one in the East—so that the Companionate would be within easy reach of all who want it.

4.

I have a letter from a Chicago attorney who suggests that a practicable way to legislate for Companionate Marriage would be to alter certain already existing laws. I quote:

"The childless marriage, such by prenuptial agreement, is here. The dissolution of this by mutual consent is here for all who are willing to 'frame' the evidence. The evidence is rarely 'framed' until all property questions are settled by agreement. The 'framing' ordinarily gets the divorce and eliminates the alimony.

"If the law makes this divorce more respectable by making it more honest, and puts the truth-teller upon at least an equal footing with the perjurer, is not this about all it can do for this situation?

"And is not this done by two relatively simple statutory changes, *i.e.:* (1) Make the divorce easier by shortening the 'abandonment' where there are no children,—say first to one year and, as public opinion permits, to, say, six months; and (2) abolish alimony where the wife has never borne children, or perhaps leave alimony to the discretion of the court, where marriage has lasted, say, three or five years?"

To these very interesting suggestions my correspondent adds, "Must not social usage evolve any further betterment of present conditions? And can it not be trusted to do so?"—To which I answer Yes to both questions. It would seem evident, however, that such changes can be hastened if their desirability can be pointed out to the public. That is one of my objects in the writing of this book.

No provision is made in the above suggestions for legalized *scientific* Birth Control. This would be an unfortunate omission, so far as the Companionate is concerned, because the methods of contraception in present general use are often ineffective, dangerous to health, and psychologically unsatisfactory. Bootleg birth control would never meet the requirements of Companionate Marriage.

5.

I understand that a bill for the establishment of Companionate Marriage was recently proposed in the California legislature. A bill for the establishing of the Companionate on a separate basis from other marriage would be likely to fail in any legislature; but three such bills as I have outlined, for the modification of marriage as we have it, might, I think, readily appeal to the common sense of any progressive and courageous legislature. It has been my hope that the legislature of Colorado might lead the way in this, as it did long ago in the establishing of the Juvenile and Family Court of Denver— a pioneer step; but as the political issue is rather acute where I am concerned, I fear such a result would be impossible for the present. At this writing the Colorado Legislature, many members of which were largely chosen and elected by the Ku Klux Klan, has before it a bill, sponsored by the Klan and by certain of the Roman Catholic clergy, for the abolition of the Juvenile Court; and it is now a question, not of whether this Legislature would adopt the Companionate, but of whether its Klan influences will so much as permit my official work in Colorado to continue on any basis. It is possible that by the time these words are in print, I shall be cut adrift by these forces from the work I founded.—And so, as I say, I hope the proposed measures will appeal to the common sense of other legislatures.

Once such laws were passed, that would by no means be the end of the changes to be made. The Companionate, once established on such a foundation, would grow and perfect itself as an institution along the lines I have indicated in earlier chapters of this book. For example, there should, in time, be a law requiring medical examination for all persons who marry, whether for the Companionate or the Family. There are persons who, by reason of infectious disease, should not be permitted even the Companionate relationship till fully cured—much less procreative marriage, into which they can now enter without let or hindrance. There are still others who might properly enter the Companionate, but who should never undertake to bring children into the world.

Under such a system of medical examination, I think it might some day become perfectly practicable for Society to expect people to confine themselves to the Companionate unless pronounced by a magistrate to be both *hygienically* and *economically* fit to undertake the Family. *I do not say that there should necessarily be a coercive law to this effect.* I think the fewer laws we have the better. But I do believe public opinion would establish at least an unwritten custom of decency and right living in this matter which would be effective in most cases. A coercive law would be objectionable if only because people it restrained would probably want to violate it; whereas the restraints of decency and good taste and fair play and the desire to see children get a fair chance in life, would operate sufficiently well. I think there are very few persons who would want to bring into the world children they clearly should not have. What they must have, and do insist on having, is a normal sex life. Parenthood is not a necessary part of that. And if the parent urge be strong, there are always children to be obtained by adoption.

In this connection let me say that I have found by long experience that most people want children. There is a common impression among people who are alarmed by the Birth Control idea that if everybody understood the technique of contraception, nobody would have children, and the race would die out. These people don't know human nature. It simply does not work out that way. And obviously, persons who don't want children are the very ones who ought not to have them. I should think the absurdity of forcing the human race to propagate by law would be so evident that even the solemn moralists would see that it is nonsense. If the human race has to be kept going by means of Obscenity Laws it had better die.

6.

I have a courteous letter from a minister in a Southern city who tells me that he sees two objections to my views on the Companionate. His first objection is that many people would marry with the intention and thought of quitting if the relationship does not suit them, *and without making any real, unselfish effort to work out their problem,* since there would be no pressure from without to compel them to do this. His second objection is that couples would *"contract marriage for pleasure, and with no recognition of the divine purpose of bearing children."* He adds, "It is one thing to believe in a home with a limited number of children, and quite another to believe so much in self-indulgence and ease that children are not wanted at all. I have never been able to see very worthy motives in marriage that coldly determines that there shall be no children."

I was very grateful for that letter. It was written in a fair and kindly spirit, which is by no means always the case with the letters I receive from orthodox Christian sources; and at the same time it states clearly two points which I have perhaps not yet met specifically enough.

Let me take the last objection first. From my long experience with all kinds of people I can positively assure this critic that the assumption that most persons would not have children if they didn't have to is an error. There are a few of whom this is true, but only a few. And obviously it is better that such persons should find their happiness and their usefulness without reproach in some field other than parenthood.

I find a tendency, regrettably frequent among the clergy, to assume not merely that people shirk parenthood if they can, but also that they must be induced to have children, either by legally imposed ignorance or by religious persuasion on grounds of "duty." People who have children ought to want them. If they don't want them they are not likely to make a success of parenthood. But an overwhelming majority of people certainly do want children and love children; and this desire on their part is not a "recognition of the divine purpose of bearing children," either. It is natural. They love children and want them about. That is far better and more generous than "duty." This assumption that people never *want* to do what is *right,* and that right acting is accomplished from a stern sense of "duty," and is made possible only by divine Grace, has some very unfortunate effects on our national habits of thought. The doctrine of Total Depravity has done enough harm in the world, and it is time to throw it overboard.

7.

Now for the first objection, that people would enter the Companionate with the intention of quitting if they didn't like it.—Well, why shouldn't they? Why assume that that means that they have no intention or expectation of liking it, and that they will put forth no effort to make a go of the marriage?   Of course if such an objection applies at all it applies to any marriage.

But anybody who knows anything about human nature and human relationships and human ties knows that most normal people don't behave that way.   A tie grows up in the physical and spiritual associations of marriage that quickly acquires a tremendous power to hold the husband and wife together.   It binds them with hoops of steel— it is an emotional bond, and it is a bond of habit.   It develops in every marriage that is based on sympathy, love, and similarity of tastes.   Sometimes, so great is its power, it even develops in marriages where these fundamentals of congeniality are lacking.   I know many uncongenial couples who are held together by this bond. They may fight, but still they have a certain affection for each other.

The important thing here to understand is that a couple entering marriage may *be mistaken* in their belief that they have a basis for life-long union, and that *in the Companionate such persons would not have to bet so heavily on that belief.*   Thus they could take the chance more readily.   And why shouldn't they?   If they marry frankly facing the fact that they *may* be mistaken, why shouldn't they be that honest?   Is being honest with themselves and with each other so dangerous?   Must we eternally refuse to face the facts and possibilities of life?   There is *obviously* the danger of making a mistaken choice in *any* marriage.   Why should people not frankly admit this and provide against the danger by arranging a way to retrace their steps if need be?   What is immoral or irresponsible about that?   No more so than the immorality and irresponsibility found in present marriage, surely!

Persons who think honestly about these matters are far more likely to make a success of marriage than those who are not honest, who take refuge in orthodox hypocrisy, who have unwanted children from "duty," or from ignorance, or accident, and who stand ready to ruin each other's lives because, as this correspondent puts it, "Jesus insisted on the permanency of marriage."

What if he did?—Are we thereby forbidden to hold our own opinions on these matters?   I object to an infallible Book as much as I do to an infallible Pope.   As a matter of fact I don't believe Jesus ever taught anything of the sort about marriage.   His followers often stupidly misunderstood him, as the record confesses. They were always reading their own traditional views into his teachings, to his great annoyance. Why may they not have done it in this case?

What I vividly feel about Jesus is this: *He consistently struck at every ancient law which he found did not accord with human need.* He offended the orthodox religionists of his day, and he would offend them to-day if he were here to comment on present-day conditions.

He used common sense about the Sabbath, and they didn't like that; and he ridiculed their fault-finding by pointing out that they had never seen anything wrong in the fact that David and his followers ate shew bread from the altar when they were hungry; and that if a man's ox fell into a pit on the Sabbath Day he would not refrain from pulling the animal out on that day—not, it is implied, unless he were a manifest idiot, so gone in theological formalism that he lacked sanity. It is my belief that Jesus would unhesitatingly attack our present system of marriage if he were here. He would see—what every minister in the land is announcing with alarm from the pulpit—that too much of its fruit is evil.

Jesus had no reverence for tradition and authority, save as these proved their practical value to society. We should do well to follow his great example in this, rather than to be aping and quoting him like parrots, as if we couldn't think and act for ourselves.

8.

This constant reference to *authority* by religionists is the thing that more than any other weakens and discredits the church to-day, and puts it out of tune with reality, and deprives it of much of its power to do good.

Jesus expressly rejected this reference back to authority, and insisted on the compulsions of present reality. "Ye have heard how it was said by them of old time . . . but I say unto you . . ." Could one ask for a sharper contrast than is afforded in that "but." He came to fulfill the law, he said. True—he came to show that growth is the law; and to fulfill it as such; and to lay upon the human race the exhortation to *grow*.

Like every preëminent teacher, Jesus was concerned, not that his pupils should memorize his words or make magic formulas of them, but rather that they should *learn to think*. The plain implication of his teaching is that it is right for people to think honestly and independently for themselves. If the Christian Church would fearlessly apply that principle of independent and honest thought it would be a very different church; and it would have a message for the world the like of which it has not uttered in the two thousand years of its existence. A clergy like that would be a clergy really following the example of the Master. Jesus would be the first to condemn any slavish acceptance of the *letter* of the views he uttered. He would disapprove all attempts to make his utterances apply like a code of fixed rules to conditions he did not have to deal with or to talk about, since they did not then exist. "The letter killeth," he said, "but the spirit giveth life." It is the spirit of his teaching, not the letter of it, that gives life.

9.

One critic has raised a question by letter as to the "mutual consent" idea in the divorce of childless couples. "Suppose," he asks, "one member of the marriage wanted to quit while the other did not? If divorce were granted in the Companionate under such conditions, it would not really be by 'mutual consent,' would it?"

I admit that the words "mutual consent" are not quite broad enough to fit precisely. But I find no satisfactory substitute. Obviously, when it happened that one party wanted to continue the marriage while the other wanted its dissolution (that being the one assumption on which divorce is granted in our courts at present, by the way) the case would have to be decided by a Judge on its individual merits.—I have seen many such cases. Each is different. Each is a problem in itself. Sometimes a psychiatrist can straighten the couple out and bring them to a basis of understanding. Often I can do it myself. Usually the party who wants the divorce would be glad to change his or her mind if the conditions of the marriage could be made bearable. But sometimes it is impossible to alter the fact that one wants the divorce and that the other does not.

Broadly speaking, it seems hardly conceivable that it could often be wise to maintain a marriage, especially a childless marriage, when it had ceased to be *marriage by mutual consent*. Lacking mutual consent in marriage, then the one alternative in logic and in fact would seem to be divorce by mutual consent. So why not call it that?

These tragedies happen. Unrequited love is common. A wife clings to a husband who no longer loves her; or a husband to a wife who is indifferent to him. No laws can change this; nor can such situations as a rule be made better by forcing the unwilling partner to remain in the union. This might happen *sometimes;* but very seldom unless the unwilling one consents voluntarily to try again, or to sacrifice his or her own preference for what, in the circumstances, seems an adequate reason.

Usually divorce is indicated when a marriage has ceased to be "by mutual consent." It is hard to see how the unloved partner in such a union could reasonably or wisely or rightly withhold "consent" to such divorce, however painful it might be to yield it, except when the rights of children were involved, or else some other vital consideration. And even when there are children, divorce is often the wiser course.

10.

I have a very moving letter from a woman in a large western city whose husband has ceased to love her, and is, with her consent, living with another woman whom he does love. This couple have separated. They remain good friends, and the man contributes to the support of their child.

"Should I be ill," she says, "he would come to my aid immediately; and he does what he can for us financially.—I see them together; and, dear Judge, it is as if a knife were plunged into my very soul, the ache is so tremendous. But what is the use—what can I or should I do? Shall I give him a divorce (He says he doesn't want it) or shall I go on as I have been, hoping against hope that something will happen which will reunite us; or shall I seek happiness and love, the latter being essential to my nature, elsewhere?

"Oh, I know there is fault—chiefly in that I kept at him during our life together, to try and save, and be less extravagant—which he has interpreted as nagging and as mental cruelty."

Now there is a child in this marriage—a child who is being wronged and injured by this situation. Whether this couple could, for the sake of their child, make some compromise in marriage for the sake of providing that child with a home, is a question that depends on many complex things. There is no rule. I have in mind some women who have maintained a home under such conditions by allowing their husbands complete liberty in such outside attachments as the one mentioned here. I have known men who have done likewise in order to find a basis on which they could continue to live with their wives and give their children a home. I have known others, who having formed such outside attachments, gave them up, and who did it for the sake of their children, without grumbling because they thought that was the way to play the game. Sometimes the tensions that result from these compromises prove unendurable to the persons involved. Sometimes the compromise is successful. It depends on the personal equation.

This woman needed expert counsel in the beginning of her marriage. So do all persons who marry. It would be so much easier to prevent these domestic crashes than it is to repair the wreck after the crash comes. This woman began marriage ignorant of certain elementary facts about masculine psychology. Probably he was as ignorant of hers. Why not provide educational facilities to warn men and women against such pitfalls? If the wife had known what she knows now, she could probably have avoided this tragedy. If her husband clearly understood her present point of view, perhaps the situation could be mended even now. Who can say? When I mediate between such persons I can often make them see their common mistakes, and renew the foundations on which their love began. Suppose there were a House of Human Welfare to which this couple could have gone for counsel—or to which they could go now. It should be provided.

The point I want to make here is that no system can be devised that will insure absolutely against such situations. But the amount of that kind of thing could be reduced to a mere fraction of what it is at present if we managed marriage differently.

II.

In connection with divorce by mutual consent, the question of alimony and property is a grave one. This man, for instance, is not supporting his wife. He would be willing to support her, but his salary does not permit him to pay the maintenance cost of two households. His wife, in order to give him his liberty, undertakes to support herself. He contributes to the support of their child.— Formerly it would have been difficult for the wife to assume the rôle of economic independence which has made the present relation possible. Women have of late years become more and more capable of self-support.

A woman of thirty-five came to me the other day and asked me to require her husband to contribute to the support of their two children. They are a divorced couple. She is making $200 a month; and she explained with pride that she would not accept a cent from him for herself. "But I do think," she added, "that he should contribute his share to the support of the children. There is no reason why that should fall wholly on me."—Now if this marriage had been a Companionate, it would have been easily possible for the couple to go their ways without the complication of alimony or anything like it.

I encounter more and more of this spirit of independence among women. It is a very hopeful thing. Some accept alimony for a little while, to tide them over after divorce till they can dig in and make a living for themselves. They expect to work. But there are others, of course, who accept the old idea that it is the duty of the husband to support his wife, whether or no; that no married woman can fairly be expected to support herself; that support for life was clearly indicated and implied in the bond; and that they are at liberty to settle down in idleness, and live on alimony for the rest of their lives, or for as long as the man can be forced to provide money. Indeed, there is a gold-digger type of woman who marries with the express intention of acquiring an alimony income for life by way of the divorce court. It is easily done—under our present marriage code—especially if the man happens to be rich and able to afford the burden without special inconvenience to himself.

In many of these cases there is an evident injustice. And yet it is impossible to lay down a general rule about it. Each case has to stand on its merits. For instance, some women cannot make a living. Often a woman has been accustomed all her life to a standard of living such that if she had to depend on what she could earn, the change of standards forced upon her would amount to descent into bitter poverty and want. To refuse alimony in such a case might be sheer cruelty. A woman used to a ten thousand or twenty thousand dollar income, but incapable, by reason of her lack of training and capacity, of making more than the wages of a ribbon counter clerk, would be destroyed by such a change of standards.

It all comes down to the human approach. Such problems should be submitted to Judges with the power, and the specialized training, to make wise human adjustments which would be fair rather than merely legal. They would seldom be perfect. We have to do the best we can. But at present we make almost no attempt at such adjustments. Justice is not at present dispensed on that plan. It is dispensed rather on a plan that is largely indifferent to equity, and to human happiness. Its chief characteristic is that it arrives at decisions and disposes of human tangles, with a minimum of inconvenience to society. It is a machine processed thing, a flivver,—not a hand-made creation in human artistry, as it should be. Artistry takes time, trouble, and money to achieve; we haven't time for it. There is nothing so cheap on earth as human lives and human happiness; and nothing so costly as art. So why bother?

12.

There are some terrible abuses in the alimony system as we have it. In my own court, recently, I tried a case before a jury twice. A young man of thirty was sued for non-support by his wife, a woman of twenty-five. They had no children. The husband, at large expense to the County, was brought back from a distant state, under a charge of non-support and desertion. The first jury disagreed because of the fact that the man and woman were both equally able to earn a living. Some of the jury could not see why the woman should not support herself.

Then the County was put to the expense of a second trial, in which the jury convicted the man on the technical arguments of the District Attorney, which one of the jurors told me later they could not escape, though they thought them unjust.

I was then compelled to order the man to pay fifty dollars a month for the support of the young woman; and he is still doing it, as the law requires.

This is happening under a statute which does not distinguish between the Companionate and the Family; and which provides simply that he must support his wife—and children. The fact that there are no children makes no difference, nor does the fact that they are not living together, nor that she could wholly support herself. She is fastened on him like a leech.

A Denver lawyer told me the other day that he lately represented a man of forty in a divorce case against the man's wife, aged twenty-eight. It was shown at the hearing, on application of the wife's lawyer for attorney fees and alimony, that the wife was employed by a large corporation at a salary of $150 a month. The husband was making $200 a month. The court ordered the husband to pay the wife's lawyer $200 attorney fees, and to pay his wife *$75 a month alimony*. Thus the husband's income was reduced to $125 a month; and the wife's income was raised, without a cent of cost to her, to a clear $225 a month. The husband had to pay her lawyer and his own lawyer, the court costs—all in addition to $75 a month alimony. Figure out for yourself how long it took that man to get out of debt, and what chance he had of finding happiness again, either in or out of marriage.—There isn't a day that I don't come in contact with these pompous stupidities of the law.

These are some of the conditions that could be remedied if we had, for the Companionate at least, a different way of dealing with questions of property and alimony.

In Family Marriage the conditions would in some ways be different, and the arrangements could justly be made different, because Family Marriage would involve obligations deliberately entered into. It would have been entered into with the clear understanding that when a man and woman have brought children into the world, the happiness and welfare of those children come before any question of the personal happiness of their parents; and that only under the urge of clear necessity could they expect divorce while their children were of an age to need their care.   There would be reason and clear justice in expecting such persons to put their children first; and ordinarily they would see the reasonableness of it and would play the game that way.

13.

It is a curious and interesting fact about divorce as we have it that the courts have habitually put the happiness of the parents first, and have made the welfare and happiness of the children a secondary matter.   Couples with children can, under the present system, get a divorce as easily as if they had no children.   And when the divorce is granted, the children simply have to make the best of the situation, and get along as they can.   Material provision is made for them, but no spiritual provision.   They have a right to both their parents; yet they are deprived of that, and of a two-parent home.   The real victims of the divorce are thus the children, who are subject to spiritual deprivations which may warp and cripple them for life.

How can we expect anything else with marriage and divorce as we have them?   It is inevitable.   For we permit couples to rush into Family Marriage to gratify a sex urge which can find no other legitimate outlet.   They often mistake that urge for the basic congeniality which should be the basis of marriage.   Romantic love without such basic congeniality is like a plant without roots.   Lacking nourishment, or soil to grow in, it dies; whereas properly nourished, it might have lasted and flourished in a life-long union.

Too late the victims of such hasty marriages discover their mistake.   Then it often happens that some relief, through divorce, is essential; *and to hold such people together is often worse for the children they ought not to have had, than divorce*.   At best it is an evil choice; for though the divorce mill may be the lesser of two evils, and though it may release the parents, and create a sort of peace where there has been strife, yet it often grinds the lives and the future of the children to pulp.   And yet, we must have it; and we shall continue to need a great deal of it till there is some safeguard against the conception of children by people who don't really love each other well enough to stick.

The contention I am making for these changes in our marriage code is in reality nothing but a continuation, another step forward, in the fight I have been making through the last twenty-eight years for the welfare and betterment of the lot of women and children. It is a fight for the rights of women and children.

Years ago a great struggle was waged between progressive forces in this country, and the reactionary forces led by certain of the clergy, for divorce. Liberalism slowly won. Women then found it possible to obtain release from brutal husbands and protection and support for their children. It was not perfect, but it was better than what we had had.

To-day it continues as a struggle to obtain for women an equality of rights, in marriage—including the right to have wanted children, with the help of Birth Control, and the right to control their destiny as individuals who are no longer in slavery.

It continues as a struggle to give to every child the right to be wanted when it is conceived, the right to be well-born, of healthy parents who love each other, and the right to a home so well founded beforehand that divorce is not likely to touch it.

More than that, it is a struggle, through the rational application of Birth Control and the rational ordering of marriage to meet the *problem of overpopulation* which now menaces the world and threatens it with fresh wars. For war has, in the past, been in the last analysis a clumsy and brutal method of keeping within bounds the population of nations that had no methods of Birth Control save dangerous abortion and unnatural infanticide.

14.

The work of settling the Western hemisphere has, for a hundred years, made population control less necessary than formerly. But now the saturation point is being reached, and already the problem, even in this vast country, is becoming acute. The difficulty is not to populate the Earth, but to avoid an overpopulation that will out-strip the food supply and lead to wars as the only method of decimation. The howl about "Race Suicide" is specious nonsense. The breeding of children for quality rather than quantity, is the next needful step. And this, I believe, may best be achieved by Birth

Control used in conjunction with such a revision of our marriage code as is here suggested. Other factors enter in, of course, but a right ordering of marriage is basic.

When this is accomplished, one of the most important fights in history for the rights of women and children will have been won. There will be more to do; but that achievement will at any rate be posted to our credit.

The ideal of marriage suggested in this book seems to me to be considerably more exacting than that evidently preferred by some of my conservative critics—who hold that marriage as we have it is all right, *and that the trouble lies with the men and women who enter it*. This is a characteristically theological view of the matter. What I maintain is that people are rather likely to be pretty decent in their conduct if our institutions and our system of education would give them a chance.

In the ideal marriage we need to seek the union of two *free* personalities, which, without the imposition of any outside force, will by *slow degrees* knit together and grow spiritually into each other.

This is not to be done in a day; and it is not accomplished by an ecclesiastical fiat which, in a five-minute ceremony, performs the magic feat, the sacramental miracle of making two strangers into "one flesh." Time alone can work that miracle.

Nor can this process of growth together be forced. If there be no freedom and spontaneity in it, it fails. The life goes from it. The consciousness of coercive authority often inhibits and blasts it. The only stimulus that can make it grow is the stimulus that comes from within. With such stimulus, men and women will voluntarily make an *effort* to grow into each other's lives; they will surmount obstacles and difficulties and misunderstandings; they will together create between them a love that is real and lasting.—But introduce social coercion, and mutual ownership of each other, and the tyranny of jealousy! Instantly the element of moral responsibility and creative energy vanishes from the marriage.

Held together now by coercive traditions, the couple abandon the efforts at understanding which would have held them together. They become no longer responsible, but irresponsible, in their mutual dealings—because society has given them over each other a tyrannical power of ownership which breeds irresponsibility as the sun breeds maggots.

The very thing which many of my critics accuse me of trying to introduce into marriage was introduced into it long ago by their authoritarian doctrines. *They,* and their predecessors in reactionary thought, have put anarchy and hate and bondage into marriage; and now, quite rightly, they are alarmed when they see the fruit which *their* method and system is bringing forth. Some of us, tired of this ecclesiastical despotism, are minded to find other ways of dealing with this human problem.

15.

In the *freedom* of the Companionate, people would have a safe opportunity to grow into each other's lives; and they would accomplish that object only if the elements of such growth were really present in their union. If such elements were lacking, they would discover the mistake, part, and go their ways.

But if such growth *did* take place, then it would be a genuine thing, a real union. Having created that union of their lives out of the physical and spiritual intimacy of their association together in the Companionate, they would then usually be able to carry this union effectively over into the graver obligations, the greater strain and stress, the more exacting duties, and the *yet closer bond* of the Family—the procreative marriage.

Thus the Family Marriage would be a step forward—a short step, easily taken, and well prepared for. It would not be a blind plunge into the unknown. And the new joys and responsibilities, the new trials and difficulties, would all serve to bring the man and woman into the kind of union which is real marriage, and real monogamy—growing constantly, and hence capable of lasting their life through, for the reason that it would be *alive,* and neither dead nor static.—They would be ready for it; they would have slowly acquired the strength for it; they would not be trying to leap twenty feet before they had learned to leap ten.

The Family would thus crown their lives. It would have grown as grows the oak, slowly. The early Companionate would be a mere sapling beside it. And thus there would be created a home which would be a safe nest for children, and a sure refuge for the makers of it.

No marriage, I think, can reach its full possibilities without children, either natural or adopted. To those who have made a success of marriage, with happy children growing up around them, I need not say that here is indeed an overflowing cup.

I do not mean that Family Marriage is necessarily the most beneficial for all persons. There are those who are not individually adapted to it, and who can find a higher personal development, either without marriage, or with the Companionate. Such persons may need to be able to put forth their undivided energies in directions with which the Family is not compatible.

But for most of us it still holds true that the Family is the ideal to reach for. Approach it gradually, grow into it by the safe route of the Companionate, and no other way of life offers such inspiring possibilities. Here is the road by which most of the race can attain greater spiritual heights than by any other. This we comprehend and feel, as by an inner vision. And that is why we cling to Marriage and will never let it go.

CHAPTER X

THE SPIRIT OF MONOGAMY

I.

I TALKED not long ago with a sad faced, faded, rather pretty little woman who a few years before had gotten a divorce from her first husband, though she had two lovely children by him, and had very soon married another man. Let us call her Mrs. Gardiner.

It was sufficiently evident that her purpose in getting the divorce was the making of this second marriage; and I recall the buzz of astonished gossip the whole transaction occasioned in her social set and among her friends when it happened. What had made it surprising was that she was not at all a sporting type of woman. She was a quiet, mouse-like little creature, gentle and cultured in her ways—very much of a home-body; the last person, in fact, that one would have suspected of falling in love with some one other than her husband, and much less of going to the extreme of seeking a divorce.

She had come to see me about her boy, who had gotten into a bit of mischief—not a serious matter. And then, as if reaching out for the relief of being able to talk honestly and perhaps confessionally, she turned the conversation toward herself.

"Judge," she said, "I would give ten years of my life if I could undo this second marriage and go back to my first husband. But I suppose it is too late. Even if Lewis would take me back, people would not understand; and I don't think I could endure the gossip. The ordeal of that first divorce and remarriage nearly killed me. —I don't know which way to turn. I am unhappy; and the children are unhappy; and I'm like one shivering beside the ashes of a fire that has died. You see—I married this second time for love. I wanted to be loved; and Lewis was indifferent. He neglected me. I couldn't stand it. Sometimes we would go for weeks without intimacies—you understand?—I am so constituted that it was hard to endure. And when I took the rôle of the aggressor, of course that made matters worse; for men want to do the pursuing. It merely repelled him."

"And so you divorced him."

"Yes. I didn't want to. I could have had an affair with Phil without getting a divorce and marrying him, of course, but I couldn't persuade myself to anything like that. And yet when I found that Phil loved me—well, I just had to have him, some way."

"And what's the trouble now? Has Phil disappointed you?"

Her brows wrinkled into a puzzled frown. "I can't make it out. At first it was wonderful. Then he sort of dropped away from me, and I from him. It's been mutual. We don't seem to have anything really in common, you know. Now with Lewis it was different. We were always companionable, and interested in the same things. But that seems to be lacking with Phil."

"You mean that when the romantic part of your present marriage died out, there was nothing left?"

"I suppose so," she answered bitterly. "It's proved a fake."

"And you thought that if you and Phil were sexually congenial," I added, "that would take care of everything else and insure the success of your marriage to him. Was that it?"

She nodded. "Why shouldn't it work out that way? It does in courtship. Two people want each other; and that makes everything—all their relations together, happy."

"Certainly," I said. "But when satiety comes, what then? Sex is important and all but indispensable in marriage—but it is not enough. No marriage can succeed without some of the homely, commonplace, substantial common interests of life to hold the two persons together and give them, so to speak, a common destiny. You misunderstood what marriage consists of."

She sat nervously fingering and turning a ring that was on one of her fingers—a wedding ring. "What I'd like to know," she said with sudden vehemence, "is how I ever let a lot of second-hand thinking trick me into what I've done. I broke up my home, I virtually deprived my children of their father, with whose help I should have raised them, and what has it amounted to for me?

"And yet, it seemed as if I *had* to have what I wanted. The strain was wrecking me. And now it's wrecking me again, because Phil has become very casual about it all. I guess I'm just made that way, Judge. But—" Here she paused, leaned toward me and almost whispered, "If I had it to do over again, there would be no more divorce nonsense. It's deadly. I'd have had an affair with Phil, and I'd have stayed married to Lewis, and it would have done far less harm than did the course I took in order to remain moral and respectable and chaste. The plain fact is that I'm no more moral and chaste this way than I would have been the other way; and that I ought to have worked this problem out in marriage, and satisfied myself without breaking up my home and substituting a sham marriage for what was, in its fundamentals, a real one.—Lewis and I had grown into each other's lives. Being rooted up and transplanted—I can't tell you what a deadly thing I have found it!"

So far nothing further has developed in the very usual and common domestic situation outlined to me by this woman. I see her occasionally, on the street or in a restaurant, or in her car. And her face lights up when she sees me, as if she were glad to meet one who knew the truth about her. Perhaps some day she will go to her first husband and tell him what she told me. In the meantime her friends take it for granted that she is happy in her status as a divorced woman remarried to the man of her choice; and she wears a non-committal mask before the world that tells nothing.

I come across many of these cases, dramatic illustrations, all, of the fact that eroticism is no fit basis for marriage; that marriages which have their foundation largely or exclusively in sex rather than sympathy and congeniality plus sex are predestined failures and that divorce is, *per se*, an evil thing.

2.

I am for monogamy and against divorce. This statement will doubtless surprise some persons who remember that I have said much from time to time in favor of divorce. But there is no inconsistency in this.

When I say I am against divorce I mean that I recognize divorce as a great social evil. This does not mean that I would refuse divorce to people, who, under the present messed-up system of marriage, stand in need of such relief. Indeed, I would make it much easier for them to obtain divorce than it is at present. But I would provide against divorce by so changing the status of marriage that fewer persons would want divorce.

What I believe in is the prevention of divorce by modifying the conditions that cause it. Merely to forbid divorce would be stupid; and to make divorce difficult to obtain is almost as stupid. But to introduce into marriage certain qualities it does not at present possess, qualities that would tend to insure the existence of a genuine spiritual union between all who marry—that would be highly intelligent.

But to obtain such a condition we would have to alter some of our current views about what is allowable in the sex relations; and such a change of tradition as that must be a matter of slow growth. Not so slow, either, if the incredibly swift social changes now taking place are evidence. Still, the fact remains that it is a matter of growth, however swift or slow the growth may be.

There can be no reasonable doubt that divorce, *per se*, is an evil. We resort to it merely to avoid worse evils; but it is itself an evil. It is an evil, in my judgment, even when it takes place between couples who have no children to complicate the situation. There is nothing to be gained, I think, by holding such persons together when their union makes them miserable—but the fact that their union does make them miserable in itself constitutes a kind of divorce; and that fact is an evil fact. Nor is it to be nullified or altered merely by holding the couple together physically in spite of the fact that they are spiritually divorced. The only excuse for doing that may be the presence of children, for whose welfare the happiness of the parents needs often to be sacrificed. Yet the status of children is often improved by such separations however regrettable the cause that make them necessary.

Of course there are many married couples who don't get along very well, but whose continued union is nevertheless practicable and desirable. There is a certain amount of stress and strain in many marriages which, I think, the parties of such marriages would not be justified in regarding as ground for divorce. I shall come back to this point later.

One fact about divorce which should be kept firmly in mind is this: that divorce is in reality a form of polygamy. We have both polygamy and monogamy in America to-day. Both seem necessary under our present sex code. I realize that this is a question of definitions; but the spiritual essentials of polygamy are certainly present in divorce, no matter what the legal definitions of polygamy may be.

3.

If we had a marriage code which made genuine monogamy possible and practicable all but a very few persons would choose monogamy. Monogamy is the preference of all who do not consider themselves at liberty unintelligently to follow their passing and badly grounded impulses.

Our present marriage code absolutely necessitates divorce as its corollary. Marriages are entered into lightly and irresponsibly and blindly because marriage is the one erotic outlet which society permits. Such marriages have in them the seeds of polygamy and divorce; and they are perhaps rather more likely to have polygamous than monogamous tendencies.

The tendency of such marriages toward impermanence has to be met by a system of easy divorce which can be entered into almost as easily and irresponsibly as marriage itself. And we have such a system of divorce, or are rapidly acquiring it. It is requisite under the circumstances.

Having, by a puritanical morality, made easy marriage a sexual necessity, we have done everything possible to introduce the elements of instability, polygamy and divorce into marriage. And yet the upholders of puritanical morality, that miserable foundation of Marriage As Is, are the ones who are most violently set on forbidding divorce.

They decry sex, and they hypocritically make of marriage the means for accomplishing sinlessly what they insist is a sin. According to them the gratification of erotic impulse is "sin," unless such gratification takes place in marriage,—in which case it is never a sin, no matter how beastly and cruel it may be. By the same token, eroticism is never anything but a sin when it expresses itself physically outside of marriage, no matter how lovely and spiritually exalted it may be.—We semi-barbarians, fed on theological fanaticism, actually believe this monstrous thing; and we contemptuously label as "pagans" all who dispute it.

No pagan love-cult has ever existed, in ancient or modern time, that has ever devised a conception of human conduct so harmful as this so-called Christian, sacramental, church-formulated, church-maintained fake that we are pleased to call marriage. The pagan world has the decency and good sense to recognize that eroticism is not marriage; it took Christendom to make eroticism and marriage morally one and inseparable by decreeing no other relation between the sexes permissible in the sight of God, and Holy Church.

That notion has come to the end of its tether. We are beginning to realize that permanent, monogamous marriage is in no sense to be identified with the helter-skelter of unstable, ill-judged unions which we lump with *real* unions under the common name of Marriage.

Such unions are no more *Marriage* in this exacting sense of the word than if no wedding had taken place. They belong in a different category from Marriage. The present mess springs largely from the fact that we insist on making the two things identical. We are driven to this because of the possible birth of children. But we would not be driven to it if, by means of birth control, the birth of children could be avoided in all but the class of unions adjudged competent for procreation and the responsibility of offspring.

4.

We are now in a position to consider some facts that bear directly on marriage. Before going into this aspect of the subject, I want, in passing, to call the reader's attention to Keyserling's "Book of Marriage." Count Keyserling's own contributions to that symposium present, from the philosophical side, certain views of marriage which I have long held, and with which I am strongly in accord. I propose to follow here a line of thought somewhat similar as it comes to me in the light of my experience with people.

One fact about marriage which railers against the institution have never been able to explain away is the stubbornness with which the human race clings to it, and the persistence of our belief in its possibilities. No amount of failure has ever been able to rob marriage of this prestige. It has certain inherent values which withstand all assaults and override all doubt and derision. Good people, who are disturbed by assaults on marriage, might as well spare themselves the worry. Assaults on marriage will merely improve the institution by subjecting its code to critical scrutiny and amendment.

The second thing to note about marriage is that it has value, constructive and creative value, in people's lives, even when it is not, superficially speaking, a success. There are hundreds and thousands of married persons who put up with varying degrees of hell, and who yet cling together for one reason or another, without quite analyzing why they do it—and muddle through. With some it is the children; with others, it is an underlying love which persists in spite of bickerings and petty quarrels. The reason for this is that marriage creates, or tends to create, a community of interest and an identity of lot. The parties are in the same boat. They tend to cling together in spite of every adverse circumstance. Only in the last extremity of misery do most persons seek divorce.

It may be concluded from this, I think, that marriage, quite apart from sex satisfaction or the rearing of children, does have a value which develops over and above these things, a clear margin of spiritual profit, if you will, to the parties of the marriage, *if they manage to stick,* and stand the gaff, and take their medicine.

Another way of putting it would be to say that one thing which makes marriage profitable to those who enter it is that it involves certain practical responsibilities which make of it a discipline; and that this is valuable whether it includes happiness or not. Marriage, in short, is beneficial and profitable and of supreme importance because it is difficult, because it is a creative art, because it is not primarily happy, and because it calls upon every nerve and sinew of the soul for the utmost effort and *fidelity of function* if genuine happiness is to be created out of the stubborn stuff of human nature male and female. That word *fidelity* has a significance in marriage which far transcends any sex code whatever, and which carries over into the realm of spiritual dynamics. Our habit of restricting the word to the commission or non-commission of a physical act betrays how beside the point is most of our reasoning about marriage.

5.

In marriage two lives unite themselves to the creation, so to speak, of a new entity, a new spiritual reality, which grows from that union as a child grows from the union of two cells. I don't see how any one who is not clean gone in material cynicism can ignore this fact, so easily verifiable in the experience of people. Certainly anybody who has had even a reasonably successful marriage must have felt it in some degree. It is true in a very high degree of persons who are highly developed, spiritually and mentally; it is true to a less degree of those who are less finely organized and less capable of putting creative effort into the art of living; but it is true, in a measure of all who marry, each in his degree. Marriage, therefore, has a first-hand, intrinsic value of a very high order; and the conditions of marriage cannot well be created by any other mode of life. It fulfills a unique and special function in the life of the individual, and hence in the life of society. It is therefore, by all means, to be preserved and fostered in ways that will enable it to fulfill its peculiar function to the best advantage.

Legal marriage has for its purpose the nurture and protection of children; but socially the significance of the institution cuts deeper than that. It is of vital import, not merely to the possible children of the marriage, but to the two parties of the marriage; and it must largely fail of its function with respect to them unless it is capable of *voluntarily* lasting through life.

It is a truism, propounded by sages since the dawn of history, that marriage offers one of the most feasible and practicable of all known roads to spiritual development. "It is not good for man to live alone." That is why we so stubbornly cling to marriage. Something grows out of it that apparently grows out of nothing else. Beginning with an erotic impulse, itself an evanescent and insubstantial thing, marriage becomes a thing of spiritual substance —one of the realest things in life.

What gives marriage its peculiar power as a developer of human life is the enormous difference of potential, both physiological and psychological, that naturally exists between man and woman. Indeed, one might say that the fundamental and important fact in marriage is that men and women cannot fully understand each other, and yet are impelled always to make an effort toward such understanding. Marriage focuses that effort.

The one sex, so to speak, is positive, and the other negative; and it is from such a combination that electricity derives. Hence, the constant stress and strain that keeps married persons living always under pressure and always more or less uncomfortable and ill at ease in their dealings with one another. Hence their tendency to make demand on each other that it is not easy to meet, *at first,* but which becomes easier to meet as this unique discipline gets in its work.

6.

Of course, it is foolish for anybody to expect unalloyed, romantic happiness—the happiness of the courtship and the honeymoon—to endure under such conditions. That is the happiness of conquest over the new and strange and how fortunate are the people who have within them the infinite variety that can keep them forever new and strange to one another. But there is one thing which is capable of keeping all marriage reasonably new and strange, and that is the infinite variety which normal activity and effort give to living, and to the job of working, playing and living shoulder to shoulder with another person.

In short, the adjustments and the variety of marriage are alike the fruit of effort, of creative effort; and the pain of that effort is lightened and sanctified and made worth while by the periods of reward and satisfaction and relaxation which are the natural fruit of such travail. That is why marriage is worth the price when it is a success and when it is contracted by persons who are so matched as to be capable of these peculiar psychological actions and reactions with respect to each other.

This is a lifetime job. That is why divorce, which interrupts the process, is a bad thing for the individual and for society. Divorce is a crippling; it is transplantation; it delays growth, and may kill the plant. Hence, we should avoid divorce, not by forbidding it to persons who unfortunately need it, but by seeing to it that permanent marriage can be contracted only under conditions which will give it a reasonable chance of success—a much bigger chance than it has at present.

The way to avoid divorce is to decrease the number of marriages that would normally end in divorce, that are predestined for divorce; and the way to accomplish that is to make eroticism less and less the chief determining and controlling factor in people's choice of their mates.

In my judgment this cannot be done while marriage, as we now have it, is the one outlet permitted to the sex impulse. We should provide another type of marriage to meet this need. Whether society could wisely permit still other forms of sex liberty than the Companionate is a matter for the future. Perhaps, with this rampant eroticism that is now the bane of society, brought under control by such a means as this, some still further development toward a sane sex code and a greater degree of sex freedom outside of procreative marriage would be possible.

7.

Of all the forces in the world that have been instrumental in producing the type of marriage most inevitably destined for the divorce court, the Christian Church stands first. It has accomplished this tragic result—with the best of intentions doubtless—by attributing to "chastity"—as to virginity—an exaggerated and fictitious value; by regarding every erotic impulse outside of wedlock as a sin; by regarding sex as "lust"; by accepting the implications of St. Paul's teaching that it is better to marry than to burn; and by making of marriage a magic rite of purification, whereby people may sin with the permission of heaven.

With such a choice as that, and under such prohibitions as that, no wonder people come to the altar in droves, a mad rout driven into marriage whether fit for it or not. How could it be otherwise? Such marriages are marriage under compulsion, marriage under the

whip of desires that will not be denied. They are not true marriages.

This is the truth about our marriage code, in spite of all our
efforts to cover up the facts, with lily-white bride veils, and by
sedulous silence on the subject of sex at all well-conducted and
well-bred weddings. It is a smirking silence, a leering silence, a
sickening hypocrisy. We have brought marriage to this pass. We
have made of it an announcement that Mr. Jones and Miss Smith
will this night cohabit, presumably for the first time in their lives,
since both are supposed to be virtuous. Thus, we, by implication,
throw on sex in marriage an abnormal and unhealthy emphasis it
would not have if sex were conventionally available in any other
relationship.

And so the Christian Church, thundering down the ages against
"the sinful lusts of the flesh" has, *by suppressing sex outside of procreative marriage,* given it an abnormal importance within marriage. And having made eroticism and marriage largely synonymous,
it can't understand why people will seek divorce. It has builded
marriage on a foundation of sand, and is shocked when the sand
crumbles.

8.

I have said that I am for monogamy and against polygamy. Let
me explain what I mean by this. I mean that it is impossible, in
my judgment, for anybody to maintain with more than one person
at a time the peculiar spiritual relationship which develops out of
marriage.

I do not attach to the words "monogamy" and "polygamy" the
purely sexual significance that they ordinarily carry. My experience with marital tangles has long since demonstrated to me that
many a marriage which is physically "monogamous" is spiritually
polygamous, though no sex derelictions enter into the situation, and
though the partners are both physically "faithful."

I have seen other marriages which remained spiritually monogamous, even though there had been "stepping out," physically, on the
part of one or both partners. I have seen still others in which

this physical stepping out was the symbol of a spiritual stepping out; and these marriages I regard as polygamous.

The point is that marriages in which the partners cling to a common course and goal in life, and travel their path through to the end together, toward a common destination and over a common road, are monogamous. That is the outstanding spiritual fact about them, regardless of what convention may say about the *liaisons* which frequently play a part in these marriages.

By the same token, where the partners abandon their thought of a common path and destination, and so break up their unique relationship in order to establish something similar to it with some one else, that marriage becomes polygamous, simply by the attitude of the persons toward each other, even though they remain physically "faithful." Polygamy is the spiritual reality back of such marriages, regardless of whether they are technically monogamous or not.

The mere fact of outside sex relations, either by the socially permitted road of divorce, or the socially forbidden road of the *liaison,* is not what makes a marriage polygamous. Such outside relations *may* make the marriage polygamous by spiritually disrupting it and spiritually turning one or both partners toward some one else; but they do not, in fact, necessarily do so. What makes a marriage polygamous is the scattering of its spiritual energies toward other intruding persons, for whatever cause, and regardless of whether there have or have not been physical sex relations with such persons. If there be no such scattering, there is no polygamy, even if there be physical adultery. I affirm this from my actual observation of hundreds of marriages, and on the ground of confidence imparted to me by hundreds of men and women.

9.

Physical "infidelity" is not, in itself, necessarily polygamous, nor is physical "fidelity," in itself, monogamous. Both are spiritual facts and must be evaluated in spiritual terms. Conventional persons are ready enough to admit that mere physical fidelity is not, itself, monogamy, and that a technical monogamy does not preclude the possibility of a spiritual polygamy, and that such a spiritual polygamy will be the *fact* of such a marriage however monogamous it may seem. The *spiritual substance* of such a marriage will be polygamous. Everybody admits that. But the persons who most readily admit that physical fidelity is not, in itself, monogamy, and that it may be coincident with spiritual polygamy, become very resentful and bewildered when confronted with what to them is the very disagreeable thought that the thing works both ways, and that polygamy no more exists by the commission of a physical act than does monogamy by abstention from such an act. Polygamy is a state of mind, a way of thought—so is monogamy. It is too bad that we are such moral cowards that we shirk the logical consequences of this self-evident truth.

The view of the Christian Church that the mere fact of physical adultery is in every case a proper ground for divorce is, to my mind, thoroughly immoral. It denotes a preoccupation with the physical aspects of conduct which Jesus, in whose name such ethical outrages are committed, would never have sanctioned. The really proper and moral ground for divorce is the fact that the parties of the marriage have already been torn apart spiritually.

Divorce is the disrupting of the marriage tie in this spiritual sense. Physical infidelity may disturb or break down the spiritual bonds of a marriage or it may fail to do so; but divorce inevitably destroys the whole structure. In this sense, divorce is deadly to marriage.

Under the system of two kinds of marriage which I am urging, the tendency would be for men and women to marry only on a basis of genuine love, well grounded in mutual sympathy and mutual fitness for such a relationship. The tendency would be for all who could marry on these terms to marry. People would prefer marriage to less satisfactory substitutes and make-shifts. The reason for this would be that love finds its best expression and fulfillment in marriage.

10.

Under the system of Companionate and Family Marriage which I am urging, the tendency would be for men and women to enter Family Marriage only on a basis of proved and steadfast love, whose quality had already been tested before the coming of children. The further tendency would be to prefer the Companionate to the un-married union.

This would be a long step forward. It would be a definite recognition of the fact that sex relations of less social significance and permanence than those of procreative marriage are socially permissible or desirable. The notion that such relationships outside of procreative marriage are not possible, or right, or socially desirable, is, in my judgment, a superstition which will in time disappear, and indeed is disappearing.

Physical loyalty in marriage will be conditioned by these changing views. I believe the time will come when it will be felt that conduct which injures or destroys the spiritual relationship of a given marriage is wrong conduct; and that sex conduct on the part of the married is to be judged by whether it does or does not destroy or disturb these spiritual bonds. I do not say that physical infidelity may not do so; I merely insist, in the light of my experience and observation, that it does not necessarily do so. What would destroy one marriage has no effect on another marriage. These matters are for individual decision, based on culture, fineness of feeling, good sense, sensitiveness and good taste.

I am aware that this statement will draw heavy fire from persons who think they are upholding the sanctity of marriage when they conceive of loyalty in terms of abstention from a physical act. Society, as a whole, does just that. Physical "loyalty" insures "respectability" even in marriages given over to evil, base, and mean passions—marriages whose one virtue is a technical chastity on the part of the husband and wife.

Under our code it is chastity, not charity, that covers a multitude of sins. Physical chastity is the most popular of the virtues. It is an easy concept for the ordinary mind to grasp since it does not demand chastity of the spirit. We are not concerned with spiritual chastity at all. As a result of this our spiritual health is bad. Our ideal of physical chastity, bereft of spiritual content, becomes simply a filthy idol; and the sooner we overturn it and find us a chastity that will be clean, happy, and unashamed, the better for this nation.

I am accused of making light of chastity. Of the sham we call

Chastity, Yes; but of the spiritual reality, which would give Sex its right place in human life and then keep it there, No! I do not think lightly of it. I believe in that kind of chastity; and I think that, in spite of so-called "religious" opposition, we shall sometime achieve it. When we do, half the misery in the world will disappear.

II.

Havelock Ellis has recently written an extremely significant article on "The Future of Marriage" for *The Saturday Review* (London), in which he sums up the problem of modern marriage with such splendid insight that I have asked and obtained his kind permission to quote some rather extended extracts. (The italics are mine.)

"Divorce," says Mr. Ellis, "may be said to be an aspect of the Protestant Reformation, an assertion of individuality and freedom and truth against what seemed the fiction of the Catholic conception of marriage. But in its achievement the sound core of the Catholic conception was overlooked. Catholic marriage represented not merely a sexual union, but a conception of life, a religious life, in which sexual union was only one of the bonds, and not so supremely important that to break it involved the dissolution of the marriage. Nor is that large conception peculiar to the Catholic Church; it is found more or less clearly in India, in China, even among primitive people in New Guinea studied by Dr. Malinowski. The Catholic Church was only peculiar in the way it supported that conception by assuming that, consent having once been given, marriage could not be dissolved by subsequent events. That was a daring way of asserting the dignity of marriage; but it was a fiction.

"Protestantism, which so clearly saw the fiction of Catholic marriage, failed to see that it also founded marriage on a fiction, and of an equally glaring and mischievous kind. The Protestant conception of marriage, which is that of the modern world generally, is rather vague, but it is in its essence secular and in its popular atmosphere romantic. That is to say, *it is narrowed down to a kind of legal sex contract which is held to be sufficiently sanctified by the promise of exclusive and permanent mutual sex love. Such a promise, even in the union of the most devoted lovers, is a fiction. It can never be kept, and the recognition that it cannot be kept, combined with the cowardly fear to acknowledge that fact, plunges our marriages into deceit and misery.* That does not, of course, mean that every married couple is entitled to enter the divorce court. There are endless gradations between the secret desire and the technical act of adultery. *What it means is that we have so strenuously inculcated this romantic fiction into the young couple that when they privately discover that it is a fiction they are overwhelmed with a sense of personal guilt, and only in rare instance dare to confide in each other and to attain that mutual sincerity and trust which might well be regarded as in itself, even in the absence of sexual fidelity, the finest form of marriage.* Our marriages are only saved from disaster—when they are saved—by a readjustment from the fictive romantic basis on to something more stable, but the change is usually painful, troublesome, and imperfect, generally leaving the feeling on both sides of disillusionment, and each party keeps hidden

Love's private tatters in a private Eden.

The divorce movement, excellent as it has been, has helped to fortify the romantic view of marriage; it has concentrated attention on the erotic side of marriage as though that were not only a highly important element but the sole content of marriage, and its diversion an adequate reason for dissolving the union.

"Nothing seems clearer than that to-day we no longer have any use for romantic fictions in marriage. We may be thankful that the youth of to-day—whatever extravagant reactions they may sometimes fall into—have been sufficiently open-eyed and level-headed to realize that fact. But we do not find presented any definite conception of the ideal of marriage on a non-romantic basis. On that account I would attach significance to Count Keyserling's essay, 'The Correct Statement of the Marriage Problem,' in 'The Book of Marriage.' It has seemed to some readers rather obscure, to some pedantic, to others grim, and many of us would propose to reformulate the statement at some points. But it yet remains the most important statement we possess of the marriage problem as it presents itself to-day, and it is well worth the study it demands.

"The point at which Count Keyserling is specially apt to repel the reader is by rejecting the ideal of the 'happy marriage.' He does not consider that marriage is, or should be, merely a 'happy' condition. It is more than a sexual union, it is the bond of two equal and independent personalities, striving through that mutual relationship to attain a self-development neither could achieve in isolation, and that process cannot fail to involve pain as well as joy; the ideal of comfort and ease may be better sought in a pig-sty. For those who find this conception too exalted there are two considerations to bear in mind. In the first place, it is a mistake to suppose that men and women are afraid of difficulty and pain; all our lives bear witness that both are accepted, even welcomed, when they seem worth while, and that marriage is the best marriage which most fully corresponds to the real image of life. Moreover, no possible form of marriage could evoke more heroism than that which, so often unnecessarily and unprofitably, is shown in our conventional marriages, alike by husbands and by wives. In the second place, as Keyserling points out, no one is bound to marry; not only is it possible to find erotic gratification outside marriage, but such gratification can never safely be made the aim of marriage. There are many people also, especially saints and artists, who would be well advised to leave marriage severely alone. It is only too easy to find warning examples. Rudolph Valentino, who was the conspicuous symbol to the world of the romantic fiction of love, believed in it himself, but, as he is reported to have confessed shortly before his death, he 'had lived in hell,' for 'fate mocks us artists.'

"If Keyserling presents what he would himself regard as a satisfyingly tragic conception of marriage, as that which we are now approaching, there are more pleasantly beneficent features about it which he scarcely seems to have adequately set forth. The loss of the pretty romantic fiction is more than fully compensated by the loss of the probable or certain disillusion. The way is open for making marriage not only, in Keyserling's phrase, an interpolar tension of two units constituting a higher unit, but also, in the large sense, an erotic companionship. The two lovers cannot expect their relationship to continue, as it began, nor is that even desirable; for there is nothing more unpleasant than the spectacle of two people so absorbed in each other that they are inapt for all the large and fruitful ends of social life. But they can always cultivate an erotic comradeship of mutual sincerity and trust constituting a deep and tender communion, even strong enough, if need be, to remove the sting from what would otherwise be infidelity, although such communion is the best protection against infidelity.

"There we are brought up to the ancient problem of jealousy. 'I found them one morning in each other's arms—and I killed them,' wrote, in his autobiography, three centuries ago, the Spanish captain, Contreras, of his wife and her lover. The justification for such high-handed action is gone; we no longer regard husband and wife as each other's property; adultery to-day seems to be regarded as less a matter for tragedy than for comedy. But the emotional basis subsists. Jealousy is natural, an animal instinct that we may observe even in our domestic animals. We become civilized and humane by conquering it, and those who are unable to do so are unfitted to deal with modern marriage. Marriage, indeed, any love relationship, must always be a discipline; but it is also an art. The rediscovery of the existence of the art of love is, indeed, one of the grounds for expecting an increase in the stability of marriage as well as in its charm. And how far marriage in any given case can admit of wider affectionate relationships must ever be a difficult and fascinating problem, to evoke the finest developments of discipline and of art."

CHAPTER XI

CHASTITY: WHAT IT IS NOT

1.

At the risk of shocking some excellent persons I propose to say some unorthodox things about "Chastity." Chastity is almost as popular in this country as 100 Per Cent Americanism. It is White, Blonde, Nordic, and Protestant, and is endorsed by the Ku Klux Klan. Roman Catholics and Jews also lay claim to it; and one reason why we look with suspicion on furriners and bolsheviks is that a good many of them are supposed to discount it.

Chastity is the "foundation of the American Home." In addition to being White, Blonde, Nordic, and Protestant, it is of the Feminine Gender, and is almost exclusively the attribute of Pure Women. Men are not required to concern themselves with Chastity so long as they are Brave. They leave it to the women they do not seduce. A Brave Man kills whoever dares to sully the Purity of "his Women"; but he is at liberty, without loss of social standing, to sully the Purity of other men's Women if he can get away with it.

Any woman whose Purity has been "sullied," and who happens to get found out, is not fit to become the wife of any self-respecting man, or to become the "mother of *his* children." He wants to be sure they are his. His point of view is well illustrated in the explanation which a certain colored minister once made to his congregation of the difference between Knowledge and Faith. "Take fo' instance," he said, "Brotha and Sista Simpson heah, with their seben fine chillun. Now Sista Simpson has *knowledge* dat dem chillun is hern; and as fo' Brotha Simpson, why he got *faith* dat dem chillun is hisn."

Back of that bit of humor lies a tragic fact. The demand for chastity in women rather than in men rests upon it, for reasons connected with the inheritance of property, and the desire of men to leave their possessions to children of their own begetting. "Purity" hadn't a thing to do with it originally. Thus it happens that, thanks to our muddleheaded thinking and our cruel superstitions on this subject, we have made of Chastity, not a genuine foundation for anything in human life, but a mythical foundation on which human happiness and human decency can be builded only with the greatest difficulty. Another demonstration of the love of money as the root of all evil.

This does not mean that I am calling Chastity a myth; I am merely saying that with the help of our ingrained puritanism we have done our best to make it one. The brand of Chastity on which we have builded the American Home is not Chastity; it is a hypocritical fake that masquerades under that name, and which lacks spiritual reality. It is a shell, a semblance, within which reside fears, negations and prohibitions, and almost nothing that can be called positively or genuinely ethical.

The thing we call Chastity inevitably involves states of mind which pass from mere impulses of natural desire into obsessions and preoccupations with sex which are often quite the opposite of Chastity. Thus our so-called Chastity becomes a forcing ground, a hot-bed, for the growth of sex obsessions and even perversions, which warp and distort the inner lives of thousands who are far from suspecting what is really happening inside of them.

There are many indications of this tendency, which has become a national trait in America, to interpret in terms of sex things which normally have nothing to do with sex—much as naughty small boys put nasty double meanings into words and phrases which really have no sexual connotation. With us, for instance, the words "morality" and "virtue" have a sexual connotation that our minds seldom escape from. To call a man "moral," or a woman "virtuous" or a youth "clean" ordinarily means one thing, continence outside of wedlock. These words, of course, have other meanings—in the dictionary; and we leave them there, thinking of them rarely.

We never get away from sex; we never quite dismiss it; it is always there—because we are forever engaged in a hand-to-hand struggle with it, a struggle which a different way of thinking about sex would render largely needless.

2.

I recently received a letter from the commandant of a military school protesting against the views I have expressed in "The Revolt of Modern Youth."

"Your solution," he wrote, "is not compatible with morality or Christianity. . . . My own youth was passed in a God-fearing home where sex was not much discussed, and I believe it is nobler to train men and women to stand sentinel at the door of their thoughts and to resist the beginnings of temptation than it is to keep up a discussion of the sordid lapses from virtue, and to be an apostle of an age wherein the conventions that have sustained society shall be confidently swept away, to be supplanted by your untried theories. Rome was not better when divorce was easier and vice rampant."

I regret the inability of this correspondent to see that the only too-well-tried theories which *he* advocates in preference to my "untried" ones are producing unending human misery; that the pet conventions of him and his kind have *not* "sustained society"; and that those very conventions are demonstrably responsible for the dangerous and often disastrous confusion that has come upon us in matters of sex conduct to-day.

In passing, I want to say a word about that old chestnut concerning the fall of Rome. Puritans have been shouting for the last thousand years that Rome fell because of divorce and laxity in sex morals. These persons should read a little history, and find out what really happened to Rome. If they would inform themselves they would find that the same conditions which produced the fall of Rome also produced demoralization in Roman social life. The social demoralization was an effect, not the primary cause. Moreover, there was nothing in that situation that can be compared with the wonderful spiritual awakening, and the growing interest in the art of living, which is taking place in America to-day.

I quote the following from Van Loon's "The Story of Mankind." It disposes of the fable just referred to:

"Two centuries of revolution and foreign war had repeatedly killed the best men among the younger generations. It had ruined the class of free farmers. It had introduced slave labor, against which no freeman could hope to compete. It had turned the cities into beehives inhabited by pauperized and unhealthy mobs of runaway peasants. It had created a large bureaucracy—petty officials who were underpaid and who were forced to take graft in order to buy bread and clothing for their families. Worst of all, it had accustomed the people to violence, to bloodshed, to a barbarous pleasure in the pain and suffering of others."

To say that changes in our present sex code, changes resulting from an effort to make life more livable, are capable of producing a national degeneration such as came about in Rome from the operation of extremely complex economic forces, is to talk nonsense.

The gentleman apparently thinks I advocate divorce and "vice," the two things to which he attributes the fall of Rome. I have already explained at some length that I consider divorce a great evil, to be provided against, not by forbidding divorce, but by so altering the basis of marriage that divorce would seldom be necessary. To deny divorce to persons who unfortunately need it, however, is to lock the door after love has fled.

Nor may moral freedom combined with moral responsibility, such as I should like to see in all sex conduct, fairly be compared with what this correspondent calls "vice." I am against vice as much as he is—perhaps more so. But my definition of vice would differ from his. *I want to see it rooted out of the human heart by enlightened freedom and culture.* With that done, conduct would take care of itself.

What I clearly see every day in connection with the work of my court, is that the order of things which this correspondent advocates as a foundation capable of sustaining society is in reality a foul quagmire—a fertile source of vice, and on the whole the most immoral of all the traditions that have been saddled on us by our "God-fearing" ancestors. Devil-worshiping ancestors, rather! Afraid of their own shadows in the sun!

The suggestion that men and women be taught to "stand sentinel at the door of their thoughts" is, in my judgment, vicious unless it be qualified. It sounds fine, and it is morally rotten. The thing for people to do is to think what they think and not be afraid of it. The "God-fearing" homes, where people must not think what they think, are sex obsessed and mephitic with hidden nastiness; and the people in them need help more than do the naked "heathen" to whom they send missionaries. People who are so ashamed and afraid of sex that they must jam the thought of it back into subjective darkness, as if it were some monster ready to spring out on them, are the people who finally get themselves into such a state that if they ever do let the monster out, God help them. They have good reason to fear it, finally. Their so-called morality has made of the sex impulse within them an abnormal thing, a diseased thing, unlovely, dangerous, and degraded—lacking in sanity, balance and a rational soul. It makes spiritual Calibans out of men and women created in the image of God. Standing sentinel at the door of their thoughts to keep temptation out, they have harbored it and kept it in. By refusing to open the doors and windows of their spiritual house, they have acquired the moldy and mildewed morality that might be expected from such conditions—the same morality which so many excellent persons insist "sustains society."

3.

I suppose everybody who knows anything about the Theater at all has heard of the play called "Rain." The central character of the play is one Sadie Thompson, a part played with wonderful power and truth by Miss Jeanne Eagels. Sadie Thompson falls into the clutches of a Missionary in the South Seas. He is one of the Praise-God Barebones type, whose mission among the natives is to make them wear hideous clothes, destroy their ancient customs and dances, and instill into their minds his own poisonous ideas of sex. This holy man has had no marital relations with his wife during the years they have been married because children would interfere in their work of spreading the Kingdom, and because intercourse for any purpose other than procreation is a sin.

Needless to say, sex is "not much discussed" in that "God-fearing home" where people put "a sentinel at the door of their thoughts." Needless to say, too, the missionary and his wife are very solemn about the brand of devil worship they have misnamed "religion."

The missionary, who knows nothing about so wicked a thing as psycho-analysis—relates to his wife a curious recurrent dream about "mountains in Nebraska," where there are no mountains. In Nebraska, however, there are a good many low hills. They rise sharply from the plain—low, graceful mounds—shaped exactly like a woman's breast.

This pure man converts Sadie Thompson from a personality of brazen courage and directness into a neurotic, distraught wraith of what she had been, afraid of the missionary's God and of Hell Fire —as she had good reason to be if she accepted such a fantasy. The Missionary wrestled with her in spirit, and in prayer, for many hours daily. He would go to her room and pray with her, while the tropic rain dripped and dripped from the eaves.—Religion and sex are emotions which it is sometimes hard to differentiate.

One night the thing so long suppressed inside of him, the monster that lay there in the recesses and depths of his subjective mind, leaps from its prison. He goes to her room; the monster within him takes her body, and is fed, at last. Then it sullenly creeps out of sight again, deep into the subjective depths where it has been so long imprisoned. And the Missionary goes from her room out into the night, and in an agony of remorse kills himself.

And in the morning Sadie Thompson, not knowing yet of his death, comes raging from her room, the cynical, brazen prostitute of old— her new-found "religion" has dropped from her like a haircloth garment. "All men are alike," she rages. "All of them pigs— pigs!"

Then comes the concluding scene, in which the missionary's wife, a broken woman now, says something about being sorry—for Sadie. And in the small broken voice that lingers in your memory once you have heard it through the magic of Miss Eagels's acting, Sadie says, "I am sorry—for everybody in the world."

If, as Aristotle said, it be the mission of tragedy to cleanse and purify the heart through terror and pity, this is tragedy.

4.

I have here told only so much of the story of "Rain" as is necessary to make intelligible the story I am about to relate. I call it my story of "Rain." It happened years ago, long before "Rain" was ever heard of. I told Miss Eagels the tale not long ago when she was in Denver, and came to watch the work of my court.

A seventeen-year-old girl, whom I shall call Sarah Nichols, walked into my chambers one day. She said she had heard of me through a friend whom I had pulled out of a scrape, and that she had come to ask for help. Sarah said she had fallen in love about a year ago with a boy whom I shall call Jack Isaacs, a very fine young Jew of an orthodox family. Jack was twenty. They had wanted to get married, but knew that his parents and hers would alike object to the match.

Sarah's father was the Rev. Joseph Nichols; and though his first name was Jewish, everything else about him was violently White, Nordic, Protestant, and One Hundred Per Cent,—*and Chaste*. Don't forget that, for thereby hangs the tale. He had been a Jew-hater and a Jew-baiter for years; and the only thing on earth he hated more than the people he mentioned in Church as the Chosen People of the God he professed to worship, was the Roman Catholic Church and everybody in it. This, in spite of the fact that his Roman Catholic brethren claimed the same God he did, and were, some of them, just as bigoted as he was, and to that extent able to see eye to eye with him.

Jack's people, on their part, being devout and orthodox Jews, were naturally inclined to respond to this sort of Christian spirit, as exhibited by such exponents of Christianity as the Rev. Joseph Nichols, with a degree of hostility that would certainly block the marriage of their minor son to Sarah.

Sarah then went on to say that she and Jack loved each other so much that they had finally been unable to resist temptation, and that as a result she was three months pregnant.

"I won't be able to keep it a secret much longer," she said while her fingers drummed nervously on the table. "And I can tell you, Judge, that I'd rather jump in the river than have to tell father or have him know about it. It would be just terrible if he knew. He'd try to shoot Jack. It would be all the worse because Jack is a Jew. As for Mother, she has already begun to look at me rather sharply and to ask pointed questions. I think she suspects."

"Could you," I asked, "approach your mother with a thing like this?"

"It would be easier than with Father," she answered. "Father would turn me out of doors—or worse. He'd call me the Scarlet Woman and the Harlot of Babylon, and he'd say I was impure and ruined."

"There are two things for you to do right now," I said. "One is to tell me all about it; and the other is to realize that you are a good girl, and that you are not to let any one convince you you are not. Get over this 'ruined' idea. If you bring a fine baby into the world and give it a proper chance in life you are doing the world a service, and don't you forget it. Don't let these superstitions touch you. Forget your fears. Will you do that?"

"I'll do anything you say," she said, a smile beginning to appear on her face. "I feel better already."

"Oh, I've just begun," I said. "The first thing I'm going to do is marry you to Jack—if I find he's the kind of fellow you say he is. He wants to marry you, doesn't he?"

"Yes, indeed; but his parents won't see it at all. Father has said such horribly uncharitable things about Jews, you know. His mouth seems to drip poison when he talks of Jews and Catholics. And besides, they want him to marry a Jewish girl when he marries. It's natural, I suppose.—Besides, how can you marry us if our parents don't consent. We are both under age, you know. Jack and I have talked all that over."

"Yes," I said, "but you're talking it over with the Judge, now. We have a right, under the law, to do a lot of things up here. I'll show you some of them."

"But I'm three months along. How will I ever get around that? It's too late even for a seven months' baby."

"There is one thing I can do, and will do, in that connection for the sake of your unborn child," I said. "The Child Welfare laws of Colorado have one big purpose, that no child shall suffer because of the sin, ignorance, or poverty of its parents. I have a right to protect your child from the social stigma that attaches in this not quite civilized country of ours to the fact of its being conceived out of wedlock. For the sake of your child, you understand, I will predate your license and your certificate of marriage sufficiently to take care of the conventional nine months. What advantage you may reap personally is incidental. By the same token we will, if necessary, provide money for your child, paying it over to you as the child's mother. But remember, it is your child's money. The state does these things *for your child, not for you.* Do you understand that clearly? So far as I am concerned, I'd like to see the State provide for you personally on the same terms; but what I am able to do for your child will serve your need, so it comes to the same thing in practice.—A lot of people call this encouraging immorality; but you and I won't worry about that, Sarah. You bring Jack here as soon as you can. I want to be sure of him. You say he is steady and has a good job. You want to marry him, don't you? You think you can make a go of it, don't you?"

"Oh, Judge, I'll be the happiest girl in the world; and with Jack —we'll just be in heaven. We'll get along. Yes, Jack has a fine job and he'll get a still better one. We'll surely make out."

"All right; bring him in. And after I've married you, I'll have a confidential talk with your mother."

She left, walking on air, saying over and over, "Oh, Judge, I'm so happy! Oh, I'm so happy!"—which struck me as better than being ruined and jumping in the river, or any of the other nonsense of so many unnecessary "American Tragedies." What I was here doing to help that *good* girl, as I have also done to help so many like her, made me feel like a fairy godfather. By the way, why aren't there any fairy godfathers in the story books?

Sarah brought Jack with her the next day. Following my custom, I sent her out of the room and had a showdown with Jack. I found him a decent, manly fellow, madly in love with Sarah and eager to take over his share of responsibility and more too. He said he had never had venereal disease, and admitted to one sex experience before his affair with Sarah. He said Sarah knew about that. Promising him my help with them, I advised him to tell his family the situation as soon as possible, and to get from them such coöperation and help as he could—since there seemed little likelihood that anything of the sort would be forthcoming from the so-called Christian wing of the alliance.

"Dad will give me hell," he remarked ruefully.

"You've got it coming to you," I said. "As you know, my boy, I do not approve what you two have done. It was not the right way to solve your difficulties. But that is past now—there is a little third party involved here and three people need my help."

"I could have got her out of this fix for fifty dollars," he observed, "by taking her to a doctor I know about, but I just couldn't think of persuading Sarah to do anything like that, though we discussed it just as soon as we knew, because she was sure we'd both be ruined. But we decided it was out of the question."

"I'm glad of that," I said heartily. "You're a brick, my boy, and so is Sarah. You are facing your difficulty in the only decent way. You'll come out all right."

Then I married them; and I arranged the dates on the license and certificate as I had promised. This covered up their violation of the conventions, and served the legal purpose for which licenses and certificates are intended just as well. I am aware that this will be shocking news to many persons who already disapprove of me as an encourager of immorality; but if such young people are to be pulled out of their scrapes and if "illegitimate" babies are to be protected from our silly social taboos, this is sometimes the only way such a situation can well be met. The point for the protection of helpless little children is unanswerable, whatever might be argued against helping the parents. Personally I believe in helping both the child and its parents and starting them off with a clean slate; but obviously helping the child means helping its parents. Help refused to the parents is help refused to their child. It is, in fact, a direct blow at the child—a blow which the laws of Colorado mercifully provide against. Another legal factor which enters into this situation and warrants the protecting and aiding of parents in such cases is "the Redemption of Offenders Act," the name of which sufficiently describes it. It exists, so far, only in Colorado.

Never shall I forget the happiness of that girl and the smiling satisfaction of her husband. They joyfully came to see me after that many times. Later I had a talk with Sarah's mother, who, like all such mothers I dealt with, proved ready enough to back up her daughter as soon as the first shock was over. And how often I have acted as "absorber" to that shock.

Following the marriage and the sharing of our confidences with Sarah's mother, it was decided that the boy and girl should for a time continue as usual in their respective homes—the marriage remaining a secret; but that later, with approaching maternity, it would be announced that Sarah and Jack had eloped. Our theory was that now that Sarah was about to become a mother, the Rev. Mr. Nichols would be overwhelmed and softened by the glad tidings. At this time it fortunately happened that the reverend gentleman had been away on his soul-saving crusades in mountain and plains towns, where there was mining or boring for oil.

By the time he returned Sarah was already showing in the waist line. The fact did not escape her father; and his attitude was not at all reassuring. It filled Sarah and her mother with dread, even though they were now armed by me with all the necessary conventional credentials.

Mr. Nichols disappointed us all by acting badly. He scowled about the house for a few hours and then began to ask questions which threw Sarah into a panic of fear. Mrs. Nichols attempted her rescue and tried to explain matters. This brought out the fact of the marriage which, he was assured, had taken place secretly several months previously. It also brought out the fact of Sarah's pregnancy—volunteered by Sarah in the hope that it would soften him toward her. Instead he went into a rage.

He marched furiously up and down the room, and demanded to know who had infringed on his parental authority and married his daughter without his consent.

Sarah told me later that, to protect me, she had intended to tell him she had lied to me about her age, and passed herself off for eighteen, but in her panic forgot it. She told him I had made the marriage, and explained that she and Jack had taken this course because they knew both families would oppose the match. "And so, Father, when Jack and I couldn't stand it any longer we went to Judge Lindsey and got married."

"What right did he have to marry you?" he thundered. "Didn't he know you were my daughter? Why, you're nothing but a kid. Your looks show it. Didn't he know it?"

"Oh, yes," she cried. "But he married us just the same."

And then the fat was in the fire. That afternoon, while I was out, the Rev. Mr. Nichols came tearing into my chambers. He paced up and down and demanded, "Where is the Judge?" When he found I was out he began speaking his mind.

This Juvenile Court business, he said, was going entirely too far. He had heard we had done things that were simply scandalous, and now he had the evidence of it in his own family; and I would have to account to him for my conduct. He was in such a rage that one of the women officers told me later she at first thought of calling in an officer to subdue him. He waited around for some time, and as I did not show up, finally went away, snorting threats that he would return.

The next day Sarah came to see me, much disturbed. She told me of her interview with her father. When she had told him of her pregnancy he accused her of having had to get married and of having committed "the supreme sin—the supreme sin," and other nonsense that to his way of thinking seemed axiomatic.

"Don't you tell him anything about the 'supreme sin,'" I warned. "You tell him you ran away and got married because you wanted to, and that I married you."

"I did," she said. "And I showed him the marriage certificate; and of course, thanks to you, Judge, if he looks up the license that will correspond to it. But I'm awfully afraid of him; and if he ever did find out, he might do something dreadful. Just now he's stumped by that certificate; the dates are all right and my baby comes just as it should." She paused. "Judge, I wonder if I hadn't better tell you the truth—about *him*. He hasn't a bit of right to be indignant about me, and my sins are none of his business.—You know, Mother hasn't gotten along with him very well for a long time. Mother is cold toward him, and he is toward her. They don't sleep together. He is ugly to her most of the time, and doesn't treat her right. He is always sneering and finding fault with her.

"One time when he was out soul-saving he met a girl who came to the church meeting—brought there by somebody. He got interested in her soul. He wanted to save her for Jesus. He said she was like scarlet, but that she would be washed white like snow if she became a bride of the Lamb. And he used to talk, looking into her eyes, and holding her hand and stroking it.—He took a fatherly attitude toward her, and it looked all right. I am sure he didn't himself realize what was going on inside of him, and that he'd have been horrified if he had known.

"He told Mother this girl had a beautiful soul, and that he was going to get her out of the clutches of certain influences in the town where he met her, and that he wanted to bring her home to live with us for a while.

"Mother, who never opposed him in anything, said, 'All right'; and Mary came. That was her name; Mary Borden. She was a funny kind of girl. She got all worked up by Father's talking and praying over her, and she said she was in love with Jesus; and that she was a Magdalene; and that she was terribly worried about the men who had lost their souls by sinning with her, and that she wondered if she couldn't save their souls as well as her own. And then she and Father would pray. Sometimes they prayed down in the living room, right before all of us. I hated it. It made me feel ashamed. It made me feel as if they'd been walking around naked. And sometimes they went upstairs and prayed in her room, by her bed— with the door open; and you could hear Father praying all over the house, and Mary sobbing.

"All this time he was ugly as sin to Mother. She put up with it and said nothing. And I tried to treat Mary decently, though the whole thing made me sick. I began to hate the thing he called religion. He got drunk on it.

"One night Mother was away. She had gone to nurse her sister, who was sick. It was a hot, sultry night in summer. I got up to go to the bathroom; and not wanting to disturb Father, I went carefully along the hall on tiptoe. As I passed father's door I saw he was not in his room. Then I came to Mary's room. The moon was shining bright—right on her bed. And,—oh, Judge, I didn't want to tell you—Father was there. I stopped stock still. I could hardly believe what I saw, or that it was actually Father. He was muttering and mumbling—and—and—well, I guess it was the shock of what I saw; at any rate I made a noise, and Father turned his head and saw me. I ran back to my room and shut the door, and sat on the edge of my bed, shivering, though the night was stifling hot.

"Pretty soon came a knock, and Father came in. Down the hall I could hear Mary, laughing and laughing like a fiend, or a demon, or a mad person—I don't know which. And Father himself acted as if he were mad. He kneeled down by the bed and began to pray for forgiveness. He asked God if he should not kill himself. Would that make up for his sin? No, he couldn't do that for fear he'd go right to Hell! His eyes had a wild light in them; and I was so sorry for him that I just put my arms around him and talked to him and tried to quiet him. And all the time I could hear Mary, laughing and laughing.

"Father said he was going to kill himself; that he might as well, now that he had killed his soul. He said he had been sinning with Mary in his heart for a long time; and that he couldn't keep his thoughts down; and that he hadn't been himself; and that all the praying he had been doing just seemed to bring him closer to Mary and to want her more. 'Am I myself?' he asked, looking at me like a maniac. 'Am I your father? Don't you think I'm some one else? Your father couldn't do such a thing! Who am I?'

"Well, I felt that I must quiet him somehow. And I told him not to worry, and that I'd never tell Mother.

"And he said, very pitifully, 'Oh, Sarah, you will never tell her?'

"'Father,' I said, 'there is no sense in your taking on this way. You are always telling how the Lord forgives other sinners; and surely he will forgive you.'

"At last I got him quieted down, and back to his room. But all that night I heard him stirring about the house, and pacing the floor. But Mary had shut her door, and there was no more from her. I didn't have any ill will toward her. I don't think she expected any such conduct from Father. The next morning she walked out of the house with her grip, and I've never seen her since.

"I had to do some tall lying to Mother to account for her depart-

ure; because Father acted so funny when she asked questions. I
took all the blame, explaining that I had lost patience with Mary
and that she had left in a huff at me, and that I thought it a good
riddance.

"But, Judge, I'll never forget the way that girl laughed that night.
I sort of got the feeling that she was—well—disappointed, you
know. I guess she had thought Father wasn't like other men. He
had been awfully strict with himself, I suppose; and he must have
had it boiling around inside of him, and the temptation was too much
for him when he tried converting a girl who could be had for the taking. If it had been some girl who vould have had to be won, I suppose he wouldn't have had the nerve to try it. I've done a lot of
thinking about it and that's the way I figure it. Maybe if he hadn't
been holding himself in so hard Mary wouldn't have been so much of
a temptation to him. But I guess he never had had anything to do
with women, except Mother; and for years he and Mother hadn't
roomed together. So you see something had to break, either his
temper and his nerves, or else his morals. Mostly it's been temper
and nerves. I've talked about it with Jack a good deal, and he
thinks that's the way of it, and that Father isn't really to blame.

"But with all that having happened, wouldn't you think I ought
to be able to go to him with a matter like this affair with Jack and
tell him the truth? The fact is he's so used to being a hypocrite
about sex that he believes his own lies. It's strange this matter
hasn't reminded him of Mary and of the consideration I showed
him, but it doesn't seem to."

"Remind him yourself," I said. "That's the solution of your
problem, Sarah. Talk to him privately. Tell him you have heard
all about the exhibition he made of himself at this court, and about
the threats he made; and then say to him, 'Father, surely I'm not
the only sinner in our family; and you always preach that the Lord
forgives sinners. You say I must have done wrong or something
to have had the Judge marry me, though you know perfectly well
that he marries scores and scores of people, and it means nothing
at all just because one gets married by him. Now let me tell you
this: he married me. Here is the centificate, and you can go and

look at the license, and you will find the dates correspond, and that I'll have my baby nine months after my marriage. I haven't any more to say about it than that, Father, and I don't think you should. Father, do you remember Mary?'

"Now," I finished, "you just recall that to him, and remind him how you stood by him, and how he got over his 'sin,' as I suppose he calls the thing that happened to him; and make an appeal to his generosity and his common sense on that basis. Do it without threats or any hint of holding a club over his head. Don't make him feel that his secret is not safe with you whatever he does; and don't frighten him or hurt him, or make him feel that you reproach him or judge him. Let him create his own attitude of mind out of the materials at hand. Remember that he is as much a helpless victim of superstition as you are—though in a different way."

A few days later Sarah came back, deliriously happy. "Father has changed altogether," she announced the instant we were alone. "He said to me, 'Don't ever mention Mary to me again. The thought of her makes me sick and ashamed. But I see what a trap it was, Sarah. I just didn't know what I was getting into when I tried to deal with Mary.—As for you, I feel differently. I've had a chance to think. I see the Judge has helped you in the only way he could. You and Jack can do whatever you like so far as I am concerned. But please forget about Mary.'

" 'Father,' I said, 'I know God has forgiven you if you have sinned; and I think that if I have committed any sin, he will forgive me. I am sorry I displeased you.—And now, you are going to be nicer and kinder to Mother than you have been, aren't you?'

" 'I didn't mean to be anything else,' he said. 'I guess it's been nervousness. But I'll do better.'

"And, Judge, he is trying, I think. He isn't really unkind at heart; but there must have been something out of order inside of him—don't you think so? It showed itself in that affair with Mary. And oh, Judge, I'm so sorry for him; because after my experience with Jack I know what it all means. Only our case is different because Jack and I are not reproaching ourselves. We had decided that since we loved each other we had a right to be all we chose to each other; and that so long as we didn't have a baby it was nobody's business but our own. But Father has always believed and taught that it *was* everybody's business, whether there was a baby or not. The trouble with us was that we didn't take the right means not to have a baby. But now I'm glad we didn't; and I'm so happy that I got onto the street car this morning singing to myself; and the conductor heard me and laughed—and I laughed, too. Why, Judge, just think how awful it would have been if Jack and I had succeeded in not having a baby. I wouldn't give my baby up for anything. Even now, before it's born, I don't see how I ever lived without it. A thing so wonderful can't be wrong."

"No, Sarah," I answered. "It isn't wrong. But you arrived at it in a way that is forbidden by society, my dear child. It might have been terribly unfortunate if there had been no one to come to who would understand you and deal with you as I did, or had there been no way to provide for your baby. That would have been the case in most states. In Colorado, you see, we have several ways of meeting this situation. For instance, I have more applications from people who want to adopt babies than there are babies to adopt. But in most states little is provided for looking after the interests of such children; and society, instead of blaming its own stupidity, blames the mothers, brands the children as illegitimate, and encourages child murder. There is no such thing, Sarah, as an illegitimate child. All states will some day so decide. By helping you and Jack in this matter I have made possible the creation of a good, socially productive, socially valuable home. But my enemies insist that the work I am doing encourages immorality and strikes at the foundations of the home. What do you think about it, Sarah?"

5.

This story has an interesting sequel. Joseph Nichols did not come in to see me after the incident with Sarah was closed; but I learned that his feelings toward me had become friendly.

Not long afterward he moved away from Denver, and took charge of a church in a town not far distant. Occasionally he made trips to Denver; and these trips increased in frequency about the time the Ku Klux Klan came into prominence. It was soon evident that he was actively identified with that movement.

It was impossible, of course, for me to have any part in an organization like the Klan. I could not be a party to the racial and religious intolerance on which it was builded.

Intolerance, like jealousy, is simply a form of fear. Biologically it is as instinctive and natural as jealousy—and when not controlled by the reason, is just as wrong and irrational. Such reactions of the blindly instinctive thing within us have to be overcome by the rational faculty; and since the vast majority of people use very little reason and a vast amount of instinct in ordering their conduct, it was of course inevitable that such an appeal to fear as the Klan now made should draw an immense response from thousands of well-intentioned persons whose emotions outran their judgment, and who doubtless would have acted quite differently if they had understood the true nature of the spasm of racial and religious feeling that was sweeping them off their feet, and making them easy prey for exploitation by the Klan leaders.

I have already quoted from a letter by Bertrand Russell, in which he speaks of the fact that "religion is the chief enemy of kindliness and decency in the modern world."—Well, here, in the activities of the Klan, was a capital example of how "religion" may become just that; and of how the basest instincts we have are capable of presenting themselves under the guise of true religion and patriotism—with which they have nothing to do. People were persuaded that certain things which gave stability to their daily lives were in peril. The thought struck them with terror. And they responded to that touch of Fear with the same spirit of blind cruelty which characterizes a mob that lynches a negro or burns him alive because he has attacked a white woman, or is merely supposed to have done so. The machinery of the law does not act swiftly enough to allay such panic. Nothing will allay it except reason and self-control; and mobs are notable for their lack of reason and self-control. A mob is merely a mass of loosely connected protoplasm acting blindly according to the laws which govern the mechanism of physical life. The Klan gave every evidence of being a mob, led by crooks who proposed to use it for their own political ends. That was why I could have nothing to do with the Klan.

One reason I shrunk from this manifestation of organized fear was that through these many years of my work in Denver I have come in contact with all kinds of people, of every race, creed, and condition of life. And what I have learned from this is that they are much alike.

6.

There are differences of temperament, there are varying notions of value, there are varying customs, there is friction that arises from such differences of manner and custom; but once you put into your philosophy a *differential,* so to speak, that is capable of adjusting itself and of making allowances for such racial and religious variations, then you find always and everywhere that people are simply human beings, neither good nor bad—all of them lovable if one understands them.

This isn't Pollyanna talk. It is the truth. I don't say it is easy to get at it in one's own conduct, but it is true. I have my own struggles in this connection. In my reflective moments I realize that the intolerance and venom which have been manifested in many quarters toward many of the beliefs set forth in this book and in "The Revolt of Modern Youth" have been the fruit of fear. And at such moments it seems very clear that it is up to me not to let fear in turn take possession of me. For fear is contagious, and it makes one hate one's adversary. It is better to try to be tolerant even toward intolerance. I am not consistently so, but that at any rate is what I more or less aim at. Heaven help us all!

Well, as I was saying, I could not have anything to do with the Klan; and probably I should have found it necessary to hit out at it sooner or later. The Klan leaders understood this perfectly, from my refusal to join the organization. Trouble was inevitable. They were plotting from the start to gain control of the dominant political party at the primary elections; and this scheme included the taking over of the Juvenile and Family Court of Denver, together with all other agencies of government. The Klan's purpose, in other words, *was to function as the government,* and to use the powers of government to make Denver safe for Protestant, Blond, Blue-Eyed Nordics and One Hundred Per Centers. Roman Catholics and Jews and "furriners" wouldn't stand a chance.

In planning to get control of the Juvenile and Family Court of Denver, the Klan selected as its candidate for the Judgeship a man who was known, and who afterward proved by his own conduct, to be utterly unworthy of the place. There was nothing for me to do but fight. I had hoped to avoid this. I had wanted for the Court the support of both political parties. This Court ought not to be made a political football; it should be out of politics, because it is a unique and special work. But there was no escaping a struggle. I fought, as I had fought before through nine or ten elections, a fight made necessary by the injection of politics into the situation.

I wish there were time to go into this in detail here; but I shall have to refer those who wish to know what is still the political side of the situation in Colorado to "The Beast," written in collaboration with Harvey O'Higgins. The enmities which I raised up by the writing of that book have never ceased to follow me with a kind of guerrilla warfare that has always made it necessary for me to spend my whole salary on campaign expenses at every election in order to stay in office and do my work.

The election of 1924 was marked by the height of the Klan hysteria. It hit Colorado like a cyclone. The Klan leaders, trafficking for money and power in the hatreds of people, races, and religions, won practically every item on its ticket *except the judgeship of my court*. I weathered the storm, though by a very close margin. I was the only candidate on the minority party ticket actively opposed by the Klan that came within gunshot of election. In view of my handicaps it was the greatest victory of the ten general elections—some hard fought—in which I had each time triumphed, often over bitter opposition.

But the fight was not over. My Klan opponent, with the backing of the Klan, demanded a recount of the ballots. This recount was conducted under the auspices of men who were members of the Klan. I need not dwell on the impropriety of the proceeding. Suf-

fice it to say that after a Klan grand jury had, as we thought illegally, ransacked the ballot boxes, and after election officials had
been duly terrorized, they *still*—by some miracle—lost the count to
me by some thirty-five votes. This was my majority out of nearly
one hundred thousand votes cast in Denver in the year of Klan
inundation.

I had run, and won, on the Democratic ticket in an election that
gave about 35,000 plurality to chief positions on the Republican
ticket of my Klan opponent. To many a political old-timer in
Denver it seemed like a political miracle.

Several weeks before this remarkable election, the Rev. Joseph
Nichols appeared in my chambers. He shook hands with me
gravely and sat down. "I just want you to understand, Judge,"
he said, "that while I am with the Klan, and am strongly in accord
with its principles, I do not approve of this fight on you. I have
come to tell you that I am for you strong; and that I am doing
all I can to protect you from Klan hostility. I shall talk privately
with all the klansmen I can get at, and argue that they ought, without saying too much, to throw their vote for you. I can get you
a lot of votes that you will otherwise lose; for most of them follow
the crowd, and don't realize what is at stake in this court. But I
have seen some good samples of your work; and I don't want to see
helpless people deprived of the aid and understanding you can
give them."

A few moments later, as he rose to go, he turned back hesitatingly.
"Sarah told me about her talks with you," he said, "and lately I've
come to understand your way of thinking. And—I told my wife
everything; so that now there is nothing on my conscience. We understand each other better."

I feel sure that Joseph Nichols, a member of the Ku Klux Klan,
brought in the thirty-five votes that elected me, and then some; and
that if it had not been for him, I would have lost that fight. But
what pleased me most was that I got Joseph Nichols's own vote.

As for Sarah and Jack, they voted for me too. They still live
in Denver and have three blooming children. Jack is making a
good living, and my conviction that I did a first rate job in that

case grows stronger and stronger as the years pass. There is no suicide in *my* story of "Rain."

7.

And now, on the basis of the facts I have just related, let us return to a consideration of Chastity, and what it is not. In the Nichols home they followed the prescription recommended by the correspondent who was brought up in a God-fearing home where sex was not much discussed, and where they "set a sentinel at the door of their thoughts"; a typical American home, in other words, where they tell you, quite sniffily and contemptuously, if you ask them, that they still believe in "Chastity" and haven't much use for people who don't.

They call it Chastity, because in this country that is largely what chastity is. We have succeeded remarkably well in creating this Purity veneer, this lid clamped down over whatever devil's broth may be simmering underneath, under an unguessable, pent power of steam. It is easier to create that kind of surface chastity than it is to create a real chastity, sweet and sound and happy to the core.

For a real chastity is a state of mind, a way, not of foregoing love, but of evaluating it. Such chastity is not easily had. It is a product of culture and freedom; and it is not necessarily in agreement with our prevailing sex traditions. As judged by those traditions it may even appear unchaste. For mere conformity to a prescribed code, a real chastity substitutes moral responsibility, common sense, good judgment, and a sincere desire to respect other people's rights. It would base sex conduct on ethics, not on a compulsory morality which has never heard of ethics and which cares nothing for what is genuine in conduct.

Unfortunately we Americans are creatures of law. We decide nothing for ourselves. We have a law for almost everything. That is why we lack the poise which is necessary for the free conduct of our personal affairs without anarchy and license. We are as unreliable, and as unstable, in matters of sex freedom as was the Rev. Joseph Nichols when he ran up against a real temptation—or as the missionary in "Rain." That's the natural result of carrying your arm, or your moral nature, in a sling of sheltering tradition.

Our conventions prescribe a technical chastity, and are satisfied with that; and the consequence is that we don't recognize genuine chastity when we see it, unless it happens to have the conventional earmarks. Lacking those it simply isn't chastity—whether it be chaste in reality or not. Thus it happens that I am continually coming into contact with instances of sex conduct which, while beyond the pale of conventional respectability, are nevertheless genuinely chaste.

We make of chastity a physical rather than a spiritual condition. A physical chastity is all that society demands as the condition of respectability, and it is all the church demands. It doesn't matter how rotten you may be inside. You may be saturated with a sex obsession for twenty-four hours of a day; you may burn with inordinate and unnatural desires; you may harbor constantly the thoughts that wither and destroy; you may be possessed by devils of repression that are wrecking you, body and soul. But be sure you retain your mask intact. Contrive to be a whited sepulchre and you can get by, no matter how rotten you may be inside. You will be respectable; society will recognize and receive you; "pure" women will not draw their skirts aside as you pass; and you on your part will socially recognize and receive all who maintain *their* masks intact. This, not the wild and ill-advised rebellions against convention that are done in the open, is what is the matter with us. It is this internal lack of straight thinking and wholesome feeling that wrecks us. Virtue is a happy condition, but there is nothing happy about this. It is as unwholesome as any other kind of moral leprosy.

8.

I am not saying that a technical, conventional chastity has no place. I am merely saying that we have made that kind of chastity into an overrated virtue, on which we insist in season and out. We lug it in by the ears even when it is clearly out of place, and preposterously unsuited to the existing circumstances. We use no reason nor common sense in dealing with this thing. Chastity is not a specified, ready-made variety of conduct; it is a state of mind and heart. By the same token unchastity is a condition of the mind and heart; not a mere departure from some prescribed line of sex conduct. Sex relations in marriage, for instance, may be, and often are, unchaste—in the absence of love—though technically they are always "chaste."

What I have frequently discovered about "chaste" people is that continence has not necessarily had the effect of ennobling or purifying their characters, as it is supposed to do; but that it has, on the contrary, often resulted in a diseased attitude of mind toward sex, and in sex obsessions, to such a degree that such persons read sex into everything, and have it always present in their consciousness. They interpret all they see in sexual terms. They can't watch a boy and a girl walking down the street without inwardly speculating as to what they will do when they are alone; they can't see such a couple dancing without at once calling attention to the closeness of their dancing, or the alleged impropriety of their movements, or to the shortness of the girl's dress, or to her lack of a brassière. They read their prurience into everything. I have noticed this infirmity in many of the clergy who preach in season and out against the sins of this generation.

Such persons are unchaste, however consistently they may cling to a technical chastity, or however they may, if unmarried, remain continent; for continence and chastity are not the same thing. The minds of such persons are too often a hot-bed, a breeding ground of exaggerated, base and even perverted desire. Sex perversions and sex obsessions spring from such states of mind—not chastity.

In other words, our conventional conception of chastity as mere continence is a lie; it is a morbid and festering substitute for a sex life which ought to be clean cut, happy, and healthy, a spontaneous and fearless condition of the mind and heart, with plenty of room in it for clean desire, cleanly expressing itself. Real goodness does not make people unhappy, though we have a puritanical notion that it does; and that if it doesn't it can't be goodness. Real chastity, likewise, does not make people unhappy; it makes them happy. Nor does real chastity cause filthy images to spring up like toadstools in the mind, nor does it obsess the whole inner life with sex and thoughts of sex; nor does it wreck health and nerves and sour the character and disposition. Finally, chastity does not make of marriage simply a permitted and legal outlet for "the sinful lusts of the flesh," because it does not look upon the lusts of the flesh as sinful.

9.

Real chastity should be happy—a frank and joyful thing, created out of discipline and desire. Chastity is the sanity of sex; it is not the death, extinction, or needless and stupid repression of sex. It is a reasonable expression of sex; and its legitimate bounds are far wider, in my opinion, than anything provided for in our present marriage conventions.

Of course this means that it does have bounds; and I think those bounds are readily definable, though they vary with individuals and with the circumstances. What determines those bounds is the educated conscience and common sense of the individual. I am unable to see that the fact that some persons lack conscience and common sense alters the situation. Society develops such qualities by having the opportunity to exercise them. To get anywhere with human affairs you have to trust people—and educate them, of course.

I dissent from the extreme of continence prescribed by our sex code; and I think the Companionate would be a reasonable compromise with our present conventions and with our present want of education and self-control in these matters of sex conduct. If such a code were once established, further freedom in this direction might later become practicable without injury to society and without any departure from sound ethics.

In a theoretically perfect condition of society restraints of any kind would not be needed, because everybody would do right, and everybody would follow his own desires only to the extent that gratification of such desires would work no injury on others. But such a state as that is so far in the indefinite future that we may restrict. ourselves here to pointing it out as a philosophical ideal. In the meantime we can work toward it, and are working toward it; and that is the reason for this revolt and for these changes that are taking place in our sex code to-day.

It is a terrible fate that has come upon mankind that the things it pronounces good and virtuous should so often be evil. And there are few evils more malignant than the stupid fake, the conventional veneer, to which we wrongfully, and almost blasphemously, give the name of Chastity.

There is nothing new about all this. I am continually startled by the evidences that come my way that thousands of persons are groping their way, both by instinct and by efforts to think things out, toward some sounder and more sincere and adequate principle of sex conduct than they have found in received tradition. That this is the case among the younger generation is evident; that it is equally true of the older generation is also evident, though not openly so. The older generation is merely more discreet about putting itself on record.

10.

I have in mind a man whose name is well known in Denver; and in his profession he is nationally known. He is a churchman highly respected by the clergy, who have little conception of his real thoughts. He could not "afford" to give expression publicly to what I am permitted here to record for him. He told me that he had radically altered his conception of what he wanted his daughter to think and feel about sex, and that he had told her so.

"I would prefer for her to have whatever sex experience she has in marriage," he said, "not because I'm concerned about the morality of it, but because I consider it safer, in view of the way society treats people who break with the conventions. But if she were to remained unmarried, I should consider it a capital misfortune if she let that interfere with her right, as a woman, to live out her sex life.

"My wife and I grew up with the old-fashioned notions; and when Isabel began to feel the pull of this younger generation talk we went right up in the air. But being confronted with the situation, we set ourselves to think it through.

"You know the old argument. Chastity is the chief of all the social virtues because the virility of a nation depends on the chastity of its women. Chastity, according to this way of reasoning, is a form of loyalty to the race, and is obligatory on people for that reason. Few persons have any doubt, I suppose, that unchastity strikes at the foundations of the home, and therefore at the very roots of the national and racial life.

"Well, in a sense, all that is undoubtedly true; but it depends on how you define chastity. We've made a catchword of it, and it needs to be made definite. I have known some wonderful women, for instance—and I know you have—who were not continent, and not conventionally pure, but who were capable of producing virile and wonderful progeny. They made good wives and mothers. There was nothing degenerate about them. And from what you tell me of the girls who come to you, it would be nonsense to lump them as degenerates, weaklings, morons, or even 'bad.' "

I laughed. "One of the most brilliant girls I ever dealt with," I told him, "took high honors in one of our greatest state universities. She had just borne an 'illegitimate' child when she entered the class in sociology; and one of the first things she did was to listen to a lecture by a learned professor, who assured the class that the mothers of illegitimate children were nearly all defectives, subnormal mentally and physically. Most of the girls I deal with who 'go wrong' are above the average in beauty, brains, and intelligence. That's what makes them so attractive. They seldom, if ever, 'get caught' or get into courts. It is the 'defective' type who mostly get into court procedures. This is, in part, responsible for her professor's ignorance. But go on with your story."

He nodded. "High spirited, wild as young hawks, overflowing with life, mature for their years—that's my daughter.

"Well, this is the way I look at it. In the first place, there's a chemistry of sex, a chemistry of love, if you will. It has its bases in the hormones secreted by the endocrine glands. That's something that wasn't known in the old days, but we are hearing plenty about it now. The action of these chemical substances, when they are released into the blood-stream, determines biologically the sexual make-up and vital characteristics of the personality.

"Now evidently a factor like that simply *Is*. You can't do away with it by denying it or bottling it up or laying it to original sin. It can no more be ignored than any other fact in nature. It must be recognized and utilized sanely. But in that case where do these doctrines about the benefits and beauties of continence come in? If it means anything it means that continence is not natural, and that that is why something instinctive within us fights it.

"I have talked to a lot of old-time doctors, conservative medical men, about this, and most of them officially take the stand that continence is beneficial, or at least harmless. I don't see them practicing their own theories, however. They are like other men; and when you find a man, doctor or layman, who has been absolutely continent before marriage, you've found a rare bird. I'll wager it would be something like one-tenth of one per cent, or somewhere near it. It's the same with the clergy. Take theological students, mostly unmarried. They are continent—oh, yes. They let women alone; but the great majority don't let themselves alone. And that isn't continence. Apparently medical men are pretty well agreed now that this does them no particular harm, except for the mental and psychological effect of fear and remorse, based on all the horrible things they have been told and taught about such forms of appeasement. But they make me tired with their talk about continence. Some think that's the best way to control the relations of the sexes outside of marriage; but I don't agree. It's unnatural, and a bad preparation for marriage, and they shouldn't be driven to such substitutes.

"Now the way I figure it is this. The best way to keep sex from getting possession of youngsters is to keep them busy; and of course the same thing applies to their elders too. Get them interested in other things and use up as much of this flood of sex energy as possible that way. That's what I tell my daughter.

" 'Sublimation,' the psycho-analysts call it. My girl is in a school I have picked with that in mind. She has plenty to do, and she's interested in doing it. If I had a boy, I'd keep him busy the same way. That is one of the most important uses of athletics for boys and girls. Keep them busy, and you've found a way to utilize the sex hormones in ways that are natural, beneficial, and productive. A lot of the girls and boys who come to you in trouble have not had that kind of guidance, and they've had time to get into mischief. Isn't that so?"

"It is," I said.

"Now that takes care of a major part of the problem, doesn't it?"

"But not all of it."

"No—by no means. That's where these sublimationists miss their step. They think you can sublimate the whole business. As I figure it, there is so much hormone that no matter how you keep these kids on the jump, there's usually a surplus of sex energy left over— not only in adolescence, but in later life. That's why I think this talk about sublimation as a means to absolute continence in strongly sexed people is bunk.

"I know women who have never married, and who ought to—who need marriage badly. They have the notion that they have sub- limated all the sex they've got in feminist careers. But I've con- cluded with respect to such people that they either haven't got much, or else that there is an unused surplus of bottled-up sex inside of them that more than accounts for their nerves and their 'peculiarities.' In addition, of course, they miss the companionship, the human ele- ments, of marriage; and they lose heavily by that.

"More than that, I've concluded that many of these people who think they have sublimated their sex impulses into something they call 'higher' have really translated them into perversions and dis- orders and a general inability to live, think, and feel right. The psycho-analysts call that 'introversion,' I believe.

"On the other hand, there are many normal men and women who find it possible to live celibate lives, and to be healthy and happy in that condition. No one rule applies to all persons. Broadly speak- ing, however, most persons need and should have a normal sex life.

"The question then, as I see it, is what's to be done with that portion of sex energy which can't be sublimated. It seems to me that other things being equal, people can't very well be benefited by its repression, and they may be harmed if such repression be carried too far. I don't think commands to self-control by any means meet this issue. Most of us have too much self-control rather than too little. We are past masters in the art of sitting on ourselves, bottling our- selves up, and playing the virtuous and chaste hypocrite, no matter what our thoughts and desires may be.

"For my part, I agree with those who hold that sex repression is and always has been, one of the causes of war. Society has been a witch's cauldron of sex phantasy, secret wishes, frustrated hope, and perverted instinct. War becomes a kind of sublimation for all this. Deny love normal expression and you transmute it into hatred. It is not for nothing that Sex is identified in our speech with Love, so that we use the word Love to indicate the activity of Sex. Think of the kindness, and the Good Will, and the sense of harmony with life that would come upon men and women if they could be at peace with Sex and with Society at one and the same time, on a saner and more workable basis of Chastity than the one the past has confined us to! I don't mean that it would bring a millennium; but I do mean that it would make the kindly virtues come easier than they do; and that the forces released by such a change would not be savage forces, but the reverse. It goes without saying, of course, that any sudden plunge into such a change would be dangerous. We are not educated for it. It would have to be a slow growth, a natural change, such as seems to be taking place in response to changed conditions of living."

"And contraception?" I asked.

"Of course! Contraception would make it possible. The lack of contraception in the past abundantly justified the fear of pregnancy and of unwanted children. It was natural that society should shut down on every sex relationship that made no provision for the care of possible children. The state didn't want to take them over. It wanted the parents to do it. But if you eliminate unwanted pregnancy, you dispose of that problem. The trouble is that we have come to attach a mystical significance to a social convention which was originally a practical measure and not mystical or religious at all."

"I don't think you are wholly right in that," I said. "Many of these sex taboos came into existence before mankind realized that intercourse had anything to do with the coming of children. There are savage tribes to-day that do not connect the two things. Primitive man regarded with superstitious awe every emphatic and important natural force; and when it came to Sex, here, along with war, and the acquisition of property, was one of the most emphatic things that happened to him. His primitive fancy, helped out by his priests and shamans did the rest. Of course, as social life became a more complicated thing, the fear of unwanted children unquestionably became an important reason for added severity in the conventions of Sex."

"It comes to the same thing," he answered. "The discovery of contraception may prove to be the most revolutionary thing that has ever happened to human society. We are just at the beginning of it. The day will come when contraception, in contrast with the clumsy methods in use at present, will amount to no more than the swallowing of a pill. And when that day comes, as it will very soon, what then? Take the eugenic possibilities of such a discovery, for instance!"

"Then you mean," I asked, "that you have laid all these cards on the table in dealing with your daughter?"

"Yes. I've done it partly with the help of books, I confess. It is hard to break through old reserves. But she and her parents have finally learned to talk about these things."

"Most persons," I observed, "would think you were running a grave risk to trust the judgment of an adolescent that far."

"Those are the counsels of fear," he said. "This takes faith. No one knows that better than you."

"I wish more people could see it," I replied.

"More *are* seeing it," he said.

CHAPTER XII

SOME OBSESSIONS: THEIR CAUSE AND CURE

1.

As I have already indicated, the now generally accepted recognition by society of the two kinds of marriage I have been discussing ("the companionate" and "the family") involves the assistance of modern science in the development of really satisfactory and adequate methods of contraception.

In the meantime it would startle a good many smug persons if they knew how widespread among young people, in every class of society, is the knowledge and use of fairly effective contraceptive devices. They make use of them as a matter of course.—I pause to remind my critics that I'm not responsible for this; and that I am merely recording what I know to be a fact.

2.

Lest some be inclined to doubt my assertion that young unmarried people are making wide use of contraceptives, let me cite one of the many evidences that have come my way.

An indignant neighbor had made a complaint concerning a noisy party that had been given by high school flappers, who served liquid refreshments that had something to do with the uproar that followed. One of the girls present at the party came to see me about it. Her name—let's call her Caroline. She is about seventeen, a very up and coming little personality, with a good mind. Outwardly she is very demure. Meeting her casually one would never suspect her of a number of things of which I learned later. Least of all did her parents and teachers suspect it.

Caroline, after explaining about the party, which has no importance in this connection, responded to some questions from me by making me a list of fifty-eight girls of high school age, known to

314

her personally, who had had at least one or more sex experiences with some youth. She checked off forty-four of them whom she said she knew positively had had such relations with boys. All of the fifty-eight in her list were more or less addicted to drink, and wild parties. Many of them were still actually in high school and most of them were there at the time of their first sex delinquency.

She said that the Dean of Girls in the school she attended knew nothing of any of these cases, and did not remotely suspect their existence. I was aware of that because I had been told that that same lady of impeccable virtue had made vigorous attacks on "Judge Lindsey's outrageous libels on the youth of Denver in his book 'The Revolt of Modern Youth' "—as though I had ever libeled any youth. I have always defended them.

Caroline then opened up a mine of information concerning this and that girl which was in line with what I have long been familiar with, and which is not believed by the "educational authorities" who assert that "less than one per cent" of their pupils "go wrong."

I immediately got in touch with nine of the girls on Caroline's list who had had relations with boys. These nine girls admitted it all, and in turn gave me the names of some boys with whom they had had relations. I talked to them separately, of course, and the names of some of the boys appeared on several of the lists. Others were on only one list.

One of these girls, aged sixteen, had had relations with twenty boys, and gave me the names of nineteen of them on the spot. I afterwards talked with most of those boys, and all of them have admitted the truth.

Nine of the girls had gone the limit with an average of five boys each. These nine of them had had such relations, collectively, more than two hundred times.

Yes, yes—I know it's shocking. But that's not what I'm telling it for. The point I want to make is that out of those more than two hundred occasions *not a single pregnancy resulted.*

I have often said that starting from any one individual case I could uncover an indefinite number, though my time and equipment and funds for such work are unfortunately very limited. Colorado doesn't exactly pour money by the shovelful into the coffers of our

Family Court. It's the criminal courts, the punishment machine of the state, that get the real money.

Not a single pregnancy resulted. Why? The question answers itself. Largely because every one of those youngsters is familiar with contraception. With such a safeguard at their command, how are you going to stop them? By force? By law?

3.

Among the facts that came out in my interview with Caroline was confirmation of what I already knew was common, that many of the girls of her acquaintance often carry a certain well-known contraceptive device in their vanity cases right alongside of lipstick and powder puff—a regular part of their armory.

"Do you carry them?" I asked.

"Sure—wouldn't I be the prize fool if I didn't? What do these fool boys care what happens to the girl? I tell you, Judge, we girls have got to look out for ourselves in this world."

Then she went on to give me a varied list of the slang names by which the device in question has come to be known—terms vividly metaphorical and quite unknown to the less imaginative Older Generation. Some of them I already knew; with others I was not familiar, since slang is a thing that changes constantly.

That this vanity case practice, as testified to by Caroline, is not uncommon I have many verifications. I know a woman, for instance, who lives in a very select boarding house in Denver, where there are a number of outwardly respectable and conventional young women of from 18 to 25 years. This woman recently told me that she knows several of these girls very well, and that they, quite as a matter of course, go thus provided against emergency.

I know another woman who, while a guest in a wealthy home, picked up a lost vanity case during a party that was being given by the beautiful and charming daughter of the house to her young friends. She opened the case in order to find out who owned it. She found out who owned it. It belonged to the daughter of the house. She also made a discovery that shocked her profoundly.

At this moment she saw the owner of the vanity case approaching with some of her friends, girls and boys. She tried to dispose of the case because she dreaded that if she gave it back to the girl, the girl would understand that she had opened it in order to find out whose it was.

They were close, and there was no graceful way of escape. But she instantly saw that they were looking for something. And their conversation revealed that it was the lost vanity case.

"I must have left it in here," said the young woman, who seemed not at all disturbed over her loss and its possible consequences in the hands of some stranger, or of her own parents.

"Is this what you were looking for?" asked the lady. "I have just picked it up."

And thus that tale ended, till it was told to me.

4.

Caroline continued her confidences. One fact that came out was that a week before she had been one of a party of high school girls and boys who went for a trip in the mountains. Their plan was to spend part of the night at a roadhouse.—A thoroughly reckless and regrettable business, I grant you. But how reckless? Well, not quite so reckless as it looked. Canny and cautious, rather. For just as the party was on the point of leaving Denver, one of the cars stopped at a drug store, and one of the boys went in and purchased the necessary precautionary measures *for the whole party.*

"You see," Caroline continued, "there is no reason why a girl should have to take all the chances because of something that can't happen to a boy. Once I went out with a boy who was afraid to go in the drug store and get preventives, because the soda jerk he knew, and who sold them to him, wasn't there. So I had to go to another drug store where there was a soda jerk I knew who would get them for me. Of course a girl has to be careful to know a girl soda jerk or a man clerk she can depend on. But it isn't that way with a boy. That kid has so little nerve you bet I'd never go out with him again."

5.

I am sorry to have to record this incident. It shocks even me, used as I am to such facts. But it is too important, and too conclusive, to omit. It is significant of a prevalent condition. People who "simply refuse to believe it" may go on wearing blinders and protesting if they will; but the facts stand, and they *mean something*. They are so patently packed with meaning that I am at a loss to understand the point of view of the excellent people who will write me letters of protest when they read this, "This isn't true. It is an exceptional case. You don't see anything of the *good* boys and girls."—But I do. Most of these kids are supposed by their parents and teachers to be absolutely moral, or at worst rather given to a liking for jazz, and cigarettes, but otherwise perfectly "straight." I hasten to add that I know many other youngsters who not only seem "straight" but are straight. I meet them here in my chambers all the time, for one reason or another, having nothing to do with their own conduct. Some come to see the court, others in behalf of friends and so on. But it is not of these that I am speaking here.

Some persons ask, "What if these things *are* true? What good does it do to tell it? Such things have always happened. We all know that."

They have *not* always happened. No such wholesale rebellion against the ancient conventions of sex has ever been known before in the history of our civilization. The reason is that this present civilization is the first of its kind. No other civilization, for example, had rubber. Rubber has revolutionized morals.

Whether you interpret these facts as evidence of a hopeless condition of moral corruption, after the manner of those who think the traditional interpretations of chastity are the Alpha and Omega of sociology and the last word on this complex question; or whether you think it a lawless and passing phase in a process of social change which will in time become orderly and amenable to legal and social control, through such devices as Companionate Marriage, for instance, depends on your way of thought. Personally I haven't a doubt about the outcome, though I regret that so many young feet are treading this perilous road, and that society is not waking up more quickly to the need for some remedy other than thundered prohibition from the pulpit, and interviews with every conservative Tom, Dick and Harry telling "what is the matter with our youth" and asking "whither are we drifting?"—Why drift?

Youth is treading this new path, not in occasional and exceptional instances, but by hundreds and even by thousands; and the new impulse has reached even into the ranks of the Older Generation, as I have already tried to show! What is the matter with the well-intentioned people who think they can stop such a process by preaching sermons, shouting denunciation, denying self-evident facts, and quoting texts to cover their own want of courage to think for themselves.

Moreover, why has sex become a secret, unacknowledged obsession in our Puritan born and Puritan bred civilization? If the Puritan outlook on life is good, why has it borne such speckled and poisonous fruit as this? Under what provocation do these boys and girls, who are at bottom not different from the boys and girls of less hectic generations, think so exclusively about sex that they apparently have no room in their heads for anything else? Why is the Older Generation of this day so restive, and so furtive, under its cloak of respectability?

6.

I answer, for the same reason that the minute the Prohibition Law was passed the American people not only became obsessed with the thought and subject of drink, but became also grossly incontinent with respect to drink, and could for a long time think and talk of nothing else,—with the difference that they talked of and sought drink openly, whereas they seek an outlet to their sex obsession secretly, and in fear. It is the same reason that causes hundreds of Americans when they land in Europe, where they can have all the drink they want, to make drunken pigs of themselves, in an orgy of release which satisfies something within them that many believe should never have been denied in the first place by anything save their own sense of voluntary decency, moderation, and restraint.

Such prohibitions and restraints work best when they come from within, as the fruit of education and culture. When imposed from without, whether in drink or with respect to sex, the ratio of safety to repression is about what you get when you plug the spout of a boiling teakettle, or hang a block of New England granite on the safety valve of a functioning steam engine. This is not to say that steam should not be controlled, or that it should be allowed to go aimlessly to waste. It *should* be controlled, and used, and made serviceable and safe.

Your attitude toward Prohibition is based on whether you believe human beings can be educated to decency and to voluntary restraint in the indulgence of an appetite, or that they must be restrained by force and law. Your attitude toward the time honored sex taboos is based on precisely the same choice.

Before Prohibition the American nation was finding itself on the liquor problem, after some decades of license, such as might be expected in a pioneer, unmatured civilization. It was educating itself slowly and steadily to a practicable ideal of temperance. The process was taking time, but it was effective. It was, however, far too slow for the busybodies who think people can be legislated into heaven. They instituted a form of direct action and bourgeois syndicalism which killed and aborted the delicate moral organism that was gestating in the spirit of this nation. The result is monstrous, but not, I believe, irrevocable. We can try again.

To-day many are piggish about drink. Too much of America drinks bad gin and worse whiskey and calls it good. We guzzle like a nation of yokels. We don't sip and taste and prefer; we swallow, gulp, and feel the kick. Such swinishness compares with good living as the fusel oil served to a longshoreman in a blind pig compares with the wine served to guests at a certain Wedding Feast in Cana of Galilee.

7.

I see the evidence on every hand. I know of a man, for instance, who is one of the leading churchmen in his community in a neighboring state. He was once a candidate for the governorship of his state. One day he addressed a Christian Endeavor meeting, and made a red hot speech for prohibition, a speech that rang with fervor against the Demon Rum.

The next day, in his hotel room in a neighboring town he drank himself into a condition of sodden idiocy, with heaven knows what horrible substitute for sound whiskey, and then went out onto the street and got into a row with a cop. The cop, not knowing that this

distinguished captive was one of the boys, locked him up; and before
the candidate's dismayed friends at City Hall could right matters
by greasing.the left palms of the right people, the opposition newspapers got hold of the story.

There is good ground for the contention that we are adopting the
wrong way to make ourselves temperate and decent. Drinking is
not intrinsically a sin, but we, with a stupid want of discrimination
and judgment, have pronounced it so, and in our minds have made it
so—and a terrible social corruption has resulted—many think far
worse than what we had before.

By the same token, sex is not a sin; the desire of a man for a
woman, and of a woman for a man, is not a sin; but we have hedged
the thing about with restrictions based primarily on the notion that
women are property. We give the notion a liberal coating of alleged
religion; and we call this hoary and disgusting fake "sex morality."
And we have kept this up so long that we have largely lost our
ability to think in terms of a genuine sex morality. In fact, we
would call a genuine sex morality "immorality" if any one had the
nerve to practice it openly to-day.

The most monstrous feature of this tragedy is that the groping,
bewildered, seething mass of people who are trying in their own way
to come at a moral substitute for this fake morality, are unable to
think their way through. The best most of them are able to do in
breaking away from the old system, is to achieve a spurious morality
themselves, just as Americans abroad, by rushing to the "American
bar" in Paris or London, only to make beasts of themselves, achieve
a spurious freedom.

Some persons credit me with advocating some such thing as that
in sex. Nothing could be further from my thought. I simply record
the facts. In sex conduct we are right now going through the
spurious freedom phase; we are grossly misbehaving in the first
childish exhilaration of revolt. But I think we shall some day
achieve something in sex very far removed from all this—something
governed by authentic tastes, and free but educated preferences—a
genuine culture in short. Neither in our past orgy of superstitious
restraint, nor in our present orgy of ill-considered license, have we
ever had such a thing; but of the two conditions, the first seems to me

to have been the more deadly, the more hopeless, the more morally
vitiating of the two. The inability of our "moral" fanatics to do
any straight thinking about this matter amply indicates how people
atrophy in a country that takes full charge of the personal morals
of its citizens.

8.

I related the case of the mountain trip indulged in by those boys
and girls to a minister of my acquaintance. "It is perfectly obvious,"
said the reverend gentleman, "what the remedy is in a case like
that. Those young people should have been chaperoned." That was
all he could contribute. The notion that a chaperon would not
have changed the real situation, namely the mental and moral condition of those children, did not seem to occur to him.

His prescription was worthless. He overlooked the deeper fact
that those children were obsessed with sex, and that that obsession
was patently the fruit of the conditions in which they had always
lived. They couldn't go off for a good healthy day's enjoyment in
the mountains. They must drop everything of the sort in order to
satisfy the starved something, the warped and crippled something,
the twisted something, that had taken possession of them. For this
they were not responsible. Whatever it was, society created it.

How society has created it I have told with some detail in "The
Revolt of Modern Youth." And I here content myself with suggesting this thought: We have a social order which, in deferring
marriage till the twenties or later, takes no count of the fact that
sexual maturity, a terrific force, arrives in the teens. It can be
sublimated. under a proper system of education, in athletics, in
music, in dancing, in study and intellectual growth, and it need not
seek a specifically sexual outlet. Our educational system should
proceed as much on this idea as possible. I know the principal of an
excellent co-educational private school, a boarding school, who never
has any trouble with the sex problem among his students. He turns
the trick, not by making rules to be broken, but simply by running
the school under a system of student self-government, and by so
allotting the work of the school that every individual student is kept

normally busy and occupied in healthful pursuits every hour of the day.

We have, however, to remember that in spite of such safeguards and such sublimation of the developing sex life of the young, the tendency to seek a specifically sexual outlet is often very marked; and neither in our educational system nor in our moral code do we intelligently cope with this fact. We fall back on easy and established social prohibitions of the sort which that wild roadhouse party of boys and girls defied in so sickening a fashion.

I call it sickening, not with reference to their natural impulse of sex, but rather with reference to their want of any sense of fitness. They were offensive. They behaved like yahoos. The standards of delicacy, good taste and good breeding would have imposed restraints on that exploit if the party had possessed them.

9.

I have been receiving a good many letters of late asking me how I reconcile some of the views I am expressing in this book with the Bible. I have one short and conclusive answer to that question. I don't reconcile it with the Bible. Moreover, I don't see why I should. Those of my views which are in accord with Holy Writ speak for themselves. Those which are not have to be classed with evolution, the roundness of the earth, and other matters which were not factors in the speculative thought of the ancient Jews. To say that modern sociology must deal with modern facts is not to flout or discount the Bible. It is to interpret that book in the corrective light of changing conditions.

One reviewer pronounces me a dangerous cross between a bolshevist and a Nietzschean. "Nietzsche," this chaste and indignant lady points out, "denied the existence of lasting moral principle or right in the conduct of life."

Well, I don't agree with that Nietzschean denial. To me there is a vast distinction between human custom and the moral law. The moral law is the important thing. Human custom is valid only so long as it conforms to this higher principle. That is why I so often find that there is small room for human customs that interfere with moral law. A custom must produce in terms that are practicable and measurably good or I am done with it, and so, in the end, is everybody else.

My creed is a simple one. I think it is up to the human race to behave in a way that will intelligently make for the happiness and welfare of the greatest number of persons; that we are to use our common sense, as individuals, in judging what conduct, in any specific situation, will do that. I think the best morality is based on happy, expansive, and generous living which reckons duly on the happiness of others, and takes pleasure in that happiness. I think such a way of living needs to be rational and not custom-bound or superstitious; and that it must be based on honest, courageous, and independent thought rather than on second-hand maxims and prohibitions accepted uncritically because they are old or are alleged to be "in accord with the experience of the race." Some are, and some are not.

10.

A moral man is concerned, not with an abstract and an arbitrary "moral law" that cares nothing for consequences and is therefore not moral, but rather with a concrete moral law which is measured by the *results* of his conduct. If a conventionally moral act produces unhappiness, he will consider whether it be truly moral and good or not; and he will be concerned not merely with the immediate consequences of such an act but with its ultimate consequences. An act which brings immediate pleasure but may bring ultimate misery is bad; while one which brings immediate pain but final pleasure is usually good.

The moral man will use his best judgment to determine such probable consequences. What is harmful is sinful, what is harmless is right or at least permissible, and what works in the long run for good, and for a greater intensity of life—that is Virtue. The only reasonable standard of value in conduct is the consequences for us and for others that lie implicit in our acts and in our thoughts. Whatever works evil is evil. Whatever produces good is good. And God requires of us, I believe, both thoughts of good will and acts of good result,—as good, at least, as we can compass. Cut-to-pattern convention, you see, has small chance in company with such principles as these.

A truly moral man will place the emphasis in conduct on something other than the usual "thou shalt not," so emphasized in the Ten Commandments. He will regard cruelty and unkindness and jealousy and malice and other similar forms of conduct and thought which are *socially permissible* as abominations in the sight of God, and will be inclined to be lenient with persons who sin because they love. It is not clear that some of the things we forbid are injurious or wrong. It is very clear, on the other hand, that many of the things we permit and applaud as right and good are really injurious and wrong to the last and lowest degree in the Seventh Circle of Hell. Our laws of social conduct are too often not concerned with right and wrong; and this is especially true with respect to sex. Marital jealousy, one of our pet social virtues, is an example of what I mean.

What many other persons would call the "moral law" I regard as not moral at all. In fact, I think it often cruel, unjust, savage, and ignoble. Take, for instance, the value we place on chastity in women. This is part of our "moral" law. It masquerades under all sorts of esthetic names. It is identified by poets with the "purity" of the lily. It implies that sex relations sully that purity. It even insists on an "immaculate conception" in order to make sure that its particular chief deity, a man-god, should be free from this taint. And then, by a special magic, it excepts married women from the general rule. They have had sex relations, but they are chaste and pure—even in a loveless marriage—all by virtue of a bit of magic called a wedding ceremony. On the other hand, some sinning sister, unmarried, who has committed the same act in an ecstasy of love, is impure, polluted, tainted and what not. What all this means is simply that women are property; and that society swats any woman who yields up her virginity irregularly by branding her with a mark of shame and making her taboo. The "moral law"— Where under heaven is there a name to fit this thing?

II.

What the ancient Jews *really* meant by "thou shalt not commit adultery" was "thou shalt not steal." And they referred to a particular kind of property—human property, chiefly women. Why not say so, and admit that possessive jealousy and property rights are back of our traditional attitude in this matter?

When I say this I am by no means making myself an advocate of adultery. I am merely saying that our conception of what should be the relations of the sexes, particularly in marriage, will have to be revised and put upon a genuinely ethical basis before we can have a right to call the thing moral. As it stands, I think our code of sex morality is Immorality with a big "I." It is a lie more immoral than all the adultery ever committed because it does more harm than all the adultery ever committed. If you don't believe it, make a review of the mess called Modern Marriage and Divorce.

When we call a woman "virtuous" do we mean that she is really virtuous? Not at all. We mean that she is presumably "chaste," by virtue of a marriage ceremony. We call her virtuous though she may be a liar, a gossip, a virago, and a terror at home, without a virtue of mind or heart to commend her. I know many such. They are not to be compared in virtue with some prostitutes; and still less with hundreds of girls and women I know who are sweet and dear and good though they have loved outside of wedlock.

I have a letter from one text spouter saying "If you had denounced these evils you tell of, and even quoted now and then from the Bible to show how wrong it all was, it would have been all right."

Don't I know it? Why, if I should denounce and bewail through all the pages of this book and demand in despairing tones what the world is coming to, and mention "our modern Sodoms and Gomorrahs" often enough, the things I have related in some of my stories wouldn't raise a ripple of denunciation from the godly. They would lap it up and call for more.

This is a trick resorted to regularly by some of the clergy in this country. They announce sermons on lurid topics, in which sex will figure largely; and they give their conventional congregations a bigger kick than they could get out of the hottest plays on the New York stage. Sometimes they try the "men only" and "women only" hokum and pack the sanctuary. They do this right in church and get away with it. How? Simply by denouncing hard enough and long enough. This saves the face of the proprieties; with that attended to, the sky is the limit.

The trouble with such brethren is that they haven't got the facts. *But I have!* And the trouble with me is that I don't put them over behind a smoke-screen of sham denunciation.

One critic writes me that the Seventh Commandment is a full and complete answer to everything I have written. In my judgment it is nothing of the sort. These "sinners" who rebel and then get caught in the conventional toils have plenty to say for themselves when once you get under their skins. And I don't see why they should not have the floor and their day in court just as soon as the *good* people of this country, who are of course *quite* without sin, and who make the laws—get through doing all the talking. What the good people demand is that their side of the matter be presented *in toto* and *ad nauseam,* and that everything on the other side be suppressed or else smothered in a feather bed of scriptural quotations. They are poor sports.

12.

If we could bring ourselves to think honestly about these matters, we could make marriage a much more genuinely monogamous institution than it is, with much less adultery in it than there is. I don't call marriages in which the parties are restive and don't love each other, or in which they desire infidelities they don't commit, *monogamous.* Monogamy is in the heart if it is anywhere. I have even known it to exist in marriages that were physically polygamous. Monogamy is in the psychology of a marriage if it is anywhere. A merely technical monogamy reduces neither the number of divorce courts nor the sum of domestic misery.

I scrutinize and question the authority of any custom to persist without currently giving an account of itself, and submitting to revision when revision is necessary. Any other plan is destructive to the very morality it professes to uphold. It is the "moral" people of this country who are undermining morality by their efforts to suppress every fact that they think might weaken their position. They can take it from me that their day is short.

What I am for is a genuine morality which will maintain a proper balance between the rights and claims of individuals on the one hand and the rights and just claims of society on the other. At present, especially in our sex conventions, we have nothing of the sort. Society claims everything; and there is no limit to its superstitious greed, avarice, and fear.

I know a man who has a savage dog. If that animal broke loose he would be a menace to the community. He would kill any one he could get at. He lunges at his steel chain and leather collar when a group of school children so much as pass within sight of his kennel. This dog is savage merely because he is kept chained. —It is the same with Sex. I don't advocate turning this savage, long confined force suddenly loose on the country, any more than I would advocate the sudden unleashing of that savage dog when a group of boys and girls were passing. Rather I advocate a system that will make such a liberty gradually possible under reasonable and kind control. It can be done. Sex is a great spiritual force. But would you know it when you see the thing glowering at you there in chains? I should think that anybody with a mind above moron capacity could see this distinction.

I am not for license, nor for the irresponsible promiscuity of free love, nor for sex orgies. But neither am I for the type of marriage that would bind people together without love and make a steel trap of wedlock. I am for decency, restraint, culture, real religion, and conduct based on the Golden Rule as Jesus taught it. Let my critics show a better prescription with their Old Testament references and their "Chastity" obsessions.

13.

"But Jesus forbade adultery," say they.

Jesus also said, "Whosoever shall smite thee on thy right cheek, turn to him the other also." He forbade the use of force, and then in a terrific burst of wrath whipped the money changers from the temple. He likewise said, "Ye have heard that it was said by them of old time, Thou shalt not commit adultery. But I say unto you that whosoever looketh on a woman to lust after her hath committed adultery with her already in his heart." By that Jesus meant just as real adultery, psychologically and spiritually, as would be

involved in the physical act. In that event there are few men on
earth who haven't committed adultery. Here was an attack on
hypocrisy and cant with a vengeance. "He that is without sin
among you, let him cast the first stone. . . ." He consigned sinners
to eternal fires of hell, and yet is said to have told the sinning girl he
did not even condemn her.

If these Bible quoters think so much of the commands of Jesus,
why don't they obey him literally and turn that other cheek; and
why don't they regard themselves as adulterers; and why—oh,
why—don't they indulge now and then in the luxury of telling the
truth? It would do them good. I derive fresh strength every time
I do it. There is no tonic like it.

What it all means is that Jesus could at times be magnificently
human, inconsistent, and even naïve. I insist that though he gave
us the most valid ethic ever propounded for human conduct, we
are not absolved by it from the moral obligation to use our noggins
and to be honest and independent in our way of thought, and to
agree with Jesus in this or disagree with him in that, and do it
openly. For instance, I don't turn the other cheek and I don't think
I ought to. Neither did Jesus when he scourged the money changers
in the temple. What magnificent humanity; what a superb, fallible
infallibility he had! How much more truly a god he was than his
orthodox followers have ever dreamed. He could be human, and
he could be inconsistent.

Jesus spoke with the voice of his time. What he taught was
valid for ever, but the language he used had to be the language
of that day if he was to get himself understood. He may have
had an intuitive knowledge of the Fourth Dimension and of the
Einstein theory and of the characteristics of electrical energy,—but
if he had talked of such things to his generation he would simply
have closed their minds to the vital part of his message. How deep
his intuitions went we can only guess; but we don't have to guess
about his intuitive common sense.

14.

If Jesus were here to-day he would speak with the outlook of this
time, and in language which this generation would understand. He

would apply to the facts of life as we have it now the same principles that he applied to life as they had it then. And though the principles would be eternally valid and eternally the same, the conclusions and judgments flowing from them would be different because the conditions would be different.

The reason the orthodox of that day crucified Jesus was that he flouted the shams and pretenses of the people about him, and stripped their orthodoxy naked to the wind of his spirit when he did it. They preferred their comfort to his truth. The orthodox of this day would treat him the same way if he should suddenly make an appearance in their respectable pulpits. They would demand of him conformity to the letter of all his former pronouncements, regardless of changes in the conditions that called them forth.

Consider his attitude toward one of their most treasured orthodox superstitions of his time. They had accused his disciples of violating the Sabbath, because being hungry, they had plucked corn in the fields on that day: "And he said unto them, have ye never read what David did, when he had need, and was an hungered, he, and they that were with him? How he went into the house of God in the days of Abiathar the high priest, and did eat the shewbread, which is not lawful to eat but for the priests, and gave also to them which were with him?

"And he said unto them, The sabbath was made for man, and not man for the sabbath.

"Therefore the Son of man is Lord also of the sabbath."

There is food for extended thought in that passage. Jesus knew the difference between a man-made taboo and a genuine law of God. And so they crucified him.

CHAPTER XIII

THE CLERGY AND CURRENT MORALS

I.

A DENVER Bible class teacher, whom I shall call Mr. James Howe, came to me in consternation some time ago with a note which he had picked up on the floor of his church, shortly after the dismissal of Sunday school.

The contents of the note had nearly shocked him into illness. It was unsigned and more or less cryptic, but its implications were plain. And since the part of the building where it had been found had been occupied just previously by a class of adolescent girls, the note constituted ample evidence, not merely that the owner of it had "gone wrong," but also that she was a highly sophisticated young woman, and had made scientific provision against mishaps. Apparently the only mishap she had overlooked was the fact that vanity cases may sometimes fall open by accident.

"Judge," he said. "I hardly slept all night. What am I to do? Why, I know every girl in that class. I had thought of them all as sweet and lovely, and I believed them pure and wholesome. I have known them since they were children; I know their parents and the homes they come from—first rate homes. They are close friends of my daughter and of my two boys. My daughter, indeed, is a member of the class; and if they were lined up before you you would say that any one of them might be she."

His hand trembled and he tapped nervously on the arm of his chair.

"Have you any reason to suppose that your daughter might have dropped this?" I asked.

"Thank God, no!" he exclaimed. "She wasn't there. God has spared me that."

"That's fine," I said. "But why do you say that God spared you?

331

332 THE COMPANIONATE MARRIAGE

I don't say anything that would sound like sarcasm, my dear man, but I can't help thinking that if he was so solicitous about you, it is rather a pity that he overlooked the parents of this other girl. Wasn't it the friends of Job who suggested that Job must have committed some sin, and that God had taken that way to punish him?"

"His ways are past finding out," he said.

"They are indeed," I thought, "and sometimes I wonder how you and members of the clergy ever found out so much about them." But this I kept to myself: for he needed sympathy and help, and I was far from wanting to hurt his feelings. So I let it pass in silence.

"Can anything be done?" he asked.

"I think so. But what's to be done may depend a good deal on your point of view. Let me tell you something about certain things in connection with your Sunday school that you apparently haven't found out, but which I have been familiar with for some time. I know one unmarried girl there who had a child last year; and there is another who came to me infected. I arranged for the confinement of the first, and I sent the other to the private physician who is in my confidence, and he cured her. I don't know whether these girls are members of the same class as the owner of this note: but these two instances will give you something to think about. For instance, the situation indicated in this note might be worse. This girl, for example, might have become pregnant or diseased, like those others, instead of getting off scott-free, as she apparently has done."

"More?" he gasped. "Do you tell me there are more? And my daughter—"

"Oh, no," I put in hastily, "neither of them was your daughter. Be easy on that score. The Lord, I suppose, you would say, has spared you—to that extent at least. But let's get back to the question and let's lay all the cards on the table. This girl has had relations outside of marriage; and she has done what so many of these modern youngsters are doing. She has taken the precaution to protect herself. Apparently then the old-time methods of teaching all youngsters to abstain from such improprieties doesn't work. I could have told you this long ago. Such methods are not working as so many think they are and they are in a large way responsible for the very conditions they forbid. More people than you know have stopped behaving themselves merely because they are afraid they will be punished by the Lord later on if they do as they please; and so far as I know, the motive which sways most of these youngsters when they *do* draw the rein on themselves is their own wish for decency, moderation and good taste in the ordering of their lives, and not the fear of hell fire.

"Give them a love for such things, just as you might give them a love for music or good books or good painting, or any kind of art, and you've got them,—with no question of rewards and punishments entering in. They get their reward in an inner satisfaction. *This esthetic craving is a sound basis for conduct.* We all yearn for beauty. We all want to be beautiful and to act beautifully. But in Sunday school is conduct presented in any such light as that? In too many of them it is not! Such Sunday schools follow the old theological lines; and they are not, in my opinion, genuinely religious lines. That is why they are failing with modern youth.

"The system of telling people to be good here and to give up things they desire here in order that they may be happy and long-lived after death is no longer working as it formerly did. For one thing, growing numbers of youth no longer accept the word of the clergy as to what things are right and what things are wrong; they no longer admit the authority of convention; they insist that they have a right to think for themselves; and I may add that they have a moral code, though you may think they haven't. If you questioned this girl—provided you were sure of her identity—and were skillful enough to get her confidence and know her real thoughts, you would find that *she* has a code.

"I don't want what I am saying to sound unsympathetic, but I do want to wake you up, my dear man. For I know what a power you are in your church and your good work; and I hate to see you misapplying your great power to inspire people. Are you willing to frankly talk this thing out with me? It isn't just a matter of trying to get hold of this particular girl, you understand; for indeed she seems pretty competent to look out for herself and to keep out of trouble with society, whatever you may think of her morals.— What you have to deal with is a situation."

"I'll talk it out with you gladly," he said. "Perhaps you are right. No one knows better than I that something is wrong in our system. It isn't for nothing that the churches are losing their grip. But this thing has floored me. I didn't believe those girls knew anything about such things, even by hearsay. I have always maintained that the statements made in your book, 'The Revolt of Modern Youth,' are an exaggeration caused by your contact with so many delinquents. And now—to think that my daughter has been intimate with those girls for years; and exposed to such corrupting influences!"

"Do you see any difference in her?"

"No—but she must know all about these things; and it's degrading, and dangerous."

"Does it degrade you to know the truth about them?"

"But—she's so young. I want to shield her."

"Ignorance is not a shield," I said. "The girl that lost that note—would you rather she knew how to take care of herself, as she evidently does, or would you have had her mind so unsullied by facts as to leave her the possible victim of unwanted pregnancy or disease?—If you want my opinion, I say that if you haven't had your daughter properly instructed at the proper time in everything that is known to science on this whole subject of contraception and prophylaxis you are far from deserving the signal mercy you think the Lord has shown you."

"But to teach them such things is to imply that they will have a right to apply the information," he protested. "It is to assume that they may have sex relations before marriage, when such a possibility should not even be debatable. The application of such knowledge in marriage is a different thing. Let them be instructed after marriage—yes; but this other thing—I find it unthinkable. And I may as well tell you, Judge, that it is being charged by your enemies that young people express the opinion that the doctrines set forth in your book, 'The Revolt of Modern Youth,' make it very easy for people to feel that they can be unconventional in sex conduct without being wicked."

"That's quite possible," I said. "But the ethical values lie in

what they choose and prefer and like and want, don't they? You
have the alternative of restraining them as best you can by bonds of
fear and ignorance, or of letting them restrain themselves by educating them to high standards of good taste, culture and discrimination;
and to an inward, real, first-hand preference for the fine and beautiful things in life and in love, and then let their conduct flow from
such tastes.—The girl who uses rouge and lipstick—teach her to
prefer the lips and cheeks that are colored by health. Teach her to
be beautiful within. But don't tell her her craving for beauty in
life and her craving for the intensities and the pleasures of living
is a sin."

"I grant all that, of course," he said. "But they *have* no cultured
preferences, and the other is the only thing that can control them."

"Take a chance on them. You'll be surprised."

He shook his head. "I don't dare. This is a Utopian vision.
You are a dreamer and an idealist. You are not practical."

"Stack your facts against those I have been collecting for more
than twenty-five years in my court," I said, "and see which of us
is dealing in bugaboos and outworn theories. Let's put it this way.
The note you have found represents *what is really going on, whether
you want it to or not*. It represents a phase of the revolt of modern
youth about which I have written over the protest of the Old Guard
of the ministry.

"The ranks of the Old Guard are dwindling to-day—mostly by
desertion. I hope you are with the deserters. Read history; trace
these processes of social change, and see how the Old Guard at first
fights them, and then inevitably succumbs before the advance of a
new and better order. History proves the Old Guard wrong. Be
guided by that; and for heaven's sake get over any notion you may
hold that the orthodox interpretations of scripture are the last
crystallized finality of revealed truth. Fewer and fewer men in the
ministry find that view any longer as reasonable. Such an interpretation of scripture, they perceive, forbids social growth; and is doing
harm.

"This note is only one of hundreds of evidences that come my
way. It is tragic that so many good men should be unwittingly

helping to produce the very demoralization of which they complain. Can't you *see* that the Old Guard are giving the young no equipment for making their own lives into original and beautiful creations of the spirit, and that it is requiring of them that they become copyists, imitators of cut-to-pattern standards which are presented to them as the final and only possible standards? When the Old Guard tell them that, they know it simply isn't true. Can't you see it?"

"These ideas of yours are very stimulating," he said slowly; "and I fear they are dangerous. Still—I don't want you to think I'm not willing to be candid. I know you are sincere, 'that you mean well.'"

"Good! Now answer me this question which you have so far failed to meet me on: Since this kind of thing *is* going on, and since the forces at work are so big that nobody can stop them from running their course, would you rather these girls were able to rely on their wit and common sense or that they should be subject to the risks involved in youth and ignorance? In other words, would you keep them ignorant if you could, or are you prepared to admit that the thing which really plays hob with them is not so much their departures from sex convention as the unwanted pregnancy and disease which they encounter ignorantly?

"Let me point out to you that you can't for the life of you distinguish in that Sunday school class which of those girls is the sinner. They remain individually as high in your esteem and as sweet and lovely as they were before you found this note. But if you could discover the owner of it, then by some black magic of theology—forgive me if I seem harsh—by some black magic of theological tradition, I say, she would be transformed into an impure and fallen creature. And the others would stay on their pedestals till you found out something about *them*. And you can bank on it that you don't know the whole story by a long shot. It isn't all in this note. Their lives are no open book to you. *I* say that what this girl has done has had no social consequences for anybody but herself. She has taken good care of that. I say further that her responsibility to society would have become acutely evident if she had fallen into the trap into which ignorance of contraception and prophylaxis might have led her. What do you say? Be honest now, there's a good fellow."

"Yes, I admit what you say of the practical consequences," he said. "Her sophistication eliminated the social consequences; and I suppose to that extent they must be admitted to have saved her and other persons from trouble and disgrace. I don't undervalue that or wish it otherwise.—But you are overlooking this girl's responsibility to God. She has violated His commandment."

"She has violated a command of custom and tradition which you *believe* and *allege* to be a command of God," I put in. "But customs which our ancestors thought were commands of God have changed, and are no longer accepted by you as other than what they are— practices, namely, which society has discarded because it finds them no longer useful or practicable, and hence no longer the Will of God. What applies to one custom applies to all. Some day we shall have a new set of sex customs, and the ministers of that day will call *those* the divine command."

"For a person who does not accept the scriptures as the inspired and final word of God, inspired in every line," he said, "that is a perfectly sound argument. But I accept the Bible as final—at least I think I do. And so, of course, I reason to a different conclusion."

"You really take it as final? You have no misgivings as to the damage such a method of interpreting scripture may do to society?"

"Yes, I have my honest doubts and questionings. But I have clung to it. You see I'm trying to be candid, Judge.—But there is another side to this. If these young people didn't know how to avoid the consequences of sexual misconduct they would be *afraid* to do such things. I admit that that is not the highest motive for rectitude, but it is socially valuable. It gets results. People must be controlled by fear, if need be, for their own good and the good of society."

"I thank you for your candor," I answered. "At this rate we may get somewhere. You admit, then, that if controlled by fear, they would still *want* to cut loose and follow their impulses,—which you, perhaps, would call their lower impulses, their lusts, stirred into

activity by Satan. But why regard these as lower impulses, since
marriage converts them into something sacred, even by your code.
If the marriage ceremony can so transform and translate them, maybe
they are not intrinsically evil, after all!   Maybe the thing needed is
merely their control, *whether in marriage or out of it*.   But you can't
bring such impulses under control by making them difficult to attain.
In fact, prohibitions intensify them, don't they?   Prohibitions, perhaps, are the very thing that make them evil.   And by prohibitions
I mean prohibitions imposed from without.   Now if we could have
prohibitions imposed from within, *created* from within, out of the
genuine desire to possess what is beautiful and lovely in life—and
to *be* lovely and beautiful, that would be different, wouldn't it?
I maintain that the one kind of prohibition is worthless and without
ethical or spiritual value; and that the other is beyond price."

He smiled.   "Well, I admit you present a fascinating picture of
the golden age; but how on earth can we put such a thing into
practice without wrecking everything?   The ice is too thin.   You
are forgetting human nature.   We haven't evolved that far."

"That's what they said when I began sending youth to the reform
school and reformatories without an officer to keep them from running away," I retorted.   "It was too big a strain, they said, to put
on human nature.   But I did it, and never lost a boy, out of
hundreds in all these years.   How did I do it?   Simply by making
sure that I had the boy *thinking straight* before I let him go, with
his railroad ticket in his pocket, and self-respect in his heart.   That's
all.   And it works with most people if you'll just take the trouble
to put it over.

"The trouble with theology and its teaching about original sin
and the fall of man, is that it holds that the human heart is wicked
and that it has to be saved in spite of itself.   Now why don't you
drop all that and commit yourself to the thesis that human beings
are only too glad to be good if they can see their way to being
so, and that when people sin they sin through astigmatic thinking?
A pox on theology.   Put some real religion in its place.   The two
things are not identical, not by a long shot."

"But what you hold is not religion," he objected.   "It's paganism.
It's mere rationalism.   You hold that a thing is justified if it is

natural or beautiful. The church teaches the opposite doctrine."

"Which it must eventually abandon," I said. "Can't you see how preposterous it is? You will find no support for this rejection of nature and of beauty in the teachings of Jesus. Consider the lilies—even Solomon in all his glory was not arrayed like one of these.

"As for rationalism, that is simply an effort to think straight and find the truth. It is a lot harder than taking the Bible in hand and saying, 'Here is all the truth; all of it; and thank God I don't have to do another lick of thinking. Thinking is such confoundedly hard work.' My dear fellow, if you want to see what kind of grapes this theological rejection of rationalism produces, by ordering people's conduct for them instead of making them responsible for their own doings, look at exhibit A, found on the floor of your church.

"Now what I say to these young people is this: You are free agents. You have the making of your own lives. The judge that must judge you is your own heart and conscience. You have ample opportunity in this age to do as you choose. Nobody can stop you, and I, for one, wouldn't stop you if I could. You need fear no punishment so long as you do not violate the rights of other persons. You may have your own code so long as you regard your neighbor's rights. So far as sex is concerned, here are the means science has discovered for preventing pregnancy and disease. With these to guard you against injuring either yourselves or others, you can now make your choice on grounds into which fear does not enter, but with which your sense of manners, taste, beauty and decency has everything to do. It narrows down to a question of what you really like, and of what you think will make you really happy, together with what you can do without injury to yourself or other people. What do you like? What do you like in pictures, in music, in literature, in sculpture, in architecture, in nature, in friendship, in religion, in love, in all the great things of life which are great because they are beautiful, and which are abominable if they are not beautiful.

"But you must be your own judge of beauty. Nobody else can tell you what you are to find beauty in. This is a personal thing, a matter of insight and personal revelation. A music lover can't convey to a person with no ear for music why music enthralls him. It is a matter of personal feeling. Religion is the same. So is fine discrimination in matters of conduct. What is cheap in the eyes of one may be lovely in the eyes of another, for our capacities differ; but it is safe to say that all normal persons have within them a sufficient instinct for beauty to guide them aright if they have been taught by the example of society and those around them, and by teachers of conduct (such as yourself, my dear Howe), to heed that inner voice and cling by preference to its admonitions. Good taste, restraint, self-discipline, sensitiveness, judgment, refinement, culture —real religion, these will lead you aright. That is what I say to them. And more than ninety per cent of them come out right by that rule.

"Now what would you like to see done—if you could order things as you wish, assuming that you are converted, let us say—only to part of the view I have been expressing."

"One of the first things I would do," he said, "would be to put some sort of restriction on the manufacture of the devices mentioned in that note. I don't mean that I am against their use. I have come around to a partial acceptance of Birth Control. What I object to is that they are within the reach of these youngsters. They are a direct inducement to sex delinquency. What you have been saying impresses me, I admit. But you want to go too fast. You know the law forbids their sale or use. I think there should be a campaign started to restrict the distribution of such devices."

"It's been done," I said. "Anthony Comstock arranged long ago to have it stopped. But I could take you to a town I know of where a great factory keeps scores of girls at work at machines which are dedicated exclusively to the service of a certain pagan goddess. The product of those machines is contraband and bootleg, and I suppose that to estimate the amount of misery, disease, unwanted pregnancy, illegitimate births, and murdered or outcast children that are thereby prevented in human society would require something bigger than the Congressional Record merely to record it.

"I know a man in Denver," I went on, "who has two sons. This man has a very religious home, like yours. His two sons have been protected all their lives against vice. When the war came, one of these sons enlisted and went to France. The other for some reason, perhaps because of his age, remained at home.

"Some time later this boy—the one who stayed home under the protection of his parents, came to me for help. He had defied his home training in spite of all 'threats of hell and hopes of paradise'; and his ignorance of sex and of contraception and of prophylaxis had failed to restrain him *by fear*, as you have suggested would be the case. He took his chance, and went the limit. He got a venereal infection. I sent him to a physician, who finally cured him. This boy also brought to me a girl—a girl who might have been in your more or less select Sunday school, my dear Howe. In his ignorance and folly he had infected *her*. Her case was so serious that an operation was necessary; and the damage was so great that she will never be able to bear a child.

"So much for the virtuous son who stayed at home with his parents to guard his morals and keep things dark, and save him from the knowledge that would have averted all that dreadful damage to himself and another person.

"Later, when I was in France, I met and talked with the other boy. I found that he had indulged himself with French girls, some of whom were probably diseased. But did he get an infection? Not he. And why? Because when the war came we chucked our Puritan prejudices. The army provided prophylaxis for soldiers. It didn't so much as say to him: 'You must behave, because if you don't you'll get infected.' Instead it instituted the most stringent regulations possible for prophylactic treatment; and I saw soldier boys standing in line waiting for such treatment. More than that, in certain places prophylactic materials were dispensed where every youth could freely receive their aid; and instructions were given for their use. And any soldier who was so careless as to get an infection was in for penalties of very great severity. Their personal morals were their own, but their health belonged to the Army, and thus their sex conduct became 'immoral' only when it involved social and military consequences.

"When the war was over, I heard a Y. M. C. A. man get up and make a talk about how our army had been the cleanest army in the world; and how our boys had come back as clean and pure as when they had left their mothers and sisters. Perhaps! But if so, the reason a large number of them came back 'clean and pure' was the hardboiled reason that an army regulation, which was never instituted by the clergy, had kept them so. I should have liked to hear the Y. M. C. A. man tell *that*.

"And thus it happened that the one boy came back from France with nothing worse than a bullet scar on his arm, and the other, at home, had a disease of which he will always carry the effects— because his parents prescribed his conduct for him, and kept him in line by keeping him ignorant.

"You believe," I continued, "that there is no substitute for this crystallized morality which you would prefer for the young. I wish you could get over the idea that it is safer and more productive of good and of happiness to prescribe people's conduct instead of urging and teaching them to make conduct a creative art. I wish you could persuade yourself that beauty and culture can go over with people on its own power, and that it does not require super- natural aids of 'thou shalt' and 'thou shalt not'—principally the latter.

"Now let me tell you a story that will show you, whether you agree with these rebels against the established order or not, that they do have a code, which they hold to, such as it is, without any supernatural aids, simply because they prefer it. I don't ask you to agree with their code, mind you, and I am far from say- ing that it is all it should be. I merely want to demonstrate to you that it exists, and that it can be trusted to operate, within its own field, without coercion or watching, among the people who hold it.

"Two girls, whom I shall call Ethel and Anne, came to me one day and asked me if I would not call in Mabel, a friend of theirs, and make Mabel behave herself.—Parenthetically let me say that I knew both of these girls very well. They were both of them sophisticated to a degree that would probably have shocked you; but they were both of them 'straight.' Neither of them had ever had a sex experience, and the extent of their improprieties amounted to no more than occasional petting, which is no longer an impeachment of a girl's morals. In other words, as conduct in such matters goes nowadays, they were what most persons would call 'moral.' My critics might not believe it, but I had had something to do with their choosing that course; though I had persuaded them into it, not by any reference to heavenly rewards and hellish punishments, but by laying the cards on the table, and expressing somewhat the same views which I have been telling to you.

" 'What has Mabel been doing?' I asked.

" 'Why,' said Ethel, 'I was at a frat dance a few months ago, and I happened to walk into a bedroom at the frat house, and there I found Mabel, with Jerry Mason. Well, Judge, believe me I backed out of that room quick, saying "excuse me." I guess they had forgotten to lock the door.'

" 'Yes,' put in Anne indignantly, "and now Jerry's got the same disease Mabel had. The little fool. She hadn't any business getting it in the first place. And now she is mean enough to pass it on. It's perfectly outrageous. She did the same thing once before to another boy, and he nearly committed suicide. She must quit it. There's no telling what harm she'll do. Won't you call her in and make her behave, and get cured? *She's immoral!'*

"Now I want you to note one thing about what those girls said. They were not asking me to stop Mabel from her unconventional conduct with Jerry or other boys. Not at all. They didn't do that kind of thing themselves, but if Mabel wanted to do it, that, they thought, was her business. They and their set did not regard it as markedly different from petting. It was a step further in intimacy, but they didn't regard it as wrong, or impure, or unchaste, or immoral. What they did regard as wrong, unchaste, and immoral was that Mabel had knowingly injured that boy.

"Their code didn't call for continence, but it did very clearly call for fair play, and the kind of morality which that implies. Their code forbade doing what would injure somebody else. For instance, it forbade a boy bringing unwanted pregnancy or disease to a girl, and it forbade a girl imparting disease to a boy.

"Their code *should* have gone further than that, of course.

Mabel's promiscuity, for instance, was not only dangerous, as events had proved, but it was cheap, and in execrable taste.

"My own feeling is that these youngsters are in terrific confusion just now, but that they are going to arrive at something sane and reasonable. In the meantime, I don't for a minute imply that the line of conduct in which they now indulge strikes me as sane, reasonable, or desirable. It is merely a part of the process of change. I explained my views on that point fully in 'The Revolt of Modern Youth.'

"Well, I got hold of Mabel; and I asked her if she did not realize what an outrageous thing she had done.

" 'But, Judge,' she said, 'I didn't mean to. I thought I was cured. I'm awfully sorry I got Jerry into such a mess. I can see now that I ought to have gotten a doctor's certificate. I'll never make such a mistake again. That fool doctor told me I was cured.'

"That was my chance at Mabel. I had never talked with her before. I told her what I thought of her conduct, of the way she was cheapening and debauching herself, and bringing herself to a point where, physically and spiritually, she would soon be burnt out. Every argument I could think of I brought to bear; and I told her stories of other girls and boys, and showed her how clearly she was on the wrong track.

"I didn't tell her her conduct was wrong by theological standards, but I showed her that it lacked wisdom.—It was Solomon who asked for wisdom, when he wanted to please God, wasn't it?—I kept an eye on Mabel after that, and she is doing very well now; and if God is angry at her she isn't aware of it.

"Wisdom and common sense seem to me much better than this miserable sinner nonsense, if you'll pardon my saying so. Wisdom and common sense are permanent building materials for people who want to live effectively and happily; but the miserable sinner talk is simply a form of fear and self-abasement. It is a form of rot and decay wherever you find it, and not all the churches in the world can make me believe that God requires it of anybody.

"Straight thinking is what is required of us all. That includes right feeling as well, and right acting. And that's religion; that's worship; that's life. We are not miserable sinners; we are simply limited human beings struggling against our limitations and gradually overcoming them. And some of us aren't strong enough and clear-headed enough to make much headway, in this life at least. Everybody needs help, my dear Howe. It is maddening to think what the churches and the clergy might do in that direction if they would quit their concern about the future life and buckle down to dealing with this, without the aid of fancy theologies that haven't the remotest thing to do with religion or the facts of daily life."

"But—" protested Howe. "You forget—" And then *he* was off. But I'm not going to quote him here, for the simple reason that we argued, not only on that occasion but on others, in a friendly war of words that lasted for hours. The way I finally got him backed into a corner where he couldn't wriggle any more was by making him come to court and see with his own eyes and hear with his own ears, what was going on.

Thus it happens that, while he does not go to the lengths I do, we nevertheless find it possible more and more to meet on common ground. He is one of the many warm friends I number among churchmen and the clergy, some of whom agree with me more than they dare to say in public, while others agree with reservations. And, of course, others don't agree at all.

2.

My purpose in recounting this talk with my friend Howe has been to bring out how fundamental is the difference between a rationalistic and esthetic way of looking at human conduct and the dogmatic way of looking at it. The one is flexible and free and able to meet conditions as they exist and to do something effective to remedy them; the other is rigid and final, it sets up a spurious claim to divine authority, and demands that the world conform. And the world, no longer to be terrified by bogies, laughs and goes its way.

How far, for instance, have that element of the clergy opposing Birth Control ever gotten in their effort to convince thinking people that contraception is a violation of God's will? Intelligent laymen are waking up to the fact that they know as much about God's will as do this element of the reactionary clergy; and this is a very healthy and hopeful condition.

When people begin to take the responsibility for their own moral decisions on their own shoulders they will begin to be moral. Theology, masquerading as divinely revealed religion, has forbidden them that right long enough; and it has thereby produced, quite without anybody intending it, a monstrous amount of ethical impotence, stupid conduct, cruelty, fear, and asinine blundering on the part of human beings who would have done well enough if they had been taught to follow that inner craving for what is just, right, and beautiful which is the common heritage of all of us.

This is in no sense to be interpreted as an attack on the clergy themselves, but simply on the system they represent and are themselves the victims of. I know many ministers who heartily agree with what I have just said, and who are eager to change the spirit and import of pastoral work in these particulars.

Those of the clergy who dissent from these ideas and who cling to the old notions are, it seems to me, the victims of their training, and except for the fiery intolerance of some of them, I do not reproach them for that.

It is natural for men to cling to what is old and tried. They see no spirit of adventure and high purpose in these new movements of society, but only folly and threatened disaster. They always tell you that Rome fell because she acted on what they claim were ideas like these. And it is characteristic of such minds that it never occurs to them to read history and find out from competent historians and economists why Rome fell.

From start to finish I find in the thinking of these clerical reactionaries not a spark of originality or power of growth. They have nothing but a kind of stubbornness which might pass for courage if it were not really a form of panic-stricken cowardice, cowering and trembling there behind the skirts of the Folkways. But in saying this, let me again emphasize that I am here making no personal references; and though I speak plainly it is, I hope, in no spirit of intolerance or rancor.

It takes all kinds of men to make a world, and ninety per cent

of the race have had their imaginations so stifled by the traditions
and theologies around them that they inevitably become conservatives.

A conservative is a person who clings to what is ready-made
because he lacks the imagination to create anything better; and he
regards as reckless and irresponsible all who disturb his fancied
security. He doesn't know that he is over a powder magazine, and
that the radical on whom he looks with such suspicion, is merely
trying to get him to move to "a better 'ole"—concerning whose
merits he is, of course, skeptical.

3.

My talk with Howe ended on a note that gave me something to
think of, and which shed an added bit of light on what follows.
I suggested that if he wanted to start a campaign to enforce the law
against the sale of contraceptives and a general exposure of these
conditions all around, here was a good place to begin. But he
became panic stricken on the spot. It had always been my experience that in cases of this kind "law enforcement" is not wanted
by the would-be enforcers if it involves a public scandal in *their*
church. He was extremely anxious that I should do nothing that
would involve the risk of publicly exposing anything wrong in *his*
Sunday school. Nothing must be done that would involve exposure, even though it might mean a cleaning up of the conditions.
Better that things should go on as they were than that the facts
become known. They would reflect on the Church, and they would
discredit him and their beloved pastor, and they would alienate
many of their valued parishioners.

For different reasons I was in entire accord with him that exposure in this case would do no good. My thought was that
exposure would needlessly bring disgrace on people who could be
set right without it. He, on the other hand, was thinking of the
institutional and social interests that would be involved and more
or less jeopardized. It was natural that he should feel so; and my
object in pointing it out here is to show how closely it parallels
certain other experiences I have had with people who denounce me
as an encourager of immorality and a lax enforcer of justice, but

who want to be shielded themselves. As I have just observed, Mr. Howe was not the only one to throw his moral theories to the winds when it involved interests in which he was personally concerned.

What I find all along the line, and what I shall demonstrate to be true in the story that follows, is that on the slightest inducement of a personal sort these staunch and conservative upholders of the established order, these shouters for morality and law enforcement, stand ready to evade the law at every turn. The law is all right—they are for it—but they don't want it to touch *them*. It is always for the other fellow. And the worst of it is that they are often guilty of unmitigated cruelty toward persons who overstep the bounds, and who happen to have no pull with them. They are like a certain Judge I know who, I have pretty good evidence, has a store of illegally owned bootleg liquor in his cellar, and who once sentenced to prison a washerwoman who had sold a quart of whiskey in her home to a prohibition agent. She had been trapped to her undoing. He is great for law enforcement when it doesn't touch himself and his friends.

4.

In a certain large church in Denver there was a minister whom I personally liked very much. He was a gentle, kindly man who was genuinely trying to do his work in a way that would please his Master; and if he ever slipped, that was because he was human —and, of course, highly theological. He and I had always been on friendly terms, but we had met only now and then. I knew that he had his doubts about my ideas of sex and sex conduct, though he approved unqualifiedly of certain other phases of my work. I may add that he numbered among his parishioners some very wealthy, powerful, and important persons.

With the encouragement, I believe, of some of these important persons, he preached a great many sermons about lawlessness in Denver. He said women and children were inadequately pro-tected, and the courts did not enforce the law. And, as I have said, he was great for law enforcement, let the lightning strike where it would, high or low, rich or poor. He was a powerful and eloquent preacher, his sermons attracted much attention, and the newspapers gave them considerable space on Monday mornings.

A thing that once made him specially eloquent was the fact that a number of sex cases had been uncovered in which girls under eighteen had gotten into trouble. It was possible to prosecute these cases under the laws against statutory rape—which is, of course, quite another thing than rape by violence. The prosecution would have been based mainly on the fact that the girls were slightly below the age of consent (eighteen years).

These cases were not prosecuted as statutory rape, partly because the girls feared the publicity and would not testify, and partly because prosecutions in most such cases are fruitless anyway—since few juries will convict a man when they know the offense was mutual, and that the girl had consented,—even though she might be below the legal age of consent.

Now it chanced that while this minister—let us call him the Rev. Jacob Fisk—was thundering for law enforcement, a most tragic thing happened. Every profession shows up with an occasional black sheep, and the ministry is, of course, no exception in that. The young assistant minister of Mr. Fisk's church was discovered debauching young boys. He was an unmarried man, effeminate in manner, and he had always been very active and efficient in his work; but he was one of those unfortunates who belong in psycho-pathic hospitals, and who nevertheless are candidates for the most drastic punishments the law can administer if their offenses are discovered. The law does not know, yet, how to deal with these people; and our prisons contain hundreds of them, their lives a living hell.

This exposure of the young assistant was, of course, a difficult matter to handle; and it threatened to develop into one of those open scandals which sometimes upset a fashionable church. The boys were called in by a member of the governing board of the church, and their parents sat in at the conference. It was agreed that the matter should be hushed up, and that the assistant minister should be quietly gotten out of town on the first outgoing train. And Mr. Fisk, after taking the boys into his office, impressed upon them very solemnly and earnestly that they were to say nothing of what had happened. He urged on them that it would disgrace and

injure the church, and that it would disgrace them and their parents.
The boys promised to say nothing.

That would have been the end of the matter if it had not happened that the father of one of the six boys involved had gone into a towering rage over this solution. He came to me and told me all about it, and asked if something could not be done. He said his wife was a member of that church, but that he wasn't, and he didn't propose to see the matter passed off that way, with that fellow turned loose to corrupt other boys.

To prove his case he brought along his boy, and the other five, whom my officer had rounded up for him before the parents knew what was happening. The officer took their affidavits and we then issued a warrant for the arrest of the assistant minister, since it was clearly not good for society that he remain at liberty. But Mr. Fisk and his leading parishioners had been too quick for us. The bird had flown.

But I am used to these very human foibles. I smoothed down the enraged father of the boy and urged him to let well enough alone, since the offender was clearly out of reach; for they hadn't been content to get him out of town. They sent him to a foreign country to make sure he was thoroughly inaccessible. I pointed out that nothing was to be gained by exposure and scandal in themselves; and that since we couldn't get our man, we didn't want to make a bad matter worse.

To Mr. Fisk I said nothing. Like a good many of his clerical brethren in Denver, he didn't know I knew a thing. Nor did he suspect that I knew of various other scandals that had been hushed up in his church on other occasions—in the interests of convention, respectability, and public morals, *even when such concealment meant that the evil involved had to be allowed to go on unchecked.*

All was quiet along the Potomac for the next six months. Mr. Fisk dropped law enforcement and talked of other matters. Then suddenly he began to gather steam. I had been guilty of more leniency; and he decided it was time to castigate me from the pulpit. I had not sent certain boys to prison, and he was going to ask why.

A friend of mine, who was also a friend of Mr. Fisk, told me what was brewing. He added that Mr. Fisk seemed satisfied that it was his duty to do what he could to lessen my chances of winning the next election, since he was sure I was becoming a "dangerous man."

I thought a moment; then I asked my friend if he would not invite Mr. Fisk to meet me at his home that evening that we might talk things over. He consented to this, and the meeting was arranged. When I got to the home of our common friend, I found the disciple of law and order looking a bit sheepish; for the sermon was to be preached the following night, and our friend had not known it was coming so quick.

Later I learned that he had said to Mr. Fisk, "Don't you think you had better talk with Judge Lindsey before you prepare that sermon? He might be able to explain some things."

"Not at all," he had answered. "I have the necessary facts. I have been hearing about these sex cases, and that there are no prosecutions. He puts these people on probation instead of punishing them."

When we got together he frankly explained what he expected to say about me. It was lively stuff.

I countered with various explanations; but they made little impression on him. "The law must be enforced," he said majestically, "regardless of your well-meaning theories."

"All right, Brother Fisk," I answered. "I have a plan for strict law enforcement which I will confide to you presently, just to get your opinion of its feasibility. But first, let me say this: you are like a good many other ministers who denounce me; you don't concern yourself sufficiently with facts, and you are, if you will pardon my frankness, confoundedly cocksure that the Lord is with you. Now there are some wise ministers; and they are getting wiser. They want to know, and they are setting themselves in humility of soul to find out the truth. A few of them even take the trouble now and then to come over to my court and learn things at first hand; but I have never seen you there."

"Of course there is no personal animus on either side," he said. "Personally I like you, Judge; but I have a duty to perform. You seem to me to deserve criticism because you are not enforcing the law as it stands in the law books. The only way to stop lawlessness is to punish offenders."

"Then you would hold," I suggested, "that punishment should be meted out, regardless of the rank and position of those concerned, and that not only should they be punished, but also any who may dare to stand between them and the justice they deserve."

"Certainly. The law is the law. It must be enforced."

"Has it ever occurred to you," I said, "that strict law enforcement is impossible if you are to have even-handed justice? There are influences, for instance; there is money. The poor man can't afford a lawyer, or if he does, he may get one that isn't worth his salt. The rich one may employ some man, the mere weight of whose reputation can often bend a jury to his will. Even-handed justice, you can take it from me, is usually a myth; and we would perhaps get just as good an *average* of justice in this country, so far as our legal deserts go, if we all cast lots to see who was to go to prison and who was to stay out.

"Now as to these rape cases, as you call them—and these youthful rapers. I know that some of them are among our prominent and well-to-do families, and that others are very poor. Some are from families who are having a desperate struggle to exist and punishment visited on them will only add to their miseries and leave them in terrible want.

"I, for one, don't want to send these people to the penitentiary, save in cases of violent rape, which is a very different matter from what you are *calling* rape. I am ready to pull the rope when some little girl or some woman has been assailed with violence. But such cases are rare. These others are simply sex cases—indiscretions mostly of youth, generally what we call in our court a 50-50 case. They ought to be handled in a different way, by psychologists, physicians, and skilled social workers who are capable of doing con-

structive work on these young offenders. We can and do rehabilitate most of them by putting them on probation and making them
behave. As for the girls, they often have as much to do with it
as the boys, and they don't want them punished in the way you
are insisting.

"Now, my dear Fisk, let me make a suggestion. You go ahead
and preach that sermon to-morrow. It may start something. I'll
profit by it. I'm willing to follow your advice and give your scheme
of law enforcement a trial if you still think I should. I'll try
hitting out."

"Well," he said, evidently pleased, yet slightly puzzled, at this
sudden surrender on my part. "I do think you should use more
severity, Judge—more severity. You can only teach these people
by severe measures. And when you do, you may be sure that I will
be the first to commend you for it from the pulpit."

"All right, my dear fellow," I said cordially. "I'll do it. I believe in starting at the top in these matters, and in getting the
fellows higher up first. They have much less excuse for wrong-
doing than those who have never had any advantages in the way
of education and right surroundings. Don't you agree that I should
begin at the top?"

"By all means," he said enthusiastically. "Make an example of
them. Be courageous, and don't care who you hit. Smite in the
name of the Lord. There are times when it is necessary to forget
the welfare of individuals and be stern."

"Quite so," I agreed. "I am glad to know that I have such
enthusiastic support from you. Do you remember the assistant
minister of your church, the one who left Denver so suddenly six
months ago?"

His form stiffened and his face flushed. "What do you know
about that?" he demanded.

"I know all about it; and I know how the thing was hushed
up."

"I was never consulted," he said.

"Oh, yes, you were consulted," I retorted. "You were consulted;
but not by me. You were consulted by certain members of your
church. Do you remember? And do you recall how you got

those kids into your office and shut the door, and said, 'Now, boys, you must not say one word about this to a living soul. You have been polluted, and it must never happen again; a frightful thing, but you must never mention it. Now remember, you have promised never to mention it.'

"They all promised, my dear Fisk. Their affidavits say they did and they relate what you said. I have those affidavits. And I have also a warrant for the arrest of your former assistant; but I couldn't connect with him and prevent him from corrupting other boys, because with your help and connivance, and that of certain of your influential parishioners, he was put on a train and shipped out. That much you know, and you were active in it; and that makes you accessory to the fact. I can't get him, but, by heavens, Brother Fisk, I can get you; and Monday morning, after your sermon and a good night's rest, we will start to enforce the law by charging you with being accessory to the debauchery of boys,— for that's exactly what you were in fact and in law. Thus your prayers that the Lord will make me see the error of my ways will have the immediate answer it seems to deserve."

He sat looking at me as if I had hit him between the eyes. His face went white; his jaw dropped. "You don't mean that! You don't mean that!" he cried. "You don't understand. You know the good name of the church was at stake. See what it would mean to the church—the awful scandal that would get out."

"Yes," I said, "I suppose that is what every individual family feels; that is what every father and mother feels about their son or daughter. The law should be enforced, but *they* should be excepted. And institutions are like persons in that. It's too bad that you and your church should have gotten into this mess, isn't it! For of course you see that your demand for impartial and— may I say—indiscriminate law enforcement, leaves no room for considering either your church or you.

"Now my inclinations in the matter are quite otherwise. I am not threatening you. I don't want to charge you with being accessory to the debauchery of the boys, because I know that though legally you are just that, actually you are not. Nor are the parishioners who helped you get rid of your assistant. It was all natural and human. I would no more do you such an injustice than you would do me the injustice of condemning me from the pulpit for not doing it. And so the serpent of evil swallows his own tail, Brother Fisk; and if you'll come over to my court some of these days I'll show the number of ways in which he can be made to do it."

Mr. Fisk slowly reached for his hip pocket, from which he drew nothing more illegal than a handkerchief. He mopped his brow and looked at me. "Good Lord," he said.

The saying that one touch of nature makes the whole world kin worked out very well in this instance. Mr. Fisk and I found ourselves talking more or less in the same language from then on. I told him some stories. Perhaps a few of them will help me make my point here, even as I made it with the Rev. Mr. Fisk.

"I suppose you know the Rev. Henry Smith, of Such and Such a church, don't you?" I asked.

He nodded.

"Well, I'm going to tell you something that will give you a fellow feeling for him. He had an assistant who did just what your assistant did; and he did just what you did when he found it out. With the help of the governing body of his church, he shipped his assistant out of town between sunset and sunrise. I know it and he knows I know it; and no man was ever more grateful for non-enforcement of the law than he is. In the circumstances he wouldn't mind my telling you about it, and I know it will go no further.

"And then there's another colleague of yours; I shan't tell you his name. Let's call him the Rev. Asa Jones. He had to cope with the same situation, except that the offender was not his assistant, but his own son—which goes to show that there is nothing so bad that it mightn't be worse.

"Some time before this disaster befell him, Mr. Jones preached a sermon in which he made an attack on me very similar to the one you are not going to make to-morrow. He claimed I had been easy on an offender. The man in question had had a child by a woman other than his wife, and he was willing to support both children, and both women, and shoulder his responsibility as best he could. There was nothing else I could do in the case itself. The money for the other woman and her child was to be paid through the court. So I let him do just that; and it seemed obvious to me that his misconduct was thus given the opportunity to bring its own natural punishment with it.

"But the Rev. Asa Jones took the hide off me, or tried to, because I hadn't sent that poor devil to the pen for ten years— a sentence which might have enforced another law, but which would have buttered no parsnips for two women and two children who were a lot more interested in their daily bread and a roof over their heads than they were in having that man punished and tortured by law, in order that some preachers of the doctrines of Jesus might feel that vengeance and punishment had been fully meted out, and that an example has been made of the criminal, and all that—to the end that others might be deterred from the same offense. I know all that line of patter, you see.

"Now listen. I have in my files letters from the Rev. Asa Jones thanking me for saving his boy from a sentence in the penitentiary for corrupting boys. I saved that young man, and I don't care who knows it. I have him in a sanitarium, a psychopathic sanitarium, where, by heaven, he had better be, and where your assistant ought to be as well. They are curing him. Some day he'll be a decent citizen again. He'll get out of there when I say so, and not before.

"Thus the Rev. Asa Jones learned what you are just finding out,—that law enforcement applied in terms of law, merely for purposes of punishment, is a thing often more devilish than the crimes the law forbids. The best possible enforcement of the law that I know of is to cure people and make good citizens of them, and let mere punishment and revenge as such go hang. If punishment be not corrective and curative in intent there is little excuse for it. It becomes itself a crime and a breeder of crime.

"Here is another instance of a case where a church covered up an offense that it would have shouted to the heavens in a demand for punishment if it hadn't struck so near home. There was a young people's meeting in the basement of a certain church as large as yours, with lots of rich and influential members who didn't like scandal. After the meeting those boys and girls, about twelve couples, turned out the lights and had a petting party in the dark. About half of them went the limit. Now these were simply cases of statutory rape, similar to the ones which you are not going to preach about to-morrow. It would have been quite a haul for any judge that wanted to 'enforce the law,' and such enforcement would have ruined quite a number of persons. Did the pastor and governing board of that church want prosecution and law enforcement—for themselves and their friends? Not they! They were more than willing to benefit by the very judicial infirmities which they had always reproached me for or at which they had at least looked askance; and I wouldn't blame them a bit if only they would think the thing through and apply a similar tolerance outside *their* fold. Most of those girls, good and bad alike, are married now, and are good wives and mothers; and as for the rest of the gang, I can assure you they don't look like candidates for the pen or the reform school.

"And I mustn't forget to tell you about Mr. Karl Karson, a very important and shining light of the Ku Klux Klan, and a member of your church. You know the hypocritical mouthings of some of the Klan on law enforcement and the protection of American womanhood, and the purity of the home. Some of its high officials are especially that way, and they object to me because I don't go in for the same line of platitudinous morality.

"Well, some time ago, just before the last election, while I was fighting the Klan very hard, there came under my care a girl who is the daughter of a man who is a leader in the educational affairs of Denver. This girl was given to the practice of a horrible perversion which has become exceedingly common in this country, especially since some of our soldiers brought it back from Europe with them. She was all too well acquainted with some thirty boys of high school age and certain men before I got hold of her. She was seventeen years old, and was diseased at the time I undertook her rehabilitation—contrary, I may say, to the advice of everybody who had tried to handle her. I sent her to a psychopathic specialist, and I kept in personal touch with her, and she is straightening out. But it isn't law enforcement, my dear brother. Instead of living with anybody and everybody, and spreading disease and perversion, she now has one lover. If some of your brother ministers had her in hand, they would forbid her that one lover and send her back to her old way of life, with dozens of lovers; or they would fix her forever in her old weakness by sending her to a reform school, where she would not reform. But I don't work that way. Under my system of dealing with her as she is, and as the necessities of her nature demand, she is rapidly becoming a normal person, and she now tells me that she and the man she is living with will soon marry. In the meantime, they are both behaving themselves so far as society at large is concerned, and the girl is no longer a source of social corruption, as she would be if the ordinary disciples of law enforcement had handled her case.

"Now shortly after I undertook her case, this girl, Marian, let me call her, came to me and said that a few evenings before, at a dance, she had met the eminent Klansman, Mr. Karl Karson. While they were dancing Mr. Karson said to her, 'Marian, I hear you are an adept at so and so.

" 'Sure I am,' she said. And forthwith made an engagement with him. She came to me with the story, not to betray the fellow, but to get my permission, if you please, to keep the date.

"Now consider how simple it would have been to have used her for a stool-pigeon. I could have let her go to him, and had my officer descend upon them at the right moment, and put that man in the pen for twenty years. No trouble at all. He is one of the bitterest enemies I have in Denver, and he is still after my scalp. He claims that I encourage immorality, that I don't enforce the law, and that I advocate free love and trial marriage. I could have enforced the law and ruined him at one stroke. And your church, incidentally, would have been involved indirectly in a bigger scandal than the one you escaped by shipping your assistant out on a late train. I could have blown their political pretensions to smithereens and had a gorgeous revenge besides. But I didn't. What I intend to do sometime is get that man into my office and tell him that if he doesn't cut out such behavior he is heading for trouble.

"The Klan demands law enforcement. Would the Klan have relished the kind I could have given them then?

"Not long ago I uncovered a homosexual ring in a Denver school. It involved thirty or forty boys, a Denver physician, and a teacher. Were the educational authorities of Denver *grateful* to have that nest of corruption cleaned up? They were not. They denounced me bitterly as a trouble maker. Why? Because the "good name" of the school system must be preserved by covering up the truth. Better have the corruption go on than have an *exposé* which would demonstrate the incompetence of persons who are supposed to know all about young people, and who claim that Lindsey is a libeler of the youth of Denver.

"Here is another. There was a man in Denver who was rabidly in favor of the prosecution of the kind of sex cases you are not going to preach about to-morrow. He wanted to give these 'rapers' hell. And to his great joy, he was put on the Grand Jury that was going to clean up the situation. He went about breathing fire and slaughter and threats of what he would do.

"Now it happened that among the witnesses called was a sixteen-year-old girl whom this fellow had himself seduced. When she entered the room he thought that she had come to expose him, among others; and driven by his guilty conscience he made a dive for the door, and got excused from that Grand Jury later. The girl, as it happened, had *not* come there to expose him, but to give other testimony, and she was immensely amused at his precipitate exit. She gave me a spirited account of it later.

"He was very prominent, my dear Fisk, very prominent, and a certain big business firm in this town would have been immensely distressed if one of its solid granite pillars had proved to be crumbling sandstone. *And what is more they would have gone to any length to muzzle any effort to expose him.* They would have had an undying grudge against me if I had told on him. I knew all about it through my confidences with the girl, which I could not betray; so I never peeped; though he had it coming to him, in view of his brazen hypocrisy in being willing to send to prison men who had done just what he had done and who didn't happen to have his money.

"That's what it comes down to all along the line. Money and power backed you in the concealment of your assistant; and money and power, in one form or another, rise up to protect their own all along the line. And what this cry for law enforcement on your part and on the part of your brother ministers really means, whether you and they know it or not, is that they are too often hounding the poor and the ignorant, and are escorting the rich and powerful into heaven over a broad, smooth, gold-paved street of respectability.

"I don't particularly blame them. It is human; and they are far from realizing the true nature of the Beast, the *respectable* Beast they serve. But it is so. And these are the things I think about when with lies and slander they attack me as an encourager of immorality, a preacher of free love, an advocate of trial marriage, and a conniver at lawlessness of all sorts.

"We are all the victims of the conditions, my dear Fisk. I am blaming nobody, and my regard and respect for your profession remains very high, even though I know the foibles of some persons in it.—What do you think?"

"I wish," he said slowly, "that we could be frank as you are and tell the truth. I think I shall some day get the courage to preach on that."

"Good!" I said. "But be careful not to lose your job. We need you here. Too many people regard *facts*, remember, as far more offensive than crime. You can't possibly make yourself more offensive than by telling the facts."

He looked at me with misery in his eyes. "But why should it be so? They are good people. They mean all right. So do I. What is this invisible thing that hems us in and keeps us earth-bound?"

"I can tell you *one* of the things it is," I answered. "These stories I have told you illustrate it; and even the story of you and your assistant would illustrate it. It doesn't mean that society is corrupt, or that organizations like the church wink at corruption or wrong doing. It simply means that they have mapped out a program which they themselves are unable to follow, and which, with very good reason, they are unwilling to follow. The reason they can't apply it is that something within them rebels when they come to the pinch. This system of theological morality is more and more refusing to work; if you try to work it, you destroy human beings, and you produce misery and work injustice. We need a system based on love and kindness and tolerance and understanding; and these howlers for law enforcement want that just as much as anybody, but they don't know they want it. They haven't been trained to that way of thinking.

"I could tell you many times as many such experiences as I have related; and perhaps it has seemed to you that these stories I have told you have been in the nature of so many cracks at the church, and the Klan, and at respectability, and at the hypocrisy of organizations that protect their own. Not at all. I am merely trying to show you what are the fruits of the unethical system of morals they uphold. They can't make a go of it. And when things go wrong, they have to step from under. If all the laws and traditions they want enforced could be enforced—and if society would stand for such a tyranny—this world would be a red hot hell, and such a breeding place for vice and crime as would make Sodom and Gomorrah wholesome and desirable by comparison.

"Don't infer that I am not for law enforcement. I am. But let the spirit and intent of the thing be different. People who come to me are *glad* to have the law enforced on them because it is applied in such a way as to save them and better them, and they know when I look them in the eye that such is my intention toward them.

"Let the forces of society, I say, learn a lesson from their own hypocrisies. Let them learn how evil is the thing they avoid by their hypocrisies, and let them openly drop this dead thing and turn to something that's alive and which is able to grow if men will but love it and desire it.

"Above all, let's get away from the idolatry that worships the Law, regardless of whether a lick of sense went into the making of it or not.   You know how Gilbert and Sullivan poked fun at it, in the words of the ridiculous Lord Chancellor:

> " 'The Law is the true embodiment
> Of everything that's excellent.
> It has no kind of fault or flaw,
> And I, My Lords, embody the Law.'

"There are many people, inside the legal profession and out of it, who carry that pompous absurdity in their hearts, and never know what bunkum it is.   And then they turn around and bewail the growing want of respect for law in this country.   What do they expect, when they pass prohibition laws forbidding people to order their own conduct in the use of alcohol; and 'obscenity' laws forbidding them not to have children if they are married; and laws against 'statutory rape' forbidding them to beget children if they are unmarried; and blue sky laws forbidding them to amuse themselves as they please on Sunday; and censorship laws telling them what they may not read, though they want to read it, or what they may not see on the stage, though they may want to see it.

"But why continue the list?   The point is that you, and your church, and the other various organizations I have mentioned, are *all* of you lacking in respect for law because the law has gotten to a point where it merits so little respect.   And the reason it merits so little respect is that its prohibitions are asinine, its punishments not curative but vengeful, and its administration managed by the very same stupid traditions that made the laws.   I'm not speaking of *all* laws, mind you, but of those we, as a people, most obviously don't want and don't respect."

5.

I leave my friend Fisk here.   I don't say he is converted; but I know he is interested.   He, too, shows up at the court now and then; and he hasn't preached that sermon yet.   And when he does lambaste me, as he does now and then, he does it in moderation—in moderation; and with a covert grin in my direction.

It was not long after this that I had my last visit with my friend

Luther Burbank. I told him of my talk with Fisk. It was one of the stories I told him that led to his exacting from me the promise that I preach his funeral sermon.

When I had finished Burbank could hardly contain himself. He sprang to his feet, fairly dancing with impatience.

"Why don't you write that?" he cried; "why don't you write that?"

"Good heavens, man," I said, "I want to hold my job and I have to live yet."

But here it is; and I dedicate it for whatever it may be worth to the memory of a man who, more than any I have known, understood that whatever is at once natural and beautiful is likely to be Good.

CHAPTER XIV

THE CASE AGAINST UNIFORM MARRIAGE AND DIVORCE

1.

THERE lies before me an ably written pamphlet on the subject of divorce, by a Roman Catholic priest. In it I find this sweeping statement: "Divorce simply shatters the individual home where it takes place."

There are two observations which might well have been added to that generalization. One is that divorce, as a rule, takes place in homes that are already shattered. The other is that divorce frequently makes possible the creation of one, two, or even three new homes which become abodes of happiness and of laughing children, and which are quite likely to be shatter-proof.

A great deal of noise is made about the destructive effects of divorce because that is superficially the most striking thing about it; but little is said of the constructive readjustments which it usually makes possible.

The reason people want divorce rather than mere separation, such as is permitted even by the Church, is that they want to be free to remarry. Many of them already know who it is they want to marry. And they therefore have in mind a constructive and creative course of action which in most cases proves successful. My experience with divorced persons is that they usually make a success of their second marriage; and that the reason they failed with the first marriage was not the lack of effort, but simply inability to make a go of it, either with some particular person or under the existing circumstances.

2.

For example, I recall the case of a young woman of very good family in Denver who married the son of a banker. This couple

364

lived together for nearly two years in Companionate Marriage; that is to say they had no children. Their childlessness, as the wife confided to me later, was deliberate. Both of them loved children. The wife in particular strongly desired them. But both of them understood, after a few months of married life, that they were incompatible, and that their marriage might prove to be a mistake. They found then what they should have learned before marriage, that they differed profoundly in taste and temperament. The physical attraction which had drawn them together lacked a foundation of congeniality of mind and spirit. They valued different things. In the haste and ignorance of youth, urged on by a mating instinct which could find a socially permitted outlet only in marriage, they had made an honest mistake; and now they were appalled at the thought that they were shackled together for life, companions in the misery they were generating between them.

Facing this frankly, they decided that it would be safer not to have children till they had had a chance to put their marriage to the test of time. They did not want to undertake the raising of a family under conditions that might subject children to the unhappiness from which they were suffering themselves. And yet they had hope that things would come out all right for them.

What I want to make clear is that these were conscientious young people; that for two years they tried the best they knew to make their marriage a success; and that while trying to find a common ground for happiness, they kept their troubles to themselves. They were prepared to go to all lengths to find a solution of the difficulty—some solution other than separation or divorce. One reason for this was their own solidity of character, and another was the fact that their families were extremely "religious," and would certainly bring pressure to bear to head off what they would consider the disgrace and sin of divorce in their family circle.

After this situation had persisted for nearly two years, the couple came to me with their difficulty, not because I had any judicial power in their case, but because they wanted my counsel. I talked with them together and separately, as is my custom, made every effort to find some ground on which they could agree, persuaded them to try out some of my suggestions for a time—which they did without success—and finally told them that divorce seemed to me the only solution in their case.

At last in spite of the protests and opposition of their families they set about obtaining a divorce. As usually happens in such instances, the whole case was cooked up beforehand in the offices of their attorneys, who served up the evidence in court with their usual skill. In short, it was divorce by collusion, and it involved perjury because the couple had no legal ground for obtaining divorce in Colorado. The "best people" do it, and they will continue to get their divorces that way so long as we continue to have prohibitive and restrictive legislation on divorce, and so long as divorce by mutual consent is not legal. Legally they were not entitled to this relief; but actually it would have been monstrous to have denied it to them. Unjust laws always get broken. That is all the more reason for doing away with them.

Within a year both of these persons had remarried. The young woman married a man considerably older than herself, whom she had never met till after her divorce. This man had himself been divorced, and his former wife has also remarried. The banker's son has remarried, and he has a baby by his second wife. His former wife has a child by her present husband. All three of these marriages have been successful. Three happy marriages have taken the place of two that were unhappy. Society has been the gainer by this readjustment.

Had these people been forced to remain together in the unions they originally and mistakenly formed, they would have consumed and destroyed one another in their unhappiness. Any children they might have had would have been warped and twisted by the same conditions. Those marriages would have remained a liability on the books of society. Mated as they were, these people were totally incompetent to carry out the responsibilities they had undertaken in marriage. Such unions were not marriage; and I am at a loss to understand how any rational process of thinking, free from theological bias or from superstition, could maintain that there was any possible good to be had, either from forcing those persons to

continue their original marriage, or to abstain from seeking another
mate with the help of the divorce courts.

3.

I could relate scores of instances such as this, where I have seen
people find their salvation in divorce—divorce which they both
wanted, and which was therefore divorce by mutual consent, and
utterly illegal. What is to be said of an ecclesiastical conservatism
that flies in the teeth of the facts, and insists that divorce is a
wholly destructive thing and that it can have no constructive function in our social life; and what is to be said of the enlightenment of
a civilization and laws that would barbarously have forced these
persons on each other for life regardless of their wishes and their
happiness and their welfare? They sought a civilized remedy, by
breaking an uncivilized law; and they sought a rational way of
life in the teeth of laws that forbade them to take it. Is it not
time that we took a square look at some of our social institutions
and put them on a basis that would at least be compatible with our
self-respect as a nation claiming to be intelligent and civilized?

What holds us back from admitting such facts and acting on
them? Several things. One of these is a belief, which has been
ground into our very bones, that marriage is a religious institution
having a mystical meaning with which we interfere at our peril.
Our most primitive ancestors, dancing and howling around their
camp-fires, and clad in skins, had similar notions about the important transactions of life, and the part played in those transactions
by their gods, goblins and ancestral ghosts. We do not hesitate
to-day to brand many of those naïve notions as degraded superstitions, and the state of mind that produced them as diseased and
degraded by *fear* of the unseen, or the little understood. We should
do well to wake up to the fact that we are as naïve to-day in our
clinging to irrational traditions as were those remote ancestors of
ours in their cruder way. We have refined some of the conceptions,
of course, but we have not greatly rationalized our conduct. One
need only consider the part played by the Bible in determining the
sociological thinking of enormous masses of our population to
understand the extent to which such reference to supposedly super-

natural authority can poison the rational faculty. Dogmatic theology is not religion; it is a disease which keeps us from finding the Kingdom of Heaven within us by asseverating that it is outside of us. It has corrupted and stultified the thought of millions. So long as this continues, the veil that separates us from those dim figures gathered in superstitious terror around the ancient campfire will remain appallingly thin.

This thought is suggested with startling vividness by certain efforts which are now being made to persuade Congress to pass a federal law for the regulation of Marriage and Divorce. This crusade for uniform marriage and divorce is not, as one might suppose, an effort to free our civilization from the incubus of outworn ideas and from the necessity of evading stupid divorce laws by collusion, trickery, perjury, and hypocrisy. Rather it is an effort to fasten the burden more securely on our shoulders. The argument is that "uniformity" would clear up the confusion which results from variations in state laws, and that the proposed legislation would represent a "middle ground," since it would allow divorce for five reasons, and would therefore be fairly "liberal" without too greatly outraging the feelings of the conservatives who would like to abolish divorce altogether if they could put over a law forbidding it.

4.

What the supporters of such a measure never call attention to is the fact that there can be no middle ground on such a question. Either you allow people to obtain divorce because they want divorce, or you don't. And if you don't, then they will fake their case, if necessary, in order to bring it within one of the five permitted grounds. They will break any prohibitive or restrictive law that can be written on this subject. They are doing it now and they will keep on doing it whenever the circumstances fail to bring their case within the statute.

This may be right or it may be wrong, according to your way of thinking about law and obedience to law—but it is at all events a fact. Let's accept it as such, and then reason from it, and see where we come out.

Not only will they break through this prohibitive and restrictive legislation exactly as they do at present, but they will do it with much greater facility than has hitherto been possible, since they will not have to travel from one part of the union to another in order to find divorce laws that suit their need. The citizen of New York state, which grants divorce only on grounds of adultery or of the disappearance of either party for five years, will not need to go to Nevada, Paris, or Yucatan, or to spend time and money establishing a fictitious residence where he does not reside. He will simply get what he wants by fraud, if need be, right at home. It is true that the interval between the interlocutory and the final decree would, under the proposed law, be one year, and that the parties could not remarry in that interval; but all things considered the difficulties and obstacles would be far less than they are at present for the citizens of such states. Citizens of Nevada would have to wait longer than they do now, but that would be the only difficulty in Nevada. Moreover, it would bring divorce more within the reach of the poor, who can't afford to travel; and this, indeed, is one of the strongest arguments for such legislation.

Considering that the persons who are advocating this federal legislation are making a point of the argument that we have too much divorce, and that this legislation would check the tendency, it would seem that whatever they know about law they know very little about how human beings act when living under laws to which they do not assent. Apparently, too, they do not realize that by putting such restrictions on marriage and divorce as they propose, they will cause people to avoid marriage and prefer the unmarried union instead.

I repeat, there can be no middle ground. The only federal legislation that can be permissible or desirable as a remedy for present conditions would grant divorce by mutual consent, and for no other reason than that the parties of the marriage want it. Having provided that basic and sane ground for divorce, the law might then reasonably go on to make provision for the regulation of alimony, the care of children, and other problems that arise from the application of this unhappy but necessary social remedy. Till divorce can be founded unqualifiedly on the consent and desire of the parties concerned, it will be a capital misfortune if Congress permits itself to be hornswoggled into this folly by well-intentioned persons who think morality can be legislated into existence, and that free-born human beings can be instructed in their domestic duties and obligations by organized minorities who think they know exactly how everything should be run.   Few nations have ever been cursed by such a flood of prohibitive and restrictive legislation as has inundated this country.   And of all our laws, those relating to divorce, Birth Control, and the sale, manufacture and consumption of liquor, have certainly taught us a lesson in lawlessness that ought to be a lesson to lawmakers for some time to come.

5.

Happily for the American people, and for the future of Marriage and Divorce in this country, Congress has so far stubbornly resisted all efforts to persuade it to pass a federal law for the regulation of Marriage and Divorce.

I say "happily" because I am one of those who profoundly distrust the intent and purpose that have inspired the proposed legislation.   I think the underlying intent of it is restrictive and meddlesome; that it is plausible but unsound; and that its real, unacknowledged purpose is to thwart certain vast social changes which are now in the making and which should have the right of way.

These changes in the folkways cannot be stopped.   They are racial; they are a response to fundamental changes in our civilization; they are resistless and inevitable; they are unerring in their response to human necessity.   Such social impulses have the validity and authority of natural law.   We may reasonably have faith in their ability to work out a wholesome result for society, even though the wisest of us cannot now predict to what final solution they will lead us.   We must trust this racial search for the best the race can discover; and at a time like the present, when this impulse is working visibly before our very eyes, what words can be found to describe the folly, the lack of faith, the puritanical cynicism, that would interfere with this divine miracle of social growth by throwing the monkey wrench of clumsy, panicky legislation into the living machinery of life!   No—the time for legislation will come when the present blind impulse and upreaching toward the light has acquired sight. Then it can be codified in law to some purpose.

6.

This movement for federal laws on Marriage and Divorce has many specious and apparently reasonable arguments to support it. I shall consider some of them here. They appear to me to have been dictated, not by sociological wisdom based on the historical perspectives of the history of Marriage, but on certain theological traditions which are even now on their way to extinction, and which are rapidly losing their authority with the American people. The American people steadily grow more religious as they become less theological.

The enactment of the proposed legislation, which is known as the Capper Bill, would have to be preceded by an amendment to the Constitution, which at present makes no provision whereby Congress can legislate on marriage and divorce. It is urged, even by some persons who do not approve of the terms and restrictions which the Capper Bill places on Divorce, that such an amendment would be desirable. Such persons hold that this amendment would at least permit Congress to try and try again; that it could pass and, if necessary, repeal divorce legislation—whereas now it can do nothing; and has to stand by and see the States, with their conflicting laws, and differing court decisions, make a mess of the situation.

It is eloquently pointed out that it is now possible for a man or woman to be married in one state and single in another; that children may be legitimate in one state and illegitimate in another; that persons who are respectably married here may be bigamists and adulterers there; that divorces are frequently obtained by changes of residence which amount to desertion; that property and inheritance rights are involved often in inextricable tangles; that divorces are frequently obtained without the defendant even knowing that suit has been brought in another state; that patent injustices are done and grave immoralities practiced under the protection of this or that state law; and that the only way out of the muddle is federal control of domestic relations.

"Let us, therefore, have at least a constitutional amendment that will make it possible to get something done," say these people, "and then liberal legislation, more liberal than the Capper Bill, which grants divorce on only five grounds, will gradually come into existence." So runs the argument of the liberal wing of this movement.

It is a good argument so far as it goes; but it does not in the least alter the fact that this legislation is at present largely molded and determined by illiberal forces who admittedly and openly propose to restrict and lessen divorce by making it harder to get, who propose to restrict divorce by means of it, and who, for twenty-five or thirty years to come, will have the chance of their lives to meddle in the affairs of their neighbors if these laws are passed.

At present the fact that individual states can make their divorce laws as liberal as they please is the one chance we have for extensive and immediate experimentation in this perplexing field. A federal law would not only slow down the whole process of adjustment indefinitely, but it would produce such social pressure that it might prove almost as effective an instrument for the fostering of lawlessness, tragedy, license, and crime as the 18th Amendment itself. Certainly one inevitable result would be an increase in the number of unmarried unions.

When the 18th Amendment was passed, I rather favored it; for I realized the necessity for some sort of control of the liquor situation. I still recognize the need for such control; but I understand now better than I did then, that morality and reasonableness of conduct cannot be made by the passing of statutes; and I know now, what many another American citizen has come to realize, the 18th Amendment has proved a poor way to obtain a desirable end.

Now the present intent of the conservative forces that favor a Marriage and Divorce amendment to the Constitution is perfectly plain. They propose to use it as a means for dictating to the American people the five grounds on which it can have divorce, and certain other (less objectionable) grounds on which it can marry. The five proposed grounds will not begin to cover the need of thousands who at present can obtain divorce on the legal merits of their case. This restriction, therefore, is extremely dangerous. We have had one lesson of this kind in the 18th Amendment and the Volstead Act, and it should be enough.

Some day a constitutional amendment of this kind may be wise; but not now—not till our notions on marriage and divorce have so changed that the amendment could not be used as a means to tyrannous and illiberal legislation. As things stand the lack of such a constitutional amendment is a precious safeguard against that element in this country who are forever trying to dictate what their neighbors shall eat, wear, think, drink, and do.

Let it be remembered that the leadership which has succeeded in forbidding the teaching of evolution in the schools of certain states *would put that restriction into the federal law if it could, that it would have a law absolutely forbidding divorce in the United States if it could, and that though it might never be able to pass a law as restrictive as that, it would nevertheless be able to prevent the passing of any really liberal divorce legislation for a very long time to come.* The Capper Bill is supposed to be fairly liberal; but it would pass much more easily the less liberal and the more restrictive it became. And we may depend upon it that before it passed Congress, it would have to be made even less liberal than it is.

Under such conditions the obvious and only safe course is not to pass any constitutional amendment that could precipitate such a disaster.

7.

Fortunately Congress is gun-shy of any more constitutional amendments, whether such amendments would permit federal marriage and divorce legislation or whether it would make the Bible the official legislative text of the United States Government, or whether it would outlaw Evolution. The lesson of the 18th Amendment has sunk deep; and it is even said that there are Congressmen who have rather violently declared that they will see the whole institution of marriage go to pot before they will ever vote for another amendment to the Constitution.

A burnt child dreads the fire; and in this instance the deadly parallel is all too plain. The 18th Amendment was passed under the auspices of a highly organized "religious" minority, who could quote yards of texts to show that strong drink is a mocker, but who knew nothing about sociology and nothing at all about human nature. It was followed by the Volstead Act, which was dictated by the same influences that had put the amendment over. And the result in terms of death, tragedy, and crime are too well known to need relating here.

Exactly the same thing is under way now with regard to marriage and divorce—particularly divorce. The auspices are the same, and we have profound and bitter reasons not to trust those auspices. Their purposes are still prohibitive and narrow. They believe in taking short cuts to morality. Unable to have their way by argument, they want it by law. The more clearly the American people can be brought to understand this fact, the less likely we are to put our heads in the noose of constitutional amendment a second time.

I have said that the more narrow and restrictive the Capper Bill can be made, the more easily it can be made a law, and that its chance of passing in Congress would be in inverse ratio to its liberality. If this fact means anything, it means that such a bill would be adopted, if at all, under auspices and under conditions of a sort that should never be entrusted with the responsibility of formulating federal legislation on a matter of such tremendous social importance. It means that the judgment used would not be sociological, scientific judgment at all, but judgment permeated and shot through with religious prejudices regarding "the sanctity of marriage" and other sentimental nonsense that obscures the issue.

That the bill would have to pass under these thoroughly dangerous and regrettable conditions is proved, as I have pointed out, by the fact that it is a compromise measure, designed to avoid the opposition of religious fanatics; so that instead of being made really liberal, it has been made "fairly liberal." It grants divorce on five grounds, instead of granting it by mutual consent—due consideration being given to the welfare of children, property rights, alimony, etc. It is therefore a compromise on a matter wherein compromise is infamous.

In principle it is not a whit different from a law that would grant divorce on no ground whatever, or on the one ground of adultery. When you steal a penny from a man you violate his right to his property as clearly as if you steal a thousand dollars from him, or a million; and when you attempt to force people to live together simply because they have married, you violate their right to order their private lives to suit themselves, regardless of whether you name one exception or a dozen. On such an issue there can be no compromise or quarter. It is a fight to the finish between enlightenment and savagery; *and it will never end.*

8.

Let it be remembered that if the Capper Bill were passed, divorce would be obtainable *only* on five grounds *throughout the United States:* Adultery, cruel and inhuman treatment, abandonment or failure to provide for a period of one year, incurable insanity, and commission of an infamous crime. At present a man or woman living in a state that has illiberal divorce laws, can escape, and seek relief elsewhere. But under the Capper Bill there would be no means of escape for persons who had reasons for wanting divorce that are now legal in at least some parts of this country. They would have no recourse then but illegal collusion and perjury; and since the five grounds allowed do not cover the reasons why most persons seek divorce, the amount of collusion, perjury, and bootleggery in the divorce courts would leap to high figures. Most persons seek divorce because they can't "get along"—and the underlying reasons why many of them don't get along are sex ignorance, temperamental incompatibility, and poverty. The Capper Bill makes no allowance for this fact. It would be hard to imagine a more stupid piece of nonsense than this ignoring of human nature. Such legislation is folly. It absolutely could not be enforced.

It is no argument to say that if the couple can't name one of the five suggested grounds, they have no fair ground for divorce. Who says they haven't? Who has the incredible presumption to pass on this question for other human beings? What infallible authority in Washington or elsewhere is deciding this complex question with such assurance? It just happens that there are many persons in this country who think there are *many* more than five reasonable grounds for divorce, *and that aside from questions involved in the welfare of children, it is absolutely nobody's business why a couple wants a divorce anyway.* I may add that the persons who hold this view are at least as capable of clear thinking as some who have had their minds fogged by what they are pleased to call their religion.

I have known couples who had done each other no wrong whatever, who had treated each other with the utmost kindness and consideration, and who were nevertheless wrecking each other's lives in marriage. They had no legal ground for divorce; and yet their need for divorce was far greater than that of the average man or woman who sues for divorce on the ground of adultery. That society now tries to hold such persons together simply goes to show the extent to which we are still steeped in barbarism.

Our courts grant divorce without question when adultery is charged, regardless of the welfare of the children of the marriage; they refuse divorce to other couples who have no children but who lack a statutory case; they refuse it no matter how strong the need for it may be—unless of course the couple fakes a statutory case, which they invariably do whenever the strictures of the law drive them to it.

The supporters of the Capper Bill have definitely let the cat out of the bag by announcing their hope and belief that the Bill would lessen divorce. Apparently they are not concerned to lessen the causes and conditions that lead to divorce—by such an expedient as Companionate Marriage, and by sex education, for instance.

Why are these persons so convinced that we should have less divorce, or that we have more of it than we need? For scientific reasons? Not at all. Their reasons are to be found in catchwords and phrases that may or may not mean something, such as "The Sanctity of the Home," "The Purity of American womanhood,"— which are easy to mouth till you begin to inquire into the sanctity of homes that are badly in need of divorce, and into the purity of marital relationships that have not the high sanctions of love and spiritual union to justify them.

There is no rationality or good faith in such an approach; it is biased and prejudiced from the start; and it betrays its real spirit in the covert assault it is making on so absolutely indispensable an institution as divorce, in an effort, not to rationalize it and expand its field of usefulness in enabling people to find mates with whom they can be happy, but to restrict it and prohibit it and grant it stingily.

As a monument to the unconscious cynicism of "religious" people toward marriage and toward human nature in marriage, the Capper Bill is perfect.

9.

The fact that the intent of this bill is clearly restrictive is sufficient proof of what its conservative and "religious" advocates are trying to do, and of the sort of tyranny they will exercise over the American people if they ever get into the saddle. They will get the same death grip on marriage as that which the advocates of the 18th Amendment got on another department of personal conduct and morality; and they will strangle every effort to rationalize and alter marriage if they can. When they get their way, heaven help the American people and American law.

Of course the leaders who are advocating the proposed legislation would deny all this. For many of them, as I have said, are far from being religious cranks, and I have no wish to underrate either their sincerity or their intelligence. I merely want to emphasize the obvious fact that the movement is *under the control* of the conservatives who regard divorce as an unmitigated curse which should be legislated out of existence if possible, and should be sternly restricted in any event. They proceed on the assumption that though divorce cannot exactly be called a crime it is at any rate a very serious sin against morality, to be ranked with other forms of sexual delinquency. These people are pointing with alarm to what they regard as a breakdown in our national morale, and as a disintegration of American marriage caused by a growing looseness of American morals. They mouth this kind of nonsense continually. In their eyes sociology is just a word, to be kept in the dictionary where so dangerous a thing belongs. The fact that it doesn't occur in the Bible is enough for them.

Let it never be forgotten that people of this type are the real power in control of this movement for federal divorce legislation. They are the ones who really dictate what that legislation must be like if it is ever to pass. It is they who are responsible for the fact

that the Capper Bill must be provided with five grounds for divorce
and no more; five grounds applicable throughout the United States;
five grounds intended to cope with the inconceivably complex human
relationships that can arise in thousands of marriages no two of
which are alike. And maybe, by the time the Bill passed Congress,
there would be less than five.

Read them again: Adultery, cruel or inhuman treatment, abandonment or failure to provide for one year, incurable insanity, and the
commission by either party of an infamous crime. By way of adding
full measure of the incredible folly of these restrictions, the bill
would forbid divorce upon the ground of adultery if there is evidence of collusion, or where both parties have been guilty of that
offense.

Upon the allowing of a divorce, an interlocutory decree would
be granted. The divorce would not become final for one year, and
during that interval neither party would be permitted to remarry.
This period would probably be extended to two or even three years,
by the time the Bill got through Congress. I heard learned judges,
at a convention of the American Bar Association not long ago,
advocating that the period before the final decree be extended to
at least two years! This is one more straw that shows the direction
of the wind. Let us beware of legislation that would go through
under such auspices.

These are the provisions of the proposed bill to which I object.
Other provisions have to do with alimony, property rights, rights
of children, etc., and are not concerned directly with the obtaining
of a divorce. Most of them seem fair enough, and since they are not
at issue I need not go into them here.

10.

The five grounds for divorce here allowed together with the long
period required for obtaining it simply invites violation of the law
by hypocrisy, lies, perjury, collusion and pretense. It leaves divorce by mutual consent still obtainable by these illegal means
while making it legally taboo. It puts nothing on honest grounds
and it refuses to call a spade a spade. The only real change which
it makes in the morals of the present divorce situation is that it

offers people strong reasons for avoiding marriage altogether on account of the amount of time involved, and because of other legislative restrictions attaching to it, and turning to the unmarried, childless union instead. This phenomenon is sufficiently common right now, and what we need are laws that will offer less inducement to such conduct and *greater inducements to enter marriage.*

Companionate Marriage, as I have already indicated elsewhere, would offer such inducements to enter marriage and to avoid illicit unions. Only two measures would be necessary for the establishment of Companionate Marriage in any state; first a law establishing divorce by mutual consent for childless people and second one sanctioning the imparting of Birth Control information.

Divorce by mutual consent should also be extended to couples who have children when, in the discretion of a court, there is no other way out of the difficulty. But the point is that the principle of divorce by mutual consent should be operative whenever divorce is granted, and that such divorce should be denied only in the interests of children. Even where children are concerned it is often far wiser not to force the parents to remain together. In the case of childless couples I think the principle of divorce by mutual consent should be operative even when only one party of the marriage wants divorce. Marriage is mutual, or it isn't marriage. And if it isn't marriage, it is divorce in fact, even though it may not be so in law. Provisions as to alimony, etc., should be made at the discretion of the court, on a basis of justice and common sense.

The only item in the whole Capper Bill to which I am willing to subscribe for federal legislation is the one which provides that a divorce which is granted in one state shall be recognized in all states. In that there is a glint of common sense.

What I can't see with respect to the Capper Bill is how there can be any wisdom in passing such a law when it cannot be made to square with human necessity and is therefore doomed to nullification from the start. It could not be enforced, and it would not be enforced because public opinion would never support it. Public opinion demands divorce by mutual consent. It will not obey or respect any law that fails to grant it. Organized Minorities are not Public Opinion, though they may pose as such.

At the same time while utterly ineffective as a regulator of divorce, this bill would work immeasurable harm in putting a stop to the experimentation which might otherwise go on in the field of divorce legislation in different states.

Indeed the central argument against federal legislation on divorce lies in the fact that federal legislation would be static and rigid whereas state legislation would enable us to progress and grow. It is a practical certainty that before very long some progressive and liberal legislature would break the evil spell of superstition and pass laws similar to those which I am here suggesting.

The present situation may be chaotic, but it is also flexible. If South Carolina grants no divorce, New Hampshire and Kentucky allow it on fourteen grounds. South Carolina follows the supposed wishes of the Almighty literally. Marriage is sacred in South Carolina. But how do you suppose South Carolina makes its sacred law work? Why, by socially, *though not legally,* permitting concubinage. You have to stay married in South Carolina after you get married, but you can maintain an outside intimacy without getting into trouble or losing social cast—that is, if you happen to be a man. If you are a woman and try any such experiments, you are an adulteress.

II.

I have recently received a letter from a woman in South Carolina telling me that her husband has a mistress whom he would marry if he could get a divorce from her. As the man's income is limited and not enough for two families, she wants to know what I think she should do about it.

If this woman could go to Nevada, she could obtain divorce on any one of several grounds and could establish residence in three months. That three months' provision for people who want to get their divorce over with and get back to work is an advantage. Since the three months' residence is merely a gesture, I don't see why Nevada doesn't abandon this pretense and make one week sufficient for establishing a residence. Why not tell the truth?

At all events, the present situation, whatever occasional confusion may result from the conflict of state laws, does have a needed flexibility, and offers a needed opportunity for differences in divorce legislation at a time when our folkways and customs are changing rapidly. They cannot change without such flexibility.

The fact that a citizen can escape from the jurisdiction, and possibly from the tyranny, of his own state laws, and avail himself of the more liberal laws of some other state, seems to me a very great advantage, not only because it gives the individual a liberty of action he has a right to, but also because it tends to nullify illiberal legislation in any state that has it.

12.

But if we have one federal Marriage and Divorce Law for the whole country, and an illiberal law at that, then what is now flexible will become rigid, and the way to experimentation in this important social field will be closed. To assume that we need no experimentation in that field would be absurd. The difficulties we are now having with the institution of marriage, and in the field of sex relations generally, are ample evidence that new adjustments in marriage are now spontaneously taking place, and that the whole matter is so complex as to defy analysis.

Anybody who thinks that such a question can be disposed of by a law that would simply introduce a little more red tape into the getting of a marriage license, and make a uniform and restricted set of conditions for obtaining divorce, is living in a fool's paradise. The present change is the result of social alterations so profound that nobody has been able to measure the full depth and breadth of them. The home as a producing economic unit disappeared with the introduction of machinery and with mass production. We no longer card our own wool, do our own weaving, churn our own butter, and make our own tools. The home is no longer a miniature producing unit helping to supply its own wants and those of a small neighborhood. Consequently the bonds that hold it together must henceforth be different from those of the past.

And yet we have judges and lawyers, and ministers and busy

club women, and heaven knows what other oracles uniting in the belief that we can put, bit and bridle on this stupendous thing by a little offhand legislation. You might as well try to make a synthetic oak tree to ornament your front yard, instead of waiting patiently for the acorn to unfold the unknown thing that is within it. It is notoriously bad practice, moreover, to pull a growing thing up by the roots to see if one can't shove its development along somehow by artificial means.

13.

I cannot too strongly emphasize here the lesson history teaches with respect to changes in human custom. Human custom *grows;* it is not *made.* Old customs decay and are cast off by society when they outlive their usefulness. Nobody legislates this process of dying and replacement. It simply happens; it happens so gradually that the thing is done before the people as a whole realize that the new order has come.

Society gains by these adjustments and changes; and yet there never has been a time when an array of panic-stricken conservatives—the Old Men of the Tribe, the Shamans, the Priests, the Old Crones, and all who are ossified of mind and timid of heart—have failed to weep, wail, tear their hair, rend their garments and split the sky with their shrieks of anguish, their ululations, and their forebodings of disaster. They want it *stopped,* at once.

These efforts at magic legislation to cope with the momentum of a thing that is commensurate with Society itself, are the most recent example of the activities of these meddlers. But they will not prevail. In the long run the processes of creative evolution will have their way. But in the meantime such persons can do a lot of harm by persuading the nation, even for a little while, to set itself in opposition to these processes of change. It is of first importance that the American nation should understand that this is the real issue. Will it permit itself to be led into an attempt so foolish and so futile?

It is true that having committed the blunder of passing the Capper Bill, Congress would probably, in time, be forced into the passing of more and more liberal laws on Divorce; but that would take a long while—and in the meantime, harm would be done and lives would be wrecked and the sex situation in this country would tend to get more and more out of hand.

One reason for the slowness of Congress to change such a law for a more liberal one would be the fact that Congress is notoriously timid when religious lobbies come to Washington to tell it what it must do if it wants to get reëlected "by the vote of the Christian people of this country." Indeed, the political fear felt in Congress toward these organized minorities is the trouble with this proposed divorce legislation right at its inception. Congressman Jones of Jump-Off has his eye on the organized "church" sentiment of his community. Naturally Congressman Jones is in no state of mind to legislate intelligently or courageously on a subject that requires civilized and enlightened judgment. He will lose his job if he shows such judgment. Thus he dare not rise above the level of the herd.

14.

Another thing about the proposed federal legislation that should be clearly understood is this: It means that the citizens of any state whose sentiments about divorce are liberal and sane would be indefinitely bound and thwarted by the illiberal prejudices of moralistic states, whose people still believe in a Seven Day Creation, and who swallow the Whale as readily as they think the Whale swallowed Jonah. These Bible-olaters are the sort who, if the record had said that Jonah swallowed the Whale, would have believed that. They would attribute to Jonah the same unlimited swallowing capacity that they have themselves.

By such legislation the moralistic states of this country would be able to dictate their "scriptural" notions about divorce to the people of other, more civilized states who refuse to let any infallible book that ever was printed do their thinking for them.

Such states have a right to their own opinions about divorce, but they have no shadow of right to impose them on other parts of the country. This is one reason why the doctrine of State Rights is a vital and important thing, to which we need to hold fast, even at the cost of some conflict and difficulty in marriage and divorce, such as we face at present on account of differences in state law.

Here is another way of putting it.—Suppose the people who happen to be in the saddle in one of our anti-evolution states, being unified in their fanaticism, and capable of cohesive action—as such minorities often are—were able, by persistent lobbying, hand in glove with fanatics from other states, to inject their ideas on evolution into federal legislation. There isn't much danger of it, of course; but suppose they could put it over. Is it not clear that such restrictive legislation would constitute a grave injustice to people in parts of the United States where evolution is generally accepted, and where science is supposed to be taught without restriction in the public schools?

There is nothing extreme about this supposition, mark you. The late William Jennings Bryan was openly for such federal legislation against the teaching of evolution; and so are his followers. They would put their belief into federal law if they could.

It is also true that they *will, if they can,* introduce into federal law their scriptural ideas on divorce; and that if they could go so far, they would forbid divorce, by federal statute, altogether, or else would restrict it to grounds of adultery. Probably they could not accomplish that much, but they *could,* for a long time to come, prevent Congress from passing any divorce legislation that would be an improvement on or a liberalization of, the Capper Bill.

In the meantime, many of those who are actively sponsoring federal legislation, and who are supporting the Capper Bill, would really like to pass a liberal divorce law if they could. But do they dare propose such a law? They do not. They know it would be defeated. So they offer an illiberal bill, which they call "fairly liberal," because they think that it is all they can get. They are quite right. It *is* all they can get. They can't even get that much. It will go through with its wings clipped some more by gentlemen from the biblical states; and if it were made more liberal than it is, it would get snowed under.

15.

For this reason these mistaken liberals had better come out of the camp of the enemy, where they do not belong, and bend their energies to persuading some enlightened state legislature to pass some really liberal divorce laws that would mince no words on the subject, and would grant divorce to people because they want it, and for no other reason.

In the meantime, I don't want to minimize the confusion that is resulting from conflicts between the laws of different states, and from the frequent refusal of state courts to recognize and give due weight to the laws of other states when these conflicting issues are involved.

It may fairly be asked what possible relief can be had, save through federal legislation, from the often tragic situations that arise from these differences. Men and women often get crushed between the upper and the nether millstone. They cry out for relief and for justice, and it is not to be had.

This is an extremely serious question. It involves the legitimacy of children; it involves property rights and inheritance; and it frequently involves charges of bigamy and adultery brought against persons who are in fact innocent of anything of the kind, and who, in other states, are in good social and legal standing.

This condition is clearly contrary to the intent of the Constitution, which contemplates secure civil rights for every American citizen, no matter in what part of the union he may live and travel. Act IV, Section 1 of the Constitution says: "Full faith and credit shall be given in each State to the public acts, records, and judicial proceedings of every other State."

16.

But here is what this full faith and credit clause amounts to in marriage and divorce, by decision of the United States Supreme Court:

"Mr. and Mrs. Haddock, husband and wife, were domiciled in New York. Mr. Haddock left his wife, and went to Connecticut where he acquired in good faith, after a lapse of years, a domicile.

In accordance with Connecticut laws, he obtained a divorce in Connecticut, notice of the action being by publication of process on the wife who remained domiciled in New York and never appeared in the action. Mrs. Haddock subsequently sued for divorce in New York and obtained personal service in that State on Mr. Haddock who pleaded his Connecticut divorce."

Disallowing the Connecticut decree, the Supreme Court held:

"If one Government, because of its authority over its own citizen, has a right to dissolve the marriage tie as to the citizen of another jurisdiction, it must follow that no Government possesses as to its own citizens power over the marriage relation and its dissolution. If the full faith and credit clause of the Constitution were recognized as to marriage and divorce it would destroy the State's power over them, and the United States would be powerless to repair the evil, for it has no delegated authority on the subject. This (marriage and divorce) must be regarded as an exception." (footnote)   (Haddock v. Haddock. No. 119, decided April 12, 1906.)"

You and I may not like this decision; we may even disagree with it; but there it is, and there it stands; and Mr. Haddock's Connecticut divorce in this case was no good because the Supreme Court upheld the right of New York State to say that, since the provisions of New York law had not been complied with, Mrs. Haddock was still the wife of Mr. Haddock. New York was upheld in its assertion of its sovereignty over a New York citizen. Connecticut could not divorce Mrs. Haddock, and hence it couldn't divorce Mr. Haddock.—You see it's a very pretty legal whirligig; and that when so serious a matter as divorce was concerned, Mr. Haddock found it about as safe as monkeying with a buzz-saw.

17.

Here is another:

Mrs. Kelsey obtained a divorce in Pennsylvania from her husband living in New York under circumstances making the decree invalid in New York. She remarried in Pennsylvania. Later she and her second husband went to New York to live. Later her first husband, who had also remarried, sued for divorce on the ground that her second marriage constituted adultery. The Supreme Court of Monroe County held that he was entitled to divorce even though his own second marriage was adulterous. The Supreme Court, Appellate Division, reversed this and held that he should have delayed his second marriage until he had obtained a divorce. Result . . . second wife held to be unlawful wife and child illegitimate. (footnote) (Kelsey v. Kelsey, 190 N. Y. S. 52, 1921 and 197 N. Y. S. 371, 1922.)

This had an interesting sequel. The first Mrs. Kelsey had married a Mr. Bell. When Mr. Bell died, she was held not entitled to claim a wife's right in his estate. It was also ruled by the Court that she could not, because of her misbehavior, have any right against Mr. Kelsey. In a word, she was nobody's wife.

To the man on the street, who reasons things out on a basis of common sense, these highly logical outpourings of the judicial mind in the Kelsey case may seem about as sensible as if they had come out of the pages of "Alice in Wonderland." But since the legalistic mind is what it is, and since it operates in courts and court decisions, presumably we shall have to make the best of it, and try to have laws that even a legalistic mind can translate into terms of justice. This is a main point made by those who favor a federal law on marriage and divorce; and it is a strong one.

More than that, there are endless possibilities for complication in connection with divorces obtained abroad, notably in Paris and Yucatan. There is plenty of dynamite wrapped up in the question, What standing would such divorces have in some of our state courts, especially if an issue of property happened to be involved? A case came up in Chicago, not long ago, where a couple who had gotten their divorce in Paris wanted to remarry. When they consulted an attorney about it, he advised them that the only safe procedure would be for them to obtain a divorce under the laws of Illinois, and *then* remarry. That, he thought, would make them perfectly safe from property complications and other forms of unpleasantness.

I cite this matter of foreign divorce, not because it has any direct bearing on the conflicts between the laws of different states, but because it shows how rich the whole problem is in possible complications. Thousands of Americans have obtained divorces abroad. Some unexpected court decision, striking like a bolt from the blue, might bring up the question of the validity of many of those divorces, of the validity of many remarriages, of the legitimacy of children, and of property rights, in a way that would be disconcerting to say the least.

18.

To come back to the Haddock case, cited above, we have here two apparently irreconcilable sets of interests in a country where the rights of citizens are supposed to be defined without equivocation. On the one hand there is the right of the State of New York to protect its own citizens from action by outside sovereignties, in this case, Mrs. Haddock; and on the other, the right of Connecticut to grant a divorce to one of its own citizens under its own laws, in this case, Mr. Haddock. And the United States Supreme Court holds that Mrs. Haddock's right was in this instance, superior—or, if you like, more fundamental. And probably it was. There are many instances of divorce obtained by husbands, or wives, in distant states under conditions such that the defendant is not effectively notified of the action, and does not even know that a divorce has been granted. A state that failed to protect its own citizens against such a patent injustice as this would clearly be recreant in its duty.

What does not seem to have occurred to many of the persons who have discussed these legal difficulties and who see no way out save by a resort to federal legislation is that this is a human, rather than a legal question; and that conflicts between states are like conflicts between persons—one side commits a wrong, and the other side retaliates, and then the fight is on.

If our state courts would get rid of some of their cold legalism, and if human minded instead of legal minded judges would decide these divorce cases on a basis of equity and common sense and justice, most of these difficulties could be avoided. A man who goes to another state and obtains a divorce without seeing to it that his wife has full opportunity to know of the suit, and to contest it if she chooses, is plainly obtaining his divorce by fraud, regardless of whether it is "legal" or not.

New York State, for example, requires that the defendant be personally notified. It might go further and require that the interests of such a defendant should be fully and adequately represented in the court where the divorce suit is brought, and it might justly refuse to recognize such a divorce if it were granted without conformity to such provisions. When the courts of another state fail to concern themselves with justice sufficiently to see that the interests of the defendant from another state are fully and fairly represented, then a wrong has been done which shocks every sense of decency and fair play. Unfortunately too many divorce courts do not attempt to dispense justice—they dispense "law." It is quite a different article.

Naturally this condition leads to trouble, needless trouble. It would be a disgrace to American law and American justice if the problem had to be adjusted by federal legislation rather than by a sincere effort to meet human need on a human basis.

19.

The effort to initiate federal divorce legislation is just the old story of trying to have so many laws, and such ingenious laws, that justice can be had by a strict application of them, apart from any effort at equity and common sense. It can't be done. The human equation is a very complex thing, especially in marital problems which really need to be met, not by ordinary judges, but by experts in human artistry.

Among all the cases wherein the divorce laws of different states have come into conflict, there probably has not been a single instance where a real effort on the part of the trial court to do justice to both parties would not have resulted in an avoidance of every one of these apparently insuperable legal difficulties. Divorce proceedings should be chancery proceedings; the decisions should be decisions in equity. The procedure should be not unlike the informal methods followed in the Juvenile and Family Court of Denver, where I try to work things out for the best interests of all concerned. Perhaps if an awakened and enlightened public opinion should demand a less legalistic attitude on the part of the judiciary there would be less of this machine-like administration of "justice" and more effort to make divorce truly curative. I suggest an application to this problem of the ethics of Jesus, and a little less effort to beat the Devil around the Stump.

It has been suggested by some that divorce cases involving the conflicting rights of citizens of different states might be brought under the jurisdiction of the federal government through some such principle as that by which the federal government intervenes between states in what is known as interstate commerce. That outrageous measure known as the Mann Act operates under this interpretation of the Constitution. It would not seem unreasonable to suppose that if the federal government can intervene and even meddle in the private affairs of men and women under the Mann Act, it could at least bestir itself to see justice done between them under some constructive law which would permit of appeal to a federal court when state laws had come into conflict.

A man and woman who were living together, unmarried, recently came from California to see me, and ask my advice as to whether they should get married. I had them examined by a psychiatrist, a skilled medical man; and he gave the professional opinion that they should not. This couple, because they had left California, and had come together to Colorado, where they continued to live "in sin," could have been arrested, prosecuted, and given a penitentiary sentence under the Mann Act. But if they had had a divorce difficulty, and were seeking justice on that score, the federal government could not have intervened.

However, since no such interpretation of the constitution as I am here suggesting seems to be available—outside the Mann Act, which puts people in prison when they break certain conventions—we shall have to get along as best we can. And my suggestion is that we do just that, without putting ourselves, by federal legislation, into the clutches of meddlers and busybodies who are intent on converting the United States Government into a theocracy ruled by The Great God DON'T.

CHAPTER XV

OUR UNWEEDED GARDEN OF EDEN

1.

I HAVE a profound conviction that what may seem radical in this book will be the conservatism of to-morrow.

I am now on the far side of fifty; and yet I expect to see within my lifetime most of the changes of code and conduct suggested in these pages. Some will take longer than that; but they will take!

What I have tried to do is to reduce to understandable terms certain as yet hardly crystallized feelings and social tendencies which many persons stand in dread of because they misinterpret them, and have never defined them in a constructive and hopeful way.

It is immoral to be afraid of reality; to distrust the truth is the ultimate infidelity; intolerance is the ultimate cowardice.

I detest that inane question asked by orators who lack ideas and would fain conceal their empty-headedness: "Whither are we drifting?" they ask.

But why drift? And how do they know we are drifting? Life seems a very purposeful thing to me. At all events, we must go forward, whether we fear to do so or not; and we have now reached a point where we should be able to do something more than float like jellyfish on this moving flood of change.

2.

My friend Luther Burbank told me that he was able, by rationalizing the life and propagation of plants, to accomplish in a few plant generations what Nature, without such rational aid, would not have attained short of many thousands of years of trial and error. Burbank believed that results far more marvelous than his horticultural miracles could be attained by the human race in a few generations if it could but summon the moral courage, and the *scientific insight,* to rationalize human life and the propagation of that life. Even a little such rationalization, he believed, would work, perhaps in the span of a man's life, a greater miracle of human advancement than the whole of recorded history can show. He had no program for this. But I think his idea was that we might advance rapidly along that road if every school child in America could be given an adequate insight into the ways and laws of Nature through some such scientific training as he would himself have imparted to a child he undertook to educate.

Such a training in the Art of Living as Luther Burbank would have imparted to children, would, I feel sure, be capable of breathing the breath of life into our present system of education. Our culture lacks a scientific base. Consequently it teaches people every thing but the thing they most need to know—how to live, the Art of Living. This is another way of saying that by laying emphasis on the authority of Fact, Burbank would have introduced an emotional content into the system of chilly abstractions which we are pleased to call "education." He dealt with realities; and he detested hazy thinking.

I think Burbank would have taught the essentials of biology first; that he would first have let the child listen with his own ears to the beating of the great heart of nature; and that he would have builded the child's life and character on that first-hand knowledge, instead of on systems of mythology. He had builded his own life on that; and he was himself as fine and subtle as light.

Burbank knew how great were the possibilities of human life, if it could only be liberated by science,—because, more than any man I have known, he felt them in himself. His was the *cogito ergo sum,* the "I think, therefore I am" of Descartes. It was all a matter of first-hand inner experience with him. There were depths within him into which he himself could only gaze and wonder. For instance, he could walk down a row of young trees, none of which had ever fruited, and choose infallibly those which were superior to their fellows; and years later these trees would prove their superiority over others that an ordinary man would have said were just as good. None of the people working with him, no matter what their knowledge and skill, could do this. He had a touch faculty they did not possess. It may be that he was the only man in the world who had it. In all his contact with life, life around him and within him, he saw with crystal clearness, and with apparently absolute intuitive knowledge what *might* be.

It was this that made an hour of his company like a glass of cold water to a desert traveler. Here was a measure of infallibility such as no ecclesiastical authority in history ever had—a thing mysteriously final and authentic. I have been the more convinced of the nature of his authority in the kingdom given him since reading his autobiography, written in collaboration with Wilbur Hall, and published posthumously, "The Harvest of the Years."

3.

Evolution, he insisted, can be rationalized and hastened. We could, if we would, accomplish within a few generations, improvements in the average level of humanity, physical, mental and moral, as miraculous as anything he himself had ever wrought with his Shasta Daisy, his Burbank Plum, or his thornless cactus. Men now living might see at least the beginning of this up-soaring of the human spirit before they died.

About us lies the world, an unweeded Garden of Eden needing the touch of creative geniuses like him. Ah, if he could have grown for us a garden of them, as he grew his plants, before he died.

He was hounded to his death—till he broke—by yokels who called him an atheist. If they had known what he might have done to shorten the snouts of their progeny by means of a little selective breeding, the fury of their attack would have been redoubled. They were quite right when they said that none of them had *descended* from monkeys. The traveling of them and their kind had all been done on a dead level.

But to the everlasting credit of America, and of the civilized world, be it said that the great human race took him to its heart and loved him. The others are best forgotten.

4.

My contact with Luther Burbank confirmed and crystallized in my mind certain beliefs I had always had about people, and about the possibilities of the right sort of education if we had it.

I have never been a eugenics crank, though my belief in eugenics itself is profound. I don't think, for instance, that we can legislate a human stud farm into existence to improve the human stock by confining mating and procreation to picked specimens, as Burbank did with his plants, or as an animal breeder does with his stock. There can be nothing of that sort. Probably it would be intolerable if there were; and the first thing our improved progeny would do, probably, would be to knock every stud farm type of eugenics firmly and decisively on the head.

I can imagine, as readily possible, however, a race so educated in biology and in every science closely allied to it, that it would possess a quickened scientific imagination which would confer on the average man as intense a repugnance of unfit parenthood as we would now feel with respect to the marriage, say, of a brother and sister. I can imagine biological Science getting the truths and the facts of life as deep into the marrow of our bones as that.

I can imagine Science conferring on us a conception and an ideal of human life, and of human loveliness, that would be more effective in improving the human stock than all the legislated eugenics ever put on paper. I can imagine a code of voluntary conduct based on such ideals; and I think such a code would give us a moral faculty capable of keeping pace with the growth of scientific knowledge. I also think that if we do not acquire some such morality as this, science, divorced from ethics, may quite possibly destroy our present civilization. One World War is a sufficient hint of what another scientifically fought war might be like, say fifty years from now.

I can imagine, too, a society that so recognized the need for leadership and light, the need of the world for geniuses to lead it, that it would breed its geniuses intensively, as Luther Burbank produced the precise apple or plum or apricot, or plumcot that he wanted. But not while things are run by the type of people who hounded Luther Burbank to his death. Oh, no. They are drunk with the Wine of the Wrath of God, and they propose to make everybody else equally sodden and incapable of thought.

I can imagine, quite easily, a state of society, right here in America, that would no longer coerce the poor, and the incompetent, and the weak, and the unfit into procreation by laws against Birth Control.

I can even imagine our getting to the point, quite soon, where we would see the unwisdom of legally tricking paupers, congenital cripples, the congenitally insane, epileptics, and sufferers from venereal disease, into reproducing their kind to fill the jails, prisons, asylums, and poorhouses, of which we are now building more and more every year. Yes, I can imagine even that idea sinking in before long.

And there are lots of other things I can imagine. Some of them I have explained at length in this book, and in "The Revolt of Modern Youth."

5.

It appears to me that nothing I have suggested passes the bounds of reason. I have not pictured a Utopia, nor have I said that such social changes would produce one. What I have urged is simply the minimum of change necessary to decent and fruitful living. In fact, most of it is already within the reach of well-to-do, educated people who order their lives with reasonable wisdom and courage. By right education and certain changes of custom, it could be brought within the reach of all.

Occasionally I get a letter from some social reformer asking why I have passed over without mention some social remedy which he thinks would transform society. My answer is that the *first* step is to see to it that children are well born, and that they spend their early years in homes where they can grow and thrive. Further, that if we were all well, strong, intelligent, and happy, many of the social remedies proposed for the betterment of our social and economic lot would be as unnecessary as poorhouses would be if there were no paupers. I don't want to make this too sweeping. I know that there are many strong, courageous and intelligent persons who get crushed, often by sheer chance and bad luck, in the wheels of society. I know that we shall sooner or later have to devise ways of salvaging such persons and putting them on their feet. But that does not invalidate the broad truth of my contention, that a very large portion of the misery in the world would disappear if we could all be well born, strong, intelligent, and reasonably happy; and that people who are *well born* usually manage to attain the other essentials. It is the weaklings, the ill born, who go under. It seems silly, does it not, to produce them by law?

6.

Some have called me a dreamer and a visionary. But I am not. I am a very practical person, as my record in Denver shows. And I have had a very practical purpose in mind in the writing of this book. That purpose is to convince as many people as possible that they do really and consciously *want* certain changes, or something approximately like them. If you can make a man *want* a thing, really want it, he will take care of the rest, and will move heaven and earth to get it.

The day is coming when enough people in this country are going to want these decent and reasonable essentials of living—this minimum I have pictured; and when they consciously want it they will get it. That will be a gain. One more rise will have been surmounted, one more summit attained.

I am not asking much. These are the foothills of achievement. Beyond lie the Mountains.

THE END

Family in America

AN ARNO PRESS / NEW YORK TIMES COLLECTION

Abbott, John S. C. **The Mother at Home:** Or, The Principles of Maternal Duty. 1834.

Abrams, Ray H., editor. **The American Family in World War II.** 1943.

Addams, Jane. **A New Conscience and an Ancient Evil.** 1912.

The Aged and the Depression: Two Reports, 1931–1937. 1972.

Alcott, William A. **The Young Husband.** 1839.

Alcott, William A. **The Young Wife.** 1837.

American Sociological Society. **The Family.** 1909.

Anderson, John E. **The Young Child in the Home.** 1936.

Baldwin, Bird T., Eva Abigail Fillmore and Lora Hadley. **Farm Children.** 1930.

Beebe, Gilbert Wheeler. **Contraception and Fertility in the Southern Appalachians.** 1942.

Birth Control and Morality in Nineteenth Century America: Two Discussions, 1859–1878. 1972.

Brandt, Lilian. **Five Hundred and Seventy-Four Deserters and Their Families.** 1905. Baldwin, William H. **Family Desertion and Non-Support Laws.** 1904.

Breckinridge, Sophonisba P. **The Family and the State:** Select Documents. 1934.

Calverton, V. F. **The Bankruptcy of Marriage.** 1928.

Carlier, Auguste. **Marriage in the United States.** 1867.

Child, [Lydia]. **The Mother's Book.** 1831.

Child Care in Rural America: Collected Pamphlets, 1917–1921. 1972.

Child Rearing Literature of Twentieth Century America, 1914–1963. 1972.

The Colonial American Family: Collected Essays, 1788–1803. 1972.

Commander, Lydia Kingsmill. **The American Idea.** 1907.

Davis, Katharine Bement. **Factors in the Sex Life of Twenty-Two Hundred Women.** 1929.

Dennis, Wayne. **The Hopi Child.** 1940.

Epstein, Abraham. **Facing Old Age.** 1922. New Introduction by Wilbur J. Cohen.

The Family and Social Service in the 1920s: Two Documents, 1921–1928. 1972.

Hagood, Margaret Jarman. **Mothers of the South.** 1939.

Hall, G. Stanley. **Senescence:** The Last Half of Life. 1922.

Hall, G. Stanley. **Youth:** Its Education, Regimen, and Hygiene. 1904.

Hathway, Marion. **The Migratory Worker and Family Life.** 1934.

Homan, Walter Joseph. **Children & Quakerism.** 1939.

Key, Ellen. **The Century of the Child.** 1909.

Kirchwey, Freda. **Our Changing Morality:** A Symposium. 1930.

Kopp, Marie E. **Birth Control in Practice.** 1934.

Lawton, George. **New Goals for Old Age.** 1943.

Lichtenberger, J. P. **Divorce:** A Social Interpretation. 1931.

Lindsey, Ben B. and Wainwright Evans. **The Companionate Marriage.** 1927. New Introduction by Charles Larsen.

Lou, Herbert H. **Juvenile Courts in the United States.** 1927.

Monroe, Day. **Chicago Families.** 1932.

Mowrer, Ernest R. **Family Disorganization.** 1927.

Reed, Ruth. **The Illegitimate Family in New York City.** 1934.

Robinson, Caroline Hadley. **Seventy Birth Control Clinics.** 1930.

Watson, John B. **Psychological Care of Infant and Child.** 1928.

White House Conference on Child Health and Protection. **The Home and the Child.** 1931.

White House Conference on Child Health and Protection. **The Adolescent in the Family.** 1934.

Young, Donald, editor. **The Modern American Family.** 1932.